DB2® Universal Database™ V8.1 Certification Exam 700

IBM Press Series—Information Management

DB2 Universal Database V8.1 Certification Exam 700 Study Guide
Sanders

DB2 Universal Database v8 for Linux, UNIX, and Windows Database Administration Certification Guide, Fifth Edition
Baklarz and Wong

Advanced DBA Certification Guide and Reference for DB2 Universal Database v8 for Linux, UNIX, and Windows
Snow and Phan

DB2 Universal Database v8 Application Development Certification Guide, Second Edition
Martineau, Sanyal, Gashyna, and Kyprianou

DB2 Version 8: The Official Guide
Zikopoulos, Baklarz, deRoos, and Melnyk

DB2 Universal Database v8 Certification Test 700 Study Guide
Sanders

Teach Yourself DB2 Universal Database in 21 Days
Visser and Wong

DB2 UDB for OS/390 v7.1 Application Certification Guide
Lawson

DB2 SQL Procedural Language for Linux, UNIX, and Windows
Yip, Bradstock, Curtis, Gao, Janmohamed, Liu, and McArthur

Business Intelligence for the Enterprise
Biere

DB2 Universal Database v8 Handbook for Windows, UNIX, and Linux
Gunning

Other Complementary DB2 Titles

DB2 Universal Database for OS/390 Version 7.1 Certification Guide
Lawson and Yevich

DB2 Universal Database v7.1 for UNIX, Linux, Windows and OS/2—Database Administration Certification Guide, Fourth Edition
Baklarz and Wong

DB2 Universal Database v7.1 Application Development Certification Guide
Sanyal, Martineau, Gashyna, and Kyprianou

DB2 UDB for OS/390: An Introduction to DB2 OS/390
Sloan and Hernandez

DB2® Universal Database™ V8.1 Certification Exam 700 Study Guide

IBM Press™

DB2® Information Management Software

Roger E. Sanders

PRENTICE HALL
Professional Technical Reference
Upper Saddle River, New Jersey 07458
www.phptr.com

Editorial/production supervision: *Donna Cullen-Dolce*
Cover design director: *Jerry Votta*
Cover desingn: *Nina Scuderi*
Manufacturing manager: *Alexis Heydt-Long*
Interior design: *Greg Adair*
Editor: *Jeffrey Pepper*
Editorial assistant: *Linda Ramagnano*
IBM Consulting Editor: *Susan Visser*

Published by Pearson Education, Inc.
Publishing as Prentice Hall Professional Technical Reference
Upper Saddle River, NJ 07458

Printed in the United States of America

Second Printing

ISBN 0-13-142465-3

Pearson Education Ltd.
Pearson Education Australia Pte. Limited
Pearson Education Singapore, Pte. Ltd.
Pearson Education North Asia Ltd.
Pearson Education Canada, Ltd.
Pearson Educación de Mexico, S.A. de C.V.
Pearson Education — Japan
Pearson Education Malaysia, Pte. Ltd.

To my mother, Nellie; to my mother-in-law, Betsy;
and to my "second mother," Mabel.

About Prentice Hall Professional Technical Reference

With origins reaching back to the industry's first computer science publishing program in the 1960s, and formally launched as its own imprint in 1986, Prentice Hall Professional Technical Reference (PH PTR) has developed into the leading provider of technical books in the world today. Our editors now publish over 200 books annually, authored by leaders in the fields of computing, engineering, and business.

Our roots are firmly planted in the soil that gave rise to the technical revolution. Our bookshelf contains many of the industry's computing and engineering classics: Kernighan and Ritchie's *C Programming Language*, Nemeth's *UNIX System Adminstration Handbook*, Horstmann's *Core Java*, and Johnson's *High-Speed Digital Design*.

PH PTR acknowledges its auspicious beginnings while it looks to the future for inspiration. We continue to evolve and break new ground in publishing by providing today's professionals with tomorrow's solutions.

PRENTICE HALL PTR

Contents

Chapter 4

Foreword

Certification has taken the world by storm. The professional benefits are widely recognized. The certified DBA is not necessarily better at his or her job than the IT worker who is not certified, but one fact is clear: If you certify, *you* will certainly be a more skilled individual than before. And who doesn't want to be better at their job?

Certification is becoming the de facto standard measurement of skills. It guarantees prospective employers a base level of knowledge, so some now require it. But while we all need jobs, let me emphasize the personal sense of achievement that comes with certification. Working with the empowerment of heightened expertise is indeed a joy.

Once you've decided to certify, you confront the choice of which study materials to use. You're holding the best in your hands. Roger Sanders guided thousands of IT professionals to their certifications through his *All-in-One DB2 Administration Exam Guide* for DB2 Version 7. No other book did such a thorough, authoritative job of teaching candidates what they needed to know.

In this new DB2 Version 8 series of certification guides, Roger does it again. He focuses on what you need to know, avoiding the extraneous. He has a gift for explaining technical information in simple, direct fashion. No other author uses language in such a skillful way to get you to your goal.

I've used Roger's books not only to certify, but as reference guides to refer to again and again. Their value stretches far beyond simply achieving certification, worthy as that goal may be.

You have the key to DB2 in your hands. Use your newfound knowledge wisely!

—Howard Fosdick,
Independent consultant and founder and former President,
International DB2 Users Group and the Midwest Database Users Group

Preface

One of the biggest challenges computer professionals face today is keeping their skill sets current with the latest changes in technology. When the computing industry was in its infancy, it was possible to become an expert in several different areas, because the scope of the field was relatively small. Today, our industry is both widespread and fast paced, and the skills needed to master a single software package can be quite complex. Because of this complexity, many application and hardware vendors have initiated certification programs to evaluate and validate an individual's knowledge of their technology. Businesses benefit from these programs, because professional certification gives them confidence that an individual has the expertise needed to perform a specific job. Computer professionals benefit, because professional certification allows them to deliver high levels of service and technical expertise, and more importantly, professional certification can lead to advancement and/or new job opportunities within the computer industry.

If you've bought this book (or if you are thinking about buying this book), chances are you have already decided you want to acquire one or more of the IBM DB2 Universal Database (UDB) V8.1 Professional Certifications available. As an individual who holds eight IBM DB2 UDB professional certifications, let me assure you that the exams you must pass in order to become a certified DB2 UDB professional are not easy. IBM prides itself on designing comprehensive certification exams that are relevant to the work environment an individual holding a particular certification will have had some exposure to. As a result, all of IBM's certification exams are designed with the following items in mind:

- What are the critical tasks that must be performed by an individual who holds a particular professional certification?
- What skills must an individual possess in order to perform each critical task?
- What is the frequency with which each critical task must be performed?

You will find that to pass a DB2 UDB certification exam, you must possess a solid understanding of DB2 Universal Database (and for some of the more advanced certifications, you must understand many of its nuances as well).

Now for the good news. You are holding in your hands what I consider to be the best tool you can use to prepare for the DB2 UDB V8.1 Family Fundamentals exam (Exam 700). When IBM learned that I was planning to write a series of study guides for the DB2 UDB V8.1 certification exams, they invited me to participate in the exam development process. Among other things, I had the opportunity to evaluate several of the beta DB2 UDB V8.1 exams before they went into production. Consequently, I have seen every exam question you are likely to encounter, and I know what concepts you will be tested on when you take the DB2 UDB V8.1 Family Fundamentals exam (Exam 700). Using this knowledge, along with copies of the beta exams, I developed this study guide, which not only covers every DB2 UDB concept you must know in order to pass the DB2 UDB V8.1 Family Fundamentals exam (Exam 700), but also covers the exam process itself and the requirements for each DB2 UDB V8.1 certification role available. In addition, you will find at the end of each chapter, sample questions that are worded just like the actual exam questions. In short, if you see it in this book, count on seeing it on the exam; if you don't see it in this book, it won't be on the exam.

About This Book

This book is divided into two parts:

- Part 1—DB2 UDB Certification (Chapter 1)

  This section consists of one chapter (Chapter 1), which is designed to introduce you to the DB2 UDB Professional Certification Program that is available from IBM. In this chapter, you will learn about the different certification roles available, along with the basic prerequisites and requirements for each role. This chapter also explains what's involved in the certification process, and it includes a tutorial on the IBM Certification Exam testing software, which you will encounter when you go to take a DB2 UDB V8.1 certification exam.

- Part 2—DB2 UDB Family Fundamentals (Chapters 2–7)

  This section consists of six chapters (Chapters 2 through 7), which are designed to provide you with the concepts you will need to master before you can pass the DB2 UDB V8.1 Family Fundamentals exam (Exam 700).

  Chapter 2 is designed to introduce you to the various products that make up the DB2 UDB Family and to the comprehensive toolset provided with

DB2 UDB V8.1. In this chapter, you will learn about the various editions of DB2 UDB available, the functionality each edition provides, the functionality each DB2 UDB client component provides, and the purpose of each add-on product that makes up the DB2 UDB Family. You will also see what DB2 UDB GUI tools are available and what each tool looks like on the Windows 2000 operating system, as well as what each tool is designed to be used for.

Chapter 3 is designed to introduce you to the concept of database security and to the various authorization levels and privileges supported by DB2 UDB V8.1. In this chapter, you will learn how and where users are authenticated, how authorities and privileges determine what a user can and cannot do while working with a database, and how authorities and privileges are given to and taken away from individual users and/or groups of individual users.

Chapter 4 is designed to introduce you to the concept of servers, instances, databases, and database objects. In this chapter, you will learn how to create a DB2 UDB database and you will see what a DB2 UDB database's underlying structure looks like, as well as how that structure is stored (physically). You will also learn how to destroy a DB2 UDB database, how to catalog and uncatalog a DB2 UDB database, what kinds of objects can exist in a DB2 UDB database, and what each object available is used for.

Chapter 5 is designed to introduce you to the GUI tools and SQL statements that can be used to create DB2 UDB database objects and manipulate user data. In this chapter, you will learn what SQL is, as well as which SQL statements are classified as Data Control Language (DCL) statements, which statements are classified as Data Definition Language (DDL) statements, and which statements are classified as Data Manipulation Language (DML) statements. You will also learn how DDL, DCL, and DML statements are used to create database objects, control access to the database objects created, and store, manipulate, and/or retrieve data stored in those objects.

Chapter 6 is designed to provide you with everything you need to know about DB2 UDB data types and table constraints. In this chapter you will learn about the various built-in data types available with DB2 UDB V8.1, as well as how built-in data types, user-defined data types, DataLinks, and extenders can be incorporated into a table object's definition. You will also learn what constraints are, what types of constraints are available, and how constraints can be incorporated into a table object's definition.

Chapter 7 is designed to introduce you to the concept of data consistency and to the various mechanisms that DB2 UDB V8.1 uses to maintain data consistency in both single- and multi-user environments. In this chapter you will learn what isolation levels are, what isolation levels are available, and how isolation levels are used to keep transactions from interfering with each other in a multiuser environment. You will also learn how DB2 UDB provides concurrency control through the use of locking, what types of locks are available, how locks are acquired, and what factors can influence overall locking performance.

The book is written primarily for IT professionals who have some experience working with DB2 Universal Database, Version 8.1 and want to take (and pass) the DB2 UDB V8.1 Family Fundamentals exam (Exam 700). However, any individual that would like to learn the basic fundamentals of DB2 UDB V8.1 will benefit from the information found in this book.

Conventions Used

Many examples of DB2 UDB administrative commands and SQL statements can be found throughout this book. The following conventions are used whenever a DB2 command or SQL statement is presented:

- **[ ]** Parameters or items shown inside of brackets are required and must be provided.
- **< >** Parameters or items shown inside of angle brackets are optional and do not have to be provided.
- **|** Vertical bars are used to indicate that one (and only one) item in the list of items presented can be specified.
- **,...** A comma followed by three periods (ellipsis) indicate that multiple instances of the preceding parameter or item can be included in the DB2 command or SQL statement.

The following examples illustrate each of these conventions:

Example 1

```
REFRESH TABLE [TableName ,...]
<INCREMENTAL | NON INCREMENTAL>
```

In this example, at least one *TableName* value must be provided, as indicated by the brackets ([ ]), and more than one *TableName* value can be provided, as indicated by the comma-ellipsis (, . . .) characters that follow the *TableName* parameter. INCREMENTAL and NON INCREMENTAL are optional, as indicated by the angle brackets (< >), and either one or the other can be specified, but not both, as indicated by the vertical bar (|).

Example 2

```
CREATE SEQUENCE [SequenceName]
<AS [SMALLINT | INTEGER | BIGINT | DECIMAL]>
<START WITH [StartingNumber]>
<INCREMENT BY [1 | Increment]>
<NO MINVALUE | MINVALUE [MinValue]>
<NO MAXVALUE | MAXVALUE [MaxValue]>
<NO CYCLE | CYCLE>
<NO CACHE | CACHE 20 | CACHE [CacheValue]>
<NO ORDER | ORDER>
```

In this example, a *SequenceName* value must be provided, as indicated by the brackets ([ ]). However, everything else is optional, as indicated by the angle brackets (< >), and in many cases, a list of available option values is provided (for example, NO CYCLE and CYCLE); however, only one can be specified, as indicated by the vertical bar (|). In addition, when some options are provided (for example, START WITH, INCREMENT BY, MINVALUE, MAXVALUE, and CACHE), a corresponding value must be provided, as indicated by the brackets ([ ]) that follow the option.

SQL is not a case-sensitive language, so even though most of the examples provided are shown in uppercase, they can be entered in any case.

Acknowledgments

A project of this magnitude requires both a great deal of time and the support of many different individuals. I would like to express my gratitude to the following people for their contributions:

Susan Visser—IBM Press, Data Management Program Manager

IBM Toronto Lab

Once again, Susan's help was invaluable—without her help, this book would not have been written. Susan paved the way for my participation in the DB2 UDB V8.1 exam development process, providing me with both the exam objectives and beta copies of the DB2 UDB V8.1 certification exams. More importantly, Susan helped me make the migration from Osborne/McGraw-Hill to IBM Press. Susan also reviewed many of the chapters as they were written, and she made sure the appropriate subject-matter experts at the IBM Toronto Lab reviewed portions of the manuscript as well.

Jan Kritter—Database Specialist, IBM SAP Integration and Support Center, Toronto

SAP

Jan did a superb job of reviewing the manuscript and providing me with feedback. Jan pointed out where I assumed the reader was already familiar with a topic (that they might not be familiar with), and he kept me honest. Because of Jan's efforts, some of the finer points you will find throughout this book were clarified or edited before the manuscript went into production.

Howard Fosdick—President FCI

Founder and Past President of IDUG and MDUG

Howard is the author of the "Configuration Strategies" column in DB2 Magazine and a recognized database certification expert. When I began this project, I turned to him for information on the database certification "industry." Howard provided me with the information I requested, and he reviewed several chapters as soon as they were completed. Howard also provided me with the Foreword for this book.

Rick Swagerman—Sr. Technical Manager, DB2 SQL and Catalog Development

IBM Toronto Lab

Rick provided me with detailed examples illustrating how the UPDATE/ DELETE NO ACTION and UPDATE/DELETE RESTRICT rules of referential constraints work. His examples were converted into some of the illustrations you see in Chapter 6, and Rick reviewed the final draft of many of these drawings for accuracy and completeness.

Paul Rivot—Director of Database Servers for Software Group

(Vera Patterson, Secretary)

Paul and Vera provided me with a copy of the DB2 Universal Developer's Edition, Version 8.1 software. This software, in turn, was used to produce the screen captures found throughout the book. The online documentation that comes with the DB2 Universal Developer's Edition was used extensively as well.

I would also like to thank my wife Beth for her help and encouragement, and for once again overlooking all of the things that did not get done while I worked on yet another book.

About the Author

Roger E. Sanders is a Database Performance Engineer with Network Appliance, Inc. He has been designing and developing database applications for more than 18 years, and he has worked with DB2 Universal Database and its predecessors since it was first introduced on the IBM PC (as part of OS/2 Extended Edition). He has written several articles for publications such as *DB2 Magazine* and *IDUG Solutions Journal*, authored a tutorial titled "Database Concurrency: DB2 Version 8.1 Family Fundamentals Certification Preparation" for IBM's DeveloperWorks Web site, presented at three International DB2 User's Group (IDUG) conferences, and is the author of the following books:

- *DB2 UDB Exploitation of NAS Technology (IBM RedBook; co-author)*
- *All-In-One DB2 Administration Exam Guide*
- *DB2 Universal Database SQL Developer's Guide*
- *DB2 Universal Database API Developer's Guide*
- *DB2 Universal Database Call Level Interface Developer's Guide*
- *ODBC 3.5 Developer's Guide*
- *The Developer's Handbook to DB2 for Common Servers*

In addition, Roger holds the following professional certifications:

- IBM Certified Advanced Database Administrator—DB2 Universal Database V8.1 for Linux, UNIX, and Windows
- IBM Certified Database Administrator—DB2 Universal Database V8.1 for Linux, UNIX, and Windows
- IBM Certified Developer—DB2 Universal Database V8.1 Family
- IBM Certified Database Associate—DB2 Universal Database V8.1 Family
- IBM Certified Advanced Technical Expert—DB2 for Clusters
- IBM Certified Solutions Expert—DB2 UDB V7.1 Database Administration for UNIX, Windows, and OS/2
- IBM Certified Solutions Expert—DB2 UDB V6.1 Application Development for UNIX, Windows, and OS/2
- IBM Certified Specialist—DB2 UDB V6/V7 User

PART 1

DB2 UDB Certification

IBM DB2 Universal Database Certification

The Professional Certification Program from IBM is recognized the world over and offers a range of certification options for IT professionals. This chapter is designed to introduce you to the various paths you can take to obtain DB2 Universal Database Certification from IBM and to let you know what you can expect when you sit down to take your first DB2 UDB certification exam.

DB2 Universal Database Certification Roles

One of the biggest trends in the IT industry today is certification. Many application/software vendors now have in place certification programs designed to evaluate and validate an individual's proficiency with their latest product release. In fact, one of the reasons the Professional Certification Program from IBM was developed was to provide a way for skilled technical professionals to demonstrate their knowledge and expertise with a particular version of an IBM product.

The Professional Certification Program from IBM is comprised of several distinct certification roles designed to guide you in your professional development. You simply select the role that's right for you, then you begin the certification process by choosing the role you wish to pursue and familiarizing yourself with the requirements for that role. The following sections are designed to help get you started by providing you with the prerequisites and requirements associated with each DB2 UDB Version 8.1 certification available.

IBM Certified Database Associate—DB2 Universal Database V8.1 Family

The *IBM Certified Database Associate—DB2 Universal Database V8.1 Family* certification is intended for entry-level DB2 UDB users who are knowledgeable about the fundamental concepts of DB2 UDB, Version 8.1 or DB2 UDB for iSeries (AS/400), V5R2. In addition to having some hands-on experience with and/or some formal training on DB2 UDB, Version 8.1 and/or DB2 UDB for iSeries (AS/400), V5R2, individuals seeking this certification should:

- Know what DB2 UDB products are available and be familiar with the various ways DB2 UDB is packaged.
- Know what DB2 UDB products must be installed in order to create a desired environment.
- Possess a strong knowledge about the mechanisms DB2 UDB uses to protect data and database objects against unauthorized access and/or modification.
- Know how to create, access, and manipulate basic DB2 UDB objects, such as tables, views, and indexes.
- Be familiar with the different types of constraints that are available and know how each is used.
- Possess an in-depth knowledge of the Structured Query Language (SQL), Data Definition Language (DDL), Data Manipulation Language (DML), and Data Control Language (DCL) statements that are available.
- Have a basic understanding of the methods used to isolate transactions from each other in a multiuser environment.
- Be familiar with the methods used to control whether a transaction acquires row-level or table-level locks.

In order to acquire the IBM Certified Database Associate—DB2 Universal Database V8.1 Family certification, candidates must take and pass one exam: the **DB2 UDB V8.1 Family Fundamentals** exam (Exam 700). The roadmap for acquiring the IBM Certified Database Associate—DB2 Universal Database V8.1 Family certification can be seen in Figure 1–1.

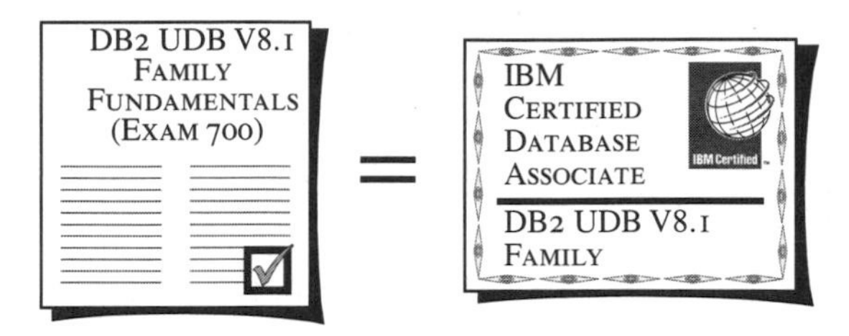

Figure 1–1 IBM Certified Database Associate—DB2 Universal Database V8.1 Family certification roadmap.

IBM Certified Database Administrator—DB2 Universal Database V8.1 for Linux, UNIX, and Windows

The *IBM Certified Database Administrator—DB2 Universal Database V8.1 for Linux, UNIX, and Windows* certification is intended for experienced DB2 UDB users who possess the knowledge and skills necessary to perform the day-to-day administration of DB2 UDB, Version 8.1 instances and databases residing on Linux, UNIX, or Windows platforms. In addition to being knowledgeable about the fundamental concepts of DB2 UDB, Version 8.1 and having significant hands-on experience as a DB2 UDB Database Administrator (DBA), individuals seeking this certification should:

- Know how to configure and manage DB2 UDB instances.
- Know how to configure client/server connectivity.
- Know how to create DB2 UDB databases.
- Possess a strong knowledge about SMS and DMS tablespaces, as well as be familiar with the management requirements of each.
- Know how to create, access, modify, and manage the various DB2 UDB objects available.
- Be able to create constraints on and between table objects.
- Possess a strong knowledge about the mechanisms DB2 UDB uses to protect data and database objects against unauthorized access and/or modification.

- Be able to obtain and modify the values of environment/registry variables.
- Be able to obtain and modify DB2 Database Manager and database configuration file parameter values.
- Know how to capture and analyze Explain information.
- Know how to use the DB2 UDB Control Center and other GUI tools available to manage instances and databases, create and access objects, create tasks, schedule jobs, and view Explain information.
- Be familiar with the functions of the DB2 Governor and the Query Patroller.
- Know how to capture and interpret snapshot monitor data.
- Know how to create and activate event monitors, as well as interpret event monitor data.
- Possess an in-depth knowledge of the EXPORT, IMPORT, and LOAD utilities.
- Know how to use the REORGCHK, REORG, REBIND, RUNSTATS, db2look, and db2move utilities.
- Know how to perform database-level and tablespace-level backup, restore, and roll-forward recovery operations.
- Have a basic understanding of transaction logging.
- Be able to interpret information stored in the administration notification log.

Candidates who have either taken and passed the **DB2 UDB V7.1 Family Fundamentals** exam (Exam 512) or acquired the IBM Certified Solutions Expert—DB2 UDB V7.1 Database Administration for UNIX, Windows, and OS/2 certification must take and pass the **DB2 UDB V8.1 for Linux, UNIX, and Windows Database Administration** exam (Exam 701) to acquire the IBM Certified Database Administrator—DB2 Universal Database V8.1 for Linux, UNIX, and Windows certification. All other candidates must take and pass both the **DB2 UDB V8.1 Family Fundamentals** exam (Exam 700) and the **DB2 UDB V8.1 for Linux, UNIX, and Windows Database Administration** exam (Exam 701). The roadmap for acquiring the IBM Certified Database Administrator—DB2 Universal Database V8.1 for Linux, UNIX, and Windows certification can be seen in Figure 1–2.

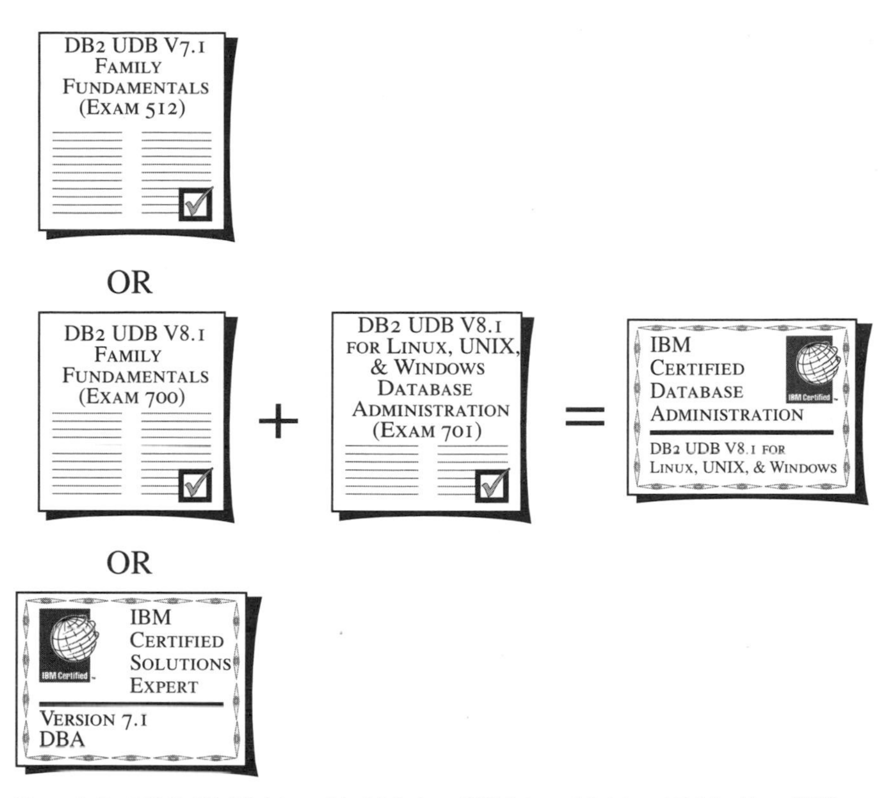

Figure 1–2 IBM Certified Database Administrator—DB2 Universal Database V8.1 for Linux, UNIX, and Windows certification roadmap.

Candidates who already hold the IBM Certified Solutions Expert—DB2 UDB V7.1 Database Administration for UNIX, Windows, and OS/2 certification may opt to take the **DB2 UDB V8.1 for Linux, UNIX, and Windows Database Administration Upgrade Exam** (Exam 706) to acquire the IBM Certified Database Administrator—DB2 Universal Database V8.1 for Linux, UNIX, and Windows certification. This exam, which is half the length and half the cost of the **DB2 UDB V8.1 for Linux, UNIX, and Windows Database Administration** exam (Exam 701), is designed to test a candidate's knowledge of the new features and functions that are provided in DB2 UDB Version 8.1. Essentially, the upgrade exam provides certified DB2 UDB Version 7.1 DBAs an accelerated approach for acquiring an equivalent Version 8.1 certification. This accelerated approach is outlined in Figure 1–3.

Figure 1–3 The accelerated approach for acquiring IBM Certified Database Administrator—DB2 Universal Database V8.1 for Linux, UNIX, and Windows certification.

IBM Certified Database Administrator—DB2 Universal Database V8.1 for z/OS and OS/390

The *IBM Certified Database Administrator—DB2 Universal Database V8.1 for z/OS and OS/390* certification is intended for experienced DB2 UDB users who possess the knowledge and skills necessary to perform the day-to-day administration of DB2 UDB, Version 8.1 instances and databases residing on z/OS and OS/390 platforms. In addition to being knowledgeable about the fundamental concepts of DB2 UDB, Version 8.1 and having significant hands-on experience as a DB2 UDB Database Administrator, individuals seeking this certification should:

- Know how to convert a logical database design to a physical database design.
- Know how to create, access, modify, and manage the various DB2 UDB objects available.
- Know how to interpret the contents of system catalogs and directories.
- Possess a strong knowledge about the activities associated with enabling stored procedures.
- Be familiar with the different types of constraints available and know how each is used.
- Possess an in-depth knowledge of the Structured Query Language (SQL), Data Definition Language (DDL), Data Manipulation Language (DML), and Data Control Language (DCL) statements that are available with DB2 UDB, Version 8.1.
- Know the difference between static and dynamic SQL.

- Know how to manage storage allocation with tools such as VSAM DELETE, VSAM DEFINE, and STOGROUP.
- Be familiar with DB2 Disaster Recovery.
- Possess a basic understanding of the different object statuses available (for example: RECP, GRECP, LPL, and RESTP).
- Be able to describe the effects of COMMIT frequency.
- Know how to capture and analyze Explain information.
- Know how to capture and analyze DB2 Trace data.
- Be able to determine the best characteristics for an index.
- Be able to describe the benefits of data sharing.
- Be able to describe the features that enable around-the-clock availability.
- Know how to use the REORG, BIND, REPAIR, UNLOAD, RUNSTATS, LOAD, and MODIFY utilities, including being able to restart a failed utility.
- Know how to use the DISPLAY, START, STOP, ALTER, RECOVER, and TERM UTILITY commands.
- Possess a basic understanding of the CHECK DATA/INDEX/LOB utility.
- Be able to demonstrate how DB2I is used.
- Be able to identify the functions of the Control Center.
- Possess a strong knowledge about the mechanisms DB2 UDB uses to protect data and database objects against unauthorized access and/or modification.

Candidates who have either taken and passed the **DB2 UDB V7.1 Family Fundamentals** exam (Exam 512) or acquired the IBM Certified Solutions Expert—DB2 UDB V7.1 Database Administration for OS/390 certification must take and pass the **DB2 UDB V8.1 for z/OS Database Administration** exam (Exam 702) to acquire the IBM Certified Database Administrator—DB2 Universal Database V8.1 for z/OS and OS/390 certification. All other candidates must take and pass both the **DB2 UDB V8.1 Family Fundamentals** exam (Exam 700) and the **DB2 UDB V8.1 for z/OS Database Administration** exam (Exam 702). The roadmap for acquiring the IBM Certified Database Administrator—DB2 Universal Database V8.1 for z/OS and OS/390 certification can be seen in Figure 1–4.

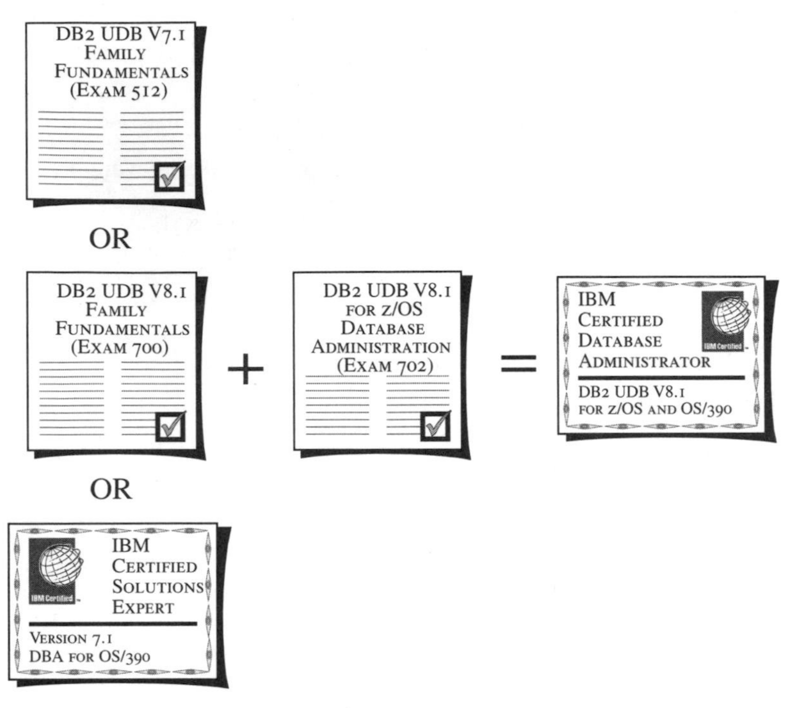

Figure 1–4 IBM Certified Database Administrator—DB2 Universal Database V8.1 for z/OS and OS/390 certification roadmap.

IBM Certified Application Developer—DB2 Universal Database V8.1 Family

The *IBM Certified Application Developer—DB2 Universal Database V8.1 Family* certification is intended for intermediate- to advanced-level application developers who possess the knowledge and skills necessary to create applications that interact with DB2 UDB for iSeries (AS/400), V5R2, and/or DB2 UDB, Version 8.1 databases residing on supported platforms, including Linux, AIX, HP-UX, Sun Solaris, Windows, zSeries (z/OS, OS/390), and iSeries (AS/400). In addition to being knowledgeable about the fundamental concepts of DB2 UDB, Version 8.1 and having strong skills in embedded SQL programming, ODBC/CLI programming, JDBC programming, or SQLJ programming, individuals seeking this certification should:

- Be familiar with the naming conventions used to identify DB2 UDB objects.
- Know how to create, access, modify, and manage the various DB2 UDB objects available.

- Possess an in-depth knowledge of the Structured Query Language (SQL), Data Definition Language (DDL), Data Manipulation Language (DML), and Data Control Language (DCL) statements that are available with DB2 UDB, Version 8.1 or DB2 UDB for iSeries (AS/400), V5R2.
- Know the difference between static and dynamic SQL.
- Possess an in-depth knowledge of the SQL functions available.
- Know when to use ODBC/CLI, JDBC, SQLJ, OLE DB, and embedded SQL.
- Be able to establish a connection to a database within an ODBC/CLI, JDBC, or SQLJ application.
- Be able to query tables across multiple databases, including federated databases.
- Be able to identify the types of cursors available, as well as know when to use cursors in an application and what their scope will be.
- Know when to use Compound SQL, parameter markers, and distributed units of work.
- Know when to use user-defined functions (UDFs) and stored procedures.
- Be able to cast user-defined data types (UDTs) within an application.
- Know what authorities and privileges are needed in order to access data with an application.
- Be familiar with the steps involved in creating an embedded SQL application.
- Know when to declare host variables, as well as how to use host variables in a query.
- Possess the ability to analyze the contents of an SQL Communications Area (SQLCA) data structure.
- Be familiar with the steps involved in creating an ODBC/CLI application.
- Be familiar with the different ODBC/CLI handle types available.
- Know how to configure a DB2 ODBC driver.
- Possess the ability to obtain and analyze ODBC/CLI diagnostic information.
- Know the correct sequence for calling ODBC/CLI functions.
- Be familiar with the steps involved in creating a JDBC application.
- Be familiar with the steps involved in creating an SQLJ application.

- Know the difference between JDBC and SQLJ.
- Be familiar with the various JDBC objects available.
- Possess the ability to obtain and analyze JDBC trace, SQL exception, and JDBC error log information.
- Know how to manage transactions across multiple databases using JTA.
- Be familiar with the DB2 Development Center.

Candidates who have either taken and passed the **DB2 UDB V7.1 Family Fundamentals** exam (Exam 512) or acquired the IBM Certified Solutions Expert—DB2 UDB V7.1 Family Application Development certification must take and pass the **DB2 UDB V8.1 Family Application Development** exam (Exam 703) to acquire the IBM Certified Application Developer—DB2 Universal Database V8.1 Family certification. All other candidates must take and pass both the **DB2 UDB V8.1 Family Fundamentals** exam (Exam 700) and the **DB2 UDB V8.1 Family Application Development** exam (Exam 703). The roadmap for acquiring the IBM Certified Application Developer—DB2 Universal Database V8.1 Family certification can be seen in Figure 1–5.

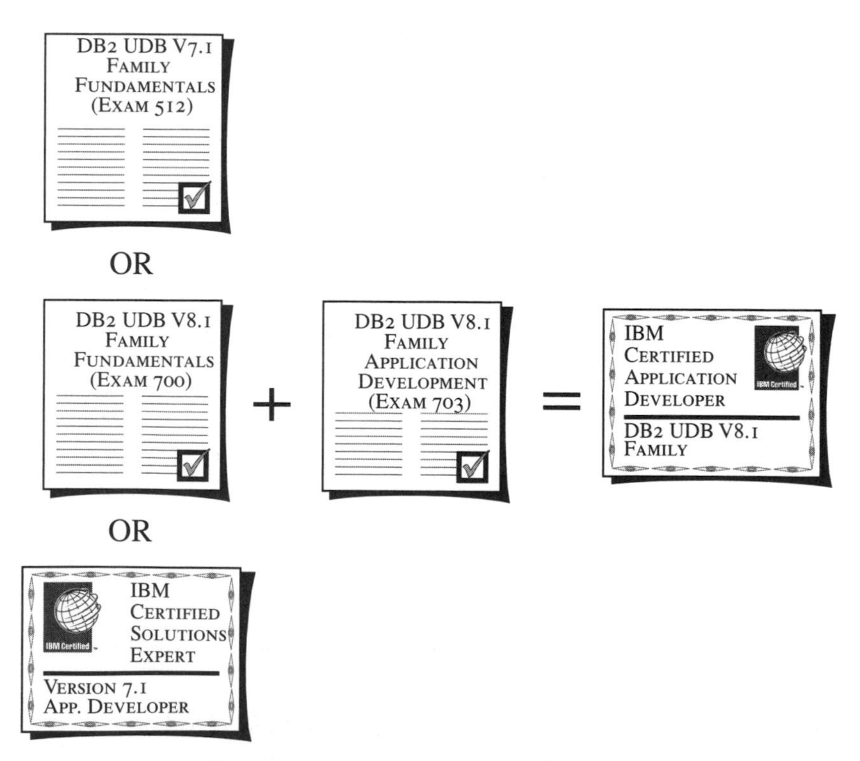

Figure 1–5 IBM Certified Application Developer—DB2 Universal Database V8.1 Family certification roadmap.

IBM Certified Advanced Database Administrator—DB2 Universal Database V8.1 for Linux, UNIX, and Windows

The *IBM Certified Advanced Database Administrator—DB2 Universal Database V8.1 for Linux, UNIX, and Windows* certification is intended for lead Database Administrators who possess extensive knowledge about DB2 UDB, Version 8.1 and who have extensive experience using DB2 UDB on one or more of the following supported platforms: Linux, AIX, HP-UX, Sun Solaris, and Windows. In addition to being knowledgeable about the more complex concepts of DB2 UDB, Version 8.1 and having significant experience as a DB2 UDB Database Administrator, individuals seeking this certification should:

- Know how to design, create, and manage both SMS and DMS tablespaces.
- Know how to design, create, and manage buffer pools.
- Be able to take full advantage of intra-parallelism and inter-parallelism.
- Be able to design and configure federated database access.
- Know how to manage distributed units of work.
- Be able to develop a logging strategy.
- Be able to create constraints on and between table objects.
- Know how to perform database-level and tablespace-level backup, restore, and roll-forward recovery operations.
- Be able to use the advanced backup and recovery features available.
- Know how to implement a standby database using log shipping, replication, failover, and fault monitoring.
- Be able to identify and modify the DB2 Database Manager and database configuration file parameter values that have the most impact on performance.
- Possess a strong knowledge of query optimizer concepts.
- Be able to tune memory and I/O.
- Be able to correctly analyze, isolate, and correct database performance problems.
- Know how to manage a large number of users and connections, including connections to host systems.

- Know how to create, configure, and manage a partitioned database spanning multiple servers.
- Be able to create and manage multidimensional clustered tables.
- Know when the creation of an index will improve database performance.
- Be able to identify and resolve database connection problems.
- Possess a strong knowledge about the external authentication mechanisms DB2 UDB uses to protect data and database objects against unauthorized access and/or modification.
- Know how to implement data encryption.

To acquire the IBM Certified Advanced Database Administrator—DB2 Universal Database V8.1 for Linux, UNIX, and Windows certification, candidates must hold the IBM Certified Database Administrator—DB2 Universal Database V8.1 for Linux, UNIX, and Windows certification, and they must take and pass the **DB2 UDB V8.1 for Linux, UNIX, and Windows Advanced Database Administration** exam (Exam 704). The roadmap for acquiring the IBM Certified Advanced Database Administrator—DB2 Universal Database V8.1 for Linux, UNIX, and Windows certification can be seen in Figure 1–6.

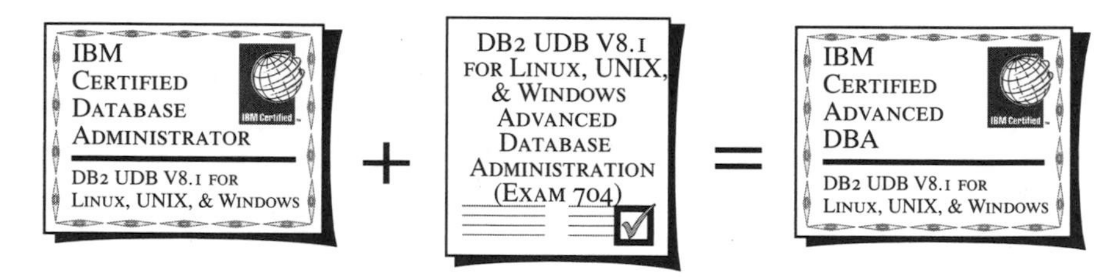

Figure 1–6 IBM Certified Advanced Database Administrator—DB2 Universal Database V8.1 for Linux, UNIX, and Windows certification roadmap.

IBM Certified Solution Designer—Business Intelligence V8.1

The *IBM Certified Solution Designer—Business Intelligence V8.1* certification is intended for individuals who are knowledgeable about IBM's Business Intelligence solutions, as well as the fundamental concepts of DB2 Universal Database, Version 8.1. In addition to having the knowledge and skills necessary to design, develop, and support Business Intelligence applications, individuals seeking this certification should:

- ➤ Be familiar with Business Intelligence terms, as well as be able to describe the benefits of Business Intelligence.
- ➤ Know how the characteristics and purpose of data marts differ from those of data warehouses.
- ➤ Know how the characteristics and purpose of operational data stores differ from those of data warehouses.
- ➤ Know how the characteristics and purpose of multidimensional databases differ from those of data warehouses.
- ➤ Know how network communications can impact Business Intelligence architecture.
- ➤ Be able to select the appropriate tools to perform transformation, extraction, data modeling, data cleansing, loading, and propagation when given Business Intelligence data and customer requirements.
- ➤ Be able to select the appropriate visualization and presentation techniques to use when given Business Intelligence data and customer requirements.
- ➤ Be able to select the appropriate analysis techniques to use when given Business Intelligence data.
- ➤ Be able to select the appropriate front-end features to use based on presentation, level of interactivity, Web-versus-FAT client, static versus dynamic, and user skill level when given customer requirements.
- ➤ Be able to define and distinguish metadata, as well as be able to describe metadata management processes and techniques.
- ➤ Know how to implement a metadata strategy when given Business Intelligence data and customer requirements.
- ➤ Know how to identify the business requirements of the customer as they relate to a Business Intelligence solution.
- ➤ Know how to define a customer's business goals and objectives, determine growth requirements, evaluate existing hardware and software, identify constraints, identify critical success factors, and determine availability and recovery requirements.
- ➤ Possess an in-depth knowledge of methods of extraction, methods for transformation, methods for cleansing, methods for workload balancing, methods for moving data, methods for scheduling, and methods for error detection and handling.

- Be able to differentiate between full differential capturing and snapshot capturing.
- Possess an in-depth knowledge of data warehouse management.
- Be able to design a solution for producing a searchable metadata repository for business users.

Candidates who have either taken and passed the **DB2 UDB V7.1 Family Fundamentals** exam (Exam 512) or acquired the IBM Certified Solutions Expert—DB2 UDB V7.1 Business Intelligence certification must take and pass the **Business Intelligence Solutions V8.1** exam (Exam 705) to acquire the IBM Certified Solution Designer—Business Intelligence V8.1 certification. All other candidates must take and pass both the **DB2 UDB V8.1 Family Fundamentals** exam (Exam 700) and the **Business Intelligence Solutions V8.1** exam (Exam 705). The roadmap for acquiring the IBM Certified Solution Designer—Business Intelligence V8.1 certification can be seen in Figure 1–7.

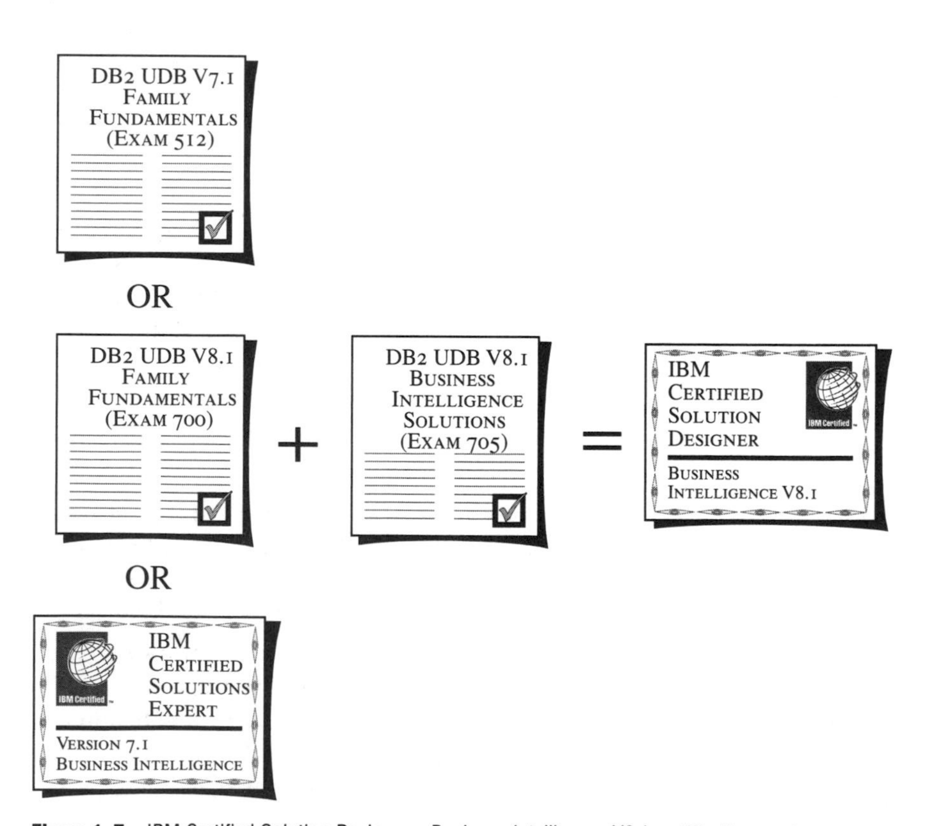

Figure 1–7 IBM Certified Solution Designer—Business Intelligence V8.1 certification roadmap.

The Certification Process

A close examination of the IBM certification roles available quickly reveals that, in order to obtain a particular DB2 UDB, Version 8.1 certification, you must take and pass one or more exams that have been designed specifically for that certification role. (Each exam is a software-based exam that is neither platform- nor product-specific.) Thus, once you have chosen the certification role you wish to pursue and familiarized yourself with the requirements for that particular role, the next step is to prepare for and take the appropriate certification exam(s).

Preparing for the Certification Exams

If you already have experience using DB2 UDB in the context of the certification role you have chosen, you may already possess the skills and knowledge needed to pass the exam(s) required for that role. However, if your experience with DB2 UDB is limited (and even if it is not), you can prepare for any of the certification exams available by taking advantage of the following resources:

- Formal Education

  IBM Learning Services offers courses that are designed to help you prepare for DB2 UDB certification. A listing of the courses that are recommended for each certification exam can be found using the Certification Navigator tool provided on IBM's "Professional Certification Program from IBM" Web site (*www.ibm.com/certify*). Recommended courses can also be found at IBM's "DB2 Data Management" Web site (*www.ibm.com/software/data/education.html*). For more information on course schedules, locations, and pricing, contact IBM Learning Services or visit their Web site.

  IBM also offers two free Computer Based Training (CBT) programs that you can download and install on your personal computer. The first of these, *CT10—DB2 UDB Programmer Fastpath* is geared towards the IBM Certified Application Developer—DB2 Universal Database V8.1 Family certification role. The second, *CT28—DB2 UDB Administration Fastpath* was written with the IBM Certified Database Administrator—DB2 Universal Database V8.1 for Linux, UNIX, and Windows certification role in mind. Both are GUI-based and interactive.

- Publications

  All the information you need to pass any of the available certification exams can be found in the documentation that is provided with DB2

UDB. A complete set of manuals come with the product and are accessible through the Information Center once you have installed the DB2 UDB software. DB2 UDB documentation can also be download from IBM's Web site in both HTML and PDF formats. (The IBM Web site that contains the DB2 UDB documentation can be found at *www.ibm.com/software/data/db2/library*.)

Self-study books (such as this one) that focus on one or more DB2 UDB certification exams/roles are also available. Most of these books can be found at your local bookstore or ordered from many online book retailers. (A listing of possible reference materials for each certification exam can be found using the Certification Navigator tool provided on IBM's "Professional Certification Program from IBM" Web site (*http://www.ibm.com/certify*).

In addition to the DB2 UDB product documentation, IBM often produces manuals, known as "RedBooks," that cover advanced DB2 UDB topics (as well as other topics). These manuals are available as downloadable PDF files on IBM's RedBook Web site (*www.redbooks.ibm.com*). Or, if you prefer to have a bound hard copy, you can obtain one for a modest fee by following the appropriate links on the RedBook Web site. (There is no charge for the downloadable PDF files.)

IBM also offers a series of six interactive online tutorials designed to prepare you for the DB2 UDB V8.1 Family Fundamentals exam (Exam 700). These tutorials can be found at *www7b.boulder.ibm.com/dmdd/library/tutorials/db2cert/db2cert_V8_tut.html*.

- Exam Objectives

  Objectives that provide an overview of the basic topics that are covered on a particular certification exam can be found using the Certification Navigator tool provided on IBM's "Professional Certification Program from IBM" Web site (*www.ibm.com/certify*). Exam objectives for the DB2 UDB V8.1 Family Fundamentals exam (Exam 700) can also be found in Appendix A of this book.

- Sample Questions/Exams

  Sample questions and sample exams allow you to become familiar with the format and wording used on the actual certification exams. They can help you decide whether you possess the knowledge needed to pass a particular exam. Sample questions, along with descriptive answers, are provided at the end of every chapter in this book. Sample exams for each DB2 UDB certification role available can be found using the Certification Exam tool provided on IBM's "Professional Certification Program from IBM" Web site (*http://certify.torolab.ibm.com*).

It is important to note that the certification exams are designed to be rigorous. Very specific answers are expected for most exam questions. Because of this, and because the range of material covered on a certification exam is usually broader than the knowledge base of many DB2 UDB professionals, you should take advantage of the exam preparation resources available if you want to guarantee your success in obtaining the certification(s) you desire.

Arranging to Take a Certification Exam

When you are confident that you are ready to take a specific DB2 UDB certification exam, your next step is to contact an IBM-authorized testing vendor. The DB2 UDB certification exams are administered by VUE, Prometric, Inc., and in rare cases by IBM (for example, IBM administers the DB2 UDB certifications free of charge at some of the larger database conferences, such as the International DB2 User's Group North American conference). However, before you contact either testing vendor, you should visit their Web site (*www.vue.com/ibm* and *www.2test.com*, respectively) and use the navigation tools provided there to locate a testing center that is convenient for you to get to. Once you have located a testing center, you should then contact the vendor and make arrangements to take the certification exam. (Contact information for the testing vendors can also be found on their respective Web sites; in some cases, you are able to schedule an exam online.)

You must make arrangements to take a certification exam at least 24 hours in advance, and when you contact the testing vendor, you should be ready to provide the following information:

- Your name (as you want it to appear on your certification certificate).
- An identification number (this can be, but does not have to be, your Social Security/Social Insurance number). If an identification number is not provided, the testing vendor will supply one.
- A telephone number where you can be reached.
- A fax number.
- The mailing address where you want all certification correspondence, including your certification welcome package, to be sent.
- Your billing address, if it is different from your mailing address.

- Your email address.
- The number that identifies the exam you wish to take (for example, Exam 700)
- The method of payment (credit card or check) you wish to use, along with any relevant payment information (such as credit card number and expiration date).
- Your company's name (if applicable).
- The testing center where you would like to take the certification exam.
- The date when you would like to take the certification exam.

Before you make arrangements to take a certification exam, you should have pencil/pen and paper handy so you can write down the test applicant identification number the testing center will assign you. You will need this information when you arrive at the testing center to take the certification exam. (If time permits, you will be sent a letter of confirmation containing the number of the certification exam you have been scheduled to take, along with corresponding date, time, and location information; if you register within 48 hours of the scheduled testing date, you will not receive a letter).

If you have already taken one or more of the certification exams offered, you should make the testing vendor aware of this and ask them to assign you the same applicant identification number that was used before. This will allow the certification team at IBM to quickly recognize when you have met all the exam requirements for a particular certification role. (If you were assigned a unique applicant identification number each time you took an exam, you should send each applicant identification number used to the certification team at IBM (certify@us.ibm.com) and ask them to combine all of your exam results under one ID.)

With the exception of the DB2 UDB V8.1 for Linux, UNIX, and Windows Database Administration Upgrade Exam (Exam 706), each certification exam costs $120.00 (in the United States). Scheduling procedures vary according to how you choose to pay for the exam. If you decide to pay by credit card, you can make arrangements to take the exam immediately after providing the testing vendor with the appropriate information. However, if you elect to pay by check, you will be required to wait until the check has been received and payment has been confirmed before you will be allowed to make arrangements to take the exam. (Prometric, Inc. recommends that if you pay by check, you write your registration ID on the front and contact them seven business days after the check is mailed. At that time, they should have received and confirmed your payment, and you should be able to make arrangements to take the exam you have paid for.)

If, for some reason, you need to reschedule or cancel your testing appointment after it is made, you must do so at least 24 hours before your scheduled test time. Otherwise, you will still be charged the price of the exam.

Taking an IBM Certification Exam

On the day you are scheduled to take a certification exam, you should arrive at the testing center at least 15 minutes before the scheduled start time to sign in. As part of the sign-in process, you will be asked to provide the applicant identification number you were assigned when you made arrangements to take the exam and two forms of identification. One form of identification must contain a recent photograph, and the other must contain your signature. Examples of valid forms of identification include a driver's license (photograph) and a credit card (signature).

Once you are signed in, the exam administrator will instruct you to enter the testing area and select an available workstation. The exam administrator will then enter your name and identification number into the workstation you have chosen, provide you with a pencil and some paper, and instruct you to begin the exam when you are ready. At that point, the title screen of the IBM Certification Exam testing software should be displayed on the computer monitor in front of you. Figure 1–8 illustrates what this screen looks like.

As you can see in Figure 1–8, the title screen of the IBM Certification Exam testing software consists of the IBM Certification Logo along with the title "Professional Certification Program from IBM," the name of the exam that is about to be administered, (for example, the title screen shown in Figure 1–8 indicates that the DB2 UDB V8.1 Family Fundamentals exam is about to be administered), and a welcome message comprised of your name and some basic information on how to get started. Before proceeding, you should:

- Verify that the exam you are about to take is indeed the exam you expected to take. If the name of the exam shown on the title screen is different from the name of the exam you had planned to take, bring this to the attention of the exam administrator immediately.
- Verify that your name is spelled correctly. The way your name appears in the welcome message shown on the title screen reflects how it has been stored in the IBM Certification database. This is how all correspondence to you will be addressed, and more importantly, this is how your name will appear on the certification credentials you will receive if you pass the exam you are about to take.

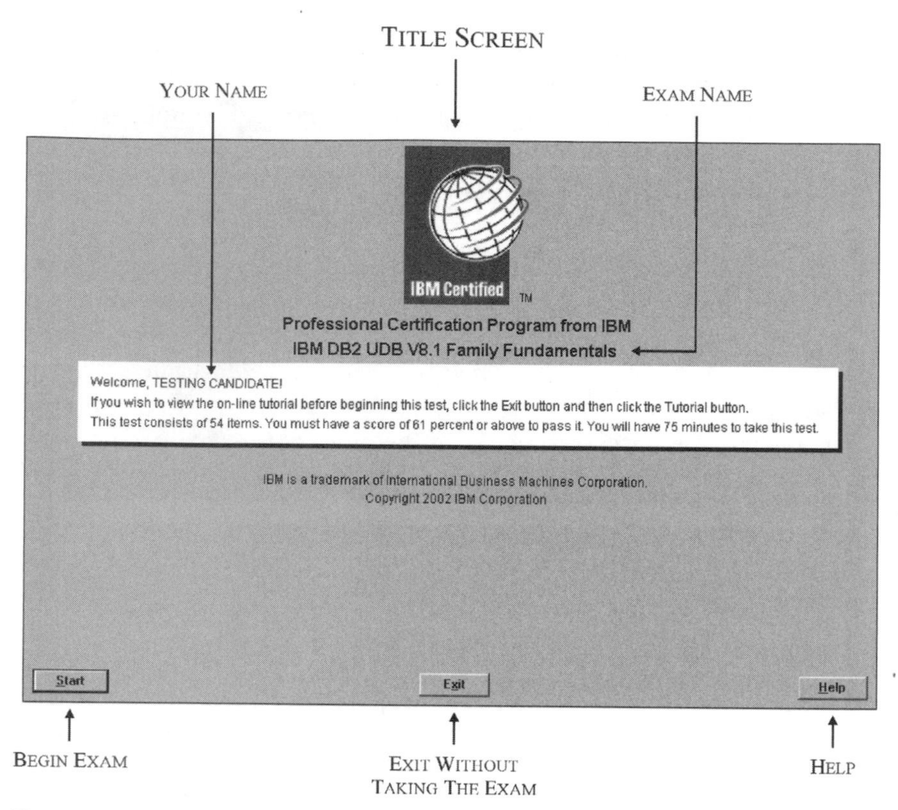

Figure 1–8 Title screen of the IBM Certification Exam testing software.

In addition to telling you which exam is about to be administered, the title screen of the IBM Certification Exam testing software lets you know how many questions you can expect to see on the exam you are about to take, what kind of score you must receive in order to pass, and the time frame in which the exam must be completed. With two exceptions, each exam contains between 50 and 70 questions and is allotted 75 minutes for completion. The DB2 UDB V8.1 for Linux, UNIX, and Windows Database Administration exam (Exam 701) is allotted 90 minutes, and the DB2 UDB V8.1 for Linux, UNIX, and Windows Database Administration Upgrade Exam (Exam 706) is allotted 40 minutes. Although each certification exam must be completed within a predefined time limit, you should never rush through an exam just because the "clock is running"; the time limits imposed are more than adequate for you to work through the exam at a relaxed, but steady pace.

When you are ready, begin by selecting the "Start" push button located in the lower left corner of the screen (refer to Figure 1–8). If instead, you would like a quick refresher course on how to use the IBM Certification Exam testing software, select the "Help" push button located in the lower right corner of the screen. (If you panic and decide you're not ready to take the exam, you can select the "Exit" push button located between the "Start" and "Help" push buttons at the bottom of the screen to get out of the testing software altogether, but I recommend you talk with the exam administrator about your concerns before selecting this push button).

If you plan to take a quick refresher course on how to use the IBM Certification Exam testing software, make sure you do so *before* you select the "Start" push button to begin the exam. Although help is available at any time, the clock does not start running until the "Start" push button is pressed. By viewing help information before the clock is started, you avoid using what could prove to be valuable testing time reading documentation instead of test questions.

Once the "Start" button on the title screen of the IBM Certification Exam testing software is selected, the clock will start running, and the first exam question will be presented in a question panel that looks something like the screen shown in Figure 1–9.

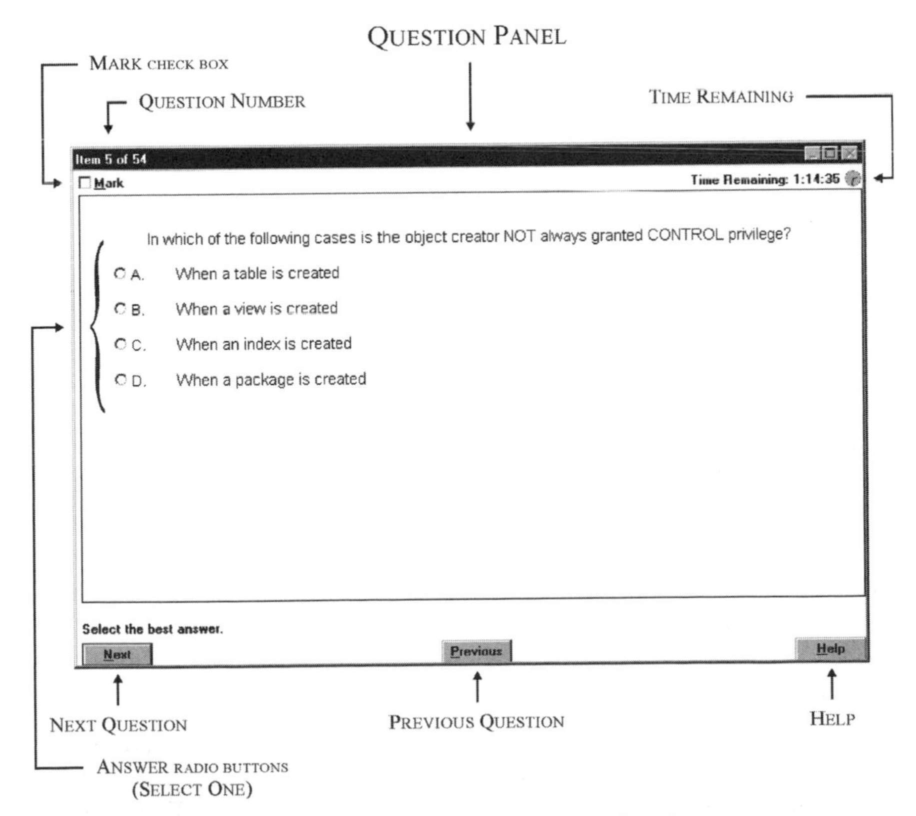

Figure 1–9 Typical question panel of the IBM Certification Exam testing software.

Aside from the question itself, one of the first things you may notice when you examine the question panel of the IBM Certification Exam testing software is the question number displayed in the top left corner of the screen. If you answer each question in the order it is presented, this portion of the screen can act as a progress indicator, because the current question number is displayed along with the total number of questions contained in the exam.

Immediately below the question number, you will find a special check box that is referred to as the "Mark" check box. If you would like to skip the current question for now and come back to it later, or if you're uncertain about the answer(s) you have chosen and would like to look at this question again after you have completed the rest of the exam, you should mark this check box (by placing the mouse pointer over it and pressing the left mouse button). When every question has been viewed once, you will be given the opportunity to review just the marked questions again. At that time, you can answer any unanswered questions remaining and/or re-evaluate any answers you provided that you have some concerns about.

Another important feature that can be found on the question panel is the "Time Remaining" information that is displayed in the top right corner of the screen. As the title implies, this area of the question panel provides continuous feedback on the amount of time you have available to finish and review the exam. If you would like to see more detailed information, such as the actual wall-clock time at which you began the exam and the time frame in which you are expected to complete the exam, you can view that information by selecting the clock icon located just to the right of the "time remaining" information. When this icon is selected (by placing the mouse pointer over it and pressing the left mouse button), a dialog similar to the one shown in Figure 1–10 is displayed.

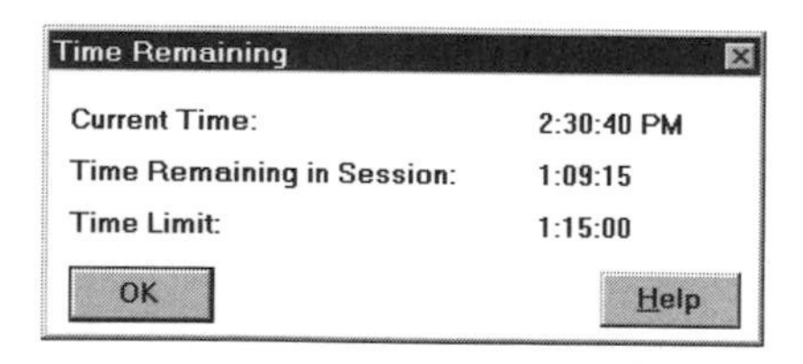

Figure 1–10 Time Remaining dialog.

Obviously, the most important part of the question panel is the exam question itself, along with the corresponding list of possible answers provided. Take the time to read each question carefully. When you have located the correct answer in the list provided, you should mark it by selecting the answer radio-button positioned just to the left of the answer text (by placing the mouse pointer over the desired answer radio-button and pressing the left mouse button). Once you have selected an answer for the question being displayed (or marked it with the "Mark" check box), you can move to the next question by selecting the "Next" push button, which is located in the lower left corner of the screen (refer to Figure 1–9).

If, at any time, you would like to return to the previous question, you can do so by pressing the "Previous" push button, located at the bottom of the screen, just to the right of the "Next" push button. And, if you would like to access help on how to use the IBM Certification Exam testing software, you can do so by selecting the "Help" push button located in the lower right corner of the screen. It is important to note that, although the "Next" and "Previous" push buttons can be used to navigate through the questions provided with the exam, the navigation process itself is not cyclic in nature—that is, when you are on the first question you cannot go to the last question by selecting the "Previous" push button (in fact the "Previous" push button will not be displayed if you are on the first question). Likewise, when you are on the last question, you cannot go to the first question simply by selecting the "Next" push button. However, there is a way to quickly navigate to a specific question from the item review panel, which we will look at shortly.

Although in most cases, only one answer in the list provided is the correct answer to the question shown, there are times when multiple answers are valid. On those occasions, the answer radio-buttons will be replaced with answer check boxes, and the question will be worded in such a way that you will know how many answers are expected. An example of such a question can be seen in Figure 1–11.

These types of questions are answered by selecting the answer check box positioned just to the left of the text *for every correct answer found.* (Again, this is done by placing the mouse pointer over each desired answer check box and pressing the left mouse button).

Once in a while, an illustration or the output from some diagnostic tool will accompany a question. You will be required to view that illustration or output (referred to as an exhibit) before you can successfully answer the question presented. On those occasions, a message instructing you to display the exhibit for the question will precede the actual test question, and a special push button called the "Exhibit" push button will be positioned at the bottom of the screen, between the "Previous" push button and the "Help" push button. An example of such a question can be seen Figure 1–12.

To view the exhibit associated with such a question, you simply select the "Exhibit" push button located at the bottom of the screen. This action will cause the corresponding exhibit panel to be displayed. (A sample exhibit panel can be seen in Figure 1–13.)

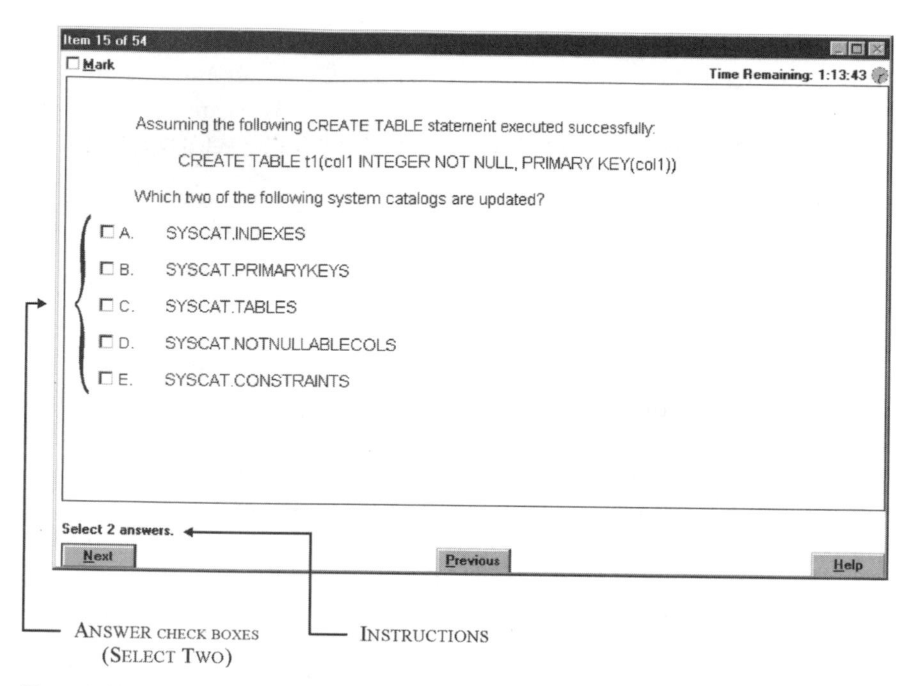

Figure 1–11 Question panel for questions expecting multiple answers.

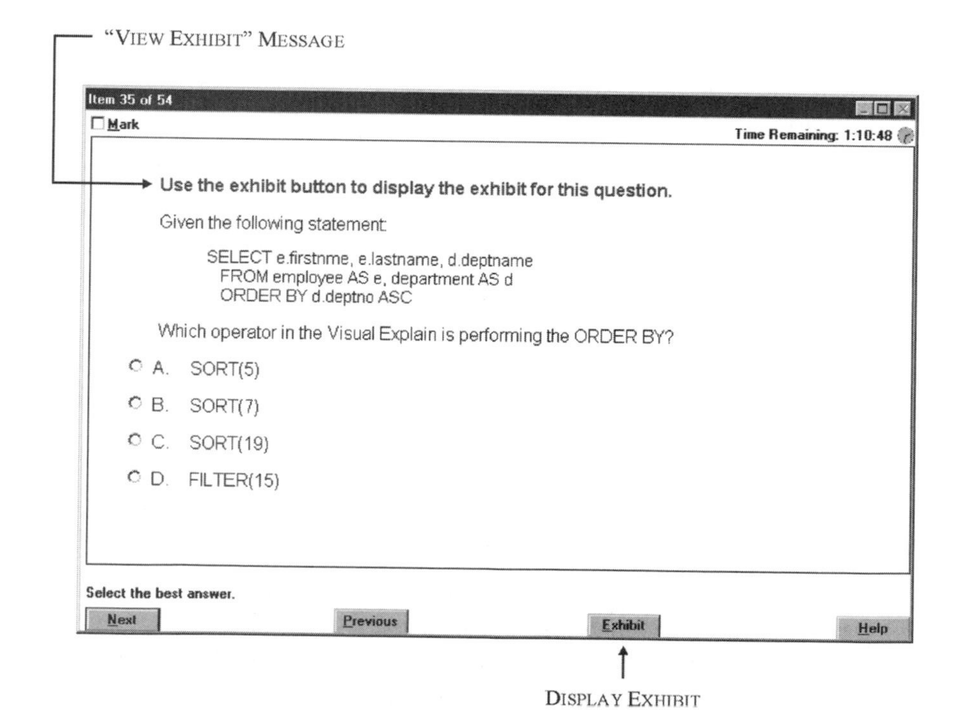

Figure 1–12 Question panel for questions that contain an exhibit.

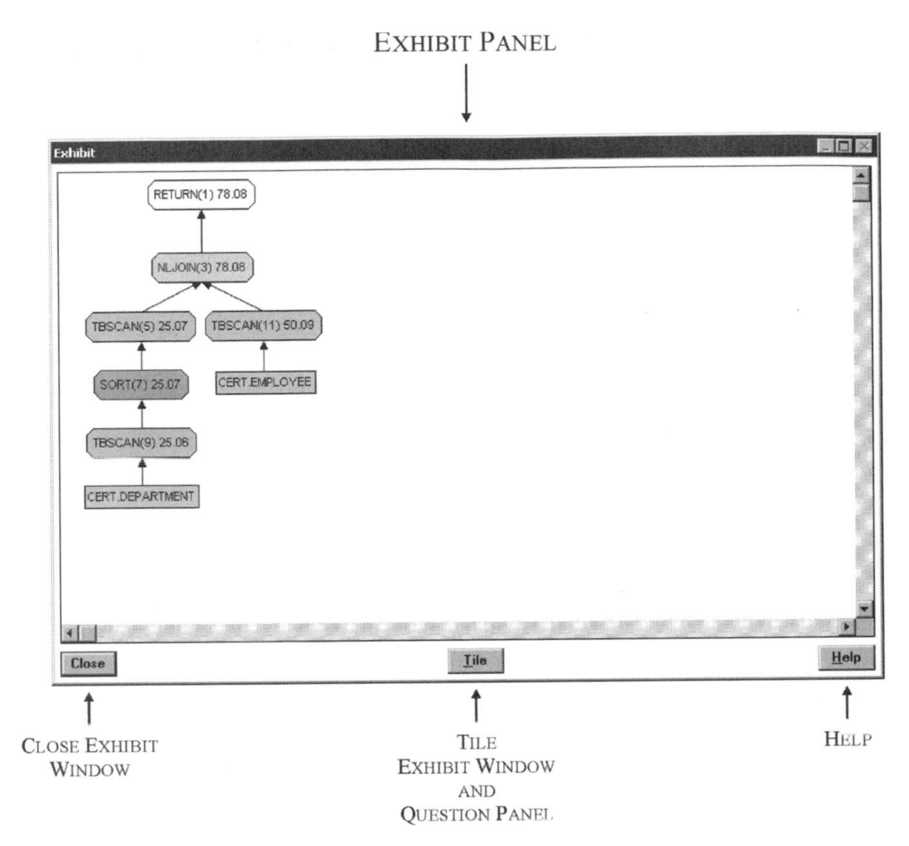

Figure 1–13 Sample exhibit panel.

Exhibit panels are relatively simple. In fact, once an exhibit panel is displayed, there are only two things you can do with it: You can close it by selecting the "Close" push button located at the bottom of the screen, or you can tile it (i.e., make it share screen real estate) with its corresponding question panel by selecting the "Tile" push button, which is located beside the "Close" push button. Aside from having to view the exhibit provided, the process used to answer questions that have exhibits is no different from the process used to answer questions that do not.

When you have viewed every exam question available (by selecting the "Next" push button on every question panel shown), an item review panel that looks something like the panel shown in Figure 1–14 will be displayed.

As you can see in Figure 1–14, the item review panel contains a numerical listing of the questions that make up the certification exam you are taking, along with the answers you have provided for each. Questions that you marked (by selecting the "Mark" check box) are preceded by the letter "M," and questions that you skipped or did not provide the correct number of answers for are assigned the answer "I" to indicate they are incomplete. By selecting the "Review Marked" push button located in the lower left corner of the screen (refer to Figure 1–14), you can quickly go back through just the questions that have been marked. When reviewing marked items in this manner, each time the "Next" push button is selected on a question panel, you are taken to the next marked question in the list until eventually you are returned to the item review panel. Likewise, by selecting the "Review Incomplete" push button located just to the right of the "Review Marked" push button, you can go back though just the questions that have been identified as being incomplete. (Navigation works the same as when the "Review Marked" push button is pressed). If instead, you would like to review a specific question, you

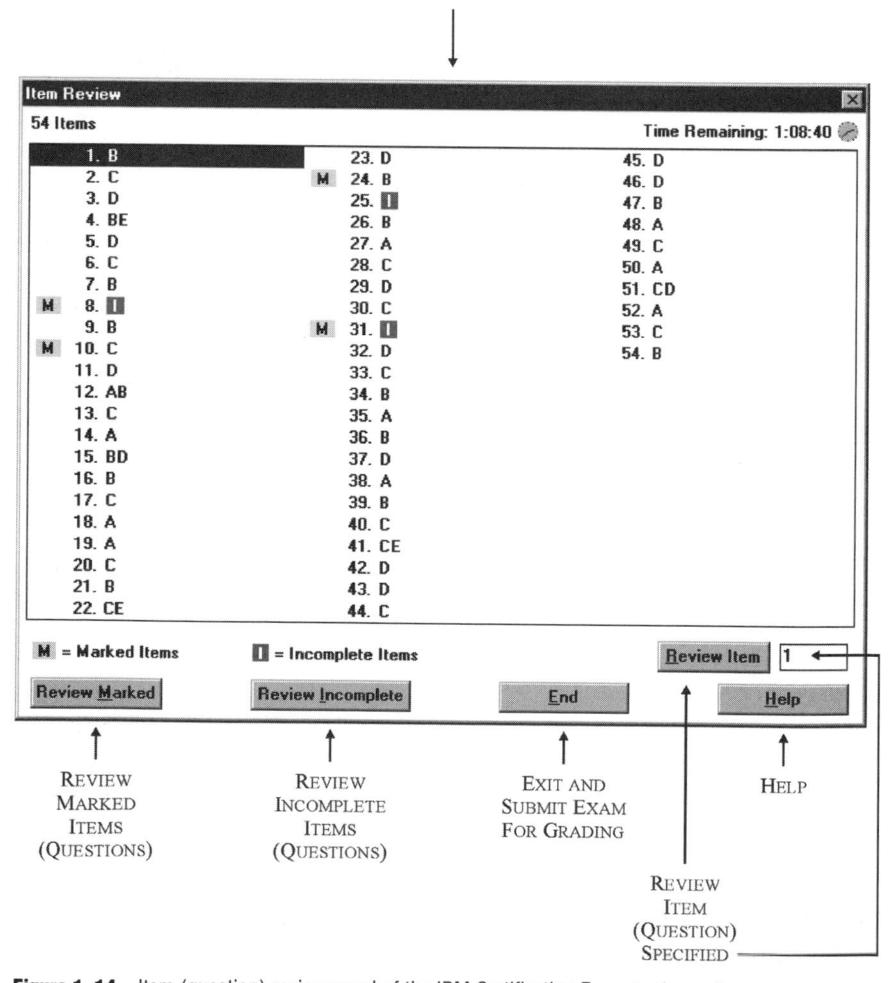

Figure 1–14 Item (question) review panel of the IBM Certification Exam testing software.

can do so by highlighting that question's number or typing that question's number in the entry field provided just to the right of the "Review Item" push button (which is located just above the "Help" push button in the lower right corner of the screen) and selecting the "Review Item" push button.

If you elect to use the "Review Item" push button to review a particular question, the only way you can return to the item review screen is by selecting the "Next" push button found on that question panel and every subsequent question panel presented until no more question panels exist.

One of the first things you should do when the item review panel is displayed is resolve any incomplete items found. (When the exam is graded, each incomplete item found is marked incorrect, and points are deducted from your final score.) Then, if time permits, you should go back and review the questions that you marked. It is important to note that when you finish reviewing a marked question, you should unmark it (by placing the mouse pointer over the "Mark check box and pressing the left mouse button) before going on to the next marked question or returning to the item review panel. This will make it easier for you to keep track of which questions have been reviewed and which have not.

As soon as every incomplete item found has been resolved, the "Review Incomplete" push button is automatically removed from the item review panel. Likewise, when there are no more marked questions, the "Review Marked" push button is removed from the item review panel. Thus, when every incomplete and marked item found has been resolved, the item review panel will look similar to the one shown in Figure 1–15.

Keep in mind that, even when the "Review Incomplete" and "Review Marked" push buttons are no longer available, you can still go back and review a specific question by highlighting that question's number or typing that question's number in the entry field provided and selecting the "Review Item" push button (refer to Figure 1–15).

As soon as you feel comfortable with the answers you have provided, you can end the exam and submit it for grading by selecting the "End" push button, which should now be located in the lower left corner of the item review panel. When this push button is selected (by placing the mouse pointer over it and pressing the left mouse button), a dialog similar to the one shown in Figure 1–16 should be displayed.

If you select the "End" push button on the item review panel before every incomplete item found has been resolved, a dialog similar to the one shown in Figure 1–17 will be displayed instead.

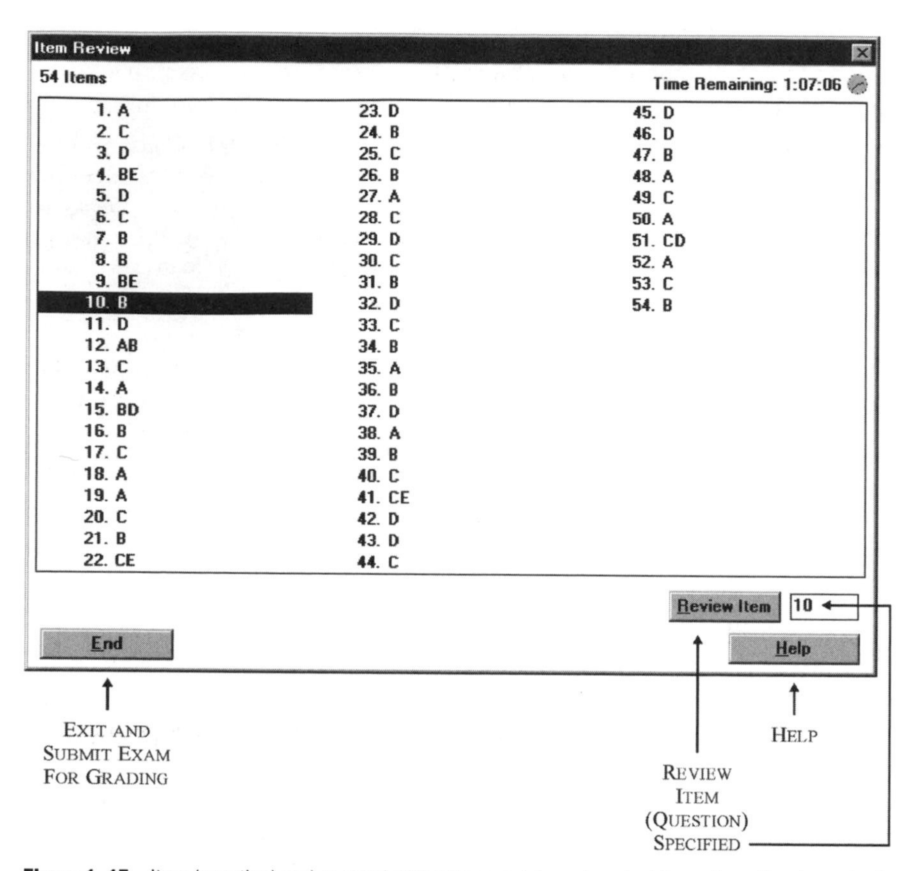

Figure 1–15 Item (question) review panel with all incomplete and marked items (questions) resolved.

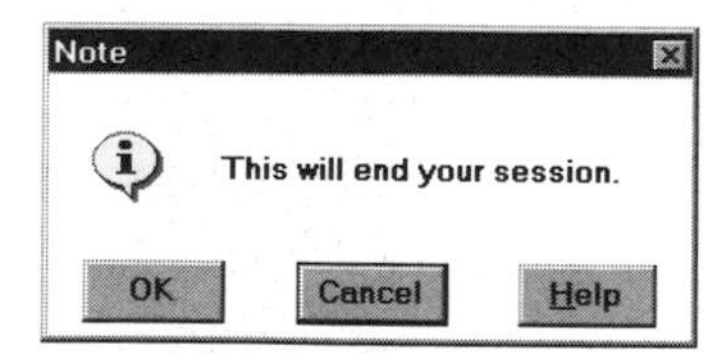

Figure 1–16 End exam session confirmation dialog.

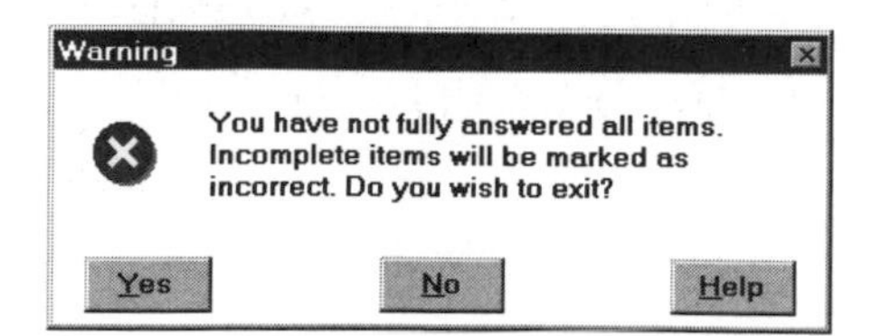

Figure 1–17 Ending exam with incomplete items warning dialog.

Both of these dialogs give you the opportunity to confirm your decision to end the exam and submit it for grading or to reconsider and continue resolving and/or reviewing exam questions. If you wish to do the former, you should select either the "OK" or the "Yes" push button when either of these dialogs is presented; if you wish to do the latter, you should select the "Cancel" or "No" push button, in which case you will be returned to the item review panel. Keep in mind that if you select the "Yes" push button when the dialog shown in Figure 1–17 is displayed, all incomplete items found will be marked as wrong and this will have a negative impact on your final score.

As soon as you confirm that you do indeed wish to end the exam, the IBM Certification Exam testing software will evaluate your answers and produce a score report that indicates whether or not you passed the exam. This report will then be displayed on an exam results panel that looks something like the panel shown in Figure 1–18, and a corresponding hard copy (printout) will be generated.

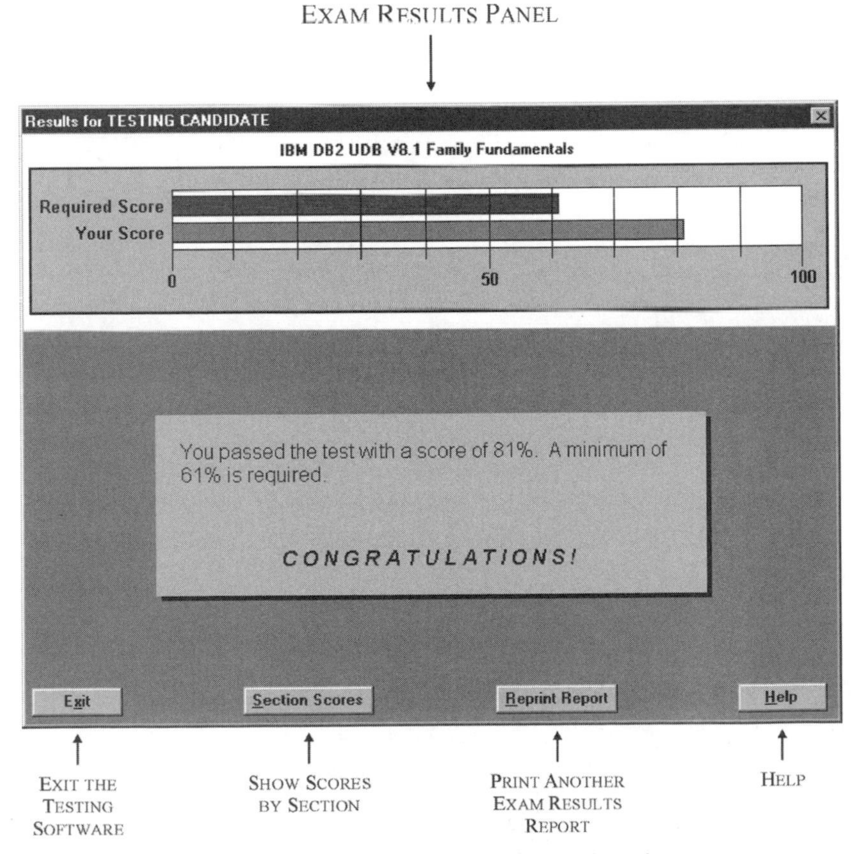

Figure 1–18 Exam results panel of the IBM Certification Exam testing software.

As you can see in Figure 1–18, the exam results panel shows the required score along with your actual score in a horizontal percent bar graph. Directly below this graph is a message that contains the percentage score you received, along with the percentage score needed to pass the exam. If you received a passing score, this message will end with the word "Congratulations!" However, if you received a score that is below the score needed to pass, the message you see will begin with the words "You did not pass the test." and your score will follow.

Each certification exam is broken into sections, and regardless of whether you pass or fail, you should take a few moments to review the score you received for each section. This information can help you evaluate your strengths and weaknesses. If you failed to pass the exam, it can help you identify the areas you should spend some time reviewing before you attempt to take the exam again. To view the section scores for the exam you have just completed, you simply select the "Section Scores" push button located at the bottom of the screen. This action will cause a section scores panel similar to the one shown in Figure 1–19 to be displayed.

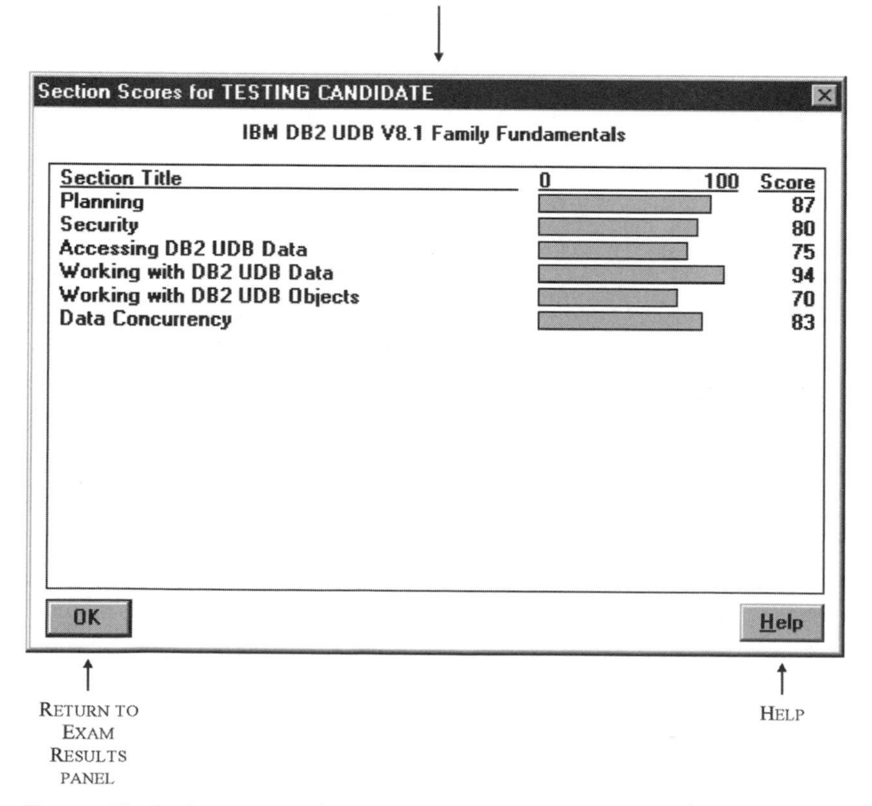

Figure 1–19 Section scores panel.

When you have finished reviewing your section scores, you may return to the exam results panel by selecting the "OK" push button located at the bottom left corner of the screen. From there, you can exit the IBM Certification Exam testing software by selecting the "Exit" push button, which is also located at the bottom left corner of the screen.

Shortly after you take a certification exam (usually within five working days), the testing vendor sends your results, along with your demographic data (i.e., name, address, phone number, etc.) to the IBM Certification Group for processing. If you passed the exam, you will receive credit towards the certification role the exam was designed for and if the exam you took completes the requirements that have been outlined for a particular certification role, you will receive an email (at the email address you provided during registration) that contains a copy of the IBM Certification Agreement and a welcome package that includes a certificate that is suitable for framing (in .PDF format), camera-ready artwork of the IBM certification logo, and guidelines for using the "IBM Certified" mark. (If this email cannot be delivered, the welcome package will be sent to you via regular mail.) You can also receive a printed certificate, along with a wallet-sized certificate, via regular mail by going to the Web site referenced in the email you receive and asking for it—you will be asked to provide your Fulfillment ID and Validation Number (also provided in the email) as verification that you have met the requirements for certification.

Upon receipt of the welcome package, you will become certified and you can begin using the IBM Professional Certification title and trademark. (You should receive the IBM Certification Agreement and welcome package within four to six weeks after IBM processes the exam results.) However, if you failed to pass the exam and you still wish to become DB2 UDB certified, you must make arrangements to take it again (including paying the testing fee again). There are no restrictions on the number of times you can take a particular certification exam; however, you cannot take the same certification exam more than two times within a 30-day period.

PART 2

DB2 UDB Family Fundamentals

Planning

*F*ifteen percent (15%) of the DB2 UDB V8.1 Family Fundamentals certification exam (Exam 700) is designed to test your ability to recognize which of the DB2 Universal Database Family products available must be installed to create a desired environment/configuration and to test your knowledge of the various tools that are provided with DB2 UDB. The questions that make up this portion of the exam are intended to evaluate the following:

- Your ability to identify the DB2 UDB products that make up the DB2 UDB Family.
- Your knowledge of the different DB2 clients available.
- Your knowledge of the nonrelational data concepts that are managed by the DB2 extenders.
- Your knowledge of data warehousing and OLTP concepts.

This chapter is designed to introduce you to the various products that make up the DB2 UDB Family and to the comprehensive set of tools that are provided to assist in administering and managing DB2 UDB instances, databases, and database objects.

Terms you will learn:

DB2 Universal Database Family
DB2 Everyplace Database Edition
DB2 Everyplace Enterprise Edition
DB2 Personal Edition

DB2 Workgroup Server Edition
DB2 Workgroup Server Unlimited Edition
DB2 Enterprise Server Edition
Database Partitioning
DB2 Personal Developer's Edition
DB2 Universal Developer's Edition
DB2 Run-Time Client
DB2 Administration Client
DB2 Application Development Client
DB2 Connect Personal Edition
DB2 Connect Enterprise Edition
DB2 Relational Connect
DB2 AVI Extender
DB2 Text Extender
DB2 Net Search Extender
DB2 XML Extender
DB2 Spatial Extender
DB2 Data Links Manager
DB2 Warehouse Manager
Query, Loading, Extraction, Transformation
Data Warehouse Center
Information Catalog Manager
Query Patroller
Query Management Facility (QMF)
DB2 OLAP Server
Control Center
Replication Center
Satellite Administration Center
Command Center
SQL Assist
Visual Explain
Task Center
Information Catalog Center
Health Center

Journal
License Center
Development Center
Information Center
Command Line Processor
Configuration Assistant

Techniques you will master:

Understanding the core components of the DB2 Universal Database Family.

Recognizing the differences between each edition of DB2 Universal Database.

Recognizing the types of DB2 UDB clients available and understanding when each is used.

Understanding what DB2 UDB extenders are available, along with what functionality each extender provides.

Understanding Data Warehouse and OLAP concepts.

Understanding what types of tools are available, along with what actions each tool has been designed to perform.

The DB2 Universal Database Family

DB2 Universal Database, Version 8.1 is the latest release of IBM's popular data management software that was first introduced in 1989. Like previous versions, DB2 UDB V8.1 runs on a wide variety of platforms (AIX, HP-UX, Linux, Solaris, Windows NT, Windows 2000, and Windows XP), and several editions are available—each of which has been designed to meet a specific business need. These editions, along with an extensive suite of add-on products that provide additional storage capability and advanced connectivity, are collectively known as the *DB2 Universal Database Family.*

The heart of the DB2 Universal Database Family is comprised of six different editions of DB2 UDB, designed to support increasingly complex database/user environments, and two developer's editions, containing a rich set of tools that can be used to develop applications that interact with DB2 UDB databases, regardless of where they reside. These editions are:

- DB2 Everyplace Database Edition
- DB2 Everyplace Enterprise Edition

- DB2 Universal Database Personal Edition
- DB2 Workgroup Server Edition
- DB2 Workgroup Server Unlimited Edition
- DB2 Enterprise Server Edition
- DB2 Personal Developer's Edition
- DB2 Universal Developer's Edition

All of the DB2 UDB editions available, along with the type of computing environment each edition is primarily designed for, can be seen in Figure 2–1.

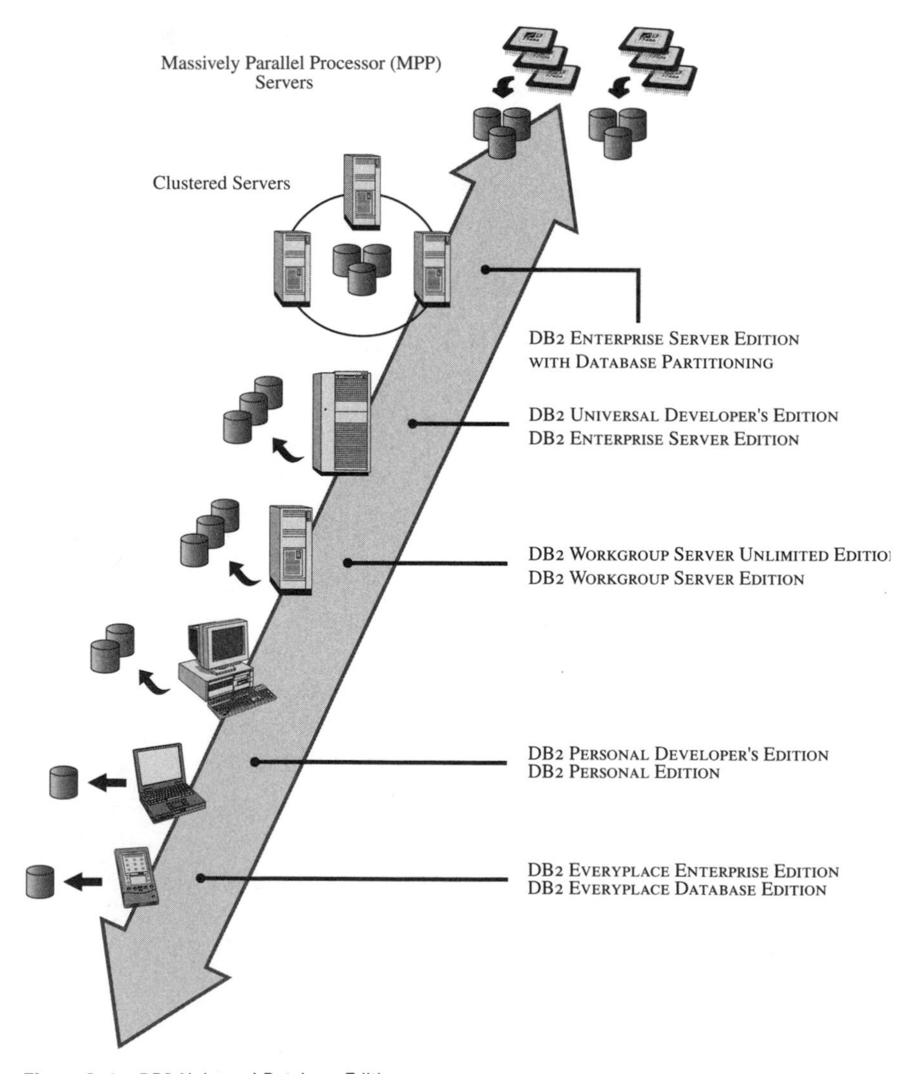

Figure 2–1 DB2 Universal Database Editions.

Each DB2 UDB edition utilizes the same database engine, recognizes ANSI Structured Query Language (SQL), and offers an abundance of graphical user interface (GUI) tools that can be used to both manage and interact with DB2 UDB databases and database objects.

DB2 Everyplace—Database Edition and Enterprise Edition

DB2 Everyplace is both a relational database management system and a synchronization server that allows enterprise applications and data to be accessed from mobile devices such as personal digital assistants (PDAs) and handheld personal computers (HPCs). With a footprint of approximately 180 kilobytes, DB2 Everyplace can be run on any of the following operating systems:

- Palm OS
- Symbian OS Version 6
- Microsoft Windows CE/Pocket PC
- Win32 (Windows NT and Windows 2000)
- QNX Neutrino, Linux, and embedded Linux devices

DB2 Everyplace is available in two editions: DB2 Everyplace Database Edition and DB2 Everyplace Enterprise Edition. DB2 Everyplace Database Edition is designed to be used by Independent Software Vendors (ISVs) and application developers who wish to create powerful mobile and embedded applications that work with DB2 Everyplace database data stored directly on a mobile device. On the other hand, DB2 Everyplace Enterprise Edition is designed to be a complete datacentric mobile synchronization server. This secure server is responsible for managing the distribution and synchronization of data between mobile device users and back-end data sources such as DB2 UDB, Informix, Oracle, Sybase, and Microsoft SQL Server. (Synchronization is performed whenever a connection to the backend data source is detected.)

The Command Line Processor (CLP) is available with both DB2 Everyplace Database Edition and DB2 Everyplace Enterprise Edition. It can be used to execute industry standard SQL statements; thus with DB2 Everyplace, users can create or drop database objects (such as tables and indexes), as well as insert, update, delete, or retrieve specific data values. Additionally, both editions of DB2 Everyplace come with a complete set of development tools that can be used to build, deploy, and support DB2 UDB applications that work with both a DB2 Everyplace database and with enterprise data stored on any supported back-end database server.

DB2 Universal Database Personal Edition

DB2 Universal Database Personal Edition (PE) is a single-user database management system that is designed to be used on Personal Computer (PC) systems running any of the following operating systems:

- Linux
- Windows NT
- Windows 2000
- Windows XP (with FixPack #4 or later)

With DB2 Universal Database Personal Edition, a user can create, manipulate, and administer any number of databases; however, each database created must reside on a storage medium managed by the PC on which the DB2 UDB software has been installed. Remote clients cannot access databases that are under DB2 Universal Database Personal Edition's control, but PCs running DB2 Universal Database Personal Edition can act as remote clients and access data stored on other DB2 UDB servers. Furthermore, DB2 Universal Database Personal Edition allows databases under its control to be managed from remote DB2 UDB servers, which makes it the perfect edition for standalone or remote office implementations that do not require multiuser capability. Figure 2–2 shows the database environment that can exist when DB2 Universal Database Personal Edition is used.

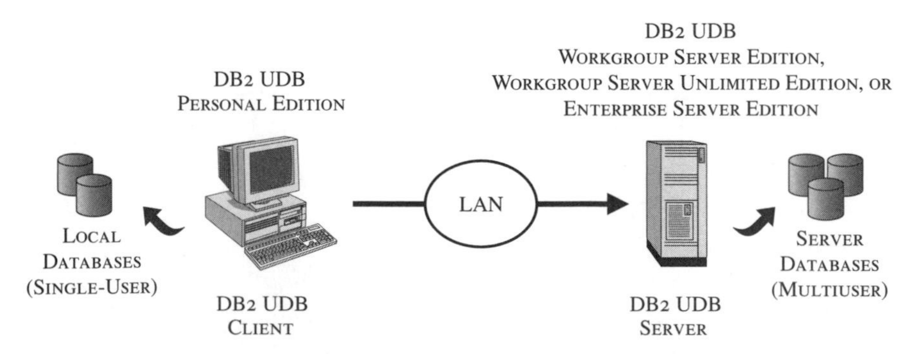

Figure 2–2 DB2 Universal Database Personal Edition database environment.

DB2 Workgroup Server Edition

DB2 Universal Database Workgroup Server Edition (DB2 WSE) is a full-function, client/server database management system designed to be used on microcomputers that have up to 4 CPUs and are running any of the following operating systems:

- AIX
- HP-UX
- Solaris
- Linux
- Windows NT
- Windows 2000
- Windows XP

For the most part, DB2 Universal Database Workgroup Server Edition is functionally equivalent to DB2 Universal Database Enterprise Server Edition. However, DB2 Universal Database Workgroup Server Edition does not provide integrated mainframe connectivity, and its feature set is somewhat limited (for example, 64-bit computing, Data Links, and external Web-based usage are not supported). Figure 2–3 shows the database environment that can exist when DB2 Universal Database Workgroup Server Edition is installed.

Remote clients can access databases that are under DB2 Universal Database Workgroup Server Edition's control, and computers running DB2 Universal Database Workgroup Server Edition can act as remote clients to other DB2 UDB servers. In both cases, client/server communications are performed using one of the following communications protocols:

- Transmission Control Protocol/Internet Protocol (TCP/IP)
- NetBIOS
- Internet Packet Exchange/Sequence Packet Exchange (IPX/SPX)
- Advanced Program-To-Program Communications (APPC)
- Named Pipes

DB2 Universal Database Workgroup Server Edition is ideal for small- to medium-sized business environments that need a full-function database server that is scalable and available over a local area network (LAN) or a wide area network (WAN). It is also useful for departments that are comprised of a small number of internal users who need a relational data store.

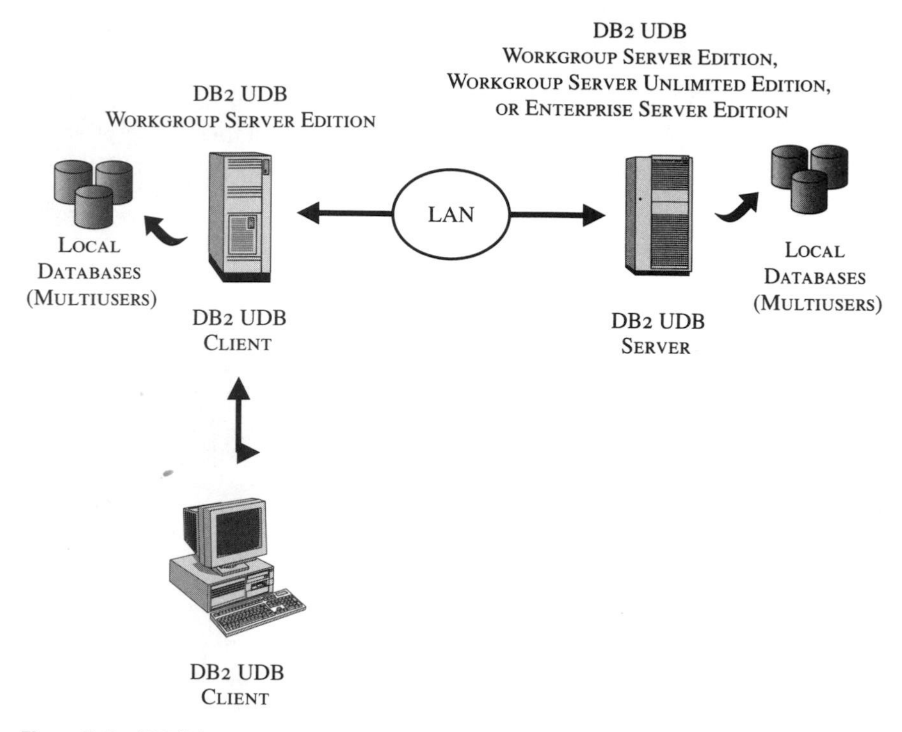

Figure 2–3 DB2 Universal Database Workgroup Server Edition database environment.

DB2 Workgroup Server Unlimited Edition

DB2 Universal Database Workgroup Server Unlimited Edition (DB2 WSUE) is essentially DB2 Universal Database Workgroup Server Edition with a simplified per-processor licensing model, as opposed to the capacity (registered user) pricing model DB2 Universal Database Workgroup Server Edition uses. And like DB2 Universal Database Workgroup Server Edition, DB2 Universal Database Workgroup Server Unlimited Edition can be used on microcomputers that are running any of the following operating systems:

- AIX
- HP-UX
- Solaris
- Linux
- Windows NT
- Windows 2000
- Windows XP

However, because its licensing model is different, DB2 Universal Database Workgroup Server Unlimited Edition provides support for external Web-based usage. This makes it the perfect choice for departmental or small business environments that need Web-based access to their data and for departments and businesses whose sheer number of users makes per-processor licensing more attractive than the capacity licensing model used by DB2 Universal Database Workgroup Server Edition.

DB2 Enterprise Server Edition

DB2 Universal Database Enterprise Server Edition (DB2 ESE) is a full-function, Web-enabled client/server database management system designed to be used on any size server that is running one of the following operating systems:

- AIX
- HP-UX
- Solaris
- Linux
- Windows NT
- Windows 2000

In addition to providing all of the functionality found in DB2 Universal Database Workgroup Server Edition, DB2 Universal Database Enterprise Server Edition comes packaged with a tightly integrated connectivity product (DB2 Connect) that allows it to participate in heterogeneous networks using the Distributed Relational Database Architecture (DRDA) protocol. This feature allows up to five DB2 Universal Database Enterprise Server Edition users to interact with iSeries and zSeries-based DB2 databases, as well as non-database host resources like CICS, VSAM, and IMS. (If more user connectivity is needed, you can purchase additional DB2 Connect user entitlements.) Figure 2–4 shows the database environment that can exist when DB2 Universal Database Enterprise Server Edition is installed.

Distributed Relational Database Architecture (DRDA) is comprised of two distinct components: an Application Requestor (AR) and an Application Server (AS). Any client that implements an Application Requestor can connect to any server that has implemented an Application Server, and any server that implements an Application Server can be accessed by any client that has implemented an Application Requestor. Thus, if only one DRDA component has been implemented on a client or a server, communication can only flow one way. With DB2 Universal Database Enterprise Server Edition, both an Application Requestor and an Application Server are implemented, so

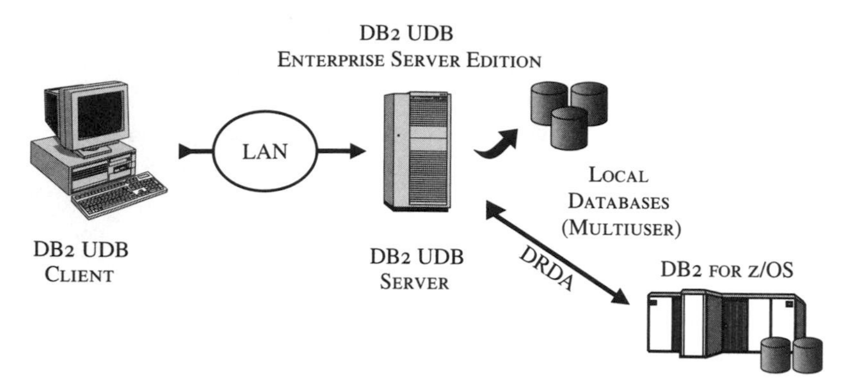

Figure 2–4 DB2 Universal Database Enterprise Server Edition database environment.

communications can flow in both directions—provided the iSeries or zSeries server that DB2 Universal Database Enterprise Server Edition is attempting to communicate with also has implemented both an Application Requestor and an Application Server.

DB2 Universal Database Enterprise Server Edition is designed to meet the database server needs of midsize to large businesses, particularly where Internet and/or enterprise connectivity is important; its scalability and reliability, coupled with its robust feature set, make it the ideal foundation for building data warehouses, online transaction processing systems, or Web-based solutions, as well as an excellent back-end for packaged solutions like ERP, CRM, or SCM.

Database Partitioning Feature

With Version 7.1, a special edition of DB2 UDB known as DB2 Universal Database Enterprise Extended Edition (EEE) had to be used if you wanted to divide (or partition) a single database into two or more sections within a large SMP workstation or across multiple workstations running the same operating system. With Version 8.1, the ability to partition a database is provided through a special feature of DB2 Universal Database Enterprise Server Edition known as the Database Partitioning Feature (DPF).

When enabled, the Database Partitioning Feature provides users with multiple benefits, including the ability to support very large databases or complex workloads and increased parallelism for administration tasks. And where DB2 Universal Database Enterprise Extended Edition was a completely different product, the Database Partitioning Feature is license-activated and does not require the installation of additional products before database partitioning can be performed. Thus, if you already have DB2 Universal Database Enterprise Server Edition installed and determine that it would be beneficial to partition one or more of the databases that are under its control, it is not necessary to remove the current installation and install a new edition. Instead, you simply purchase a Database Partitioning Feature license for each server you plan to create database partitions on.

Figure 2–5 illustrates how the Data Partitioning Feature can be used in conjunction with DB2 Universal Database Enterprise Server Edition to produce a clustered database server environment.

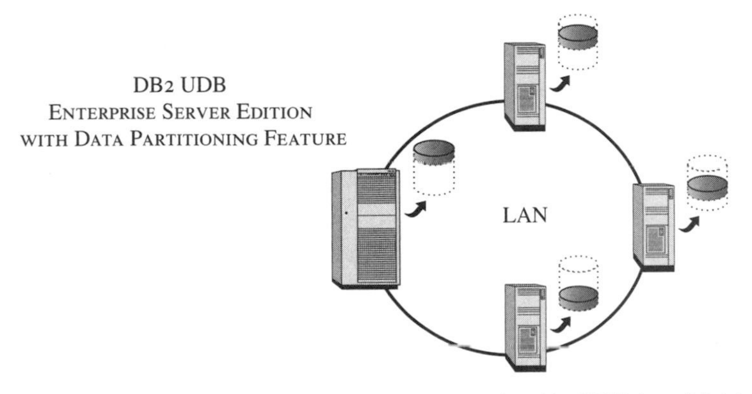

Figure 2–5 Clustered database server environment produced by DB2 Universal Database Enterprise Server Edition and the Data Partitioning Feature.

DB2 Personal Developer's Edition

DB2 Personal Developer's Edition contains both the single-user database management system that is provided with DB2 Universal Database Personal Edition and a software development toolkit (SDK) that can be used to develop desktop applications that interact with single-user databases that fall under DB2 Universal Database Personal Edition's control. Using the tools provided with the DB2 Personal Developer's Edition, a developer can construct applications that interact with DB2 UDB databases, using a wide variety of available methods:

- Embedded Structured Query Language (SQL)
- IBM's Call Level Interface (CLI), which is comparable to Microsoft's Open Database Connectivity (ODBC) interface
- DB2 UDB's rich set of Application Programming Interfaces (APIs)
- Java Database Connectivity (JDBC)
- SQLJ

The toolkit provided with DB2 Personal Developer's Edition contains a set of libraries and header files for each programming language supported

(COBOL, FORTRAN, C, C++, and Java), a set of sample programs to help with your development efforts, and an SQL precompiler/binder, which is used to process source code files containing embedded SQL so that they can be compiled and linked by a conventional compiler. Like DB2 Universal Database Personal Edition, DB2 Personal Developer's Edition is designed to be used on Personal Computer (PC) systems that are running any of the following operating systems:

- Linux
- Windows NT
- Windows 2000
- Windows XP (with FixPack #4 or later)

Furthermore, applications developed with the toolkit provided with DB2 Personal Developer's Edition can be run on any PC on which DB2 Personal Developer's Edition or DB2 Universal Database Personal Edition has been installed.

DB2 Universal Developer's Edition

DB2 Universal Developer's Edition is designed to be used by Independent Software Vendors and application developers who wish to build solutions that utilize the latest DB2 Universal Database technologies available. This comprehensive developer's package includes each edition of DB2 Universal Database except DB2 Everyplace, all three DB2 UDB clients, both editions of DB2 Connect, all of the DB2 Extenders, the DB2 Warehouse Manager, DB2 Intelligent Miner, and the same software development toolkit that comes with DB2 Personal Developer's Edition. However, because DB2 Universal Developer's Edition provides an application developer with a package that contains all of the tools needed to design, build, and prototype applications for deployment on any DB2 client or server platform available at a relatively low cost, none of the software provided in this package can be used to establish a production system.

DB2 Universal Database Clients

In order to create a client/server environment, you must have some kind of client software installed on the workstation that will serve as the client before communications with a server can be established. Consequently, most DB2 Universal Database editions contain the software needed to set up two or more types of clients. Three types of DB2 Universal Database clients are available:

- DB2 Run-Time Client
- DB2 Administration Client
- DB2 Application Development Client

Any one of these three clients can be created (by installing the appropriate client software) on any number of workstations; however, the type of client you elect to create for a given workstation should be determined by the requirements of that workstation. For example, if a particular workstation will only be used to execute a database application that interacts with a database stored on a DB2 UDB server, it would need to be set up as a DB2 Run-Time Client (by installing the DB2 Run-Time Client software appropriate for the operating system found on that workstation). As you can see from this example, in order to know which client to create for a given situation, you need to understand how each of the three clients available differ and when each one should be used.

DB2 Run-Time Client

The DB2 Run-Time Client provides workstations running a variety of operating systems with the ability to access DB2 UDB databases that are controlled by one or more DB2 UDB and/or DB2 Connect servers. This client is a lightweight client that provides basic connectivity, which allows client workstation users to issue interactive SQL statements that access data stored on a DB2 UDB/DB2 Connect server. Likewise, the DB2 Run-Time Client allows applications using ODBC/CLI, JDBC, SQLJ, and OLE DB to run on a client workstation and interact with data stored on a DB2 UDB/DB2 Connect server.

DB2 Run-Time Client software is available for the following operating systems:

- AIX
- HP-UX
- Solaris
- Linux
- Windows NT
- Windows 2000

Although the DB2 Run-Time Client provided with earlier versions of DB2 UDB contained GUI facilities, such as the Configuration Assistant, most of those facilities have been removed in Version 8.1 to reduce storage space requirements. In fact, the only GUI tool available with the Version 8.1 DB2 Run-Time Client is the ODBC/CLI Administration tool.

Figure 2–6 shows the environment that can exist when the DB2 Run-Time Client is used to access a DB2 UDB server.

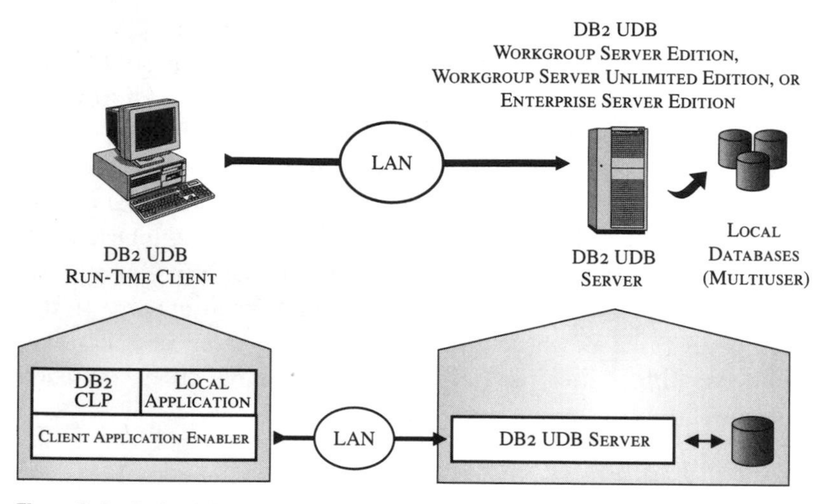

Figure 2–6 Typical DB2 client-server environment.

DB2 Administration Client

Like the DB2 Run-Time Client, the DB2 Administration Client provides workstations running a variety of operating systems with the ability to access DB2 UDB databases that are controlled by one or more DB2 UDB and/or DB2 Connect servers. However, where the DB2 Run-Time Client provides basic connectivity capabilities, the DB2 Administration Client provides basic connectivity and the ability to perform administrative operations on DB2 UDB databases that reside on a DB2 UDB/DB2 Connect server from a client workstation. To help with this endeavor, the DB2 Administration Client comes with a rich set of administrative tools (the Control Center and the Configuration Assistant) as well as support for Thin Clients.

DB2 Administration Client software is available for the following operating systems:

- AIX
- HP-UX
- Solaris
- Linux
- Windows NT
- Windows 2000

DB2 Application Development Client

Like the other clients, the DB2 Application Development Client provides workstations running a variety of operating systems with the ability to access DB2 UDB databases that are controlled by one or more DB2 UDB and/or DB2 Connect servers. However, unlike the other clients, the DB2 Application Development Client also provides a collection of both GUI and non-GUI tools and components that can be used to develop, test, and run applications designed to interact with databases that reside on DB2 UDB/DB2 Connect servers. As you might imagine, the application development tools provided with the DB2 Application Development Client are the same as those provided with the DB2 Developer's editions (the Development Center, a set of libraries and header files for each programming language supported, a set of sample programs to help with your development efforts, and an SQL precompiler/binder, which is used to process source code files containing embedded SQL so that they can be compiled and linked by a conventional compiler). The Application Development Client includes the tools and components provided with the DB2 Administration Client product as well.

DB2 Application Development Client software is available for the following operating systems:

- AIX
- HP-UX
- Solaris
- Linux
- Windows NT
- Windows 2000

Other DB2 Universal Database Products

Along with the DB2 UDB editions that make up the core of the DB2 Universal Database Family, several other products designed to expand and enhance the functionality and capabilities of DB2 UDB are available. These products, which make up the remainder of the DB2 Universal Database Family, are:

- DB2 Connect
- DB2 Relational Connect
- DB2 Extenders
- DB2 Data Links Manager

- DB2 Warehouse Manager
- Information Catalog Center
- DB2 Query Patroller
- Query Management Facility
- DB2 OLAP Server

The following sections describe each of these products.

DB2 Connect

DB2 Connect provides a robust, highly scalable communication infrastructure that is used to connect PCs and LAN-based workstations to mainframe and minicomputer databases managed by DB2 for z/OS, DB2 for MVS/ESA, DB2 for VSE/VM, and DB2 for AS/400. DB2 Connect also allows DB2 UDB applications to interface with a wide variety of off-the-shelf products, such as spreadsheets (Lotus 1-2-3 and Microsoft Excel), decision-support tools (BusinessObjects, Brio and Impromptu, and Crystal Reports), non-DB2 databases (Lotus Approach and Microsoft Access), and client/server application development tools (PowerSoft, PowerBuilder, and Borland Delphi). DB2 Connect is an add-on product that must be purchased separately unless DB2 Universal Database Enterprise Server Edition is installed; a limited-use version is provided with DB2 Universal Database Enterprise Server Edition. Once DB2 Connect is installed and configured, DB2 UDB applications that run on Linux, UNIX, and Windows platforms can work with any supported database/product transparently. However, in order for the reverse to be true (i.e., DB2 UDB applications that run on mainframes and minicomputers can interact with DB2 UDB databases stored on Linux, UNIX, and Windows platforms), DB2 Connect Enterprise Edition or higher must be installed on the Linux, UNIX, or Windows workstation.

DB2 Connect is available in several editions and each is designed to address specific data access and usage growth needs. The DB2 Connect editions that are available are:

- DB2 Connect Personal Edition
- DB2 Connect Enterprise Edition
- DB2 Connect Application Server Edition
- DB2 Connect Unlimited Edition

DB2 Connect Personal Edition (PE). DB2 Connect Personal Edition provides direct connectivity between Linux and Windows workstations and mainframe/iSeries database servers. It is designed for traditional two-tier client-server environments in which each client application connects directly to the desired database on the server. This edition of DB2 Connect does not accept inbound requests for data and cannot be used with multiuser systems and multiuser application servers.

DB2 Connect Enterprise Edition (EE). DB2 Connect Enterprise Edition provides direct connectivity between Linux, UNIX, and Windows workstations and mainframe/iSeries database servers. It is designed for two-tier client-server applications where the use of a mid-tier gateway server is desirable. Unlike DB2 Connect Personal Edition, DB2 Connect Enterprise Edition accepts inbound client requests and is suitable for use in environments where the number of concurrent users can easily be determined or where the number of registered users is relatively small. However, this edition of DB2 Connect is not suitable in environments where multitier client server applications or Web-based applications are used, because determining the number of concurrent users in such environments is not practical and licensing every registered user may be cost-prohibitive.

DB2 Connect Application Server Edition (ASE). DB2 Connect Application Server provides the same functionality as DB2 Connect Enterprise Edition; this edition is designed to provide a cheaper alternative to DB2 Connect Unlimited Edition for environments in which one or more multitier applications will access enterprise data with regular frequency, and the growth of the number of users of these applications is expected to be slow or minimal over time.

DB2 Connect Unlimited Edition (UE). DB2 Connect Unlimited Edition essentially provides an unlimited number of both DB2 Connect Personal Edition and DB2 Connect Enterprise Edition licenses; this edition is designed to provide a pricing alternative for environments where either a large amount of access to enterprise data is needed today or a large amount of mainframe access will be needed sometime in the future.

DB2 Relational Connect

DB2 Relational Connect works in conjunction with DB2 Universal Database Enterprise Server Edition to provide native read access to Informix IDS, Oracle, Sybase, and Microsoft SQL Server databases. Essentially, DB2 Relational Connect allows you to combine data stored in other DBMSs with data that is being managed by DB2 UDB; differences between DB2 UDB functions and data types are mapped so that a collection of different databases can be viewed and manipulated as if they were managed by a single resource. DB2 Relational Connect is an add-on product that must be purchased separately. Typically, it is used to create a federated database environment or to make data stored in another DBMS product available to the DB2 Data Warehouse Center.

DB2 Extenders

In most relational database systems, data is stored according to its data type, and DB2 Universal Database is no exception. Therefore, in order to store a wide variety of data, DB2 UDB contains a rich set of built-in data types, along with a set of functions designed to manipulate each data type provided. DB2 UDB also allows users to create their own data types (known as user-defined types) and supporting functions (known as user-defined functions) to better handle data that does not map directly to one of the built-in data types. Building on this capability, the developers of DB2 UDB created several sets of user-defined data types and user-defined functions for the sole purpose of managing specific kinds of data. Collectively, these sets of user-defined data types and functions are referred to as *extenders*, because they extend the basic functionality and capabilities of a DB2 UDB database. Currently, five different extender products are available. They are:

- DB2 Audio, Video, and Image (AVI) Extender
- DB2 Text Extender
- DB2 Net Search Extender
- DB2 XML Extender
- DB2 Spatial Extender

DB2 Audio, Video, and Image Extender. As the name implies, the DB2 Audio, Video, and Image Extender contains a set of user-defined data types and functions that allow a DB2 UDB database to store and manipulate non-traditional data such as audio clips, movies, and pictures. The data types and functions that are provided by the DB2 Audio, Video, and Image Extender can be used just like any of the built-in data types and functions in SQL statements. And because SQL can be used to construct multi-data-type queries, this extender provides a lot of flexibility when searching for information. For example, a query could be written to locate a particular movie by searching for its description, the date it was recorded, or its total playing time. Additionally, the Query By Image Content (QBIC) capability provided with this extender can be used to locate images that have a particular color combination, or that have colors and/or textures that are similar to those of another image.

DB2 Text Extender. The DB2 Text Extender contains a set of user-defined data types that can store complex text documents in a DB2 UDB database and a set of user-defined functions that can extract key information from such documents, regardless of where they are stored (text documents can be stored either in a DB2 UDB database or in a file system that is accessible to the DB2 Database Manager). This extender's strength comes from IBM's powerful linguistic search and text-mining technology; this technology allows users to construct queries that will search through any kind of text document, including most word processing documents for:

- A specific word.
- A specific phrase.
- A particular word sequence.
- Word variations (such as plural forms of a word or the word in a different tense).
- Synonyms of a particular word.
- Similar-sounding words.
- Words that have a similar spelling.
- Words that have a particular pattern (for example, all words that begin with the characters "data").

DB2 Net Search Extender. The DB2 Net Search Extender provides application developers using Net.Data, Java, or DB2's Call Level Interface (CLI) with a way to integrate the search functionality provided by the DB2 Text Extender into their applications. Because the DB2 Net Search Extender is similar to, but performs faster than, the DB2 Text Extender, it can be particularly advantageous when used with Internet applications, where search performance on large indexes can be critical and the ability to scale the processing of concurrent queries is needed. The key features the DB2 Net Search Extender provides include the following:

- The ability to create multiple indexes on a single column (indexing proceeds without acquiring row-level locks).
- The ability to create indexes across multiple processors.
- The ability to search for a particular word or phrase.
- The ability to search for words that have a similar spelling.
- The ability to perform wildcard searches (for example, search for all words that begin with the characters "net").
- The ability to control how search results are sorted.
- The ability to limit the number of search results returned.

- The ability to search for tags or sections (with or without using Boolean operations).

It is important to note that unlike other DB2 extenders, which provide their functionality through a set of user-defined data types and user-defined functions, the DB2 Net Search Extender provides its functionality through a set of stored procedures.

DB2 XML Extender. The DB2 XML Extender contains a set of user-defined data types and functions that can be used to store extensible markup language (XML) documents in a DB2 UDB database (as character data) and to manipulate such documents, regardless of where they are stored (either in a DB2 UDB database or in a file system that is accessible to the DB2 Database Manager). The DB2 XML Extender can be used to decompose (extract) XML elements from a document and store them in columns and tables; it can also compose (create) new XML documents from existing character and numerical data or previously extracted XML data. And because the same powerful search capabilities provided with the DB2 Text Extender are available with the DB2 XML Extender, specific items can be quickly located within a set of XML documents.

DB2 Spatial Extender. Traditionally, geo-spatial data has been managed by specialized Geographic Information Systems (GISs) that because of their design, have been unable to integrate their spatial data with business data stored in other relational database management systems and/or data sources. However, shortly after DB2 Universal Database, Version 5.0 was released, IBM, together with Environmental Systems Research Institute (ESRI), a leading manufacturer of spatial database systems, created a set of user-defined data types for describing spatial data (for example, points, lines, and polygons) and a set of user-defined functions to query spatial objects (for example, to find area, endpoints, and intersects). This set of user-defined data types and functions make up the DB2 Spatial Extender.

The DB2 Spatial Extender can be used to store, generate, and analyze spatial information about geographic features. With this extender, spatial data can be stored along with nonspatial business information in the same DB2 UDB database and presented in a three-dimensional format. This capability allows businesses to make geospatial business-intelligence decisions without having to physically move data from one location to another.

DB2 Data Links Manager

The DB2 Data Links Manager allows you to manage and manipulate data that resides in both unstructured files (for example, audio clips, images, and video streams) and in a DB2 UDB database. Files that are stored outside of a

DB2 UDB database reside in file systems that are accessible to the DB2 Database Manager and are managed as if they were stored inside the database; the DB2 Data Links Manager takes control of the file system and allows DB2 UDB to provide enhanced access control over all files that reside in the file system, ensuring referential integrity is maintained and the files become part of backup and restore operations (which are crucial for data management in transactional environments). And because files linked to a DB2 database by the DB2 Data Links Manager are backed up asynchronously whenever a file reference is stored in a DATALINK column, the data backup image produced is smaller and can be generated more quickly than if the file data was stored directly in the database itself (for example, as a LOB).

The DB2 Data Links Manager can also maximize application performance and reduce network traffic by strategically storing external files close to where they will be needed. Furthermore, little or no change is required in existing DB2 UDB applications; they can often take advantage of the DB2 Data Links Manager as soon as it has been installed.

DB2 Data Links Manager is an add-on product that must be purchased separately. It is available for the following operating systems:

- AIX
- Solaris
- Windows NT
- Windows 2000

File systems supported include:

- AIX Journaled File System (JFS)
- Solaris UNIX File System (UFS)
- Windows NT File System (NTFS)

DB2 Data Warehouse Center and Warehouse Manager

Collecting and storing data is a process that almost every business performs. However, in order to make business intelligence decisions that are based on data that has been collected, you must have the right tools, and more importantly, the data must exist in a format suitable for analysis. Often, this means that data must be extracted from the system in which it resides, cleansed, transformed, and then loaded into one or more data warehouses (or data marts), which must be updated on a regular basis and managed themselves.

The DB2 Data Warehouse Center and the DB2 Warehouse Manager are designed to help you create and maintain DB2 UDB data warehouses. The

DB2 Data Warehouse Center, which is an add-on product that must be purchased separately unless DB2 Universal Database Enterprise Server Edition is installed, has the capability to extract, transform, and load data into a data warehouse. Furthermore, the DB2 Data Warehouse Center has the ability to move data between multiple source and target systems without having to go through a centralized server. This allows data warehouses to be constructed in a much more efficient manner.

The DB2 Warehouse Manager provides enhanced extract, transform, and load (ETL) functionality not found in the DB2 Data Warehouse Center. (In fact, DB2 Warehouse Manager contains one of the most powerful distributed ETL job-scheduling systems in the industry.) It also provides full refresh and incremental update data movement options, and it can take advantage of IBM's integrated data replication functions. The DB2 Warehouse Manager is an add-on product that must be purchased separately, and it is packaged with three additional tools that are designed to help simplify data warehouse management. These tools are:

- Information Catalog Manager
- Query Patroller
- Query Management Facility (QMF)

Information Catalog Manager. The Information Catalog Manager provides metadata management and repository functionality that helps end users find, understand, and access information stored in a DB2 UDB data warehouse. The Information Catalog Manager automatically registers shared information objects, and it can be populated from the DB2 Data Warehouse Center, as well as from a variety of other tools, including Query Management Facility (QMF), Brio, Business Objects, Cogos, Hyperion Essbase, and popular desktop tools, such as Microsoft Excel and Lotus 1-2-3.

Query Patroller. As the number of users interacting with a data warehouse increases, the response time associated with each individual query tends to decline. That's because when multiple queries reach the data warehouse at the same time, the core database's load manager must spend time handling query switching, and the overhead involved with switching has a negative impact on performance. DB2 Query Patroller provides a way for database administrators (DBAs) to both control the execution of queries and manage the resources required by those queries, by prioritizing and scheduling all queries in such a way that switching overhead is minimized while resource utilization is maximized. DB2 Query Patroller also provides a way for DBAs to set individual user and group priorities, as well as user query cost thresholds. This capability ensures that a data warehouse delivers query results to its most important users first. Furthermore, it has the ability to limit usage of system resources by stopping "runaway" queries before they can start.

Because DB2 Query Patroller is closely integrated with DB2's SQL optimizer, it performs cost analysis on queries as they are submitted, and then schedules and dispatches those queries so that the load is balanced whenever possible. This is accomplished by performing an Explain operation to check the cost of a query; if the value returned exceeds the query cost threshold assigned to the user (or the group the user is a member of), DB2 Query Patroller places the query on hold and runs it at a later time. DB2 Query Patroller then frees up the user's desktop to perform other work (including submitting other queries) while waiting for the original query results to be returned.

Query Management Facility. The Query Management Facility is a tightly integrated and powerful query and reporting tool that can be used with any DB2 relational database management system. It provides an environment that is easy to use, yet powerful enough for application developers; with the Query Management Facility, users can quickly build queries and reports through its interactive interface, integrate query results with a wide variety of tools (such as spreadsheets, personal databases, and Web browsers), and restrict user access to sensitive data and valuable system resources.

DB2 OLAP Server

DB2 OLAP Server allows you to create an online analytical processing (OLAP) environment using DB2 Universal Database. This product is based on OLAP technology that was developed by Hyperion Solutions Corporation (which is marketed as Hyperion Essbase), and it can be used to create a wide range of multidimensional planning, analysis, and reporting applications that interact with data warehouses. The DB2 OLAP Server contains over 100 built-in functions, including financial, statistical, and mathematical functions, and it has the capability to store multidimensional databases as sets of relational database tables. And, because the DB2 OLAP Server is built on Hyperion Essbase technology, it provides the same functionality as Hyperion Essbase and supports the widely adopted Hyperion Essbase Application Programming Interface (API), which is accessible by a broad range of front-end analysis tools and business applications, as well as by standard SQL query tools. You also have the option of using the Essbase Application Manager and Essbase commands to create a DB2 OLAP application and its associated databases.

DB2 OLAP Server is an add-on product that must be purchased separately; however, most editions of DB2 Universal Database come with a scaled-down version of DB2 OLAP Server, known as the DB2 OLAP Starter Kit. (The

DB2 OLAP Starter Kit provides the same functionality as DB2 OLAP Server, but only for three concurrent users.)

How DB2 Universal Database Products Are Packaged

We have just seen the majority of the products that make up the DB2 Universal Database Family and we have seen that some of these products are add-on products that must be purchased separately. When you purchase a particular edition of DB2 Universal Database, you automatically receive a set of products, as well as the core DB2 UDB database engine. Table 2–1 shows the set of products that are found in each DB2 Universal Database edition available.

Table 2–1 Products That Come with Each DB2 Universal Database Edition Available

DB2 UDB Edition	Products Provided
Everyplace Database Edition	Everyplace Database Edition
DB2 Everyplace Enterprise Edition	DB2 Everyplace Enterprise Edition
DB2 Universal Database Personal Edition	DB2 Universal Database Personal Edition IBM Developer Kit, Java Technology Distributed Debugger for Java Stored Procedures Complementary Products Net Search Extender (single user) DB2 Spatial Extender (single user) Audio, Video, and Image (AVI) Extender WebSphere Studio Site Developer Advanced (trial)
DB2 Universal Database Workgroup Server Edition	DB2 Universal Database Workgroup Server Edition DB2 Administration Client DB2 Run-Time Client IBM Developer Kit, Java Technology Distributed Debugger for Java Stored Procedures Complementary Products Net Search Extender (five-user limit) DB2 Spatial Extender (five-user limit) Audio, Video, and Image (AVI) Extender WebSphere Studio Site Developer Advanced (trial) WebSphere MQ QMF for Windows (trial)

Table 2–1 Products That Come with Each DB2 Universal Database Edition Available *(Continued)*	
DB2 UDB Edition	**Products Provided**
DB2 Universal Database Workgroup Server Unlimited Edition	DB2 Universal Database Workgroup Server Unlimited Edition DB2 Administration Client Run-Time Client IBM Developer Kit, Java Technology Distributed Debugger for Java Stored Procedures Complementary Products Audio, Video, and Image (AVI) Extender WebSphere Studio Site Developer Advanced (trial) WebSphere MQ QMF for Windows (trial)
DB2 Universal Database Enterprise Server Edition	DB2 Universal Database Enterprise Server Edition DB2 Administration Client DB2 Run-Time Client IBM Developer Kit, Java Technology Distributed Debugger for Java Stored Procedures Complementary Products Audio, Video, and Image (AVI) Extender WebSphere Studio Site Developer Advanced (trial) WebSphere MQ QMF for Windows (trial) Data Management Tools (Try & Buy)
DB2 Personal Developer's Edition	DB2 Universal Database Personal Edition DB2 Connect Personal Edition DB2 Application Development Client IBM Developer Kit, Java Technology Distributed Debugger for Java Stored Procedures Complementary Products DB2 Net Search Extender DB2 Spatial Extender Audio, Video, and Image (AVI) Extender WebSphere Studio Site Developer Advanced (trial) Borland Products (30-day trial)—Borland Delphi Enterprise, Borland C++ Builder Enterprise, Borland Kylix Enterprise
DB2 Universal Developer's Edition	DB2 Universal Database Personal Edition DB2 Universal Database Workgroup Server Edition DB2 Universal Database Enterprise Server Edition DB2 Connect Personal Edition DB2 Connect Enterprise Edition DB2 Data Links Manager

(*continued*)

Table 2–1 Products That Come with Each DB2 Universal Database Edition Available *(Continued)*

DB2 UDB Edition	Products Provided
	DB2 Net Search Extender DB2 Spatial Extender DB2 Warehouse Manager DB2 Intelligent Miner Scoring DB2 Intelligent Miner Modeling DB2 Intelligent Miner Visualization Audio, Video, and Image (AVI) Extender DB2 Administration Client DB2 Application Development Client DB2 Run-Time Client IBM Developer Kit, Java Technology Distributed Debugger for Java Stored Procedures Complementary Products DB2 Everyplace Software Development Kit WebSphere Application Server, Advanced Developer Edition WebSphere Studio Site Developer Advanced (trial) WebSphere MQ QMF for Windows Data Management Tools—DB2 Web Query Tool, DB2 Table Editor, DB2 High Performance Unload (Try & Buy), Recovery Expert (Try & Buy), Performance Expert (Try & Buy) DB2 Everyplace Enterprise Edition Borland Products (30-day trial)—Borland Delphi Enterprise, Borland C++ Builder Enterprise, Borland Kylix Enterprise

DB2 Universal Database's Comprehensive Tool Set

With the exception of DB2 Everyplace, each edition of DB2 Universal Database, along with the DB2 Administration Client, comes with a comprehensive set of tools designed to assist in administering and managing DB2 UDB instances, databases, and database objects. The majority of these tools have a graphical user interface (GUI); however, many of the tasks that can be performed with the GUI tools provided can also be performed by issuing equivalent DB2 UDB commands from the operating system prompt. The following sections describe the most commonly used GUI tools available.

The Control Center

Of all the DB2 UDB GUI tools available, the Control Center is the most important and versatile one provided. The Control Center presents a clear, concise view of an entire system and serves as the central point for managing systems and performing common administration tasks. From the Control Center, users can:

- Create and delete instances.
- Create and delete (drop) DB2 UDB databases.
- Catalog and uncatalog databases.
- Configure instances and databases.
- Create, alter, and drop buffer pools, tablespaces, tables, views, indexes, aliases, triggers, schemas, and user-defined data types (UDTs).
- Manage users and groups.
- Grant and revoke authorities and privileges.
- Load, import, or export data.
- Reorganize data and collect table statistics.
- Back up and restore databases and tablespaces.
- Replicate data between systems.
- Manage database connections.
- Monitor resources and track events that take place.
- Analyze queries.
- Schedule jobs to run unattended.

From the Control Center, users can also open other Control Centers, launch other tools, perform data warehousing tasks, and work with DB2 commands. Figure 2–7 shows how the Control Center looks on a Windows 2000 server.

The Control Center is comprised of the following elements:

- A *menu bar*, which allows users to perform any of the Control Center functions available.
- A *toolbar*, which can be used to launch the other DB2 UDB GUI tools available. Figure 2–8 identifies the tools that can be invoked directly from the Control Center tool bar.

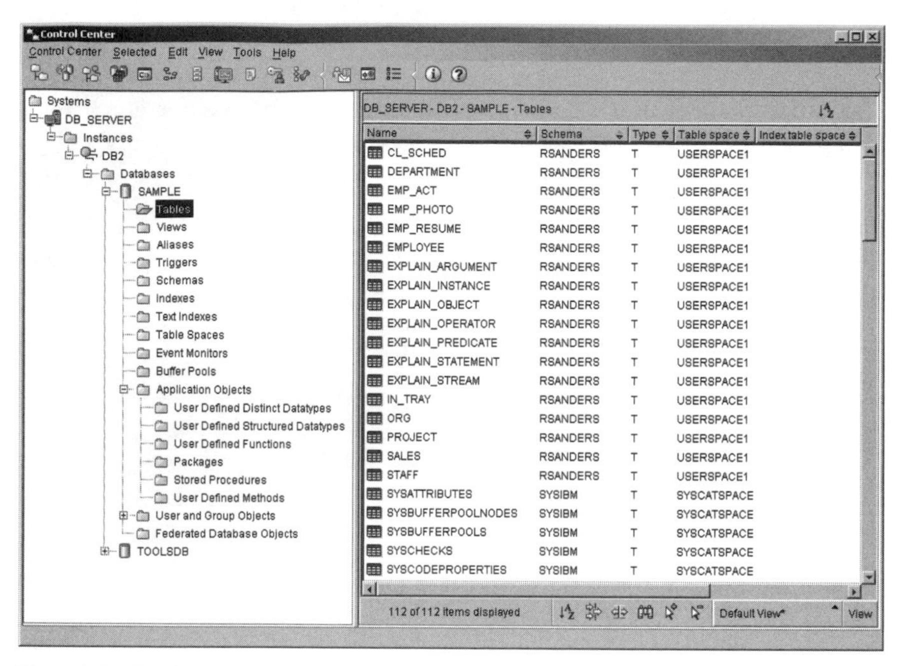

Figure 2–7 The Control Center.

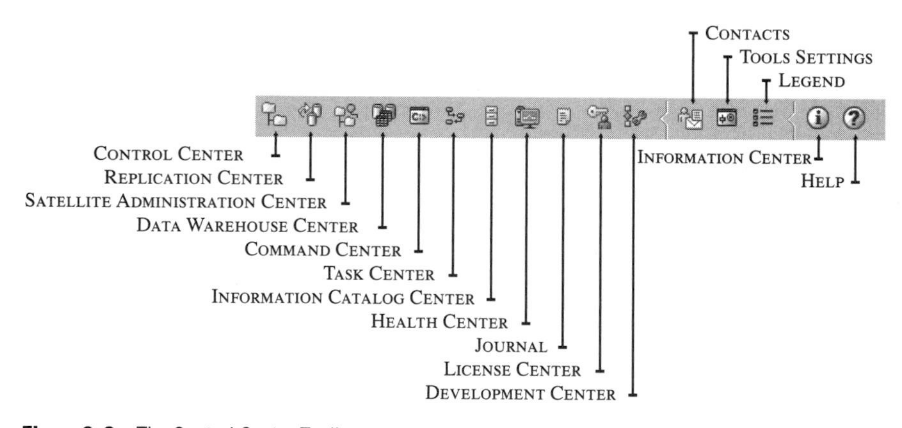

Figure 2–8 The Control Center Toolbar.

It is important to note that every tool that can be invoked from the Control Center toolbar can also be invoked from the Control Center's menu bar.

- An *objects pane* (located on the left-hand side of the Control Center), which contains a hierarchical representation of every object type that can be managed from the Control Center.
- A *contents pane* (located on the right-hand side of the Control Center), which contains a listing of existing objects that correspond to the object

type selected in the objects pane. (For example, if the Tables object type were selected in the objects pane, a list of all tables available would be listed in the contents pane.)

As you can see in Figure 2–7, every object listed in the contents pane is preceded by an icon intended to identify the type of object being described in the list. A wide variety of icons are used, and a list of all icons available, along with their corresponding object type, can be seen by viewing the Legend dialog, which can be accessed from the Control Center's menu bar. Figure 2–9 shows what the Legend dialog looks like on a Windows 2000 server.

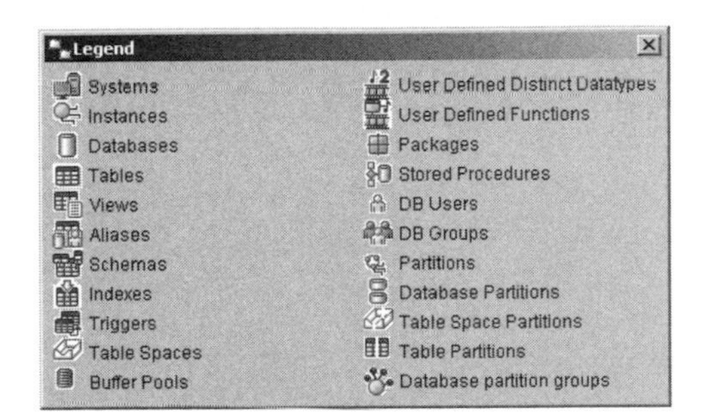

Figure 2–9 The Legend dialog.

Users can perform specific tasks on any object by selecting the object from the list and clicking the right mouse button; a pop-up menu that lists every action available for that particular object will be displayed, and the user simply selects the desired action from the menu.

The Replication Center

The Replication Center is an interactive GUI application that allows users to administer data replication between a DB2 UDB database and any other relational database, whether that database is a DB2 database or not. Using the Replication Center, users can:

- Define replication environments.
- Create replication control tables.
- Register replication sources.
- Create subscription sets.
- Add members to a subscription set.
- Apply designated changes from one location to another.

➤ Synchronize data in two locations.

➤ Monitor the replication process.

➤ Perform basic troubleshooting for replication operations.

Figure 2–10 shows what the Replication Center looks like on a Windows 2000 server.

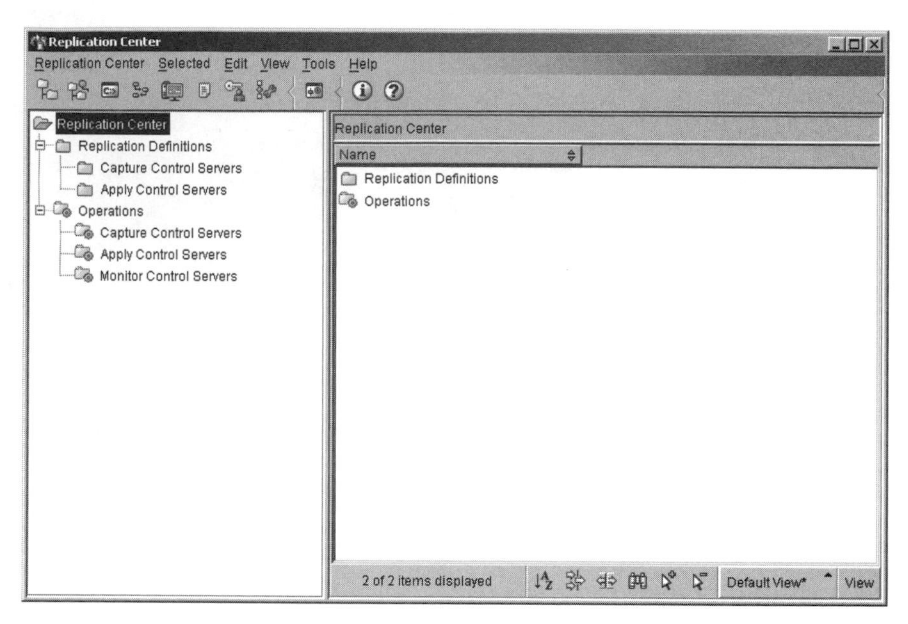

Figure 2–10 The Replication Center.

The Satellite Administration Center

The Satellite Administration Center is a GUI application that allows users to set up and administer a group of DB2 servers that perform the same business function. These servers, known as satellites, all run the same application and have the same DB2 UDB database definition needed to support a particular application. With the Satellite Administration Center, users create a group and then define satellites as members of this group. This group of satellites can then be administered as a single entity, as opposed to having to administer each satellite separately. If additional DB2 servers that perform the same business function are acquired later, they are simply added to the group as additional satellites.

Information about a satellite environment is stored in a central database referred to as the satellite control database. This database records, among other things, which satellites are in the environment, the group each satellite belongs to, and which version of an end-user business application a satellite is currently running. This database resides on a DB2 UDB server known as the DB2 control server, and it must be cataloged and accessible to the Control Center before the Satellite Administration Center can interact with it.

Groups of satellites are administered by creating batch scripts to set up and maintain the database definition that supports a business application on each satellite in a group. Each satellite then regularly connects to its satellite control server and downloads any scripts that apply to it. The satellite executes these scripts locally and uploads the results back to the satellite control database. This process of downloading batch scripts, executing them, and reporting the results of the batch execution back to the satellite control database is known as synchronization. A satellite synchronizes to maintain its consistency with the other satellites that belong to its group.

The Data Warehouse Center

The Data Warehouse Center is a set of GUI tools that allows users to build, access, and manage DB2 UDB data warehouses. With the Data Warehouse Center, users can automate the extraction, transformation, and loading process that must be performed to populate a data warehouse, as well as schedule, maintain, and monitor each phase of this process. The Data Warehouse Center can also be used to:

- Set up a data warehouse.
- Create a star schema.
- Set up DB2 and non-DB2 data sources.
- Set up access to a data warehouse.
- Calculate statistics.
- Manage metadata and the control database.

Figure 2–11 shows what the Data Warehouse Center looks like on a Windows 2000 server.

The Command Center

The Command Center is an interactive GUI application that allows users to:

- Execute SQL statements, DB2 commands, and operating system commands—operating system commands must be preceded by an exclamation mark (!).

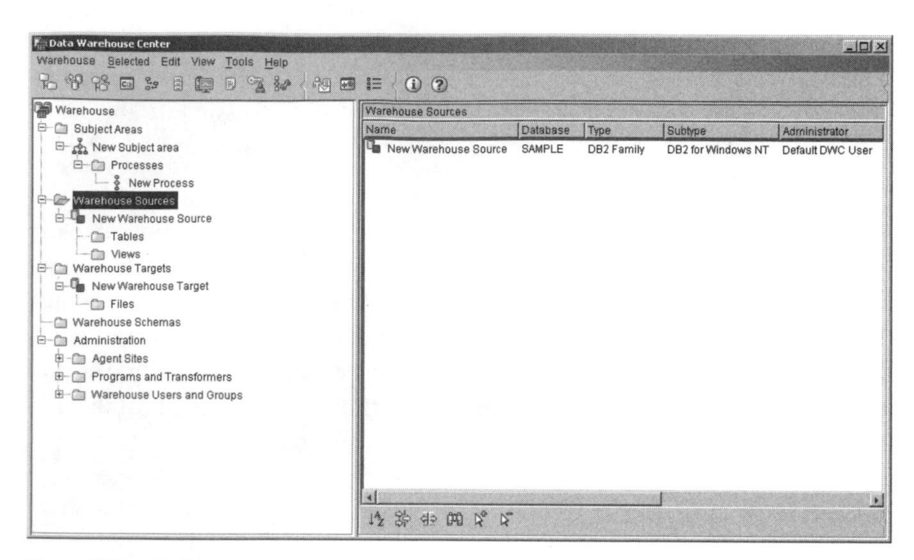

Figure 2–11 The Data Warehouse Center.

- View the results of the execution of SQL statements and DB2 commands and see the result data set produced in response to a query.
- Save the results of the execution of SQL statements and DB2 commands to an external file.
- Create and save a sequence of SQL statements and DB2 commands to a script file that can be used by the Task Center. (Such a script file can then be scheduled to run at a specific time or frequency.)
- Use the SQL Assist tool to build complex queries.
- Examine the execution plan and statistics associated with a SQL statement before (or after) it is executed.

Figure 2–12 shows what the Command Center looks like on a Windows 2000 server.

As you can see in Figure 2–12, the Command Center is comprised of four different individual pages: the *Interactive* page, the *Script* page, the *Query Results* page, and the *Access Plan* page. On the Interactive page, users can enter and execute an SQL statement or a DB2 command. On the Script page, users can execute commands in sequence, create and save a script, run an existing script, or schedule a task. On the Query Results page, users can see the results of any query executed. On the Access Plan page, users can see the access plan for any explainable statement that was specified on the Interactive page or the Script page. (If more than one SQL statement is specified on the Script page, an access plan will only be created for the first statement.)

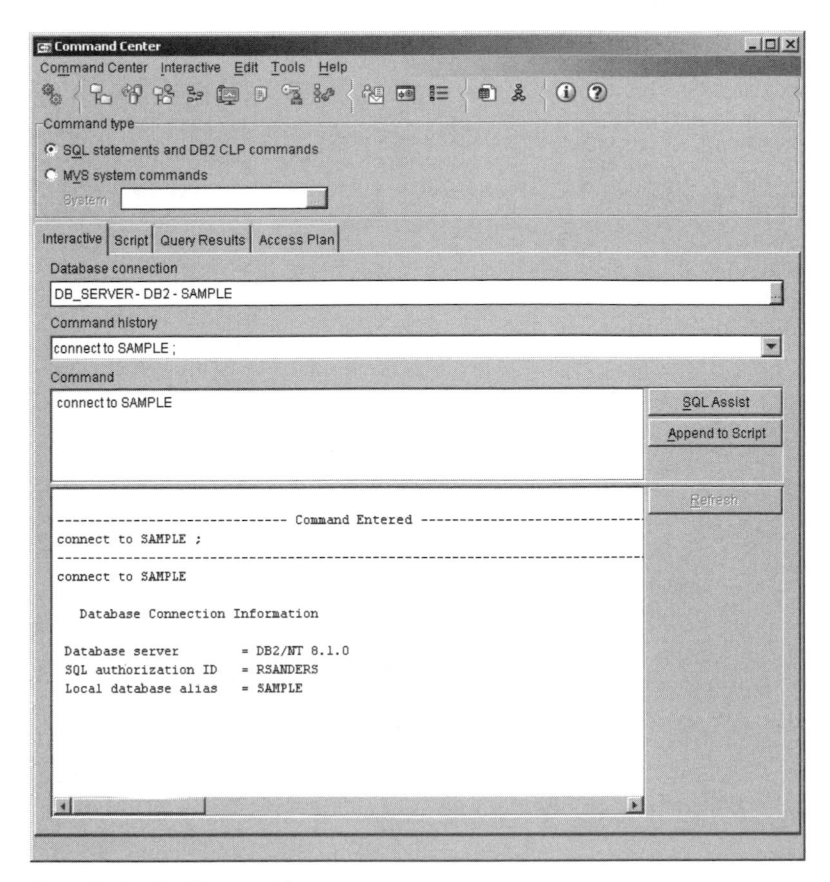

Figure 2–12 The Command Center.

SQL Assist

SQL Assist is an interactive GUI application that allows users to visually construct complex SELECT, INSERT, UPDATE, and DELETE SQL statements and examine the results of their execution. SQL Assist is invoked directly from the Command Center, and once the desired SQL statement has been constructed inside SQL Assist, it can be written back to the Command Center, where it can then be executed immediately or saved to a script file where it can be executed later using the Task Center. Figure 2–13 shows what the SQL Assist tool looks like on a Windows 2000 server after it has been used to build a complex query. Figure 2–14 shows how the results of this query would be displayed if the query were executed from within SQL Assist (by selecting the "Run" push button located at the bottom right corner of the screen).

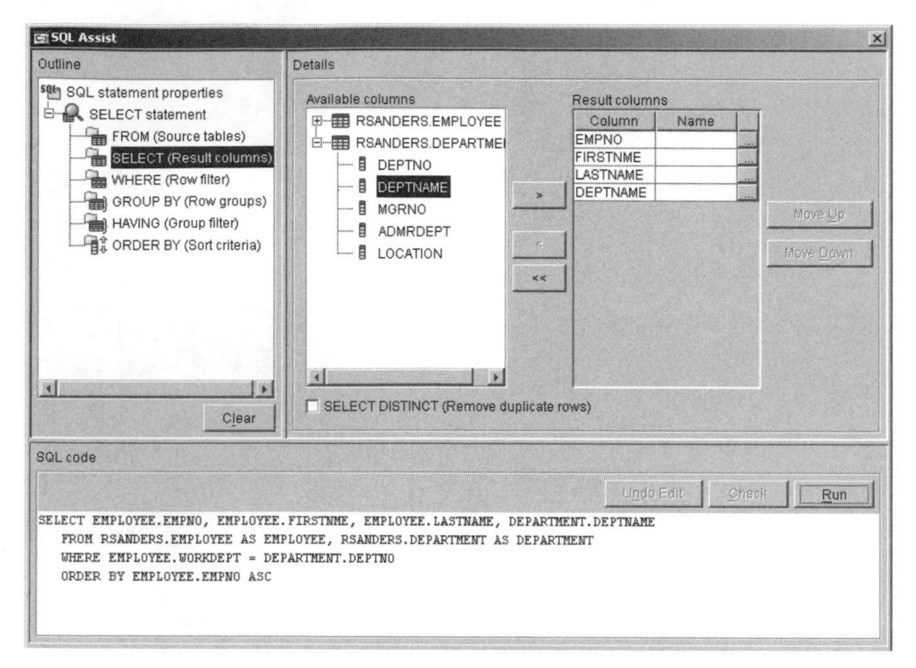

Figure 2–13 SQL Assist.

Query Result

	EMPNO	FIRSTNME	LASTNAME	DEPTNAME
1	000010	CHRISTINE	HAAS	SPIFFY COMPUTER SERVICE DIV.
2	000020	MICHAEL	THOMPSON	PLANNING
3	000030	SALLY	KWAN	INFORMATION CENTER
4	000050	JOHN	GEYER	SUPPORT SERVICES
5	000060	IRVING	STERN	MANUFACTURING SYSTEMS
6	000070	EVA	PULASKI	ADMINISTRATION SYSTEMS
7	000090	EILEEN	HENDERSON	OPERATIONS
8	000100	THEODORE	SPENSER	SOFTWARE SUPPORT
9	000110	VINCENZO	LUCCHESSI	SPIFFY COMPUTER SERVICE DIV.
10	000120	SEAN	O'CONNELL	SPIFFY COMPUTER SERVICE DIV.
11	000130	DOLORES	QUINTANA	INFORMATION CENTER
12	000140	HEATHER	NICHOLLS	INFORMATION CENTER
13	000150	BRUCE	ADAMSON	MANUFACTURING SYSTEMS
14	000160	ELIZABETH	PIANKA	MANUFACTURING SYSTEMS
15	000170	MASATOSHI	YOSHIMURA	MANUFACTURING SYSTEMS
16	000180	MARILYN	SCOUTTEN	MANUFACTURING SYSTEMS
17	000190	JAMES	WALKER	MANUFACTURING SYSTEMS
18	000200	DAVID	BROWN	MANUFACTURING SYSTEMS
19	000210	WILLIAM	JONES	MANUFACTURING SYSTEMS
20	000220	JENNIFER	LUTZ	MANUFACTURING SYSTEMS
21	000230	JAMES	JEFFERSON	ADMINISTRATION SYSTEMS

OK

Figure 2–14 The Query Results dialog.

Visual Explain

Visual Explain is a GUI application that allows users to view the details of the access plan (including the statistics in the system catalogs) chosen by the DB2 optimizer for a given SQL statement without actually executing the statement.

With Visual Explain, each table, view, and index used, along with the operation performed on each, is represented in a diagram as nodes, and the actual flow of data is represented as links between each node. This information allows users to quickly view the statistics used at the time a particular query was optimized, determine whether or not an index would improve access to a table, obtain information about the cost required to perform a particular operation, and understand how tables have been joined. Armed with this information, administrators can make database design changes, and application developers can fine-tune SQL statements to improve overall performance.

Like SQL Assist, Visual Explain can be invoked directly from the Command Center. However, unlike SQL Assist, Visual Explain can also be invoked from the Control Center menu bar. If invoked from the Command Center, Visual Explain can generate access plan information for complex queries that have been created with SQL Assist. Figure 2–15 shows what the Visual Explain tool might look like on a Windows 2000 server when invoked from the Command Center.

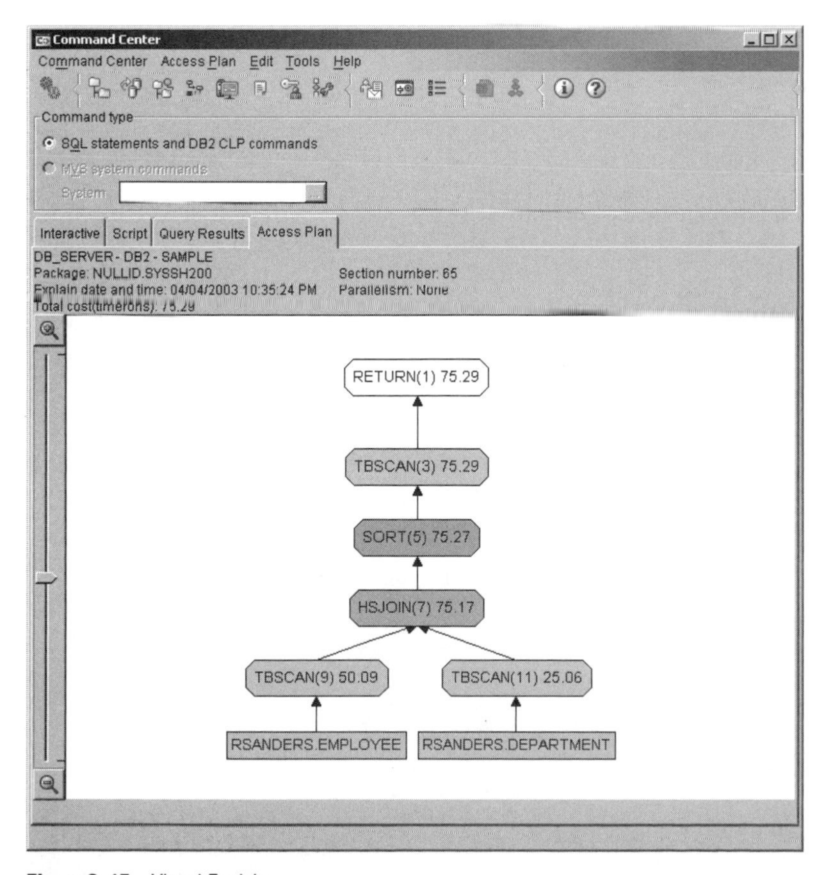

Figure 2–15 Visual Explain.

Before Visual Explain can be used, Explain tables must be added to the appropriate database. Additionally, if Visual Explain is to be used from the Command Center, the *Automatically generate access plan* Command Center option must be turned on before the query to be explained is executed. Often, the DB2 Database Manager will attempt to create Explain tables automatically the first time Visual Explain is used. Explain tables can also be created by executing the script EXPLAIN.DDL, which can be found in the *misc* subdirectory of the *sqllib* directory where the DB2 Universal Database product was installed. Refer to the header portion of this file for specific information on how to execute it.

The Task Center

The Task Center is an interactive GUI application that allows users to schedule tasks, run tasks, and send notifications about completed tasks to other users. A task is a script together with any associated success conditions, schedules, and notifications. Users can create a task within the Task Center, generate a task by saving the results from a DB2 dialog or wizard, create a script within another tool and save it to the Task Center, or import an existing script. Such scripts can contain DB2 commands, SQL statements, or operating system commands.

The Task Center uses success code sets (the return codes or range of return codes that, if received, indicate the task was executed successfully) to evaluate the success or failure of any task it executes. Return codes that fall outside the range specified are considered failures. Furthermore, the Task Center evaluates the SQLCA return code of every SQL statement executed in a DB2 script, and if any statement fails, the entire task fails.

In addition to evaluating the success or failure of a particular task, the Task Center can perform one or more actions if a particular task succeeds and perform other actions if the same task fails. The Task Center can also be configured to perform one or more actions each time a scheduled task completes, regardless of whether the task executed successfully or failed.

Figure 2–16 shows what the Task Center looks like on a Windows 2000 server.

If you run a script from the Task Center, instead of from the Command Center or a command prompt, the results will be logged in the Journal. Using the Journal, you can see a list of jobs that use a particular script along with the status of all scheduled jobs.

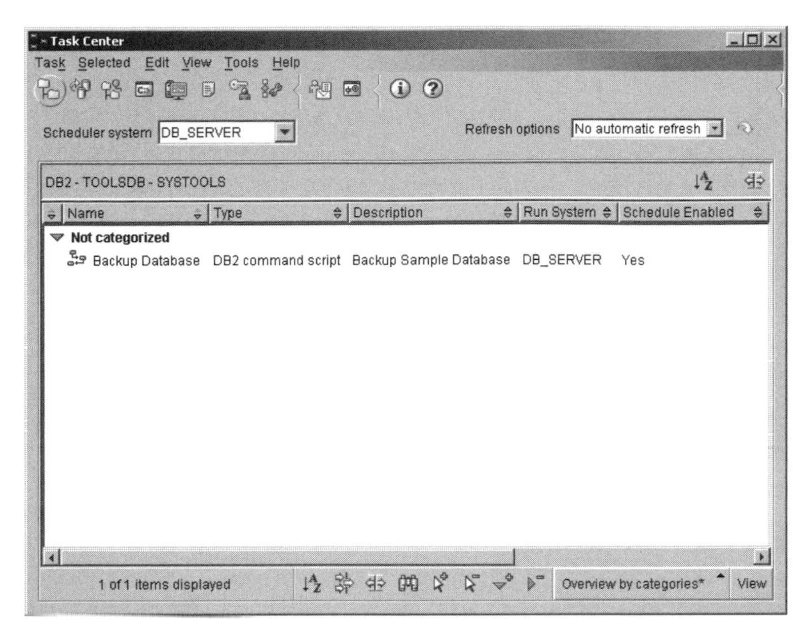

Figure 2–16 The Task Center.

The Information Catalog Center

The Information Catalog Center is an interactive GUI application that allows users to manage descriptive data (business metadata) about source information. This metadata typically contains items such as the type of information being referenced, a description of the information, what the information contains, who owns and updates it, where it is stored, and how to get to it. Essentially, the Information Catalog Center does for an organization what an electronic card catalog does for a library, and more.

With the Information Catalog Center, users can search for specific objects stored in the information catalog, view any relationships that an object participates in, view an object's lineage, and create comments for objects. Users with the appropriate authority can also create new objects for a particular information catalog.

The Information Catalog Center helps administrators organize metadata objects by requiring that each object be based on an object type and by allowing administrators to define relationship types and additional object types. Furthermore, the Information Catalog Center provides security at the object level, so privileges are set for each object, allowing greater control of business information.

The Health Center

The Health Center is an interactive GUI application that allows users to monitor the state of the database environment. Whenever DB2 UDB is active, a background process continuously monitors a set of health indicators for problem areas. If the current value of a health indicator is outside the acceptable operating range, as defined by its warning and alarm thresholds, the health monitor generates an alert. (DB2 UDB comes with a set of predefined threshold values, which can be customized to meet your needs.)

With the Health Center, users can:

- View the status of the database environment. An icon indicating the alert level for a particular object (or for any objects contained by that object) is displayed beside every object listed in the Health Center's navigation tree. If that icon is a green diamond, the corresponding object does not currently have any alerts.
- View the alerts associated with a particular instance or database. When an object in the Health Center's navigation tree is selected, the alerts for that object are displayed in the pane located just to the right of the navigation tree.
- View detailed information, along with recommended actions to take, for a particular alert. When a particular alert item is selected, a dialog containing a notebook is displayed. The first page of this notebook shows detailed information about the alert. The second page recommends actions to take to correct the situation that caused the alert to occur.
- Configure the health monitor settings for a specific object and specify the default settings for an object type or for all objects within an instance.
- Select which contacts will receive an email or pager message whenever an alert occurs.
- Review a historical list of all alerts generated for a particular instance.

Figure 2–17 shows what the Health Center looks like on a Windows 2000 server.

The Journal

The Journal is an interactive GUI application that tracks historical information about tasks, database actions and operations, Control Center actions,

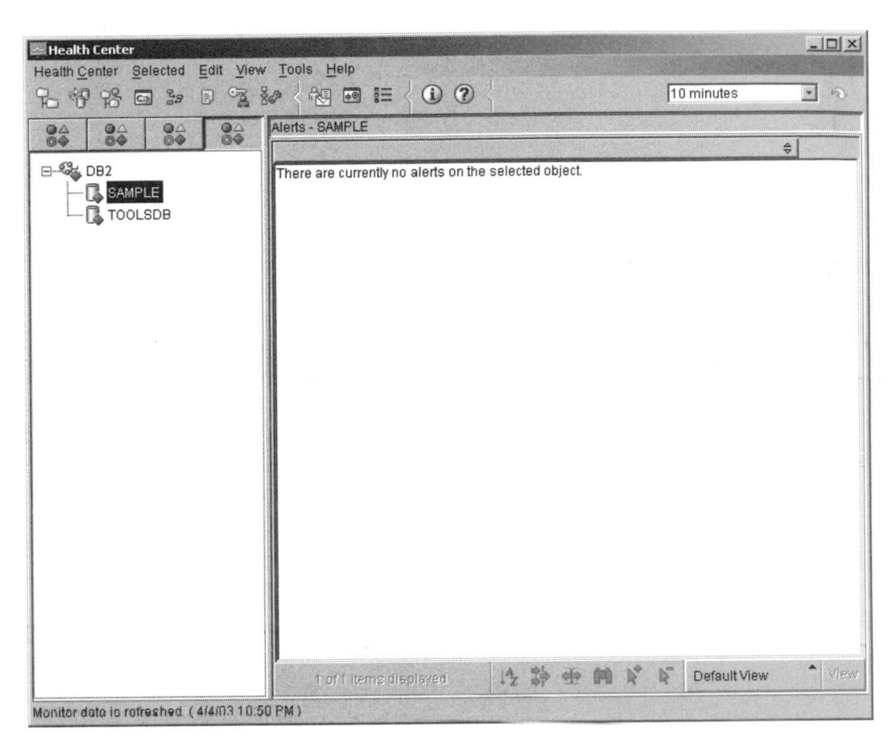

Figure 2–17 The Health Center dialog.

messages, and alerts. To present this information in an organized manner, the Journal uses several different views. They are:

➤ Task History

➤ Database History

➤ Messages

➤ Notification Log

The *Task History* view shows the results of tasks that have already been executed. This view contains one entry for each individual task (regardless of how many times the task was executed) and allows users to:

➤ View details of any task that has been executed.

➤ View the results any task that has been executed.

➤ Edit any task that has been executed.

➤ View execution statistics associated with any task that has been executed.

➤ Remove any task execution record from the Journal.

The *Database History* view shows information stored in a database's recovery history file. The recovery history file is automatically updated whenever any of the following operations are performed:

- Database or tablespace backup
- Database or tablespace restore
- Roll-forward recovery
- Load
- Table reorganization

The *Messages* view shows a running history of messages that were issued from the Control Center and any other GUI tool, and the *Notification Log* view shows information from the administration notification log.

Figure 2–18 shows what the Messages view of the Journal looks like on a Windows 2000 server.

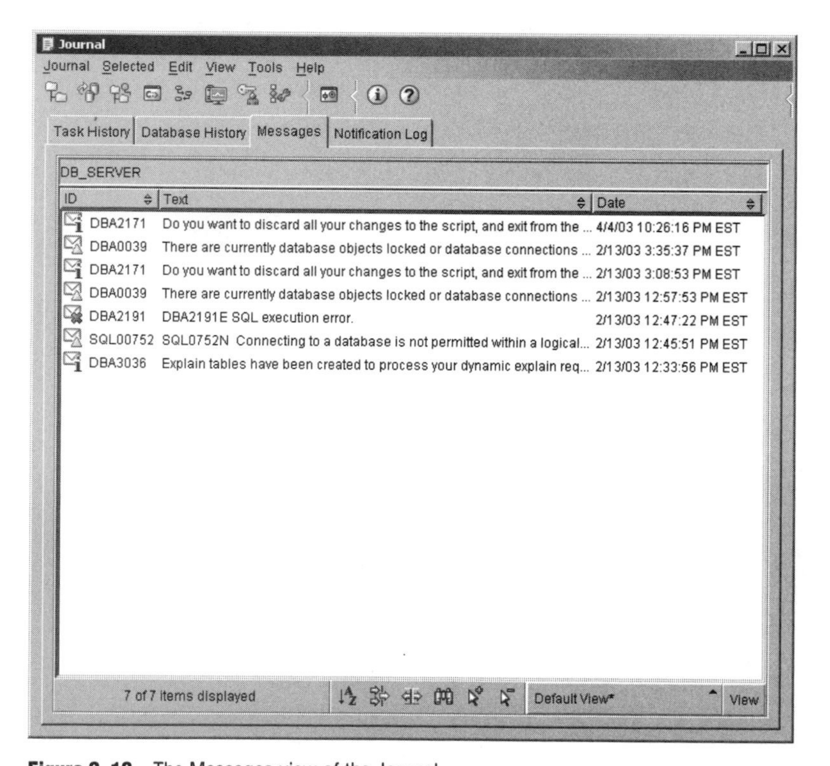

Figure 2–18 The Messages view of the Journal.

The License Center

The License Center is an interactive GUI application that allows users to view information about the license associated with each DB2 UDB product installed on a particular system. Such information includes processor status information, concurrent users policy information, license information, and user statistics or details. This tool can also be used to add or remove licenses or registered users, change license type policies, change the number of concurrent users, change the number of licensed processors, change the number of internet processor licenses, and configure a particular system for proper license monitoring. Figure 2–19 shows what the License Center looks like on a Windows 2000 server.

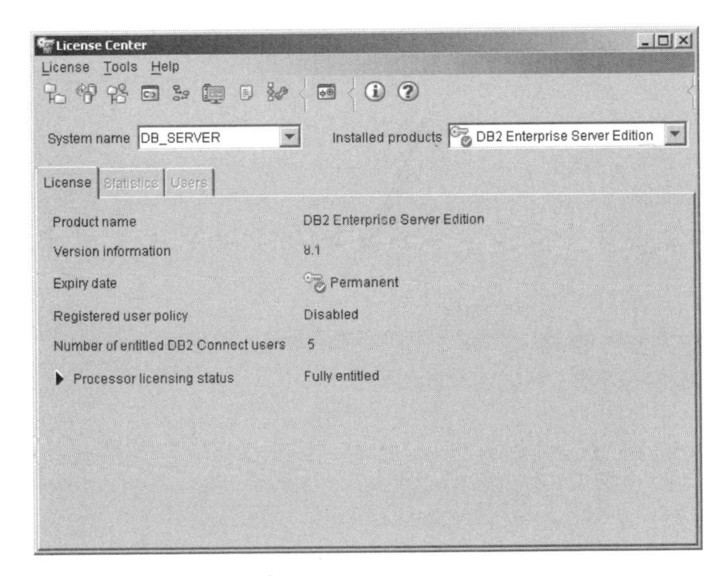

Figure 2–19 The License Center.

The Development Center

The Development Center is an interactive GUI application that provides users with a single development environment that supports the entire DB2 UDB Family. With the Development Center, users can:

- Create, build, and deploy Java and SQLJ stored procedures.
- Create, build, and deploy SQL scalar, SQL table, and OLE DB table user-defined functions.
- Create, build, and deploy user-defined functions that read MQSeries® messages.

➤ Create, build, and deploy user-defined functions that extract data from XML documents.

➤ Debug SQL stored procedures using the integrated debugger.

➤ Create and build structured data types.

➤ View and work with database objects, such as tables, triggers, and views.

Figure 2–20 shows what the Development Center looks like on a Windows 2000 server.

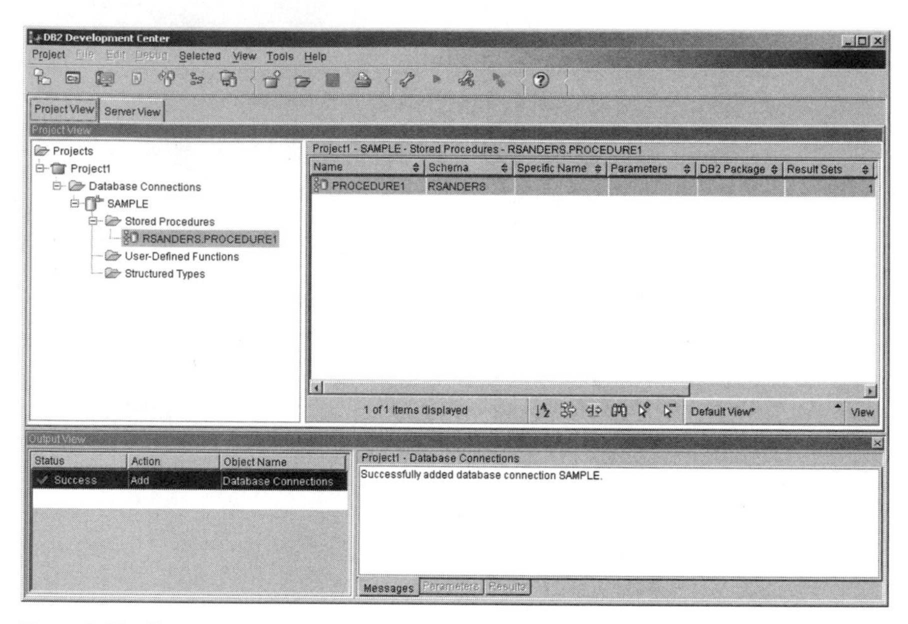

Figure 2–20 The Development Center.

The Development Center also provides a DB2 Development Add-In for each of the following development environments:

➤ Microsoft Visual C++

➤ Microsoft Visual Basic

➤ Microsoft Visual InterDev

With these add-ins, users can easily access the features of the Development Center directly from a Microsoft development environment. This makes it easier to develop and incorporate stored procedures and user-defined functions into a DB2 UDB application development.

The Information Center

The Information Center is an interactive GUI application that allows users to access an electronic copy of the DB2 Universal Database product documentation. The Information Center makes it easy to quickly locate desired information, because it divides the available product documentation into distinct categories. A list of major topics for each category is presented in separate views. The views available include:

Tasks. This view can be used to locate instructions on how to perform a particular task. Topics presented with this view include common tasks users can perform with the Control Center, along with other major administration and application development tasks.

Concepts. This view can be used to see which DB2 UDB online manuals are available and to look for information in a particular book.

Reference. This view can be used to locate reference information. This view is designed to provide quick access to information contained in the DB2 UDB reference manuals (the *Command Reference*, the *SQL Reference*, the *Call Level Interface Guide and Reference*, and the *Administrative API Reference*).

Troubleshooting. This view can be used to quickly locate detailed information about any problem encountered while using DB2 UDB. Often, this information contains recommendations that, when followed, will lead to problem resolution.

Samples. This view can be used to view descriptions of, and the source code for, the sample programs that are provided with any Developer's Edition of DB2 UDB or a DB2 UB Application Development Client. When the sample programs provided are viewed using the Information Center, they are formatted with color and hypertext links to make them easier to understand.

Tutorials. This view can be used to locate tutorials that can be used to quickly learn how to perform a particular task or use a particular tool that is part of the DB2 UDB Family.

After selecting the most appropriate view available, the user drills down through the list of topics provided until the desired topic is found. Then, when the appropriate topic has been selected, the corresponding page of the DB2 UDB documentation will be displayed in a Web browser window.

Figure 2–21 shows what the Information Center looks like on a Windows 2000 server.

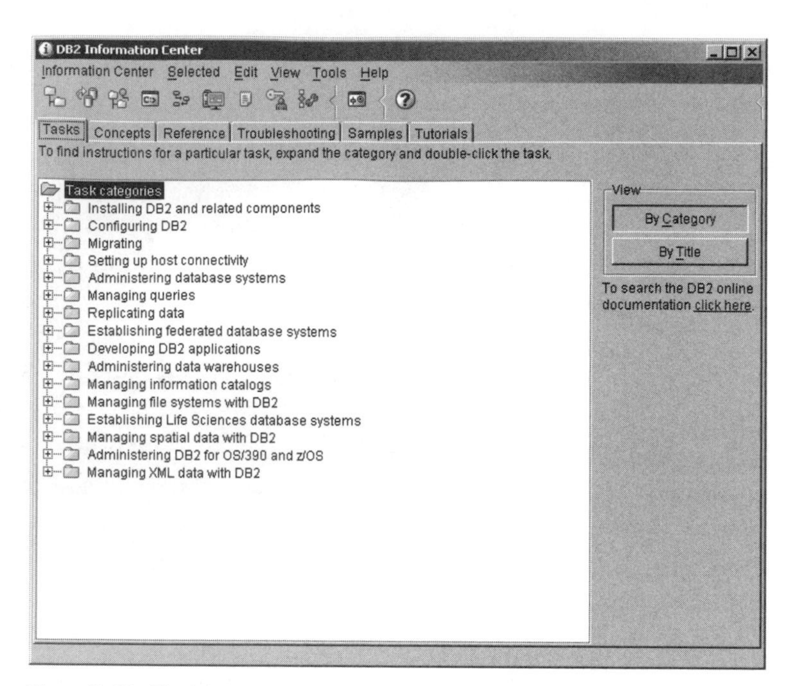

Figure 2–21 The Information Center.

The Command Line Processor

The Command Line Processor (CLP) is a text-oriented application that allows users to issue DB2 UDB commands, system commands, and SQL statements, as well as view the results of the statements/commands executed. The Command Line Processor can be run in three different modes:

Command mode. When the Command Line Processor is run in command mode, the user simply enters a DB2 UDB command, system command, or SQL statement, preceded by the characters "db2", at the system prompt. (For example, the command connect to SAMPLE would be entered as db2 connect to SAMPLE). If the command contains characters that have a special meaning to the operating system being used, it must be enclosed in quotation marks to ensure that it will be properly executed (for example, db2 "select count(*) from employee"). If the command to be executed is too long to fit on a single line, a space followed by the line continuation character (\) can be placed at the end of the line that is to be continued, and the rest of the command can follow on a new line.

Interactive Input mode. When the Command Line Processor is run in interactive input mode, the "db2" prefix is automatically provided (as characterized by the **db2 =>** input prompt). To run the Command Line Processor in interactive input mode, you simply enter the command "db2" at the system prompt. To exit out of interactive, you enter the command "quit" at the Command Line Processor prompt. Aside from that, the rules that apply to using the command mode of the Command Line Processor also apply to using the interactive input mode.

Batch mode. When the Command Line Processor is run in batch mode, it is assumed that all commands and/or SQL statements to be executed have been stored in an ASCII text file. (The characters "db2" should not precede the commands/statements stored in this file.) To run the Command Line Processor in batch mode, you simply enter the command db2 –f *xxxxxxxx* (where *xxxxxxxx* is the name of the file that contains the set of commands that are to be executed) at the system prompt.

Figure 2–22 shows what the Command Line Processor looks like on a Windows 2000 server when it is run in interactive input mode.

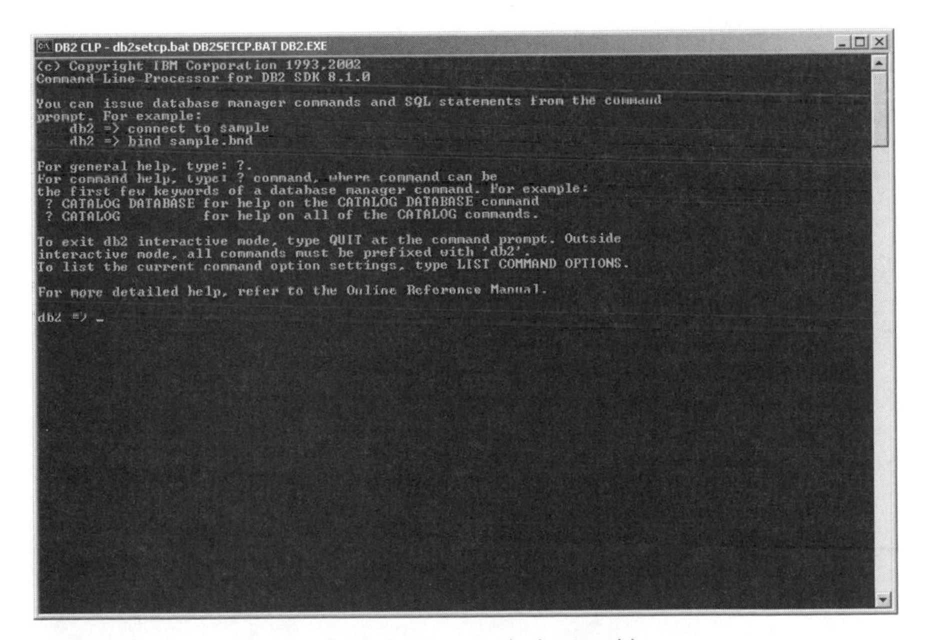

Figure 2–22 The Command Line Processor (in interactive input mode).

There are various command-line options that can be specified when the Command Line Processor is invoked; a list of all options available can be obtained by executing the command LIST COMMAND OPTIONS, either from the system prompt or the Command Line Processor prompt (when the Command Line Processor is run in interactive input mode).

The Configuration Assistant

The Configuration Assistant (Figure 2–23) is an interactive GUI application that allows users to configure clients so they can access databases stored on remote DB2 servers; in order to access an instance or database on another server or system, that system must be cataloged in the node directory of the client workstation, and information about the database must be cataloged in the database directory of the client workstation. The Configuration Assistant provides a way to maintain a list of databases to which users/applications can connect. With it, users can quickly catalog nodes and databases without having to know the inherent complexities involved with performing these tasks. The Configuration Assistant can also act as a lightweight alternative to the Control Center in situations where the complete set of GUI tools available have not been installed.

From the Configuration Assistant, users can:

- Add new database objects.
- Work with or delete existing database objects.
- Bind applications.
- Set DB2 registry parameters.
- Configure the DB2 Database Manager.
- Configure ODBC/CLI parameters.
- Import and export configuration information.

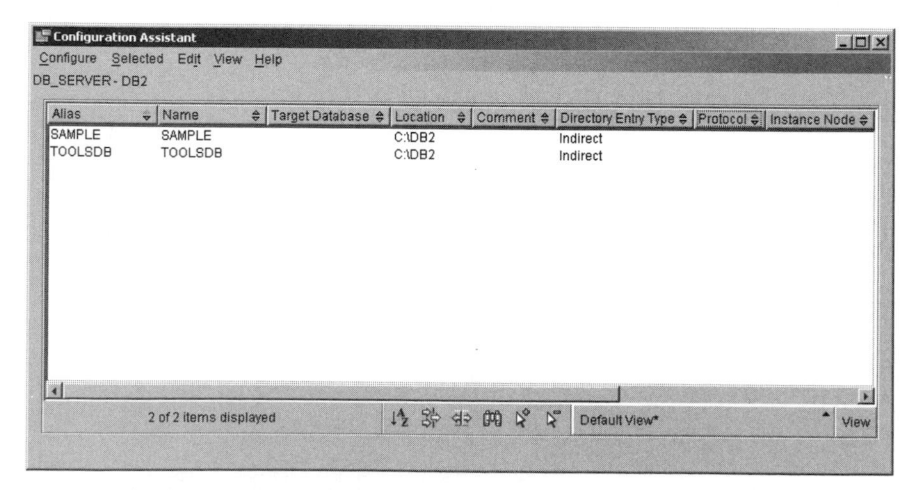

Figure 2–23 The Configuration Assistant.

- Change passwords.
- Test connections.

Figure 2–23 shows what the Configuration Assistant looks like on a Windows 2000 server.

Practice Questions

Question 1

Which of the following is the best client to use to allow users to execute ad-hoc queries, using the Command Line Processor, that retrieve data from a DB2 UDB server?

❍ A. DB2 Run-Time Client

❍ B. DB2 Administration Client

❍ C. DB2 Application Development Client

❍ D. DB2 CLP Support Client

Question 2

A client application on OS/390 must access a DB2 UDB database on a Solaris Server. At a minimum, which of the following products must be installed on the Solaris workstation?

❍ A. DB2 Connect Enterprise Edition

❍ B. DB2 UDB Workgroup Server Edition

❍ C. DB2 UDB Workgroup Server Edition and DB2 Connect Enterprise Edition

❍ D. DB2 UDB Enterprise Server Edition and DB2 Connect Enterprise Edition

Question 3

A developer needs to build an application on a Linux workstation that will access a database on an OS/400 server. At a minimum, which of the following products must be installed on the Linux workstation?

❍ A. DB2 Personal Developer's Edition

❍ B. DB2 Universal Developer's Edition

❍ C. DB2 Personal Developer's Edition and DB2 Connect Enterprise Edition

❍ D. DB2 Connect Developer's Edition

Question 4

Which of the following products is used to manage extensible markup language documents?

❍ A. DB2 AVI Extender

❍ B. DB2 Text Extender

❍ C. DB2 XML Extender

❍ D. DB2 Spatial Extender

Question 5

Which of the following is used to create and debug user-defined functions?

❍ A. SQL Assist

❍ B. Control Center

❍ C. Command Center

❍ D. Development Center

Question 6

Which two of the following are performed by the DB2 Warehouse Manager?

❑ A. Query

❑ B. Extraction

❑ C. Categorization

❑ D. Replication

❑ E. Transformation

Question 7

Which two of the following allow you to perform administrative tasks against database objects?

❑ A. Control Center

❑ B. Command Center

❑ C. Command Line Processor

❑ D. Task Center

❑ E. Health Center

Question 8

Which of the following tools is used to automate backup operations?

❍ A. Control Center

❍ B. Command Center

❍ C. Command Line Processor

❍ D. Task Center

Question 9

Which of the following maintains a history of all warnings and errors generated by the Control Center?

❍ A. Journal

❍ B. Health Center

❍ C. Information Center

❍ D. Visual Explain

Question 10

Which of the following tools can be used to determine if the creation of an index will improve query performance?

❍ A. Control Center

❍ B. SQL Assist

❍ C. Visual Explain

❍ D. Development Center

Answers

Question 1

The correct answer is **A.** The DB2 Run-Time client provides basic connectivity that allows client workstation users to issue interactive SQL statements that access data stored on a DB2 UDB/DB2 Connect server; the DB2 Administration Client provides basic connectivity, along with the ability to perform administrative operations on DB2 UDB databases that reside on a DB2 UDB/DB2 Connect server; and the DB2 Application Development Client provides basic connectivity, along with a collection of tools and components that can be used to develop, test, and run applications that are designed to interact with databases that reside on DB2 UDB/DB2 Connect servers.

Question 2

The correct answer is **C.** DB2 Connect Enterprise Edition is an add-on product for DB2 UDB that allows data to be moved between Linux, UNIX, and Windows DB2 servers and iSeries- and zSeries-based DB2 servers. Because some editions of DB2 UDB must be installed before DB2 Connect can be used, and because DB2 Connect is needed in this case to provide communications between the Solaris server and the OS/390 client, answers A and B are both wrong. The question states "at a minimum, which . . . products must be installed . . ." and since DB2 Universal Database Enterprise Server Edition comes packaged with a limited version of DB2 Connect, DB2 Connect does not need to be installed along with DB2 UDB Enterprise Server Edition, so answer D is also incorrect.

Question 3

The correct answer is **B.** Because DB2 Personal Developer's Edition can only be used to develop applications that work with local databases, and because DB2 Personal Developer's Edition must be used with DB2 Connect Personal Edition, not DB2 Connect Enterprise Edition, answers A and C can be eliminated. And since there is no DB2 Connect Developer's Edition, the correct answer is B.

Question 4

The correct answer is **C.** The DB2 XML Extender contains a set of data types and functions that can be used to store extensible markup language (XML) documents in a DB2 UDB database. The DB2 Audio, Video, and Image (AVI) Extender contains a set of data types and functions that can be used to store and manipulate nontraditional data such as audio clips, movies, and pictures in a DB2 UDB database; the DB2 Text Extender contains a set of data types and functions that can be used to store complex text documents in a DB2 UDB database and to extract key information from such documents; and the DB2 Spatial Extender contains a set of user-defined data types that can be used to describe spatial data (for example, points, lines, and polygons) and a set of user-defined functions that can be used to query spatial objects (for example, to find area, endpoints, and intersects).

Question 5

The correct answer is **D.** The Development Center is an interactive GUI application that can be used to create, build, debug, and deploy stored procedures, structured data types, and user-defined functions.

Question 6

The correct answers are **B** and **E.** The DB2 Warehouse Manager extracts, transforms, and loads data into a data warehouse.

Question 7

The correct answers are **A** and **C.** The Control Center presents a clear, concise view of an entire system and it serves as the central point for managing systems and performing common administration tasks. The Command Line Processor (CLP) is a text-oriented application that allows users to issue DB2 UDB commands, system commands, and SQL statements, as well as view the results of the statements/commands executed. Because the administrative tasks that can be performed with the Control Center have corresponding DB2 UDB commands, both the Control Center and the Command Line Processor can be used to perform administrative tasks against a database and its objects.

Question 8

The correct answer is **D.** The Task Center is an interactive GUI application that allows users to schedule tasks, run tasks, and send notifications about completed tasks to other users. Because a task can be generated by saving the results from the Backup Database wizard, the Task Center can be used to automate backup operations.

Question 9

The correct answer is **A.** The Journal is an interactive GUI application that tracks historical information about tasks, database actions and operations, Control Center actions, messages, and alerts; the Messages view of the Journal shows a running history of messages that were issued from the Control Center as well as any other GUI tool.

Question 10

The correct answer is **C.** Visual Explain is a GUI application that allows users to view the details of the access plan (including the statistics in the system catalogs) chosen by the DB2 optimizer for a given SQL statement without actually executing the statement. This information allows users to quickly view the statistics that were used at the time a particular query was optimized and determine, among other things, whether or not an index would improve access to a table, which in turn would improve query performance.

Security

Nine percent (9%) of the DB2 UDB V8.1 Family Fundamentals certification exam (Exam 700) is designed to test your knowledge about the mechanisms DB2 Universal Database uses to protect data and database objects against unauthorized access and modification. The questions that make up this portion of the exam are intended to evaluate the following:

- Your ability to identify the methods that can be used to restrict access to data stored in a DB2 UDB database.
- Your ability to identify each authorization level used by DB2 UDB.
- Your ability to identify each privilege used by DB2 UDB.
- Your ability to identify how specific authorizations and/or privileges are given to a user.

This chapter is designed to introduce you to the various authorization levels and privileges that are available with DB2 Universal Database and to the tools that are used to give or revoke one or more authorizations/privileges to users and groups.

Terms you will learn:

Authentication
Authentication Type
Kerberos
Trusted Client
Untrusted Client

Authorities

Privileges

System Administrator authority

System Control authority

System Maintenance authority

Database Administrator authority

Load authority

Database Privileges

Object Privileges

`GRANT`

`REVOKE`

Techniques you will master:

Understanding how users are authenticated and how to control where authentication takes place.

Understanding how DB2 Universal Database controls data access through a wide variety of authorities and privileges.

Understanding the differences between authorities and privileges, and knowing how they compliment each other to protect data.

Recognizing the types of authorities available and knowing what each one allows a user to do.

Recognizing the types of privileges available and knowing what each one allows a user to do.

Understanding how authorities can be given to (granted) or taken away from (revoked) users and groups.

Understanding how privileges can be given to (granted) or taken away from (revoked) users and groups.

Controlling Database Access

It has been said that one of the fastest growing crimes in America today is an act known as "identity theft." By obtaining the right information, an identity thief can borrow large amounts of money or make expensive purchases in someone else's name, leaving that individual in alarming financial shape. So, just where can this information, which should be closely guarded, be found? Chances are it has been collected and entered into somebody's database. (Think about the paperwork you had to fill out the last time you started a new job, opened a new bank account, or bought a new car. More likely than not, the information you provided on that paperwork—information that identifies who you are—was transferred to a database for future use.)

Every database management system must be able to protect data against unauthorized access and/or modification. DB2 Universal Database uses a combination of external security services and internal access control mechanisms to perform this vital task. In most cases, three different levels of security are employed: The first level controls access to the instance a database was created under, the second controls access to the database itself, and the third controls access to the data and data objects that reside within the database.

Authentication

The first security portal most users must pass through on their way to gaining access to a DB2 UDB instance or a database is a process known as *authentication*. The purpose of authentication is to verify that a user really is who they say they are. Typically, authentication is performed by an external security facility that is not part of DB2 UDB. This security facility may be part of the operating system (as is the case with AIX, Solaris, Linux, HP-UX, Windows 2000/NT, and many others), it may be a separate add-on product (for example, Distributed Computing Environment (DCE) Security Services), or it may not exist at all (which, by default, is the case with Windows 95, Windows 98, and Windows Millennium Edition). If a security facility does exist, it must be presented with two specific items before a user can be authenticated: a unique user ID and a corresponding password. The user ID identifies the user to the security facility, while the password, which is information that is known only by both the user and the security facility, is used to verify that the user is indeed who they claim to be.

Because passwords are a very important tool for authenticating users, you should always require passwords at the operating system level if you want the operating system to perform the authentication for your database. Keep in mind that on most UNIX operating systems, undefined passwords are treated as NULL, and any user that has not been assigned a password will be treated as if they have a NULL password—from the operating system's perspective, this will be evaluated as being a valid match.

Where Does Authentication Take Place?

Because DB2 UDB can reside in environments comprised of multiple clients, gateways, and servers, each of which may be running on a different operating system, deciding where authentication is to take place can be a daunting task. So to simplify things, DB2 UDB uses a parameter in the DB2 Database Manager configuration file associated with every instance to determine how and where users are to be authenticated. The value assigned to this configuration parameter, often referred to as the *authentication type*, is set initially when an instance is created. (On the server side, the authentication type is specified during the instance creation process; on the client side, the authentication type is specified when a remote database is cataloged, which is usually performed using the Configuration Assistant.) Only one authentication type exists for each instance, and it controls access to that instance, as well as to all databases that fall under the instance's control.

In Version 8.1 of DB2 UDB, the following authentication types are available:

SERVER. Authentication occurs at the server workstation, using the security facility provided by the server's operating system. (The user ID and password provided by the user wishing to attach to an instance or connect to a database are compared to the user ID and password combinations stored at the server to determine whether the user is permitted to access the instance/database.) By default, this is the authentication type used when an instance is first created.

SERVER_ENCRYPT. Authentication occurs at the server workstation, using the security facility that is provided by the server's operating system. However, the password provided by the user wishing to attach to an instance or connect to a database stored on the server may be encrypted at the client workstation before it is sent to the server workstation for validation.

CLIENT. Authentication occurs at the client workstation or database partition where a client application is invoked, using the security facility that is provided by the client's operating system, assuming one is available. If no security facility is available, authentication is handled in a slightly different manner. (The user ID and password provided by the user wishing to attach to an instance or connect to a database are compared to the user ID and password combinations stored at the client/node to determine whether the user is permitted to access the instance or the database.)

KERBEROS. Authentication occurs at the server workstation, using a security facility that supports the Kerberos security protocol. The Kerberos security protocol is a protocol that performs authentication as a third-party service by using conventional cryptography to create a shared secret key. The key becomes the credentials used to verify the identity of users whenever local or network services are requested; this eliminates the need to pass a user ID and password across the network as ASCII text. (If both the client and the server support the Kerberos security protocol, the user ID and password provided by the user wishing to attach to an instance or connect to a database are encrypted at the client workstation and sent to the server for validation.) It should be noted that the KERBEROS authentication type is only supported on clients and servers that are using the Windows 2000, Windows XP, or Windows .NET operating system. In addition, both client and server workstations must either belong to the same Windows domain or belong to trusted domains.

KRB_SERVER_ENCRYPT. Authentication occurs at the server workstation, using either the KERBEROS or the SERVER_ENCRYPT authentication method. If the client's authentication type is set to KERBEROS, authentication is performed at the server using the Kerberos security system. On the other hand, if the client's authentication type is set to anything other than KERBEROS or if the Kerberos authentication service is unavailable, the server acts as if the SERVER_ENCRYPT authentication type was specified, and the rules of this authentication method apply.

Just as the authentication type for an instance on a server is set when the instance is first created, an authentication type is usually specified at each client workstation that will communicate with a server. Furthermore, the combination of authentication types specified at both the client and the server determine which authentication method is actually used. Figure 3–1 shows the combination of client and server authentication types that should be used when users are to be authenticated at the client workstation. Figure 3–2 shows the combinations of client and server authentication types that should be used when users are to be authenticated at the server.

Trusted Clients Versus Untrusted Clients

As you can see in Figure 3–1, if both the server and the client are configured to use the CLIENT authentication type, authentication occurs at the client workstation (if the database is a nonpartitioned database) or at the database

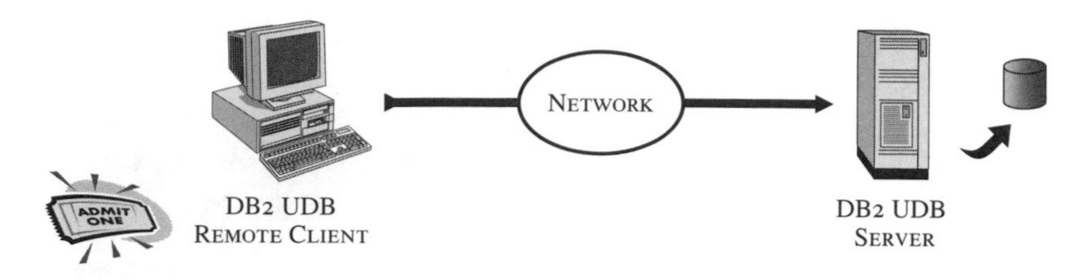

Client Authentication Type	Server Authentication Type	Authentication Type Used
CLIENT	CLIENT	CLIENT

Figure 3–1 Authentication type combinations to use for client authentication.

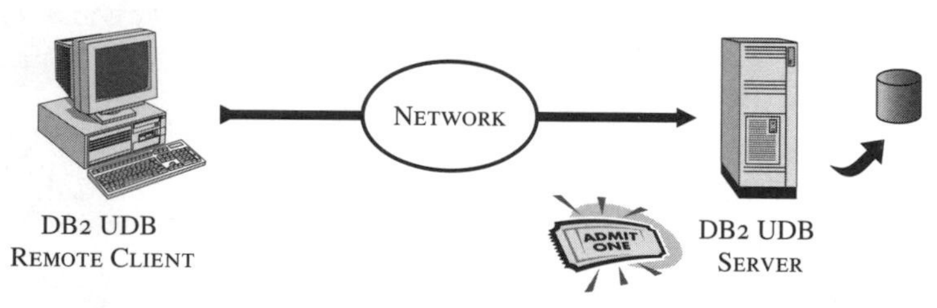

Client Authentication Type	Server Authentication Type	Authentication Type Used
SERVER	SERVER	SERVER
SERVER	SERVER_ENCRYPT	SERVER
SERVER_ENCRYPT	SERVER_ENCRYPT	SERVER_ENCRYPT
KERBEROS	KERBEROS	KERBEROS
KERBEROS	KRB_SERVER_ENCRYPT	KERBEROS
KRB_SERVER_ENCRYPT	KRB_SERVER_ENCRYPT	KRB_SERVER_ENCRYPT
SERVER	KRB_SERVER_ENCRYPT	SERVER_ENCRYPT
SERVER_ENCRYPT	KRB_SERVER_ENCRYPT	SERVER_ENCRYPT

Figure 3–2 Authentication type combinations to use for server authentication.

partition where the client application is invoked from (if the database is a partitioned database), using the security facility that is provided by the client's operating system. But what happens if the client workstation is using an operating system that does not contain a tightly integrated security facility, and no separate add-on security facility has been made available? Does such a configuration compromise security? The answer is no. However, in such environments, the DB2 Database Manager for the instance at the server must be able to determine which clients will be responsible for validating users and which clients will be forced to let the server handle user authentication. To make this distinction, clients that use an operating system that contains an integrated security facility (for example, Windows NT, Windows 2000, all supported versions of UNIX, MVS, OS/390, VM, VSE, and AS/400) are classified as *trusted clients*, and clients that use an operating system that does not provide an integrated security facility (for example, Windows 95, Windows 98, and Windows Millennium Edition) are classified as *untrusted clients*.

The *trust_allclnts* parameter of a DB2 Database Manager configuration file helps the DB2 Database Manager for an instance on a server anticipate whether its clients are to be treated as trusted or untrusted. If this configuration parameter is set to `YES` (which is the default), the DB2 Database Manager assumes that any client that accesses the instance is a trusted client and that authentication will take place at the client. However, if this configuration parameter is set to `NO`, the DB2 Database Manager assumes that one or more untrusted clients will be used to access the server; therefore, all users must be authenticated at the server. (If this configuration parameter is set to `DRDAONLY`, only MVS, OS/390, VM, VSE, and OS/400 clients will be treated as trusted clients.) It is important to note that regardless of how the *trust_allclnts* parameter is set, whenever an untrusted client attempts to access an instance or a database, user authentication always takes place at the server.

In some situations, it may be desirable to authenticate users at the server, even when no untrusted clients will need access. In such situations, the *trust_clntauth* configuration parameter of a DB2 Database Manager configuration file can be used to control where trusted clients are to be validated. By accepting the default value for this parameter (which is `CLIENT`), authentication for trusted clients will take place at the client workstation. However, if the value for this parameter is changed to `SERVER`, authentication for all trusted clients will take place at the server.

Authorities and Privileges

Once a user has been authenticated and an attachment to an instance or a connection to a database has been established, the DB2 Database Manger evaluates any *authorities* and *privileges* that have been assigned to the user (these can be assigned directly to a user, or they can be obtained indirectly from group privileges that have been assigned to a group the user is a member of) to determine what operations the user is allowed to perform. Authorities convey a set of privileges and/or the right to perform high-level administrative and maintenance/utility operations against an instance or a database. Privileges, on the other hand, convey the rights to perform certain actions against specific database resources (such as tables and views). Together, authorities and privileges act to control access to the DB2 Database Manager for an instance, to one or more databases running under that instance's control, and to a particular database's objects. Users can only work with those objects for which they have been given the appropriate authorization—that is, the required authority or privilege. Figure 3–3 provides a hierarchical view of the authorities and privileges that are recognized by DB2 UDB.

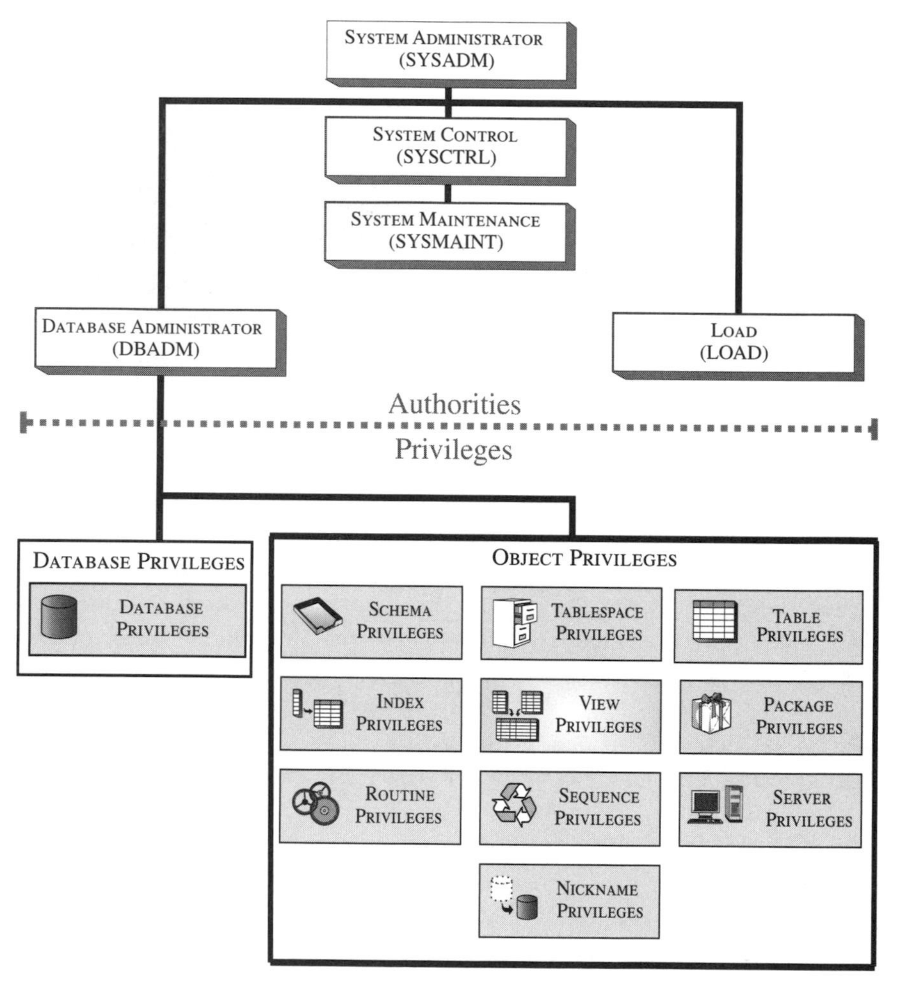

Figure 3–3 Hierarchy of the authorities and privileges available with DB2 UDB.

Authorities

DB2 UDB uses five different levels of authority to control how users perform administrative and/or maintenance operations against an instance or a database. These five levels are:

- System Administrator (SYSADM) authority
- System Control (SYSCTRL) authority
- System Maintenance (SYSMAINT) authority
- Database Administrator (DBADM) authority
- Load (LOAD) authority

The first three of these levels apply to the DB2 Database Manager instance (and to all databases that are managed by that instance), while the remaining two apply only to specific databases within an instance. Furthermore, the three instance-level authorities can only be assigned to groups; the names of the groups that are assigned these authorities are stored in the DB2 Database Manager configuration file that is associated with the instance. Conversely, the two database-level authorities can be assigned to an individual user and/or to a group of users; groups and users that have been assigned database-level authorities are recorded in the system catalog tables of the database to which the authority applies.

System Administrator authority

System Administrator (SYSADM) authority is the highest level of administrative authority available with DB2 UDB. Users that have been given this authority are allowed to run any available DB2 UDB utilities, execute any DB2 UDB command, perform any SQL operation, and control all objects within an instance, including databases, database partition groups, buffer pools, tablespaces, tables, views, indexes, schemas, aliases, data types, functions, procedures, triggers, packages, servers, and event monitors. In addition, users who have been given this authority are allowed to perform the following tasks:

- Migrate an existing database to make it compatible with a new version of DB2 UDB.
- Modify the parameter values of the DB2 Database Manager configuration file associated with the instance—including specifying which groups have System Control and/or System Maintenance authority. (The DB2 Database Manager configuration file is used to control the amount of system resources allocated to a single instance.)
- Give (grant) Database Administrator authority to groups and/or individual users.
- Take away (revoke) Database Administrator authority from groups and/or individual users.

SYSADM authority can only be assigned to a group, and this assignment is made by storing the appropriate group name in the *sysadm_group* parameter of the DB2 Database Manager configuration file associated with a particular instance. Individual membership in the group itself is controlled through the security facility used on the workstation where the instance has been defined.

System Control authority

System Control (SYSCTRL) authority is the highest level of system/instance control authority available with DB2 UDB. Users that have been given this authority are allowed to perform maintenance and utility operations against both a DB2 Database Manager instance and any databases that fall under that instance's control. However, because SYSCTRL authority is designed to allow special users to maintain an instance containing sensitive data that they most likely do not have the right to access, users who are granted this authority do not implicitly receive authority to access the data stored in the databases they are allowed to perform maintenance and utility operations on. On the other hand, because a connection to a database must exist before some utility operations can be performed, users who are granted SYSCTRL authority for a particular instance also receive the privileges needed to connect to each database under that instance's control.

Users with SYSCTRL authority (or higher) are allowed to perform the following tasks:

- Update a database, node, or distributed connection services (DCS) directory (by cataloging/uncataloging databases, nodes, or DCS databases).
- Modify the parameter values of one or more DB2 database configuration files. (A database configuration file is used to control the amount of system resources allocated to a single database during normal operation.)
- Force users off the system.
- Create or destroy (drop) a database.
- Create, alter, or drop a tablespace.
- Make a backup image of a database or a tablespace.
- Restore an existing database using a backup image.
- Restore a tablespace using a backup image.
- Create a new database from a database backup image.
- Perform a roll-forward recovery operation on a database.
- Start or stop a DB2 Database Manager instance.

- Run a trace on a database operation.
- Take database system monitor snapshots of a DB2 Database Manager instance or any database under the instance's control.
- Query the state of a tablespace.
- Update recovery log history files.
- Quiesce (restrict access to) a tablespace.
- Reorganize a table.
- Collect catalog statistics using the RUNSTATS utility.

Like SYSADM authority, SYSCTRL authority can only be assigned to a group. This assignment is made by storing the appropriate group name in the *sysctrl_group* parameter of the DB2 Database Manager configuration file that is associated with a particular instance. Again, individual membership in the group itself is controlled through the security facility that is used on the workstation where the instance has been defined.

System Maintenance authority

System Maintenance (SYSMAINT) authority is the second highest level of system/instance control authority available with DB2 UDB. Users that have been given this authority are allowed to perform maintenance and utility operations against any database that falls under an instance's control—but not against the instance itself. Like SYSCTRL authority, SYSMAINT authority is designed to allow special users to maintain a database containing sensitive data that they most likely do not have access to. Therefore, users who are granted this authority do not implicitly receive authority to access the data stored in the databases they are allowed to perform maintenance and utility operations on. However, because a connection to a database must exist before some utility operations can be performed, users who are granted SYSMAINT authority for a particular instance automatically receive the privileges needed to connect to each database under that instance's control.

Users with SYSMAINT authority (or higher) are allowed to perform the following tasks:

- Modify the parameter values of one or more DB2 database configuration files.
- Make a backup image of a database or a tablespace.
- Restore an existing database using a backup image.
- Restore a tablespace using a backup image.

- Perform a roll-forward recovery operation on a database.
- Start or stop a DB2 Database Manager instance.
- Run a trace on a database operation.
- Take database system monitor snapshots of a DB2 Database Manager instance or any database under the instance's control.
- Query the state of a tablespace.
- Update recovery log history files.
- Quiesce (restrict access to) a tablespace.
- Reorganize a table.
- Collect catalog statistics using the RUNSTATS utility.

Like SYSADM and SYSCTRL authority, SYSMAINT authority can only be assigned to a group. This assignment is made by storing the appropriate group name in the *sysmaint_group* parameter of the DB2 Database Manager configuration file that is associated with a particular instance. Again, individual membership in the group itself is controlled through the security facility that is used on the workstation where the instance has been defined.

Database Administrator authority

Database Administrator (DBADM) authority is the second highest level of administrative authority (below SYSADM) available with DB2 UDB. Users that have been given this authority are allowed to run most DB2 UDB utilities, issue database-specific DB2 commands, perform most SQL operations, and access data stored in any table in a database. However, they can only perform these functions on the database for which DBADM authority is held.

Users with DBADM authority (or higher) are allowed to perform the following tasks:

- Query the state of a tablespace.
- Update recovery log history files.
- Quiesce (restrict access to) a tablespace.
- Reorganize a table.
- Collect catalog statistics using the RUNSTATS utility.

On the other hand, only users with DBADM authority (or SYSADM authority) are allowed to:

- Read database log files.
- Create, activate, and drop event monitors.
- Give (grant) database privileges to groups and/or individual users.
- Take away (revoke) any privilege from any group and/or individual user, regardless of how it was granted.

Unlike SYSADM, SYSCTRL, and SYSMAINT authority, DBADM authority can be assigned to both individual users and groups. This assignment is made by executing the appropriate form of the `GRANT` SQL statement (which we will look at shortly). When a user is given DBADM authority for a particular database, they automatically receive CONNECT, CREATETAB, BINDADD, CREATE_NOT_FENCED, and IMPLICIT_SCHEMA database privileges for that database as well.

Any time a user with SYSADM or SYSCTRL authority creates a new database, they automatically receive DBADM authority on that database. Furthermore, if a user with SYSADM or SYSCTRL authority creates a database and is later removed from the SYSADM or SYSCTRL group (i.e., their SYSADM or SYSCTRL authority is revoked), they retain DBADM authority for that database until it is explicitly removed (revoked).

Load authority

Load (LOAD) authority is a special database level of administrative authority that has a much smaller scope that the DBADM authority. Users that have been given this authority, along with INSERT and in some cases DELETE privileges on a particular table are allowed to bulk load data into that table, using either the AutoLoader utility (`db2atld` command) or the `LOAD` command/API. LOAD authority is designed to allow special users to perform bulk-load operations against a database that they most likely cannot do anything else with. This authority level provides a way for Database Administrators to allow more users to perform special database operations without having to sacrifice control.

In addition to being able to load data into a database table, users with LOAD authority (or higher) are allowed to perform the following tasks:

- Query the state of a tablespace using the `LIST TABLESPACES` command.
- Quiesce (restrict access to) a tablespace.
- Collect catalog statistics using the RUNSTATS utility.

Like DBADM authority, LOAD authority can be assigned to both individual users and groups. This assignment is made by executing the appropriate form of the `GRANT` SQL statement.

Privileges

As mentioned earlier, privileges are used to convey the rights to perform certain actions on specific database resources to both individual users and groups. With DB2 UDB, two distinct types of privileges exist: *database privileges* and *object privileges.*

Database privileges

Database privileges apply to a database as a whole, and for most users, they act as identification that gets verified at the second security checkpoint that must be cleared before access to data is provided. Figure 3–4 shows the different types of database privileges available.

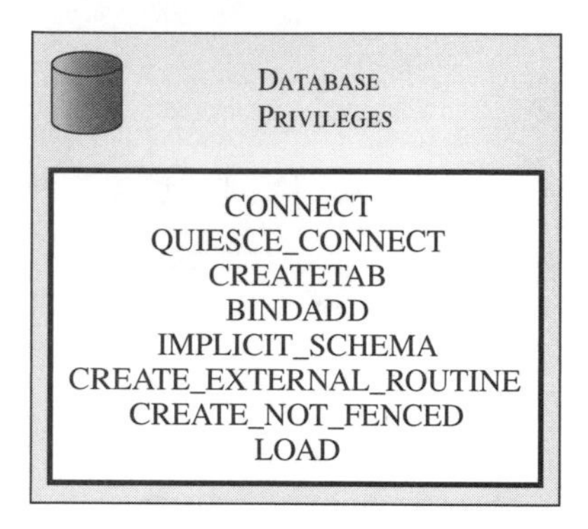

DATABASE
PRIVILEGES
CONNECT
QUIESCE_CONNECT
CREATETAB
BINDADD
IMPLICIT_SCHEMA
CREATE_EXTERNAL_ROUTINE
CREATE_NOT_FENCED
LOAD

Figure 3–4 Database privileges available with DB2 UDB.

As you can see in Figure 3–4, eight different database privileges exist. They are:

CONNECT. Allows a user to establish a connection to the database.

QUIESCE_CONNECT. Allows a user to establish a connection to the database while it is quiesced (while access to it is restricted).

CREATETAB. Allows a user to create new tables in the database.

BINDADD. Allows a user to create packages in the database (by precompiling embedded SQL application source code files against the database and/or by binding application bind files to the database).

CREATE_EXTERNAL_ROUTINE. Allows a user to create a procedure that can be invoked by applications and other database users and store it in the database.

CREATE_NOT_FENCED. Allows a user to create unfenced user-defined functions (UDFs) and store them in the database. (Unfenced UDFs are UDFs that are considered "safe" enough to be run in the DB2 Database Manager operating environment's process or address space. Unless a function is registered as being unfenced, the DB2 Database Manager insulates its internal resources in such a way that they cannot be utilized by that function.)

IMPLICIT_SCHEMA. Allows a user to implicitly create a new schema in the database by creating an object and assigning that object a schema name that is different from any of the schema names already existing in the database.

LOAD. Allows a user to bulk-load data into one or more existing tables in the database.

At a minimum, a user must have CONNECT privilege on a database before they can work with any object in that database.

Object privileges

Unlike database privileges, which apply to a database as a whole, object privileges only apply to specific objects within a database. These objects include schemas, tablespaces, tables, indexes, views, packages, routines, sequences, servers, and nicknames. Because the nature of each available database object varies, the individual privileges that exist for each object can vary as well. The following sections describe the different sets of object privileges that are available with DB2 UDB.

Schema privileges. Schema privileges control what users can and cannot do with a particular schema. (A schema is an object that is used to logically classify and group other objects in the database; most objects are named using a naming convention that consists of a schema name, followed by a period, followed by the object name.) Figure 3–5 shows the different types of schema privileges available.

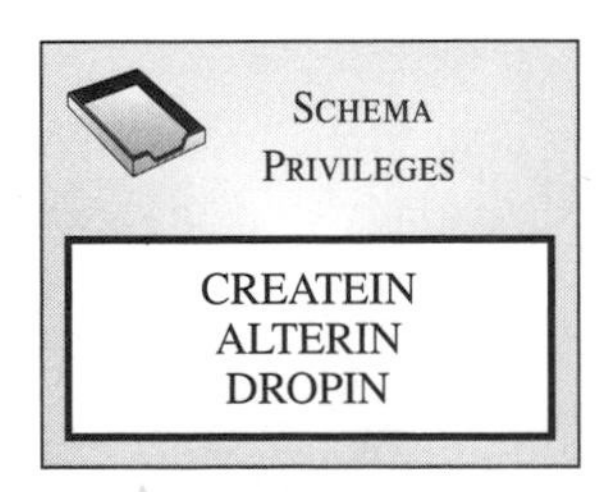

Figure 3–5 Schema privileges available with DB2 UDB.

As you can see in Figure 3–5, three different schema privileges exist. They are:

CREATEIN. Allows a user to create objects within the schema.

ALTERIN. Allows a user to change the comment associated with any object in the schema or to alter any object that resides within the schema.

DROPIN. Allows a user to remove (drop) any object within the schema.

Objects that can be manipulated within a schema include tables, views, indexes, packages, user-defined data types, user-defined functions, triggers, stored procedures, and aliases. The owner of a schema (usually the individual who created the schema) automatically receives these privileges, along with the right to grant any combination of these privileges to other users and groups.

Tablespace privileges. Tablespace privileges control what users can and cannot do with a particular tablespace. (Tablespaces are used to control where data in a database physically resides.) Figure 3–6 shows the different types of tablespace privileges available.

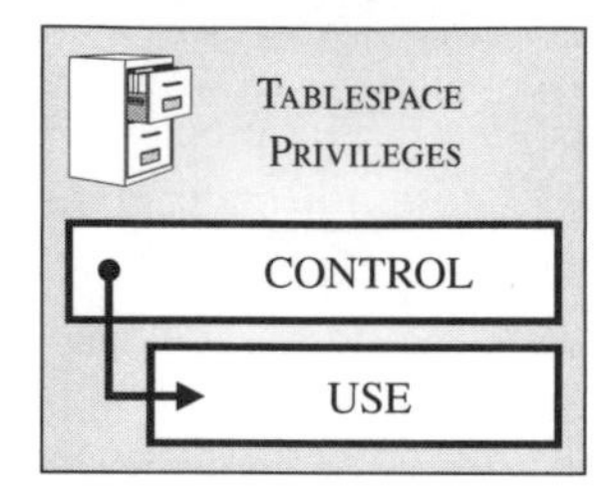

Figure 3–6 Tablespace privileges available with DB2 UDB.

As you can see in Figure 3–6, two different tablespace privileges exist. They are:

CONTROL. Provides a user with every tablespace privilege available, allows the user to remove (drop) the tablespace from the database, and gives the user the ability to grant to or revoke from other users and groups the USE tablespace privilege. (Only users who hold SYSADM or DBADM authority are allowed to grant and revoke CONTROL privileges for an object.)

USE. Allows a user to create tables within the tablespace. (This privilege is used to control which tablespaces a particular user is allowed to create tables in.)

The owner of a tablespace (usually the individual who created the tablespace) automatically receives CONTROL privilege and USE privilege for that tablespace. By default, whenever a new database is created, the USE privilege for tablespace USERSPACE1 is given to the group PUBLIC; however, this privilege can be revoked.

The USE privilege cannot be used to provide a user with the ability to create tables in the SYSCATSPACE tablespace or in any system temporary tablespace that might exist.

Table privileges. Table privileges control what users can and cannot do with a particular table in a database. (A table is a logical structure that is used to present data as a collection of unordered rows with a fixed number of columns.) Figure 3–7 shows the different types of table privileges available.

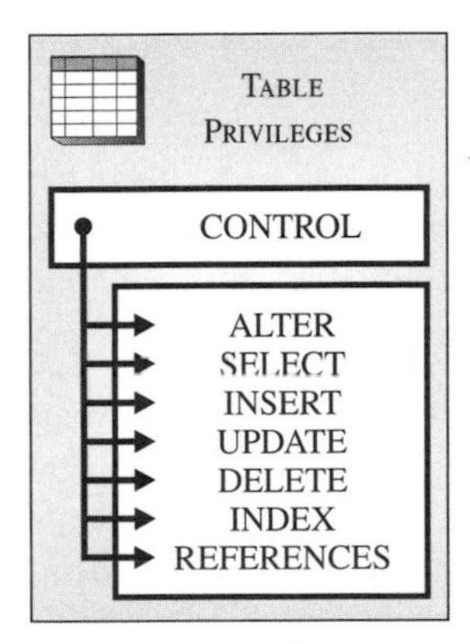

Figure 3–7 Table privileges available with DB2 UDB.

As you can see in Figure 3–7, eight different table privileges exist. They are:

> **CONTROL.** Provides a user with every table privilege available, allows the user to remove (drop) the table from the database, and gives the user the ability to grant to or revoke from other users and groups any available table privileges (except the CONTROL privilege).
>
> **ALTER.** Allows a user to execute the `ALTER TABLE` SQL statement against the table. In other words, allows a user to add columns to the table, add or change comments associated with the table and/or any of its columns, create a primary key for the table, create a unique constraint for the table, create or drop a check constraint for the table, and create triggers for the table (provided the user holds the appropriate privileges for every object referenced by the trigger).
>
> **SELECT.** Allows a user to execute a `SELECT` SQL statement against the table. In other words, allows a user to retrieve data from a table, create a view that references the table, and run the EXPORT utility against the table.
>
> **INSERT.** Allows a user to execute the `INSERT` SQL statement against the table. In other words, allows a user to add data to the table and run the IMPORT utility against the table.
>
> **UPDATE.** Allows a user to execute the `UPDATE` SQL statement against the table. In other words, allows a user to modify data in the

table. (This privilege can be granted for the entire table or limited to one or more columns within the table.)

DELETE. Allows a user to execute the `DELETE` SQL statement against the table. In other words, allows a user to remove rows of data from the table.

INDEX. Allows a user to create an index for the table.

REFERENCES. Allows a user to create and drop foreign key constraints that reference the table in a parent relationship. (This privilege can be granted for the entire table or limited to one or more columns within the table, in which case only those columns can participate as a parent key in a referential constraint.)

The owner of a table (usually the individual who created the table) automatically receives CONTROL privilege, along with all other available table privileges, for that table. If the CONTROL privilege is later revoked from the table owner, all other privileges that were automatically granted to the owner for that particular table are not automatically revoked. Instead, they must be explicitly revoked in one or more separate operations.

Index privileges. The index privilege controls what users can and cannot do with a particular index. (An index is an ordered set of pointers that refer to one or more key columns in a base table; indexes are used to improve query performance.) Figure 3–8 shows the only index privilege available.

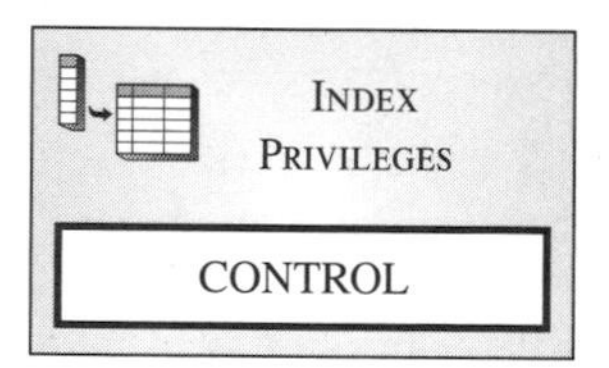

Figure 3–8 Index privilege available with DB2 UDB.

As you can see in Figure 3–8, only one index privilege exists. That privilege is the CONTROL privilege, which allows a user to remove (drop) the index from the database. Unlike the CONTROL privilege for other objects, the CONTROL privilege for an index does not provide a user with the ability to grant to or revoke from other users and groups any available index privilege. That's because only users who hold SYSADM or DBADM authority are allowed to grant and revoke CONTROL privileges for an object.

The owner of an index (usually the individual who created the index) automatically receives CONTROL privilege for that index.

View privileges. View privileges control what users can and cannot do with a particular view. (A view is a virtual table residing in memory that provides an alternative way of working with data that resides in one or more base tables.) Figure 3–9 shows the different types of view privileges available.

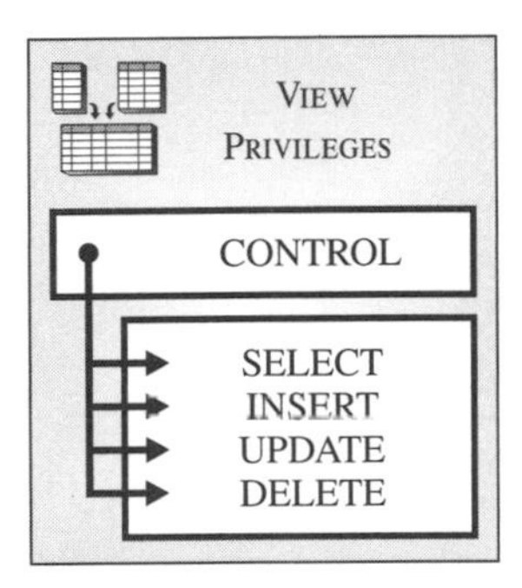

Figure 3–9 View privileges available with DB2 UDB.

As you can see in Figure 3–9, five different view privileges exist. They are:

> **CONTROL.** Provides a user with every view privilege available, allows the user to remove (drop) the view from the database, and gives the user the ability to grant to or revoke from other users and groups any available view privileges (except the CONTROL privilege).
>
> **SELECT.** Allows a user to retrieve data from the view, create a second view that references the view, and run the EXPORT utility against the view.
>
> **INSERT.** Allows a user to add data to the view.
>
> **UPDATE.** Allows a user to modify data in the view. (This privilege can be granted for the entire view or limited to one or more columns within the view.).
>
> **DELETE.** Allows a user to remove rows of data from the view.

In order to create a view, a user must hold appropriate privileges on each base table the view references. Once a view is created, the owner of that view (usually the individual who created the view) automatically receives all available view privileges—with the exception of the CONTROL privilege—for that view. A view owner will only receive CONTROL privilege for the view if they also hold CONTROL privilege for every base table the view references.

Package privileges. Package privileges control what users can and cannot do with a particular package. (A package is an object that contains the information needed by the DB2 Database Manager to process SQL statements in the most efficient way possible on behalf of an embedded SQL application.) Figure 3–10 shows the different types of package privileges available.

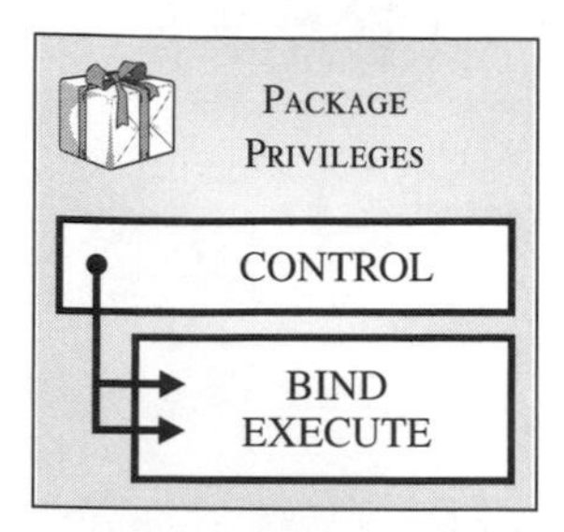

Figure 3–10 Package privileges available with DB2 UDB.

As you can see in Figure 3–10, three different package privileges exist. They are:

> **CONTROL.** Provides a user with every package privilege available, allows the user to remove (drop) the package from the database, and gives the user the ability to grant to or revoke from other users and groups any available package privileges (except the CONTROL privilege).
>
> **BIND.** Allows a user to rebind or add new package versions to a package that has already been bound to a database. (In addition to the BIND package privilege, a user must hold the privileges needed to execute the SQL statements that make up the package before the package can be successfully rebound.)
>
> **EXECUTE.** Allows a user to execute the package. (A user that has EXECUTE privilege for a particular package can execute that package, even if they do not have the privileges that are needed to execute the SQL statements stored in the package. That is because any privileges needed to execute SQL statements in a package are implicitly granted to the package user. It is important to note that for privileges to be implicitly granted, the creator of the package must hold privileges as an individual user or as a member of the group PUBLIC—not as a member of another named group.)

The owner of a package (usually the individual who created the package) automatically receives CONTROL privilege, along with all other available package privileges, for that package. If the CONTROL privilege is later revoked from the package owner, all other privileges that were automatically granted to the owner for that particular package are not automatically revoked. Instead, they must be explicitly revoked in one or more separate operations.

Users who have EXECUTE privilege for a package that contains nicknames do not need additional authorities or privileges for the nicknames in the package; however, they must be able to pass any authentication checks performed at the data source(s) in which objects referenced by the nicknames are stored, and they must hold the appropriate authorizations and privileges needed to access all referenced objects.

Routine privileges. Routine privileges control what users can and cannot do with a particular routine. (A routine can be a user-defined function, a stored procedure, or a method that can be invoked by several different users.) Figure 3–11 shows the different types of routine privileges available.

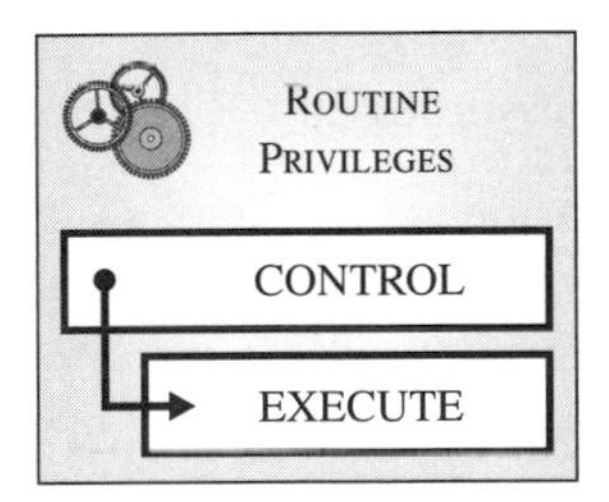

Figure 3–11 Routine privileges available with DB2 UDB.

As you can see in Figure 3–11, two different routine privileges exist. They are:

> **CONTROL.** Provides a user with every routine privilege available, allows the user to remove (drop) the routine from the database, and gives the user the ability to grant to or revoke from other users and groups any available routine privileges (except the CONTROL privilege).
>
> **EXECUTE.** Allows a user to invoke the routine, create a function that is sourced from the routine (provided the routine is a function), and reference the routine in a DDL statement or when creating a constraint.

The owner of a routine (usually the individual who created the routine) automatically receives CONTROL and EXECUTE privileges for that routine. If the CONTROL privilege is later revoked from the owner, the EXECUTE privilege will be retained and must be explicitly revoked in a separate operation.

Sequence privileges. Sequence privileges control what users can and cannot do with a particular sequence. (A sequence is an object that can be used to generate values automatically—sequences are ideal for generating unique key values. Applications can use sequences to avoid the possible concurrency and performance problems that can occur when unique counters residing outside the database are used for data generation.) Figure 3–12 shows the different types of sequence privileges available.

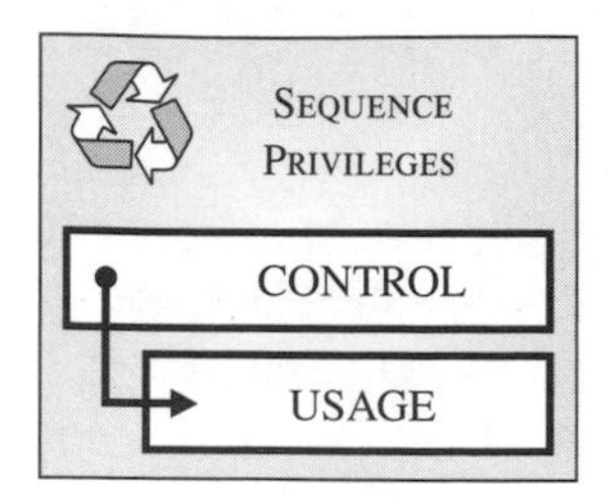

Figure 3–12 Sequence privileges available with DB2 UDB.

As you can see in Figure 3–12, two different sequence privileges exist. They are:

> **CONTROL.** Provides a user with every sequence privilege available, allows the user to remove (drop) the sequence from the database, and gives the user the ability to grant to or revoke from other users and groups any available sequence privileges (except the CONTROL privilege).
>
> **USAGE.** Allows a user to use the `PREVVAL` and `NEXTVAL` expressions that are associated with the sequence. (The `PREVVAL` expression returns the most recently generated value for the specified sequence; the `NEXTVAL` expression returns the next value for the specified sequence.)

The owner of a sequence (usually the individual who created the sequence) automatically receives CONTROL and USAGE privilege for that sequence. If the CONTROL privilege is later revoked from the owner, the USAGE privilege will be retained and must be explicitly revoked in a separate operation.

Server privileges. The server privilege controls what users can and cannot do with a particular federated database server. (A DB2 federated system is a distributed computing system that consists of a DB2 server, known as a *federated server*, and one or more data sources to which the federated server sends queries. Each data source consists of an instance of some supported relational database management system—such as Oracle—plus the database or databases that the instance supports.) Figure 3–13 shows the only type of server privilege available.

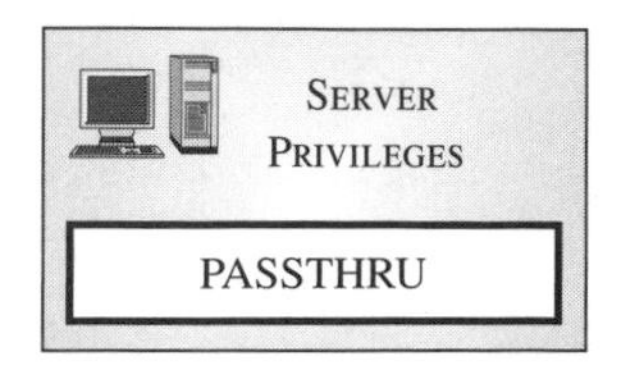

Figure 3–13 Server privilege available with DB2 UDB.

As you can see in Figure 3–13, only one server privilege exists. That privilege is the PASSTHRU privilege, which allows a user to issue Data Definition Language (DDL) and Data Manipulation Language (DML) SQL statements (as pass-through operations) directly to a data source via a federated server.

Nickname privileges. Nickname privileges control what users can and cannot do with a particular nickname. (When a client application submits a distributed request to a federated database server, the server forwards the request to the appropriate data source for processing. However, such a request does not identify the data source itself; instead, it references tables and views within the data source by using nicknames that map to specific table and view names at the data source. Nicknames are not alternate names for tables and views in the same way that aliases are; instead, they are pointers by which a federated server references external objects.) Figure 3–14 shows the different types of nickname privileges available.

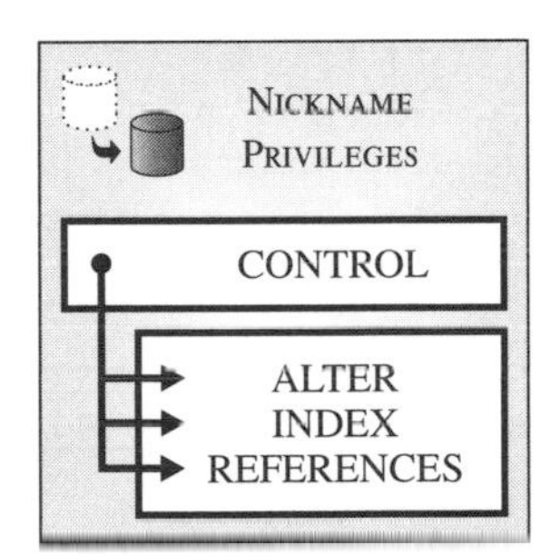

Figure 3–14 Nickname privileges available with DB2 UDB.

As you can see in Figure 3–14, four different nickname privileges exist. They are:

CONTROL. Provides a user with every nickname privilege available, allows the user to remove (drop) the nickname from the database, and gives the user the ability to grant to or revoke from other users and groups any available nickname privileges (except the CONTROL privilege).

ALTER. Allows a user to change column names in the nickname, add or change the DB2 data type that a particular nickname column's data type maps to, and specify column options for a particular nickname column.

INDEX. Allows a user to create an index specification for the nickname.

REFERENCES. Allows a user to create and drop foreign key constraints that reference a nickname in a parent relationship. (This privilege can be granted for the entire nickname or limited to one or more columns within the nickname.)

The owner of a nickname (usually the individual who created the nickname) automatically receives CONTROL privilege, along with all other available nickname privileges, for that nickname. If the CONTROL privilege is later revoked from the nickname owner, all other privileges that were automatically granted to the owner for that particular nickname are not automatically revoked. Instead, they must be explicitly revoked in one or more separate operations.

Requirements for Granting and Revoking Authorities and Privileges

Not only do authorization levels and privileges control what a user can and cannot do, they also control what authorities and privileges a user can grant to and revoke from other users and groups. A list of the authorities and privileges a user who has been given a specific authority level or privilege is allowed to grant and revoke is shown in Table 3–1.

Table 3–1 Requirements for Granting/Revoking Authorities and Privileges

If a User Holds ...	They Can Grant ...	They Can Revoke ...
System Administrator (SYSADM) authority	System Control (SYSCTRL) authority	System Control (SYSCTRL) authority
	System Maintenance (SYSMAINT) authority	System Maintenance (SYSMAINT) authority
	Database Administrator (DBADM) authority	Database Administrator (DBADM) authority
	Load (LOAD) authority	Load (LOAD) authority
	Any database privilege, including CONTROL privilege	Any database privilege, including CONTROL privilege
	Any object privilege, including CONTROL privilege	Any object privilege, including CONTROL privilege
System Control (SYSCTRL) authority	The USE tablespace privilege	The USE tablespace privilege
System Maintenance (SYSMAINT) authority	No authorities or privileges	No authorities or privileges

Table 3–1 Requirements for Granting/Revoking Authorities and Privileges *(Continued)*		
If a User Holds ...	**They Can Grant ...**	**They Can Revoke ...**
Database Administrator (DBADM) authority	Any database privilege, including CONTROL privilege Any object privilege, including CONTROL privilege	Any database privilege, including CONTROL privilege Any object privilege, including CONTROL privilege
Load (LOAD) authority	No authorities or privileges	No authorities or privileges
CONTROL privilege on an object (but no other authority)	All privileges available (with the exception of the CONTROL privilege) for the object the user holds CONTROL privilege on	All privileges available (with the exception of the CONTROL privilege) for the object the user holds CONTROL privilege on
A privilege on an object that was assigned with the `WITH GRANT OPTION` option specified	The same object privilege that was assigned with the `WITH GRANT OPTION` option specified	No authorities or privileges

Granting Authorities and Privileges

There are three different ways that users (and groups) can obtain database-level authorities and database/object privileges. They are:

Implicitly. When a user creates a database, they implicitly receive DBADM authority for that database, along with several database privileges. Likewise, when a user creates a database object, they implicitly receive all privileges available for that object along with the ability to grant any combination of those privileges (with the exception of the CONTROL privilege), to other users and groups. Privileges can also be implicitly given whenever a higher-level privilege is explicitly granted to a user (for example, if a user is explicitly given CONTROL privilege for a tablespace, they will implicitly receive the USE privilege for that tablespace as well). Keep in mind that such implicitly assigned privileges are not automatically revoked when the higher-level privilege that caused them to be granted is revoked.

Indirectly. Indirectly assigned privileges are usually associated with packages; when a user executes a package that requires privileges to execute that the user does not have (for example, a package that deletes a row of data from a table requires the DELETE privilege on that table), the user is indirectly given those privileges for the express purpose of executing the package. Indirectly granted privileges are temporary and do not exist outside the scope in which they are granted.

Explicitly. Database-level authorities, database privileges, and object privileges can be explicitly given to or taken from an individual user or a group of users by any user that has the authority to do so. To explicitly grant privileges on most database objects, a user must have SYSADM authority, DBADM authority, or CONTROL privilege on that object. Alternately, a user can explicitly grant any privilege they were assigned with the WITH GRANT OPTION specified. To grant CONTROL privilege for any object, a user must have SYSADM or DBADM authority; to grant DBADM authority, a user must have SYSADM authority.

Granting and Revoking Authorities and Privileges from the Control Center

One way to explicitly grant and revoke database-level authorities, as well as several available privileges, is by using the various authorities and privileges management dialogs that are provided with the Control Center. These dialogs are activated by highlighting the appropriate database or object name shown in the Control Center panes and selecting either *Authorities* or *Privileges* from the corresponding database or object menu. Figure 3–15 shows the menu items that must be selected in the Control Center in order to activate the Table Privileges dialog for a particular table. Figure 3–16 shows how the Table Privileges dialog might look immediately after a table is first created. (A single check mark under a privilege means that the individual or group shown has been granted that privilege; a double check mark means the individual or group has also been granted the ability to grant that privilege to other users and groups.)

To assign privileges to an individual user from the Table Privileges dialog (or a similar authorities/privileges dialog), you simply identify a particular user by highlighting their entry in the recognized users list—if the desired user is not in the list, they can be added by selecting the "Add User" push button—and assign the appropriate privileges (or authorities) using the "Privileges"

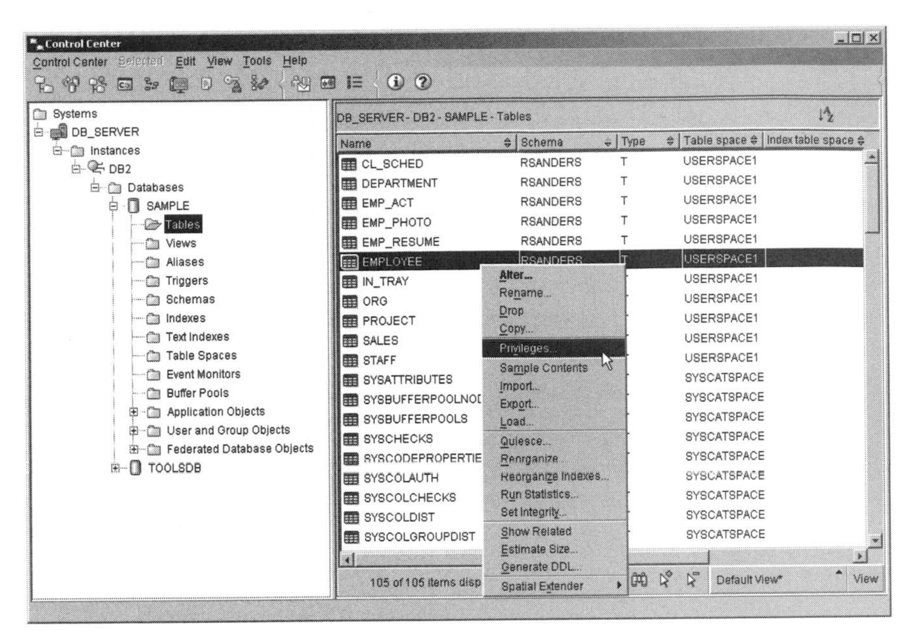

Figure 3–15 Invoking the Table Privileges dialog from the Control Center.

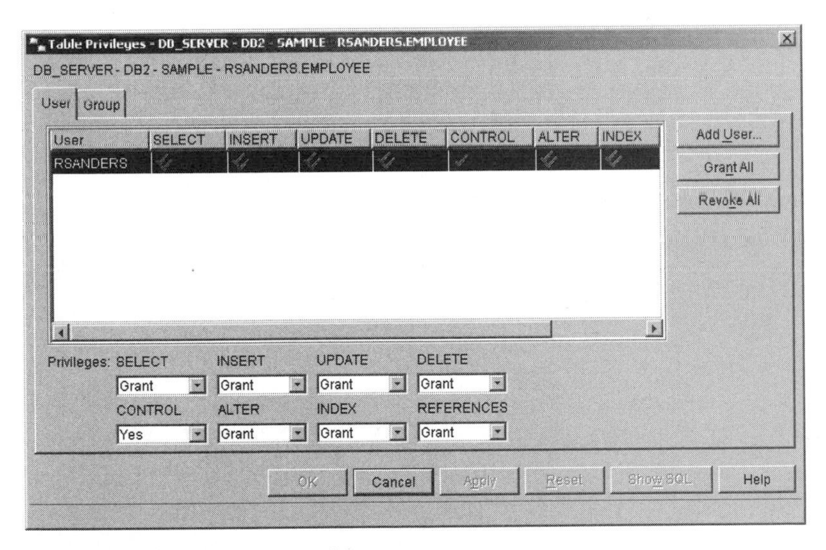

Figure 3–16 The Table Privileges dialog.

(or "Authorities") drop-down list or the "Grant All" or "Revoke All" push buttons. To assign privileges to a group of users, you select the "Group" tab to display a list of recognized groups and repeat the process (using the "Add Group" push button instead of the "Add User" push button to add a desired group to the list if they are not already there).

Granting Authorities and Privileges with the GRANT SQL Statement

Not all privileges can be explicitly given to users/groups with the privileges management dialogs available. However, in situations where no privileges dialog exists (and in situations where you elect not to use the Control Center), database-level authorities and database/object privileges can be explicitly given to users and/or groups by executing the appropriate form of the GRANT SQL statement. The syntax for the GRANT SQL statement varies according to the authority or privilege being granted—the following sections show the syntax used to grant each database-level authority and database/object privilege available.

Database-level authorities and privileges

```
GRANT [DBADM | Privilege, ...] ON DATABASE TO
[Recipient, ...]
```

where:

Privilege	Identifies one or more database privileges that are to be given to one or more users and/or groups.
Recipient	Identifies the name of the user(s) and/or group(s) that are to receive DBADM authority or the database privileges specified.

Schema privileges

```
GRANT [Privilege, ...] ON SCHEMA [SchemaName] TO
[Recipient, ...] <WITH GRANT OPTION>
```

where:

Privilege	Identifies one or more schema privileges that are to be given to one or more users and/or groups.
SchemaName	Identifies by name the specific schema that all schema privileges specified are to be associated with.
Recipient	Identifies the name of the user(s) and/or group(s) that are to receive the schema privileges specified.

Tablespace privilege

```
GRANT USE OF TABLESPACE [TablespaceName]
TO [Recipient, ...]
<WITH GRANT OPTION>
```

where:

TablespaceName	Identifies by name the specific tablespace that the USE privilege is to be associated with.
Recipient	Identifies the name of the user(s) and/or group(s) that are to receive the USE privilege.

Table privileges

```
GRANT [ALL <PRIVILEGES> |
   Privilege <( ColumnName, ... )>  , ...]
ON TABLE [TableName] TO [Recipient, ...]
<WITH GRANT OPTION>
```

where:

Privilege	Identifies one or more table privileges that are to be given to one or more users and/or groups.
ColumnName	Identifies by name one or more specific columns that UPDATE or REFERENCES privileges are to be associated with. This option is not used if *Privilege* is not equal to UPDATE or REFERENCES.
TableName	Identifies by name the specific table that all table privileges specified are to be associated with.
Recipient	Identifies the name of the user(s) and/or group(s) that are to receive the table privileges specified.

Index privilege

```
GRANT CONTROL ON INDEX [IndexName] TO [Recipient, ...]
```

where:

IndexName	Identifies by name the specific index that the CONTROL privilege is to be associated with.
Recipient	Identifies the name of the user(s) and/or group(s) that are to receive the CONTROL privilege.

View privileges

```
GRANT [ALL <PRIVILEGES> |
   Privilege <( ColumnName, ... )>  , ...]
ON [ViewName]
TO [Recipient, ...]
<WITH GRANT OPTION>
```

where:

Privilege — Identifies one or more view privileges that are to be given to one or more users and/or groups.

ColumnName — Identifies by name one or more specific columns that UPDATE privilege is to be associated with. This option is not used if *Privilege* is not equal to UPDATE.

ViewName — Identifies by name the specific view that all view privileges specified are to be associated with.

Recipient — Identifies the name of the user(s) and/or group(s) that are to receive the view privileges specified.

Package privileges

```
GRANT [Privilege, ...] ON PACKAGE <SchemaName.>
[PackageID] TO [Recipient, ...] <WITH GRANT OPTION>
```

where:

Privilege — Identifies one or more package privileges that are to be given to one or more users and/or groups.

SchemaName — Identifies by name the schema in which the specified package is found.

PackageName — Identifies by name the specific package that all package privileges specified are to be associated with.

Recipient — Identifies the name of the user(s) and/or group(s) that are to receive the package privileges specified.

Routine privileges

```
GRANT EXECUTE ON [RoutineName |
   FUNCTION <SchemaName.> * |
   METHOD * FOR [TypeName] |
   METHOD * FOR <SchemaName.> * |
   PROCEDURE <SchemaName.> *]
TO [Recipient, ...]
<WITH GRANT OPTION>
```

where:

RoutineName — Identifies by name the routine that the EXECUTE privilege is to be associated with.

TypeName — Identifies by name the type in which the specified method is found.

SchemaName — Identifies by name the schema in which all functions, methods, or procedures—including those that may be created in the future—are to have the EXECUTE privilege granted on.

Recipient — Identifies the name of the user(s) and/or group(s) that are to receive the EXECUTE privilege.

Sequence privilege

```
GRANT USAGE ON SEQUENCE [SequenceName] TO PUBLIC
```

where:

SequenceName — Identifies by name the specific sequence that the USAGE privilege is to be associated with.

Server privilege

```
GRANT PASSTHRU ON SERVER [ServerName] TO [Recipient, ...]
```

where:

ServerName — Identifies by name the specific server that the PASSTHRU privilege is to be associated with.

Recipient — Identifies the name of the user(s) and/or group(s) that are to receive the PASSTHRU privilege.

Nickname privileges

```
GRANT [ALL <PRIVILEGES> | Privilege <( ColumnName,
... )>  , ...] ON [Nickname] TO [Recipient, ...]
<WITH GRANT OPTION>
```

where:

Privilege — Identifies one or more nickname privileges that are to be given to one or more users and/or groups.

ColumnName — Identifies by name one or more specific columns that the REFERENCES privilege is to be associated with. This option is not used if *Privilege* is not equal to REFERENCES.

Nickname — Identifies by name the specific nickname that all privileges specified are to be associated with.

Recipient — Identifies the name of the user(s) and/or group(s) that are to receive the nickname privileges specified.

If the WITH GRANT OPTION clause is specified with the GRANT statement, the user and/or group receiving the privileges specified is given the ability to grant the privilege received (except for the CONTROL privilege) to other users. In all cases, the value specified for the *Recipient* parameter can be any combination of the following:

USER [*UserName*]	Identifies a specific user that the privileges specified are to be given to.
GROUP [*GroupName*]	Identifies a specific group that the privileges specified are to be given to.
PUBLIC	Indicates that the specified privilege(s) are to be given to the special group PUBLIC. (All users are a member of the group PUBLIC).

GRANT SQL statement examples

Now that we've seen the basic syntax for the various forms of the GRANT SQL statement, let's take a look at some examples.

Example 1. A server has both a user and a group named TESTER. Give the group TESTER the ability to bind applications to the database SAMPLE:

```
CONNECT TO SAMPLE
GRANT BINDADD ON DATABASE TO GROUP tester
```

Example 2. Give all table privileges available (except CONTROL privilege) for the table PAYROLL.EMPLOYEE to the group PUBLIC:

```
GRANT ALL PRIVILEGES ON TABLE payroll.employee TO
PUBLIC
```

Example 3. Give user USER1 and user USER2 the privileges needed to perform just DML operations on the table DEPARTMENT using the view DEPTVIEW:

```
GRANT SELECT, INSERT, UPDATE, DELETE ON deptview TO
USER user1, USER user2
```

Example 4. Give user JOHN_DOE the privilege needed to query the table INVENTORY, along with the ability to grant this privilege to other users whenever appropriate:

```
GRANT SELECT ON TABLE inventory TO john_doe WITH
GRANT OPTION
```

Example 5. Give user USER1 the ability to run an embedded SQL application that requires package GET_INVENTORY:

```
GRANT EXECUTE ON PACKAGE get_inventory TO USER user1
```

Example 6. Give user USER1 the ability to use a user-defined function named PAYROLL.CALC_SALARY that has an input parameter of type CHAR(5) in a query:

```
GRANT EXECUTE ON FUNCTION payroll.calc_salary(CHAR(5))
TO USER user1
```

Example 7. Give user USER1 the ability to define a referential constraint between the tables EMPLOYEE and DEPARTMENT using column EMPID in table EMPLOYEE as the parent key:

```
GRANT REFERENCES(empid) ON TABLE employee TO USER user1
```

Example 8. Give the group PUBLIC the ability to modify information stored in the ADDRESS and HOME_PHONE columns of the table EMP_INFO:

```
GRANT UPDATE(address, home_phone) ON TABLE emp_info
TO PUBLIC
```

Revoking Authorities and Privileges with the REVOKE SQL Statement

Just as there is an SQL statement that can be used to grant database-level authorities and database/object privileges, there is an SQL statement that can be used to revoke database-level authorities and database/object privileges. This statement is the REVOKE SQL statement, and like the GRANT statement, the syntax for the REVOKE statement varies according to the authority or privilege being revoked—the following sections show the syntax used to revoke each database-level authority and database/object privilege available.

Database-level authorities and privileges

```
REVOKE [DBADM | Privilege, ...] ON DATABASE FROM
[Forfeiter, ...] <BY ALL>
```

where:

Privilege — Identifies one or more database privileges that are to be taken from one or more users and/or groups.

Forfeiter — Identifies the name of the user(s) and/or group(s) that are to lose DBADM authority or the database privileges specified.

Schema privileges

```
REVOKE [Privilege, ...] ON SCHEMA [SchemaName] FROM
[Forfeiter, ...] <BY ALL>
```

where:

Privilege	Identifies one or more schema privileges that are to be taken from one or more users and/or groups.
SchemaName	Identifies by name the specific schema that all schema privileges specified are to be associated with.
Forfeiter	Identifies the name of the user(s) and/or group(s) that are to lose the schema privileges specified.

Tablespace privilege

```
REVOKE USE OF TABLESPACE [TablespaceName] FROM
[Forfeiter, ...] <BY ALL>
```

where:

TablespaceName	Identifies by name the specific tablespace that the USE privilege is to be associated with.
Forfeiter	Identifies the name of the user(s) and/or group(s) that are to lose the USE privilege.

Table privileges

```
REVOKE [ALL <PRIVILEGES> | Privilege, ...] ON TABLE
[TableName] FROM [Forfeiter, ...] <BY ALL>
```

where:

Privilege	Identifies one or more table privileges that are to be taken from one or more users and/or groups.
TableName	Identifies by name the specific table that all table privileges specified are to be associated with.
Forfeiter	Identifies the name of the user(s) and/or group(s) that are to lose the table privileges specified.

Index privilege

```
REVOKE CONTROL ON INDEX [IndexName] FROM [Forfeiter,
...] <BY ALL>
```

where:

IndexName	Identifies by name the specific index that the CONTROL privilege is to be associated with.

Forfeiter	Identifies the name of the user(s) and/or group(s) that are to lose the CONTROL privilege.

View privileges

```
REVOKE [ALL <PRIVILEGES> | Privilege, ...] ON
[ViewName] FROM [Forfeiter, ...] <BY ALL>
```

where:

Privilege	Identifies one or more view privileges that are to be taken from one or more users and/or groups.
ViewName	Identifies by name the specific view that all view privileges specified are to be associated with.
Forfeiter	Identifies the name of the user(s) and/or group(s) that are to lose the view privileges specified.

Package privileges

```
REVOKE [Privilege, ...] ON PACKAGE <SchemaName.>
[PackageID] FROM [Forfeiter, ...] <BY ALL>
```

where:

Privilege	Identifies one or more package privileges that are to be taken from one or more users and/or groups.
SchemaName	Identifies by name the schema in which the specified package is found.
PackageName	Identifies by name the specific package that all package privileges specified are to be associated with.
Forfeiter	Identifies the name of the user(s) and/or group(s) that are to lose the package privileges specified.

Routine privileges

```
REVOKE EXECUTE ON [RoutineName |
   FUNCTION <SchemaName.> * |
   METHOD * FOR [TypeName] |
   METHOD * FOR <SchemaName.> * |
   PROCEDURE <SchemaName.> *]
FROM [Forfeiter, ...] <BY ALL> RESTRICT
```

where:

RoutineName	Identifies by name the routine that the EXECUTE privilege is to be associated with.

TypeName	Identifies by name the type in which the specified method is found.
SchemaName	Identifies by name the schema in which all functions, methods, or procedures—including those that may be created in the future—are to have the EXECUTE privilege revoked on.
Forfeiter	Identifies the name of the user(s) and/or group(s) that are to lose the package privileges specified.

Sequence privilege

```
REVOKE USAGE ON SEQUENCE [SequenceName] FROM PUBLIC
```

where:

SequenceName	Identifies by name the specific sequence that the USAGE privilege is to be associated with.

Server privilege

```
REVOKE PASSTHRU ON SERVER [ServerName] FROM
[Forfeiter, ...] <BY ALL>
```

where:

ServerName	Identifies by name the specific server that the PASSTHRU privilege is to be associated with.
Forfeiter	Identifies the name of the user(s) and/or group(s) that are to lose the PASSTHRU privilege.

Nickname privileges

```
REVOKE [ALL <PRIVILEGES> | Privilege, ...] ON
[Nickname] FROM [Forfeiter, ...] <BY ALL>
```

where:

Privilege	Identifies one or more nickname privileges that are to be given to one or more users and/or groups.
Nickname	Identifies by name the specific nickname that all privileges specified are to be associated with.
Forfeiter	Identifies the name of the user(s) and/or group(s) that are to lose the nickname privileges specified.

The BY ALL syntax is optional and is provided as a courtesy for administrators who are familiar with the syntax of the DB2 for OS/390 REVOKE SQL statement. Whether it is included or not, the results will always be the same—the privilege(s) specified will be revoked from all users and/or groups specified, regardless of who granted it originally.

In all cases, the value specified for the *Forfeiter* parameter can be any combination of the following:

USER [*UserName*]	Identifies a specific user that the privileges specified are to be taken from.
GROUP [*GroupName*]	Identifies a specific group that the privileges specified are to be taken from.
PUBLIC	Indicates that the specified privilege(s) are to be taken from the special group PUBLIC. (All users are a member of the group PUBLIC.)

REVOKE SQL statement examples

Now that we've seen the basic syntax for the various forms of the REVOKE SQL statement, let's take a look at some examples.

Example 1. A server has both a user and a group named Q045. Remove the ability to connect to the database named SAMPLE from the group Q045:

```
CONNECT TO SAMPLE
REVOKE CONNECT ON DATABASE FROM GROUP q045
```

Example 2. Revoke all table privileges available (except CONTROL privilege) for the table DEPARTMENT from the user USER1 and the group PUBLIC:

```
REVOKE ALL PRIVILEGES ON TABLE department FROM user1,
PUBLIC
```

Example 3. Take away user USER1's ability to use a user-defined function named CALC_BONUS:

```
REVOKE EXECUTE ON FUNCTION calc_bonus FROM USER user1
```

Example 4. Take away user USER1's ability to modify information stored in the ADDRESS and HOME_PHONE columns of the table EMP_INFO, regardless of who granted it:

```
REVOKE UPDATE(address, home_phone) ON TABLE emp_info
FROM user1 BY ALL
```

Authorities and Privileges Needed to Perform Common Tasks

So far, we have identified the authorities and privileges that are available, and we have examined how these authorities and privileges are granted and revoked. But to use authorities and privileges effectively, you must be able to determine which authorities and privileges are appropriate for an individual user and which are not. Often, a blanket set of authorities and privileges is assigned to an individual, based on their job title and/or their job responsibilities. Then, as the individual begins to work with the database, the set of authorities and privileges they have is modified as necessary. Some of the more common job titles used, along with the tasks that usually accompany them and the authorities/privileges needed to perform those tasks, can be seen in Table 3–2.

Table 3–2 Common Job Titles, Tasks, and Authorities/Privileges Needed

Job Title	Tasks	Authorities/Privileges Needed
Department Administrator	Oversees the departmental system; designs and creates databases.	System Control (SYSCTRL) authority or System Administrator (SYSADM) authority (if the department has its own instance).
Security Administrator	Grants authorities and privileges to other users and revokes them, if necessary.	System Administrator (SYSADM) authority or Database Administrator (DBADM) authority.
Database Administrator	Designs, develops, operates, safeguards, and maintains one or more databases.	Database Administrator (DBADM) authority over one or more databases and System Maintenance (SYSMAINT) authority, or in some cases System Control (SYSCTRL) authority, over the same databases.
System Operator	Monitors the database and performs routine backup operations. Also performs recovery operations if needed.	System Maintenance (SYSMAINT) authority.

Table 3–2 Common Job Titles, Tasks, and Authorities/Privileges Needed *(Continued)*		
Job Title	**Tasks**	**Authorities/Privileges Needed**
Application Developer/ Programmer	Develops and tests database/DB2 Database Manager application programs; may also create test tables and populate them with data.	CONNECT and CREATETAB privilege for one or more databases, BINDADD and BIND privilege on one or more existing packages, one or more schema privileges for one or more schemas, and one or more table privileges for one or more tables.
User Analyst	Defines the data requirements for an application program by examining the database structure using the system catalog views.	CONNECT privilege for one or more databases and SELECT privilege on the system catalog views.
End User	Executes one or more application programs.	CONNECT privilege for one or more databases and EXECUTE privilege on the package associated with each application used. If an application program contains dynamic SQL statements, SELECT, INSERT, UPDATE and DELETE privileges for one or more tables may be needed as well.
Information Center Consultant	Defines the data requirements for a query user; provides the data needed by creating tables and views and by granting access to one or more database objects.	Database Administrator (DBADM) authority for one or more databases.
Query User	Issues SQL statements (usually from the Command Line Processor) to retrieve, add, update, or delete data. (May also save results of queries in tables.)	CONNECT privilege on one or more databases, SELECT, INSERT, UPDATE, and DELETE privilege on each table used, and CREATEIN privilege on the schema in which tables and views are to be created.
Adapted from Table 6 on Pages 261–262 of the IBM DB2 Administration Guide – Implementation manual.		

Practice Questions

Question 1

Which of the following is NOT a valid method of authentication that can be used by DB2 UDB Version 8.x?

❍ A. SERVER

❍ B. SERVER_ENCRYPT

❍ C. CLIENT

❍ D. DCS

Question 2

Assuming USER1 has no authorities or privileges, which of the following will ONLY allow USER1 to add data to table EMPLOYEE?

❍ A. CONTROL

❍ B. INSERT

❍ C. UPDATE

❍ D. INSERT WITH GRANT OPTION

Question 3

In a client-server environment, which two of the following can be used to verify passwords?

❑ A. System Catalog

❑ B. Client Applications

❑ C. Client Operating System

❑ D. DB2 Database Manager

❑ E. Application Server

Question 4

A table called DEPARTMENT has the following columns:

DEPT_ID
DEPT_NAME
MANAGER

Which of the following will ONLY allow USER1 to modify the DEPT_NAME column?

- ❍ A. GRANT ALTER ON TABLE department TO user1
- ❍ B. GRANT ALTER (dept_name) ON TABLE department TO user1
- ❍ C. GRANT UPDATE ON TABLE department TO user1
- ❍ D. GRANT UPDATE (dept_name) ON TABLE department TO user1

Question 5

An index named EMPID_X exists for a table called EMPLOYEE. Which of the following will allow USER1 to drop the index?

- ❍ A. GRANT DELETE ON TABLE employee TO user1
- ❍ B. GRANT DELETE ON INDEX empid_x TO user1
- ❍ C. GRANT INDEX ON TABLE employee TO user1
- ❍ D. GRANT CONTROL ON INDEX empid_x TO user1

Question 6

USER1 holds CONTROL privilege on table TABLE1. Which two of the following statements is USER1 allowed to execute?

- ❑ A. GRANT CONTROL ON table1 TO user2
- ❑ B. GRANT LOAD ON table1 TO user2
- ❑ C. GRANT INSERT, UPDATE ON table1 TO user2 WITH GRANT OPTION
- ❑ D. GRANT BINDADD ON table1 TO PUBLIC
- ❑ E. GRANT ALL PRIVILEGES ON table1 TO PUBLIC

Question 7

A user with SYSADM authority issues the following statement:

GRANT ALL PRIVILEGES ON TABLE payroll.employee TO user1 WITH GRANT OPTION

Which of the following statements is USER1 authorized to execute?

- ❍ A. GRANT CONTROL ON TABLE payroll.employee TO user2
- ❍ B. GRANT UPDATE ON TABLE payroll.employee TO user2
- ❍ C. GRANT CREATE_EXTERNAL_ROUTINE ON TABLE payroll.employee TO user2
- ❍ D. GRANT LOAD ON TABLE payroll.employee TO user2

Question 8

A user-defined function named U.UDF1 that takes an input parameter of type INTEGER has been created by USER1. Which two of the following statements would give USER2 the privileges needed to use function U.UDF1 in a query?

- ❑ A. GRANT USE ON FUNCTION u.udf1 TO user2
- ❑ B. GRANT EXECUTE ON FUNCTION u.udf1 TO user2
- ❑ C. GRANT USE ON FUNCTION u.udf1 (INTEGER) TO user2
- ❑ D. GRANT EXECUTE ON PACKAGE u.udf1 (INTEGER) TO user2
- ❑ E. GRANT EXECUTE ON FUNCTION u.* TO user2

Question 9

What does the following statement do?

GRANT REFERENCES (col1, col2) ON TABLE table1 to user1 WITH GRANT OPTION

- ❍ A. Gives USER1 the ability to refer to COL1 and COL2 of table TABLE1 in queries, along with the ability to give this authority to other users and groups.
- ❍ B. Gives USER1 the ability to refer to COL1 and COL2 of table TABLE1 in views, along with the ability to give this authority to other users and groups.
- ❍ C. Gives USER1 the ability to define a referential constraint on table TABLE1 using columns COL1 and COL2 as the parent key of the constraint.
- ❍ D. Gives USER1 the ability to define a referential constraint on table TABLE1 using columns COL1 and COL2 as the foreign key of the constraint.

Question 10

USER1 is the owner of TABLE1. Assuming USER1 only holds privileges for TABLE1, which of the following is the best way to remove all privileges USER1 holds?

❍ A. REVOKE CONTROL ON table1 FROM user1

❍ B. REVOKE ALL PRIVILEGES ON table1 FROM user1

❍ C. REVOKE CONTROL ON table1 FROM user1
REVOKE ALL PRIVILEGES ON table1 FROM user1

❍ D. REVOKE ALL ON table1 FROM user1

Question 11

A view named V.VIEW1 is based on a table named T.TABLE1. A user with DBADM authority issues the following statement:

GRANT INSERT ON v.view1 TO user1 WITH GRANT OPTION

Which of the following statements is USER1 authorized to execute?

❍ A. GRANT INSERT ON t.table1 TO user2

❍ B. GRANT CONTROL ON v.view1 TO user2

❍ C. GRANT ALL PRIVILEGES ON v.view1 TO user2

❍ D. GRANT INSERT ON v.view1 TO user2

Question 12

Which of the following will provide all users with the ability to perform DDL, but not DML, operations on table T.TABLE1?

❍ A. GRANT ALL PRIVILEGES ON t.table1 TO ALL USERS

❍ B. GRANT ALTER, INDEX ON t.table1 TO ALL USERS

❍ C. GRANT ALL PRIVILEGES ON t.table1 TO PUBLIC

❍ D. GRANT ALTER, INDEX ON t.table1 TO PUBLIC

Answers

Question 1

The correct answer is **D.** In Version 8.x of DB2 UDB, the following authentication types are available: SERVER, SERVER_ENCRYPT, CLIENT, KERBEROS, and KRB_SERVER_ENCRYPT. (Although DCS was a valid method of authentication in DB2 UDB Version 7.x, it is no longer supported in Version 8.x.)

Question 2

The correct answer is **B.** The CONTROL privilege gives USER1 the ability to do everything with the EMPLOYEE table (alter the table definition, retrieve data, insert data, update data, delete data, create indexes, define referential constraints, and grant any combination of table privileges to others); the UPDATE privilege only allows USER1 to modify existing data in the EMPLOYEE table; and the INSERT WITH GRANT OPTION allows USER1 to add data to the EMPLOYEE table and to grant that privilege to other users/groups.

Question 3

The correct answers are **C** and **E.** Authentication is performed by an external security facility that is not part of DB2 UDB, so answers A and D are automatically eliminated. The security facility used to authenticate users is often part of the operating system and the combination of authentication types specified at both the client and the server determine which authentication method is actually used.

Question 4

The correct answer is **D.** The first GRANT statement (answer A) provides USER1 with the ability to alter the table definition for the DEPARTMENT table; the second GRANT statement (answer B) is not valid because you can only specify column names with the UPDATE and REFERENCES privilege; and the third GRANT statement (answer C) provides USER1 with the ability to change the data stored in any column of the UPDATE table.

Question 5

The correct answer is **D.** The first GRANT statement (answer A) provides USER1 with the ability to delete rows from the EMPLOYEE table; the second GRANT statement (answer B) is not valid because DELETE is not an index privilege (DELETE is a table or view privilege); and the third GRANT statement (answer C) provides USER1 with the ability to create indexes for the EMPLOYEE table. The only thing that a person who has CONTROL privilege for an index can do with that index is delete (drop) it.

Question 6

The correct answers are **C** and **E.** The first GRANT statement (answer A) is not valid because only users with System Administrator (SYSADM) authority or Database Administrator (DBADM) authority are allowed to explicitly grant CONTROL privilege on any object; the second GRANT statement (answer B) is not valid because LOAD is not a table privilege (LOAD is a database privilege); and the fourth GRANT statement (answer C) is not valid because BINDADD is not a table privilege (BINDADD is a database privilege). However, a user with CONTROL privilege on a table can grant any table privilege (except the CONTROL privilege), along with the ability to give that privilege to other users and/or groups to anyone—including the group PUBLIC.

Question 7

The correct answer is **B.** The first GRANT statement (answer A) is not valid because only users with System Administrator (SYSADM) authority or Database Administrator (DBADM) authority are allowed to explicitly grant CONTROL privilege on any object; the third GRANT statement (answer C) is not valid because CREATE_EXTERNAL_ROUTINE is not a table privilege (CREATE_EXTERNAL_ROUTINE is a database privilege); and the last GRANT statement (answer D) is not valid because LOAD is not a table privilege (LOAD is a database privilege).

Question 8

The correct answers are **B** and **E.** The first and third GRANT statements (answers A and C) are not valid because USE is not a routine privilege (USE is a tablespace privilege); and the fourth GRANT statement (answer D) is not valid because U.UDF1 is a user-defined function—not a package (this GRANT statement is attempting to grant package privileges on a function and will fail).

Question 9

The correct answer is **C.** The REFERENCES table privilege allows a user to create and drop foreign key constraints that reference a table in a parent relationship. This privilege can be granted for the entire table or limited to one or more columns within the table, in which case only those columns can participate as a parent key in a referential constraint. (This particular GRANT statement also gives USER1 the ability the ability to give the REFERENCES privilege for columns COL1 and COL2 to other users and groups.)

Question 10

The correct answer is **C.** The owner of a table automatically receives CONTROL privilege, along with all other available table-level privileges, for that table. If the CONTROL privilege is later revoked from the table owner, all other privileges that were automatically granted to the owner for that particular table are not automatically revoked. Instead, they must be explicitly revoked in one or more separate operations. Therefore, both REVOKE statements shown in answer C must be executed in order to completely remove all privileges USER1 holds on TABLE1 since they are the table owner.

Question 11

The correct answer is **D.** The first GRANT statement (answer A), when executed, would attempt to give USER2 INSERT privilege on table T.TABLE1—since USER1 does not have the authority needed to grant this privilege, this statement would fail; the second GRANT statement (answer B) is not valid because only users with System Administrator (SYSADM) authority or Database Administrator (DBADM) authority are allowed to explicitly grant CONTROL privilege on any object—again, USER1 does not have the authority needed to grant this privilege; and the third GRANT statement (answer C), when executed, would attempt to give USER2 every privilege (except the CONTROL privilege) on view V.VIEW1—since USER1 does not have the authority needed to grant these privileges, this statement would also fail.

Question 12

The correct answer is **D.** The first and second GRANT statements (answers A and B) are not valid because "ALL USERS" is not a valid clause of the GRANT statement; and the third GRANT statement (answer C) is not valid because it gives the group PUBLIC every table privilege available (except the CONTROL privilege). The last GRANT statement is correct because it only gives the group PUBLIC (all users) the privileges needed to execute Data Definition Language (DDL) statements against the table T.TABLE1.

Accessing DB2 UDB Data

Fifteen percent (15%) of the DB2 UDB V8.1 Family Fundamentals certification exam (Exam 700) is designed to test your knowledge of the different objects that are available with DB2 Universal Database and to test your ability to create a DB2 UDB database. The questions that make up this portion of the exam are intended to evaluate the following:

- Your ability to identify and locate DB2 UDB servers.
- Your ability to construct a DB2 UDB database.
- Your ability to identify the different objects that are available with DB2 UDB.

This chapter is designed to introduce you to instances and databases, to walk you through the database creation process, and to provide you with an overview of the various objects that can be developed once a database has been created.

Terms you will learn:

System
Instance
DB2 Database Manager
Database
Registry Variables
Instance Configuration File
Database Configuration File
Recovery History File

Transaction Log Files
Buffer Pools
Containers
Tablespaces
Create Database Wizard
System Catalog Tables
Directory Files
System Database Directory
Local Database Directory
Node Directory
Database Connection Services (DCS) Directory
Add Database Wizard
Access Profiles
DB2 Discovery
Tables
Rows
Columns
Record
Field
Value
Base Table
Result Table
Summary Table
Declared Temporary Table
Typed Table
Indexes
Views
Aliases
Schemas
Triggers
Subject Table
Trigger Event
Trigger Activation Time
Set of Affected Rows

Trigger Granularity

Triggered Action

Transition Variables

Transition Tables

Trigger Cascading

User-Defined Data Types (UDTs)

User-Defined Functions (UDFs)

Sequences

Techniques you will master:

Understanding how DB2 UDB databases are created.

Understanding how local and remote DB2 UDB databases and servers are cataloged and uncataloged.

Understanding what the system database directory, local database directory, node directory, and Database Connection Services (DCS) directory are used for.

Recognizing the types of objects that are available and understanding when each is to be used.

Servers, Instances, and Databases

DB2 Universal Database sees the world as a hierarchy of objects. Workstations (or servers) on which DB2 UDB has been installed occupy the highest level of this hierarchy. During the installation process, program files for a background process known as the *DB2 Database Manager* are physically copied to a specific location on the server and an *instance* of the DB2 Database Manager is created. Instances occupy the second level in the hierarchy and are responsible for managing system resources and databases that fall under their control. Although only one instance is created initially, several instances can exist. Each instance behaves like a separate installation of DB2 UDB, even though all instances within a system share the same DB2 Database Manager program files (which were copied to the workstation during the installation process). And although multiple instances share the same binary code, each runs independently of the others and has its own environment (which can be modified by altering the contents of its associated configuration file).

Every instance controls access to one or more databases. Databases make up the third level in the hierarchy and are responsible for managing the storage, modification, and retrieval of data. Like instances, databases work independently of each other. Each database has its own environment (also controlled by a configuration file), as well as its own set of grantable authorities and privileges to govern how users interact with the data and database objects it controls. Figure 4–1 shows the hierarchical relationship between systems, instances, and databases.

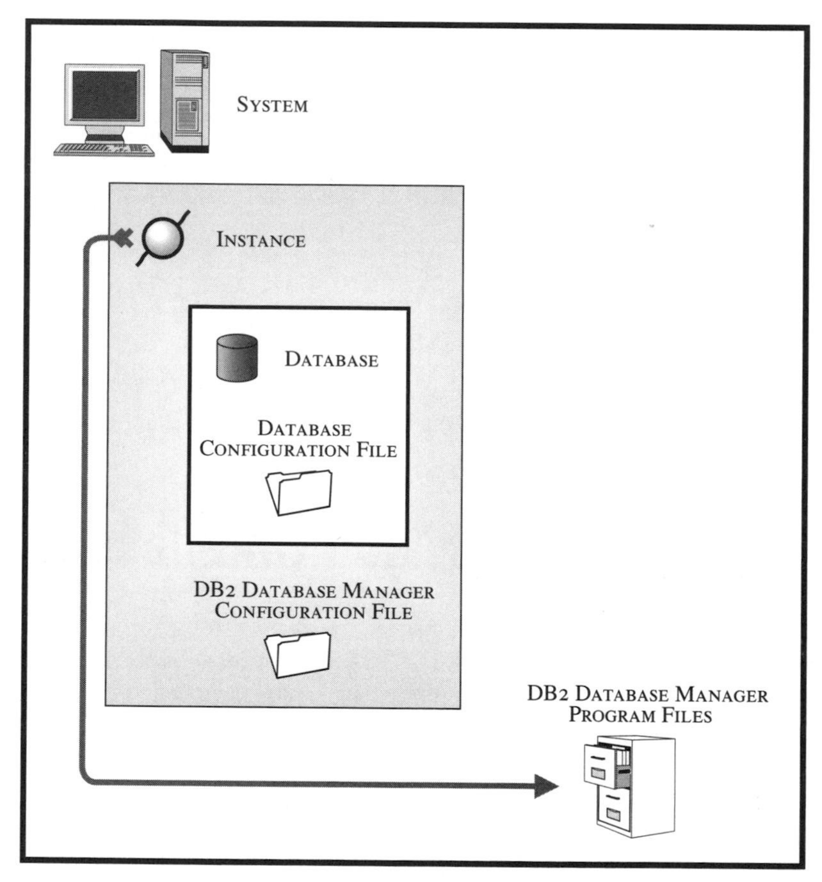

Figure 4–1 Hierarchical relationship between systems, instances, and databases.

What Makes Up a DB2 UDB Database?

From a user's perspective, a database is a collection of tables (preferably related in some way) that are used to store data. However, from a database administrator's viewpoint, a DB2 UDB database is much more; a database is an entity that is comprised of many physical and logical components. Some of these components help determine how data is organized, while others determine how and where data is physically stored. So how do you create a database and allocate storage space for it? Before you can answer that question, you must have a basic understanding of the different types of objects that are used by DB2 UDB.

DB2 UDB Objects

DB2 UDB uses both a logical and a physical storage model comprised of several different, yet related, objects. Four types of objects exist. They are:

- System objects
- Recovery objects
- Storage objects
- Database (or data) objects

System objects

System objects consist of registry variables, instance configuration files, and individual database configuration files. Registry variables are set at the system level and affect every instance that resides on a particular server. Instance configuration files (also known as DB2 Database Manager configuration files) are created and assigned to individual instances during the instance creation process. Values in an instance's configuration file control how resources are allocated for that particular instance, and changes to them affect every database that falls under that instance's control. (Values for many of the parameters in an instance configuration file can be modified to improve overall performance or increase concurrency.) Database configuration files are created and assigned to individual databases during the database creation process. Values in a database's configuration file control how resources are allocated for that particular database, and changes to them can improve performance or increase capacity, depending upon the type of activity the database encounters.

Recovery objects

Recovery objects consist of transaction log files and recovery history files. By default, one recovery history file and three transaction log files are automatically created when a database is created. Recovery history files are used, together with database backup images and transaction files, to coordinate database recovery operations. The recovery history file contains information about every backup operation executed, while transaction log files contain records of recent database operations performed. In the event a database has to be recovered from an application, user, or system error, events stored in the transaction log files can be replayed to return the database to a consistent (database consistency is described in detail in Chapter 7) and stable state, or to return a database to the state it was in up to the point in time that the error occurred, if roll-forward recovery is enabled. You cannot modify transaction log files or recovery history files directly; however, you will find that their contents are important should you need to repair a database that has been destroyed or damaged.

Storage objects

Storage objects control where data is physically stored and how data is moved between storage and memory during normal operation. Three types of storage objects are used. They are:

- Buffer pools
- Containers
- Tablespaces

Buffer pools. A buffer pool is a section of memory that has been reserved for the sole purpose of caching data pages as they are read from physical storage. Whenever data is needed to resolve a query, the page that the data is stored on (data is stored in sections called *pages*) is located in physical storage and transferred to a buffer pool, where it is then read and/or modified. If the page is modified, it is copied back to physical storage; however, all pages read stay in memory until the space they occupy is needed or until all connections to the database are terminated. Furthermore, whenever a page of data is retrieved, the DB2 Database Manager uses a set of heuristic algorithms to try to determine which pages will be needed next—those pages are retrieved as well (this is referred to as *prefetching*). Retaining all pages loaded and prefetching are done to improve overall performance; data can be accessed much faster when it is stored in memory than when it is stored on disk.

Containers. A container is some form of physical storage that the DB2 Database manager has reserved access to. A container can be a directory that may or may not already exist, a fixed-size, preallocated file that may or may not already exist, or a physical (raw) device that is recognized by the operating system. (On Linux and UNIX operating systems, a physical device can be any logical volume that uses a character special interface; on Windows operating systems, a physical device is any unformatted partition or any physical disk.)

Tablespaces. Tablespaces are used to control where data is physically stored and to provide a layer of indirection between a table and one or more containers in which the table's data actually resides. A single tablespace can span many containers, but each container can only belong to one tablespace. When a tablespace spans multiple containers, data is written in a round-robin fashion (in groups of pages called *extents*) to each container assigned to that tablespace; this helps balance data across all containers that belong to a given tablespace.

Two types of tablespaces can exist: system managed space (SMS) tablespaces and database managed space (DMS) tablespaces. With SMS tablespaces, only directory containers can be used for storage, and the operating system's file manager is responsible for controlling how that space is used. With DMS tablespaces, only file and/or device containers can be used for storage, and the DB2 Database Manager is responsible for controlling how the space is used.

If you look closely at how DB2 UDB manages data, you will discover that, depending upon how a table has been defined, each corresponding record can be stored as three distinct values: as a regular data value, which is how values produced by an application, user, or trigger are stored; as an index value, which is how all related index data values are stored; and as one or more long data values, which is how each long data and large object (LOB) value is stored. Consequently, three types of tablespaces can exist: regular, long, and temporary. As you might imagine, regular data and index data can reside in regular tablespaces, while long field data and large object data can reside in long tablespaces. Temporary tablespaces, on the other hand, are used for a much different purpose. Temporary tablespaces are classified as either system or user—system temporary tablespaces are used to store internal temporary data generated when some types of operations are performed (for example, sorting data, reorganizing tables, creating indexes, and joining tables), while user temporary tablespaces are used to store declared global temporary tables, which in turn, are used to store application specific data for a brief period of time.

Database (or data) objects

Database objects—otherwise known as data objects—are used to logically store and manipulate data, as well as to control how all user data (and some system data) is organized. Data objects include tables, indexes, views, aliases, schemas, triggers, user-defined data types, user-defined functions, and sequences. We will examine each of these objects in more detail a little later.

Creating a DB2 UDB Database with the CREATE DATABASE Command

Now that you have a basic understanding of the types of DB2 UDB objects available, let's look at how a database is created. There are two ways to create a DB2 UDB database: by using the Create Database Wizard or by using the CREATE DATABASE command. Because the Create Database Wizard is essentially a graphical user interface (GUI) for the CREATE DATABASE command, we will look at the command method first.

In its simplest form, the syntax for the CREATE DATABASE command is:

```
CREATE [DATABASE | DB] [DatabaseName] <AT NODE>
```

where:

DatabaseName Identifies the unique name to be assigned to the database to be created.

The only value you must provide when executing this form of the CREATE DATABASE command is the name to assign the database once it is created. This name:

- Can only consist of the characters a–z, A–Z, 0–9, @, #, $, and _.
- Cannot begin with a number.
- Cannot begin with the letter sequences "SYS", "DBM", or "IBM".
- Cannot be the same as the name already assigned to another database within the same instance.

Of course, a much more complex form of the CREATE DATABASE command, which provides you with much more control over database parameters, is available, and we will look at it shortly. But for now, let's look at what happens when this form of the CREATE DATABASE command is executed.

What Happens When a DB2 UDB Database Is Created

Regardless of how the process is initiated, whenever a new database is created, the following tasks are performed, in the order shown:

1. All physical directories needed are created in the appropriate location.

Information about each database created is stored in a special hierarchical directory tree. Where this directory tree is actually created is determined by information provided with the CREATE DATABASE command—if no location information is provided, this directory tree is created in the location specified by the *dftdbpath* DB2 Database Manager configuration parameter associated with the instance the database is being created under. The root directory of this hierarchical tree is assigned the name of the instance the database is associated with. This directory will contain a subdirectory that has been assigned a name corresponding to the partition's node. If the database is a partitioned database, this directory will be named NODE*xxxx*, where *xxxx* is the unique node number that has been assigned to the partition; if the database is a nonpartitioned database, this directory will be named NODE0000. The node-name directory, in turn, will contain one subdirectory for each database that has been created under the node—the name assigned to each subdirectory corresponds to the database token that has been assigned to the database (the subdirectory for the first database created will be named SQL00001, the subdirectory for the second database will be named SQL00002, and so on.) Figure 4–2 illustrates how this directory hierarchy typically looks in a nonpartitioned database environment.

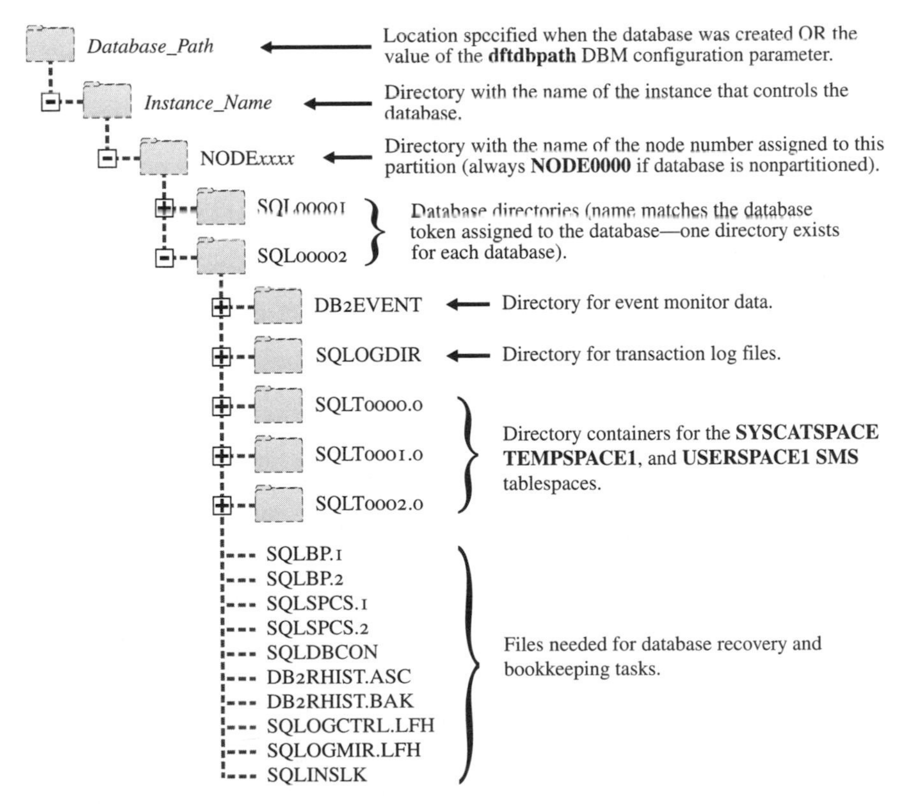

Figure 4–2 Typical directory hierarchy tree for a nonpartitioned database.

Never attempt to modify this directory structure or any of the files stored in it. Such actions could destroy one or more databases or make them unusable.

2. Files that are needed for database recovery and other bookkeeping tasks are created.

After the appropriate database-name directory has been created, the following files are created in that directory:

SQLBP.1. This file contains buffer pool information.

SQLBP.2. This file is a backup copy of SQLBP.1.

SQLSPCS.1. This file contains tablespace information.

SQLSPCS.2. This file is a backup copy of SQLSPCS.1.

SQLDBCON. This file contains database configuration information.

DB2RHIST.ASC. This file contains historical information about backup operations, restore operations, table load operations, table reorganization operations, tablespace alterations, and similar database changes (i.e., the recovery history file).

DB2RHIST.BAK. This file is a backup copy of DB2RHIST.ASC.

SQLOGCTL.LFH. This file contains information about active transaction log files. Recovery operations use information stored in this file to determine how far back in the logs to begin the recovery process.

SQLOGMIR.LFH. This file is a mirrored copy of SQLOGCTL.LFH.

SQLINSLK. This file contains information used to ensure that a database is only assigned to one instance of the DB2 Database Manager.

A subdirectory named SQLOGDIR is also created, and three files (named S0000000.LOG, S0000001.LOG, and S0000002.LOG) are created in this subdirectory. These three files are used to store transaction log records as SQL operations are performed against the database.

3. The database is cataloged in the system and local database directory (a system and/or local database directory is created first if they don't already exist).

DB2 Universal Database uses a set of special files to keep track of where databases are stored and to provide access to those databases. Because the information stored in these files is used like the information stored in an office-building directory is used, they are referred to as directory files. Whenever a database is created, these directories are updated with the database's name and an alias. (We'll take a closer look at the directory files available when we look at cataloging databases.) If specified, a comment and code set values are also stored in these directories.

4. One buffer pool is created.

During the database creation process, a buffer pool is created and assigned the name IBMDEFAULTBP. On Linux and UNIX platforms, this buffer pool is 1,000 4K (kilobyte) pages in size; on Windows platforms, this buffer pool is 250 4K pages in size. The actual memory used by this buffer pool (and for that matter, by any other buffer pools that may exist) is allocated when the first connection to the database is established and freed when all connections to the database have been terminated.

5. One system temporary tablespace and two regular tablespaces are created.

Once the buffer pool IBMDEFAULTBP has been created, three tablespaces associated with this buffer pool are created. These three tablespaces are:

- A regular tablespace named SYSCATSPACE1, which is used to store the system catalog tables and views (which we will look at next) associated with the database.
- A regular tablespace named USERSPACE1, which is used to store all user-defined objects (such as tables, indexes, and so on) along with user data, index data, and long value data.
- A system temporary tablespace named TEMPSPACE1, which is used as a temporary storage area for operations such as sorting data, reorganizing tables, and creating indexes.

Unless otherwise specified, all three of these tablespaces will be SMS tablespaces with an extent size of 32 4k pages; characteristics for each of these table spaces can be provided as input to the Create Database Wizard or the `CREATE DATABASE` command.

6. Four schemas are created.

During the database creation process, the following schemas are created: SYSIBM, SYSCAT, SYSSTAT, and SYSFUN. A special user named SYSIBM is made the owner of each.

7. The system catalog tables and views are created and initialized.

Once the tablespace SYSCATSPACE has been created, a special set of tables, known as the *system catalog tables*, are constructed and populated within that tablespace. The DB2 Database Manager uses these system catalog tables to keep track of information like database object definitions, database object dependencies, database object privileges, column data types, and table constraints. A set of system catalog views is created along with the system catalog tables, and these views are typically used when accessing data stored in the system catalog tables. The system catalog tables and views cannot be modified with SQL statements. Instead, they are modified by the DB2 Database Manager whenever:

- A database object (such as a table or index) is created, altered, or deleted.
- Authorizations and/or privileges are granted or revoked.
- Statistical information is collected for a table.
- Packages are bound to the database.

In most cases, the complete characteristics of a database object are stored in one or more system catalog tables when the object is created. However in some cases, such as when triggers and constraints are defined, the actual SQL statement used to create the object is stored instead.

8. The database configuration file for the database is initialized.

Some of the parameters in the database configuration file (such as code set, territory, and collating sequence) will be set using values that were specified as input for the Create Database Wizard or `CREATE DATABASE` command. Others will be assigned system default values.

9. A set of utility programs are bound to the database.

Before some of the DB2 UDB utilities available can work with a database, the packages needed to run those utilities must be created. Such packages are created by binding a set of defined DB2 Database Manager bind files to the database (the set of bind files used are stored in the utilities bind list file *db2ubind.lst*).

10. Authorities and privileges are granted to the appropriate users.

To connect to and work with a particular database, a user must have the authorities and privileges needed to use that database. Therefore, whenever a new database is created, the following authorities and privileges are granted:

- DBADM authority, along with CONNECT, CREATETAB, BINDADD, CREATE_NOT_FENCED, IMPLICIT_SCHEMA, and LOAD privileges, are granted to the user who created the database.
- USE privilege on the tablespace USERSPACE1 is granted to the group PUBLIC.

- CONNECT, CREATETAB, BINDADD, and IMPLICIT_SCHEMA privileges are granted to the group PUBLIC.
- SELECT privilege on each system catalog table is granted to the group PUBLIC.
- EXECUTE privilege on all procedures found in the SYSIBM schema is granted to the group PUBLIC.
- EXECUTE WITH GRANT privilege on all functions found in the SYSFUN schema is granted to the group PUBLIC.
- BIND and EXECUTE privileges for each successfully bound utility are granted to the group PUBLIC.

The CREATE DATABASE Command

So how do you create a database that uses a DMS tablespace to hold the system catalog tables? Or a database whose tablespaces are to have an extent size of 64? You can create these and other databases by using any combination of the options available with the `CREATE DATABASE` command. The complete syntax for this command is:

```
CREATE [DATABASE | DB] [DatabaseName] <AT DBPARTITION-
NUM>
```

or

```
CREATE [DATABASE | DB] [DatabaseName]
<ON [Path]>
<ALIAS [Alias]>
<USING CODESET [CodeSet] TERRITORY [Territory]>
<COLLATE USING [CollateType]>
<NUMSEGS [NumSegments]>
<DFT_EXTENT_SZ [DefaultExtentSize]>
<CATALOG TABLESPACE [TS_Definition]>
<USER TABLESPACE [TS_Definition]>
<TEMPORARY TABLESPACE [TS_Definition]>
<WITH "[Description]">
<AUTOCONFIGURE <USING [Keyword] [Value] ,... >
    <APPLY [DB ONLY | DB AND DBM | NONE>>
```

where:

DatabaseName	Identifies the unique name to be assigned to the database to be created.

Path	Identifies the location (drive and/or directory) where the directory hierarchy and files associated with the database to be created are to be physically stored.
Alias	Identifies the alias to be assigned to the database to be created.
CodeSet	Identifies the code set to be used for storing data in the database to be created. (In a DB2 UDB database, each single-byte character is represented internally as a unique number between 0 and 255. This number is referred to as the *code point* of the character; assignments of code points to every character in a particular character set are called the *code page*; and the International Organization for Standardization term for a code page is *code set*.)
Territory	Identifies the territory to be used for storing data in the database to be created.
CollateType	Identifies the collating sequence (i.e., the sequence in which characters are ordered for the purpose of sorting, merging, and making comparisons) to be used by the database to be created. (Valid values include COMPATABILITY, IDENTITY, NLSCHAR, and SYSTEM.)
NumSegments	Identifies the number of segments that will be created and used to store files for each SMS tablespace used by the database to be created (SYSCATSPACE, USERSPACE1, and TEMPSPACE1 only).
DefaultExtentSize	Identifies the default extent size to be used whenever a tablespace is created and no extent size is specified during the creation process.
Description	A comment used to describe the database entry that will be made in the database directory for the database to be created. The description must be enclosed by double quotation marks.
Keyword	One or more keywords recognized by the AUTOCONFIGURE command. (Valid values include mem_percent, workload_type, num_stmts, tpm, admin_priority, is_populated, num_local_apps, num_remote_apps, isolation, and bp_resizable—

refer to the DB2 UDB Command Reference for more information on how the AUTOCONFIGURE command is used).

Value Identifies the value that is to be associated with the Keyword specified.

TS_Definition Specifies the definition that is to be used to create the tablespace that will be used to hold the system catalog tables (SYSCATSPACE), user-defined objects (USERSPACE1), and/or temporary objects (TEMPSPACE1). The syntax used to define a system managed (SMS) tablespace is:

```
MANAGED BY SYSTEM
USING ( '[Container]' ,... )
<EXTENTSIZE [ExtentSize]>
<PREFETCHSIZE [PrefetchSize]>
<OVERHEAD [Overhead]>
<TRANSFERRATE [TransferRate]>
```

The syntax used to define a database managed (DMS) tablespace is:

```
MANAGED BY DATABASE
USING ( [FILE | DEVICE] '[Container]'
   NumberOfPages ,... )
<EXTENTSIZE [ExtentSize]>
<PREFETCHSIZE [PrefetchSize]>
<OVERHEAD [Overhead]>
<TRANSFERRATE [TransferRate]>
```

where:

Container Identifies one or more containers to be used to store data that will be assigned to the tablespace specified. For SMS tablespaces, each container specified must identify a valid directory; for DMS FILE containers, each container specified must identify a valid file; and for DMS DEVICE containers, each container specified must identify an existing device.

NumberOfPages Specifies the number of 4K pages to be used by the tablespace container.

ExtentSize Specifies the number of 4K pages of data that will be written in a round-robin fashion to each tablespace container.

PrefetchSize	Specifies the number of 4K pages of data that will be read from the specified tablespace when data prefetching is performed.
Overhead	Identifies the I/O controller overhead and disk-seek latency time (in number of milliseconds) associated with the containers that belong to the specified tablespace.
TransferRate	Identifies the time, in number of milliseconds, that it takes to read one 4K page of data from a tablespace container and store it in memory.

Now that we have seen the complete syntax for the `CREATE DATABASE` command, let's go back to our original question. The way you would create a database that uses a DMS tablespace to hold the system catalog tables would be to execute a `CREATE DATABASE` command that looks something like this:

```
CREATE DATABASE SAMPLEDB ON E:
USING CODESET 1252
TERRITORY US
COLLATE USING SYSTEM
CATALOG TABLESPACE MANAGED BY DATABASE
  (FILE 'E:\SYSCATSPACE.DAT', 5000)
```

When executed, this statement would create a database that

- Is physically located on drive E:.
- Has been assigned the name SAMPLEDB.
- Recognizes the United States/Canada code set. (The code page, along with the territory, is used to convert alphanumeric data to binary data that is stored in the database.)
- Uses a collating sequence that is based on the territory used (which in this case is United States/Canada).
- Will store the system catalog in a DMS table space that uses the file SYSCATSPACE.DAT as its container. (This file is stored on drive E: and is capable of holding up to 5,000 pages that are 4k in size.)
- Is created using default values for all other parameters not specified (i.e., USERSPACE1 and TEMPSPACE1 will be SMS tablespaces, extent sizes will be 32, etc.).

Creating a DB2 UDB Database with the Create Database Wizard

If you have ever installed software on a computer using a graphical installation program, more than likely, the interface you used is what is known as a *wizard*. A wizard is a GUI tool consisting of a sequenced set of dialogs that have been designed to guide a user through the steps needed to perform a complex operation. More often than not, the dialogs (often referred to as pages) that make up a wizard are processed in the order that they appear; thus, they orchestrate a step one, step two, step three . . . input scenario. The Create Database Wizard is no exception, and the pages it contains are designed to capture information about the characteristics of the database to be created.

In Chapter 2, we saw that the Control Center is the most important and versatile GUI tool DB2 UDB has to offer. We also saw that the Control Center is comprised of several elements, including:

- An objects pane (located on the left-hand side of the Control Center), which contains a hierarchical representation of every object type that can be managed from the Control Center.
- A contents pane (located on the right-hand side of the Control Center), which contains a listing of existing objects that correspond to the object type selected in the objects pane. (For example, if the Tables object type were selected in the objects pane, a list of all tables available would be listed in the contents pane.)

By highlighting the *Databases* object shown in the objects pane of the Control Center and clicking the right mouse button, you will bring up a menu that contains a list of options available for database objects. The Create Database Wizard is invoked by selecting *Create*, followed by *Database Using Wizard...* from this menu. Figure 4–3 shows the Control Center menu items that must be selected in order to activate the Create Database Wizard; Figure 4–4 shows what the first page of the Create Database Wizard looks like when it is activated.

Once the Create Database Wizard is displayed, you simply follow the directions shown on each panel presented to define the characteristics of the database that is to be created. (These same characteristics can be specified through the various options available with the `CREATE DATABASE` command.) When you have provided enough information for the DB2 Database Manager to create the database, the "Finish" push button displayed in the

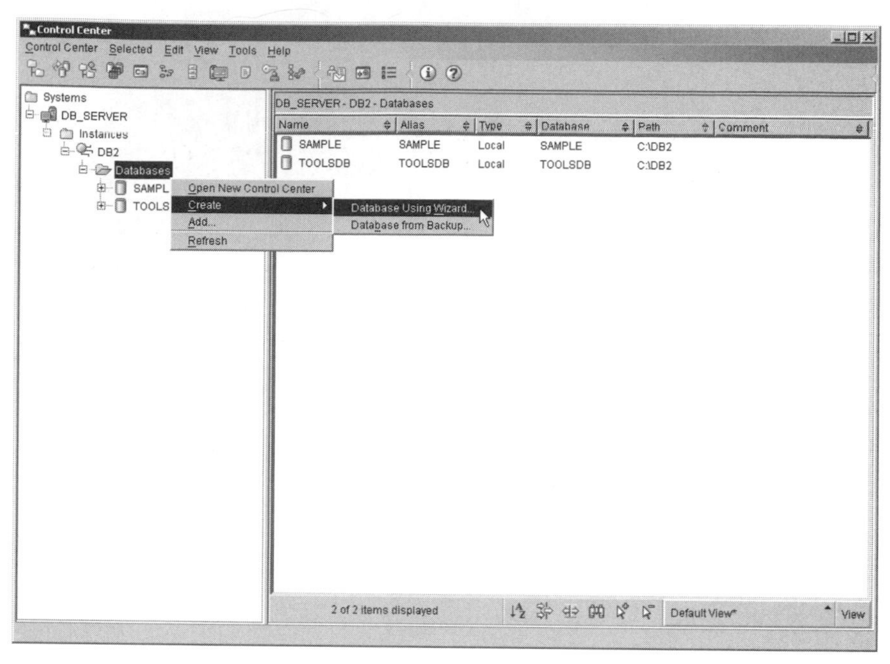

Figure 4–3 Invoking the Create Database Wizard from the Control Center.

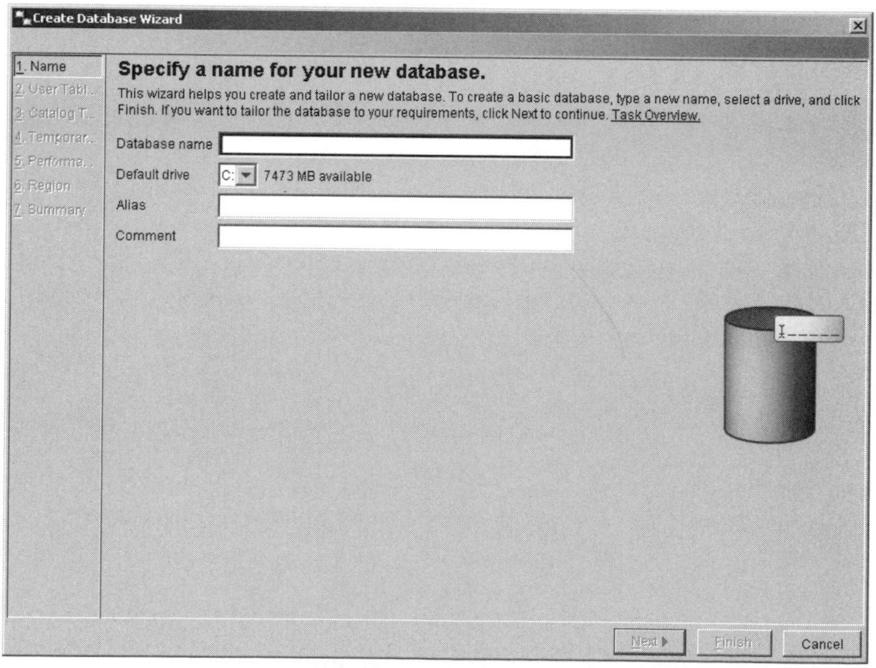

Figure 4–4 The first page of the Create Database Wizard.

lower right corner of the wizard (see Figure 4–4) will be enabled. When this button is selected, the specified database will be created.

Deleting a DB2 UDB Database

Suppose you create a test database that mirrors a production database, so you can develop a new application without affecting your production environment. When the development process is complete and the test database is no longer needed, you might want to get rid of it, so the storage space it occupied can be used for other things. This brings up an interesting question: How do you go about destroying a DB2 UDB database?

Just as there are two ways to create a DB2 UDB database, there are two ways to destroy one: by using the Control Center or by using the `DROP DATABASE` command. By highlighting the object shown in the objects pane of the Control Center that corresponds to the database to be destroyed and right-clicking the mouse button, you can display a menu that contains a list of options available for that particular database. If you then select the *Drop* item from this menu, you will be presented with a Confirmation dialog, where you will be asked to confirm your decision to delete the database (the name of the database you are about to delete will be displayed in this dialog in an effort to prevent you from accidentally deleting the wrong one). Once you confirm that the database specified is to be deleted, its contents are destroyed, its entry is removed from both the system and the local database directory, and its tablespace storage containers are made available for other databases to use. Figure 4–5 shows the Control Center menu items that must be selected in order to drop (delete) an existing database.

A database can also be deleted by executing the `DROP DATABASE` command. The syntax for this command is:

```
DROP [DATABASE | DB] [DatabaseAlias] <AT DBPARTITIONNUM>
```

where:

DatabaseAlias Identifies the alias assigned to the database to be destroyed.

So, if you wanted to destroy a database that has the name and alias TEST_DB, you could do so by executing a `DROP DATABASE` command that looks like this:

```
DROP DATABASE TEST_DB
```

It is important to remember that only users with System Administrator (SYSADM) authority or System Control (SYSCTRL) authority are allowed to drop an existing a database.

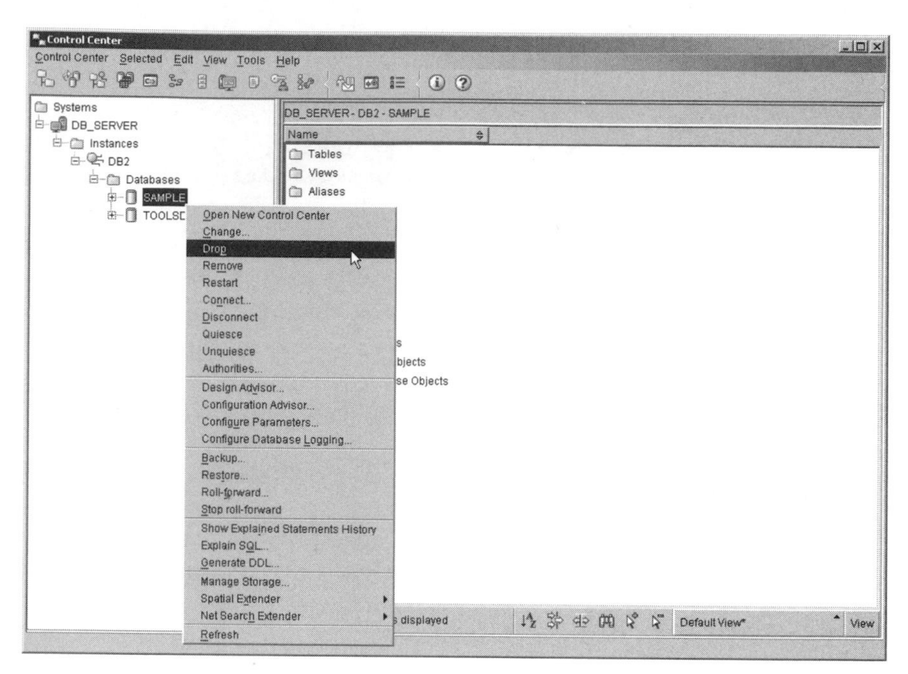

Figure 4–5 Destroying a database from the Control Center.

DB2 UDB's Directory Files

Earlier we saw that when a database is created, that database is cataloged in the system and local database directory. So what are the system and local database directories and why must a database be cataloged in them? If you recall, when we examined the CREATE DATABASE command, we saw that a database can physically reside anywhere on a system. Because of this, each DB2 Database Manager instance must know where databases that fall under its control physically reside, as well how to establish connections to those databases on behalf of users and/or applications. To keep track of this information, DB2 UDB uses a special set of files that are known as *directory files* (or *directories*). Four types of directories exist:

- System database directory
- Local database directory
- Node directory
- Database Connection Services (DCS) directory

The System Database Directory

The system database directory resides in a file named *sqldbdir* that is created automatically when the first database for an instance is created. Information about the new database is then recorded in the system database directory, and as additional databases are cataloged, information about those databases is recorded as well. (Databases are implicitly cataloged when they are created; databases can be explicitly cataloged using the Control Center or the CATALOG DATABASE command.) Each entry recorded in the system database directory contains the following information:

- The database name provided when the database was created (or explicitly cataloged).
- The alias assigned to the database (which is the same as the database name, if no alias has been specified).
- Descriptive information about the database (if that information has been provided).
- The location of the local database directory file that contains additional information about the database.
- The database entry type, which tells whether or not the database is an *indirect* database (which means that it resides on the same workstation as the system database directory file).
- Other system information, including the code page the database was created under.

The contents of the system database directory or a local database directory file can be viewed by executing the LIST DATABASE DIRECTORY command. The syntax for this command is:

```
LIST [DATABASE | DB] DIRECTORY <ON [Location]>
```

where:

Location Identifies the drive or directory where one or more databases are stored.

If no location is specified when this command is executed, the contents of the system database directory file will be displayed. On the other hand, if a location is specified when this command is executed, the contents of the local database directory file that exists for that particular location will displayed.

The Local Database Directory

Any time a DB2 UDB database is created in a new location (i.e., a drive or a directory), a local database directory file is also created at that location. Information about that database is then recorded in the local database directory, and as other databases are created in that location, information about those databases is recorded in the local database directory as well. Thus, while only one system database directory exists for a particular instance, several local database directories can exist, depending upon how databases have been distributed across the storage available.

Each entry recorded in a local database directory contains the following information:

- The database name provided when the database was created.
- The alias assigned to the database (which is the same as the database name, if no alias has been specified).
- Descriptive information about the database (if that information has been provided).
- The name of the root directory of the hierarchical tree used to store information in the database.
- Other system information, including the code page the database was created under.

As mentioned earlier, the contents of a local database directory file can be viewed by executing the `LIST DATABASE DIRECTORY` command.

The Node Directory

Unlike the system database directory and the local database directory, which are used to keep track of what databases exist and where they are stored, the node directory contains information regarding how and where remote systems or instances can be found. A node directory file is created on each client workstation the first time a remote server or instance is cataloged. As other remote instances/servers are cataloged, information about those instances/servers is recorded in the node directory as well. Entries in the node directory are then used in conjunction with entries in the system database directory to make connections and instance attachments to DB2 UDB databases stored on remote servers.

Each entry in the node directory contains, among other things, information on the type of communication protocol to be used to communicate between the client workstation and the remote database server. DB2 UDB supports the following communications protocols:

- Named pipe
- NetBIOS
- Transmission Control Protocol/Internet Protocol (TCP/IP) (which is used today in an overwhelming majority of cases)
- Advanced Peer-to-Peer Networking (APPN)
- Advanced Program-to-Program Communications (APPC)
- Advanced Program-to-Program Communications/Logical Unit (APPCLU)

The contents of the node directory file can be viewed by executing the `LIST NODE DIRECTORY` command. The syntax for this command is:

```
LIST <ADMIN> NODE DIRECTORY <SHOW DETAIL>
```

(If the ADMIN option is specified when this command is executed, information about administration servers will be displayed.)

The Database Connection Services (DCS) Directory

In Chapter 2, we saw that DB2 Connect is an add-on product used to provide connections to DRDA Application Servers, such as:

- DB2 for OS/390 or z/OS databases on System/370 and System/390 architecture host computers.
- DB2 for VM and VSE databases on System/370 and System/390 architecture host computers.
- iSeries databases on Application System/400 (AS/400) and iSeries computers.

Because the information needed to connect to DRDA host databases is different from the information used to connect to LAN-based databases, information about remote host or iSeries databases is kept in a special directory known as the Database Connection Services (DCS) directory. Whenever an entry is found in the DCS directory that has a database name that corresponds to the name of a database stored in the system database directory, the specified Application Requester (which in most cases is DB2 Connect) will forward all SQL requests made to the remote DRDA server where the database resides.

The contents of the DCS directory file can be viewed by executing the `LIST DCS DIRECTORY` command. The syntax for this command is:

```
LIST DCS DIRECTORY
```

It is important to note that the DCS directory only exists if the DB2 Connect product has been installed.

Cataloging and Uncataloging a DB2 UDB Database

Because a database is implicitly cataloged as soon as it is created, most users never have to concern themselves with the cataloging process. However, if you need to catalog a previously uncataloged database, if you want to set up an alternate name for an existing database, or if you need to access a database stored on a DB2 UDB server from a client and you do not have access to the Configuration Assistant, you will need to be familiar with the other tools that

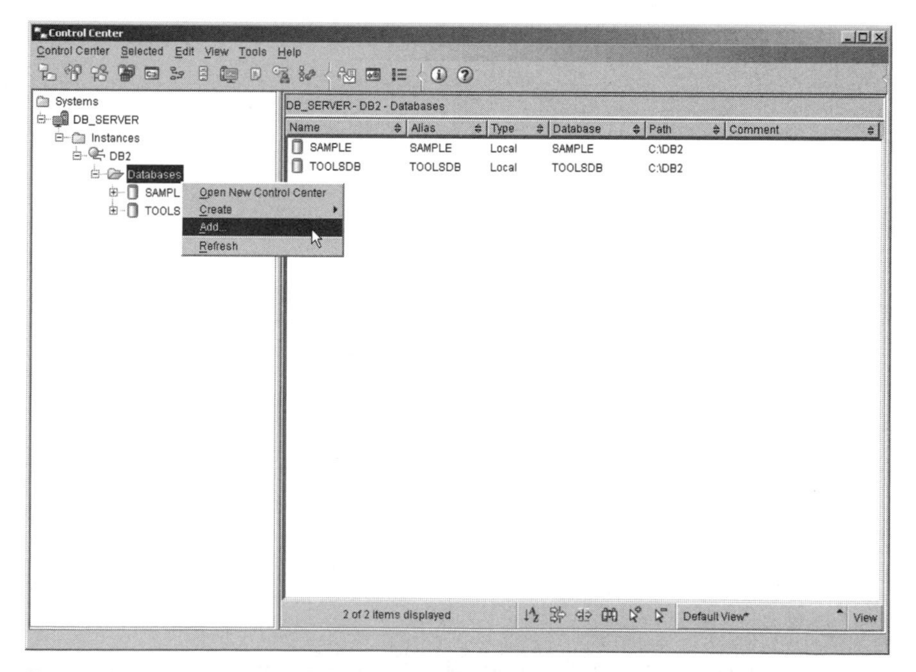

Figure 4–6 Invoking the Add Database dialog from the Control Center.

can be used to catalog databases. Fortunately, cataloging a database is a relatively straightforward process that can be done using the Control Center and the CATALOG DATABASE command, as well as the Configuration Assistant.

Earlier, we saw that by highlighting the *Databases* object shown in the objects pane of the Control Center and right-clicking the mouse button, you will bring up a menu that contains a list of options available for database objects. The dialog used to catalog databases (the Add Database dialog) is invoked by selecting *Add...* from this menu. Figure 4–6 shows the Control Center menu items that must be selected in order to activate the Add Database dialog; Figure 4–7 shows what the Add Database dialog looks like when it is first activated.

You can also catalog a database by executing the CATALOG DATABASE command. The syntax for this command is:

```
CATALOG [DATABASE | DB] [DatabaseName]
<AS [Alias]>
<ON [Path] | AT NODE [NodeName]>
<AUTHENTICATION [AuthenticationType]>
<WITH "[Description]">
```

where:

DatabaseName	Identifies the name assigned to the database to be cataloged.
Alias	Identifies the alias to be assigned to the database to be cataloged.
Path	Identifies the location (drive and/or directory) where the directory hierarchy and files associ-

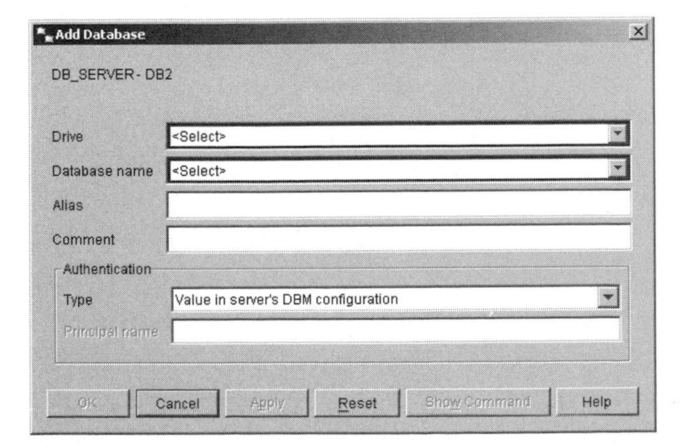

Figure 4–7 The Add Database dialog.

	ated with the database to be cataloged are physically stored.
NodeName	Identifies the node where the database to be cataloged resides. The node name specified should match an entry in the node directory file (i.e., should correspond to a node that has been cataloged).
AuthenticationType	Identifies where and how authentication is to take place when a user attempts to access the database. (Valid values include: SERVER, CLIENT, SERVER_ENCRYPT, and KERBEROS TARGET PRINCIPAL *PrincipalName*, where *PrincipalName* is the fully qualified Kerberos principal name for the target server.)
Description	A comment used to describe the database entry that will be made in the database directory for the database to be cataloged. The description must be enclosed by double quotation marks.

So, if you wanted to catalog a database that has the name TEST_DB and physically resides in the directory /home/db2data, you could do so by executing a `CATALOG DATABASE` command that looks something like this:

```
CATALOG DATABASE TEST_DB AS TEST_DB
ON /home/db2data
AUTHENTICATION SERVER
```

Since a database must be cataloged before a user/application can connect to it, you're probably wondering why you would ever want to uncatalog a database. Suppose you are running an older version of DB2 UDB, and when you upgrade, you decide to completely uninstall the old DB2 UDB software before installing the latest release. To prevent this software upgrade from having an impact on your existing databases, you could simply uncatalog them before you uninstall the old version of DB2 UDB, then catalog them again after the new DB2 UDB software has been installed. (Migration may or may not be necessary.)

Just as there are two different ways to catalog a DB2 UDB database when the Configuration Assistant is unavailable, there are two ways to uncatalog one: by using the Control Center or by using the `UNCATALOG DATABASE` command. By highlighting the object shown in the objects pane of the Control Center that corresponds to the database to be removed from the database catalog and right-clicking the mouse button, you can display a menu that contains a list of options that are available for that particular database. If you then select the *Remove* item from this menu, you will be presented with a Confirmation dialog, where you will be asked to confirm your decision to uncatalog the database (the name of the database you are about to uncatalog will be displayed in this dialog in an effort to prevent you from accidentally uncataloging the wrong one). Once you confirm that the database specified is to be uncataloged, its entry is removed from both the system and the local database directory; however, the database itself is not destroyed, nor are its tablespace storage containers made available for other databases to use. Figure 4–8 shows the Control Center menu items that must be selected in order to uncatalog an existing database.

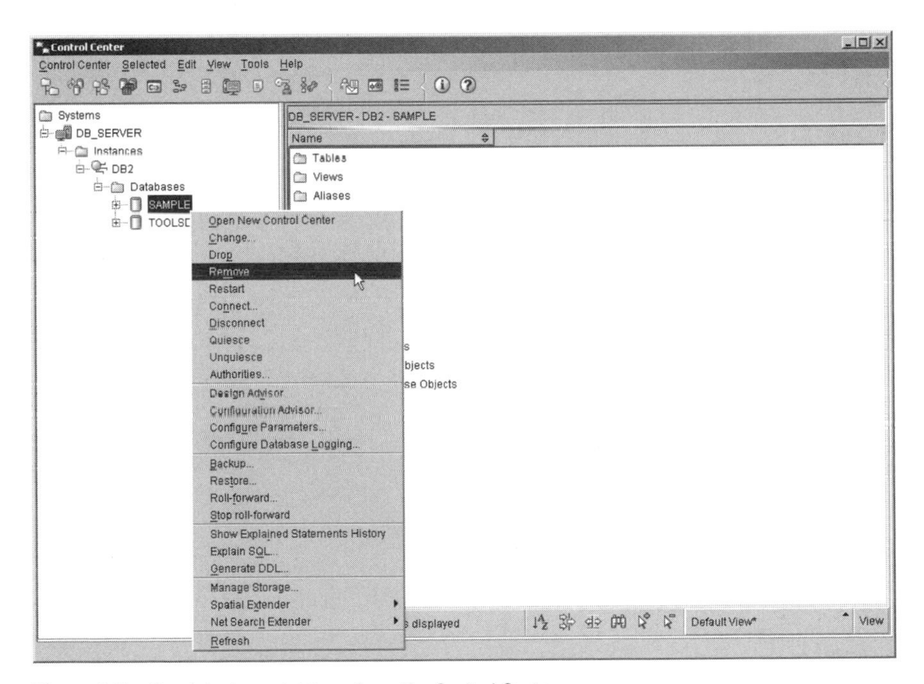

Figure 4–8 Uncataloging a database from the Control Center.

A database can also be uncataloged by executing the `UNCATALOG DATABASE` command. The syntax for this command is:

```
UNCATALOG [DATABASE | DB] [DatabaseAlias]
```

where:

DatabaseAlias Identifies the alias assigned to the database to be uncataloged.

So, if you wanted to uncatalog a database that has the name and alias TEST_DB, you could do so by executing an UNCATALOG DATABASE command that looks like this:

```
UNCATALOG DATABASE TEST_DB
```

Cataloging and Uncataloging a Node

The process used to catalog nodes (servers) is significantly different from the process used to catalog databases. Instead of being explicitly cataloged as needed, nodes are usually implicitly cataloged whenever a remote database is cataloged using the Configuration Assistant. However, if you desire to explicitly catalog a particular node, you can do so by executing the CATALOG ... NODE command that corresponds to the communications protocol that will be used to access the server being cataloged. Several forms of the CATALOG ... NODE command are available, including:

- CATALOG APPC NODE
- CATALOG APPN NODE
- CATALOG LDAP NODE
- CATALOG NAMED PIPE NODE
- CATALOG NETBIOS NODE
- CATALOG TCPIP NODE

The syntax for all of these commands is very similar, the major difference being that many of the options available with each are specific to the communications protocol the command has been tailored for. Because TCP/IP is certainly the most common communications protocol used today, let's take a look at the syntax for that form of the CATALOG ... NODE command.

The syntax for the CATALOG TCPIP NODE command is:

```
CATALOG <ADMIN> TCPIP NODE [NodeName]
REMOTE [HostName]
SERVER [ServiceName]
<SECURITY SOCKS>
<REMOTE INSTANCE [InstanceName]>
<SYSTEM [SystemName]>
<OSTYPE [SystemType]>
<WITH "[Description]">
```

where:

NodeName	Identifies the alias to be assigned to the node to be cataloged. This is an arbitrary name created on the user's workstation and used to identify the node.
HostName	Identifies the host name, as it is known to the TCP/IP network. (This is the name of the server where the remote database you are trying to communicate with resides.)
ServiceName	Identifies the service name or the port number that the DB2 Database Manager instance on the server uses to communicate with.
InstanceName	Identifies the name of the server instance to which an attachment is to be made.
SystemName	Identifies the DB2 system name that is used to identify the server workstation.
SystemType	Identifies the type of operating system being used on the server workstation. (Valid values include: AIX, WIN, HPUX, SUN, OS390, OS400, VM, VSE, SNI, SCO, and LINUX.)
Description	A comment used to describe the node entry that will be made in the node directory for the node to be cataloged. The description must be enclosed by double quotation marks.

If you wanted to catalog a node for an AS/400 server workstation named DB2HOST and assign it the alias DB2_TCPIP, you could do so by executing a `CATALOG TCPIP NODE` command that looks something like this:

```
CATALOG TCPIP NODE DB2_TCPIP
REMOTE DB2HOST
SERVER 5000
OSTYPE OS400
WITH "A remote TCP/IP node"
```

Regardless of which `CATALOG ... NODE` command was used to catalog it, any node can be uncataloged by executing the `UNCATALOG NODE` command. The syntax for this command is:

```
UNCATALOG NODE [NodeName]
```

where:

NodeName	Identifies the alias assigned to the node to be uncataloged.

So if you wanted to uncatalog the node that was cataloged in the previous example, you could do so by executing an UNCATALOG NODE command that looks like this:

```
UNCATALOG NODE DB2_TCPIP
```

Cataloging and Uncataloging a DCS Database

Aside from the fact that neither the Control Center nor the Configuration Assistant can be used, the process used to catalog a Database Connection Services (DCS) database is very similar to the process used to catalog a regular DB2 UDB database. A DCS database is cataloged by executing the CATALOG DCS DATABASE command. The syntax for this command is:

```
CATALOG DCS [DATABASE | DB] [Alias]
<AS [TargetName]>
<AR [LibraryName]>
<PARMS [ParameterString]>
<WITH "[Description]">
```

where:

Alias	Identifies the alias of the target database to be cataloged. This name should match an entry in the system database directory associated with the remote node.
TargetName	Identifies the name of the target host or iSeries database to be cataloged.
LibraryName	Identifies the name of the Application Requester (AR) library loaded and used to access the remote database listed in the DCS directory.
ParameterString	Identifies a parameter string to be passed to the AR when it is invoked. The parameter string must be enclosed by double quotation marks.
Description	A comment used to describe the database entry that will be made in the DCS directory for the database to be cataloged. The description must be enclosed by double quotation marks (").

So, if you wanted to catalog a DCS database that has the name TEST_DB and is a DB2 for z/OS database, you could do so by executing a CATALOG DCS DATABASE command that is similar to this:

```
CATALOG DCS DATABASE TEST_DB
AS DSN_DB
WITH "DB2 z/OS database"
```

Keep in mind that an entry for the database TEST_DB would also have to exist in the system database directory before the entry this command creates in the DCS database directory could be used to connect to the z/OS database.

Entries in the DCS database directory can be removed by executing the UNCATALOG DCS DATABASE command. The syntax for this command is:

```
UNCATALOG [DATABASE | DB] [DatabaseAlias]
```

where:

DatabaseAlias	Identifies the alias assigned to the DCS database to be uncataloged.

Thus, if you wanted to uncatalog the DCS database cataloged in the previous example, you could do so by executing an UNCATALOG DCS DATABASE command that looks like this:

```
UNCATALOG DCS DATABASE TEST_DB
```

Cataloging Remote Databases with the Add Database Wizard

As you can see, cataloging a local database is a relatively simple process. However, cataloging a remote database is a little more involved, because both the database and the node the database is stored on must be cataloged together. (The entry in the system database directory must have a corresponding entry in the node directory.) That's why the Add Database Wizard (not to be confused with the Add Database dialog that is invoked from the Control Center) was created. This tool, which is activated from the Configuration Assistant, is designed to capture information about the characteristics of databases that are to be cataloged, then use that information to make the appropriate entries in the database and node directories. Figure 4–9 shows the Configuration Assistant menu items that must be selected in order to activate the Add Database Wizard; Figure 4–10 shows what the first page of the Add Database Wizard looks like when it is activated.

The first thing you will notice when you activate the Add Database Wizard is that there are three methods that you can use to catalog a database. They are:

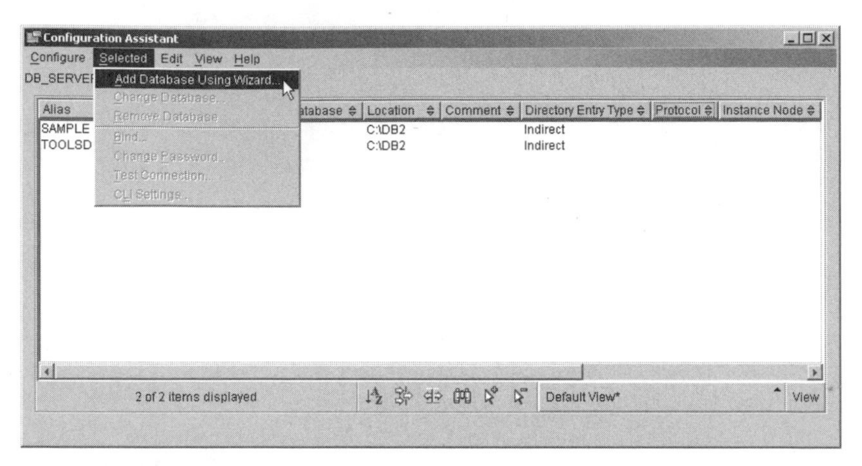

Figure 4–9 Invoking the Add Database Wizard from the Configuration Assistant.

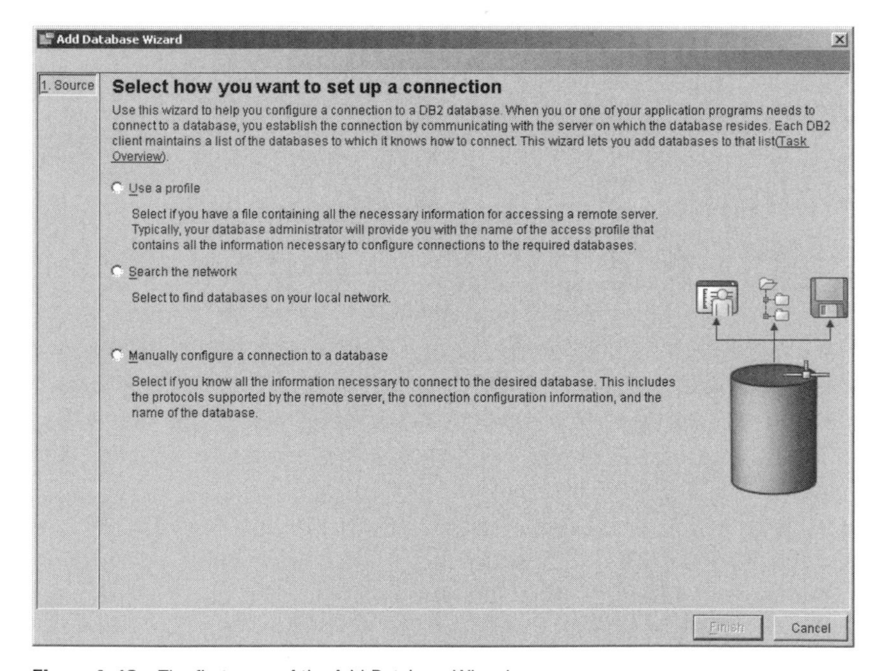

Figure 4–10 The first page of the Add Database Wizard.

➤ Automated configuration using an access profile

➤ Automated configuration using network discovery

➤ Manual configuration

From a user's perspective, using an access profile or network discovery is the easiest way to catalog a database; manual configuration requires knowledge of where the database is physically located, along with the characteristics of the communications protocols used on both the client and the server. However, before a user can take advantage of either of the automated configuration options available, the database administrator must either generate a set of access profiles or set up the DB2 Discovery services on each appropriate DB2 UDB server.

Access Profiles

An access profile contains the information a client workstation needs to catalog a remote database stored on a DB2 UDB server. Two types of access profiles exist: *server access profiles* and *client access profiles*. Server access profiles are created on DB2 UDB server workstations and contain information about all instances and databases that have been cataloged on the server. Client access profiles, on the other hand, are used to copy information about the cataloged databases and/or the settings (DB2 Database Manager configuration, CLI/ ODBC settings, etc.) found on one client workstation to other client workstations. Both types of profiles can then be exported from one DB2 system and imported to another.

Since you do not need to provide detailed communications information when access profiles are used, they are ideal for configuring a large number of clients. If you have a large number of clients to configure, you should also consider making use of LDAP (the Lightweight Directory Access Protocol). LDAP lets you store catalog information in one centralized location. Each client just needs to be able to access the centralized location to connect to any database that has been made available in the network.

DB2 Discovery

DB2 Discovery also allows you to easily catalog a remote server and a database without having to know any detailed communication-specific information. Here's how DB2 Discovery works. When invoked from a client workstation, DB2 Discovery broadcasts a discovery request over the network, and each DB2 server on the network that has been configured to support the discovery process responds by returning a list of instances found on the server, information about the communication protocol each instance supports, and a list of databases found within each instance. The Control Center and the Configuration Assistant can then use this information to catalog any instance or database returned.

To process a discovery request, DB2 Discovery can use one of two methods: *search* and *known*. When the search discovery method is used, the entire network is searched for valid DB2 servers/databases, and a list of all servers, instances, and databases found is returned to the client, along with the communications information needed to catalog each one. In contrast, when the known discovery method is used, the network is searched for a specific server using a specific communications protocol. (Since the client knows the name of the server and the communications protocol used, the server is said to be "known" by the client.) Again, when the specified server is located, a list of all instances and databases found on the server is returned to the client, along with the information needed to catalog each one.

A search discovery can take a very long time (many hours) to complete if the network the client and server are on contains hundreds of machines. Furthermore, some network devices, such as routers, may actually block a search discovery request.

Manual Configuration

If you know the details of the communications setup between a client and a server, you can manually configure a database connection using the Add Database Wizard. In this case, you are prompted by a series of wizard pages to provide information similar to that required by the `CATALOG DATABASE` and `CATALOG ... NODE` commands. This information includes the communications protocols supported by the server instance containing the database to be cataloged, the communications protocol information needed to configure a connection to the server instance, the name of the server, and the name of the database on the server.

Database Objects

Earlier, we saw that a DB2 UDB database is comprised of four distinct types of objects:

- System objects
- Recovery objects
- Storage objects
- Database objects

We have also seen how system objects, recovery objects, and storage objects come into play whenever a new database is created. Now, let's turn our attention to database objects. Database objects, also known as data objects, are used to control how all user data (and some system data) is stored and organized. Data objects include:

- Tables
- Indexes
- Views
- Aliases
- Schemas
- Triggers
- User-defined data types
- User-defined functions
- Sequences

Tables

A table is a logical database object that acts as the main repository in a database. Tables present data as a collection of unordered rows with a fixed number of columns. Each column contains values of the same data type or one of its subtypes, and each row contains a set of values for every column available. Usually, the columns in a table are logically related, and additional relationships can be defined between two or more tables. The storage representation of a row is called a *record*, the storage representation of a column is called a *field*, and each intersection of a row and column is called a *value*. Figure 4–11 shows the structure of a simple database table.

With DB2 UDB, five types of tables are available:

Base tables. User-defined tables designed to hold persistent user data.

Result tables. DB2 Database Manager-defined tables populated with rows retrieved from one or more base tables in response to a query.

Summary tables. User-defined tables whose column definitions are based on the results of a query that is also used to populate the table. Summary tables are used to improve query performance.

Declared temporary tables. User-defined tables used to hold non-persistent data temporarily, on behalf of a single application. Declared temporary tables are explicitly created by an application

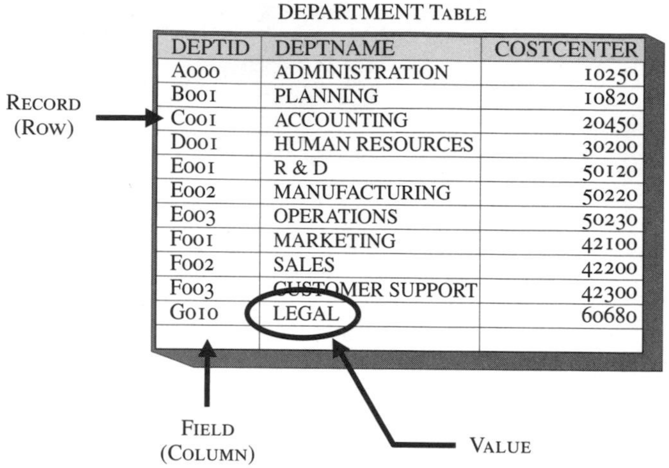

DEPARTMENT TABLE

DEPTID	DEPTNAME	COSTCENTER
A000	ADMINISTRATION	10250
B001	PLANNING	10820
C001	ACCOUNTING	20450
D001	HUMAN RESOURCES	30200
E001	R & D	50120
E002	MANUFACTURING	50220
E003	OPERATIONS	50230
F001	MARKETING	42100
F002	SALES	42200
F003	CUSTOMER SUPPORT	42300
G010	LEGAL	60680

RECORD (ROW)

FIELD (COLUMN)

VALUE

Figure 4–11 A simple database table.

when they are needed and implicitly destroyed when the application that created them terminates its last database connection.

Typed tables. User-defined tables whose column definitions are based on the attributes of a user-defined structured data type.

Data associated with base tables, summary tables, and typed tables is physically stored in tablespaces—the actual tablespace used is specified during the table creation process.

Indexes

An index is an object that contains an ordered set of pointers that refer to rows in a base table. Each index is based upon one or more columns in the base table they refer to, yet they are stored as separate entities. Figure 4–12 shows the structure of a simple index, along with its relationship to a base table.

Indexes are used primarily to enforce record uniqueness and to help the DB2 Database Manager quickly locate records in response to a query. Indexes can also provide greater concurrency in multiuser environments—because records can be located faster, acquired locks do not have to be held as long. However, there is a price for these benefits: Additional storage space is needed whenever indexes are used, and performance can actually decrease when new data is added to a base table and existing data is modified. In both cases, the operations performed must be applied to both the base table and to any corresponding indexes.

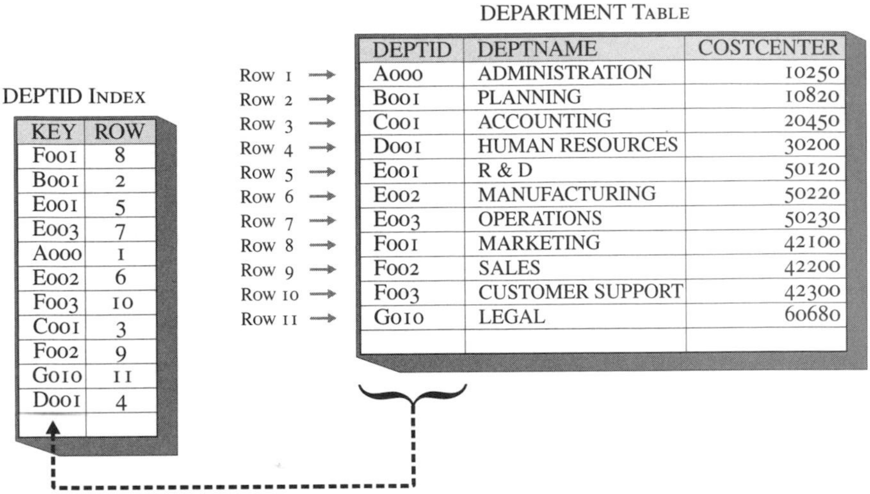

DEPTID INDEX

KEY	ROW
F001	8
B001	2
E001	5
E003	7
A000	1
E002	6
F003	10
C001	3
F002	9
G010	11
D001	4

DEPARTMENT TABLE

	DEPTID	DEPTNAME	COSTCENTER
Row 1 →	A000	ADMINISTRATION	10250
Row 2 →	B001	PLANNING	10820
Row 3 →	C001	ACCOUNTING	20450
Row 4 →	D001	HUMAN RESOURCES	30200
Row 5 →	E001	R & D	50120
Row 6 →	E002	MANUFACTURING	50220
Row 7 →	E003	OPERATIONS	50230
Row 8 →	F001	MARKETING	42100
Row 9 →	F002	SALES	42200
Row 10 →	F003	CUSTOMER SUPPORT	42300
Row 11 →	G010	LEGAL	60680

Figure 4–12 A simple index.

Views

Views are used to provide a different way of looking at the data stored in one or more base tables. Essentially, a view is a named specification of a result table that is populated whenever the view is referenced in an SQL statement. Like base tables, views can be thought of as having columns and rows. And in most cases, data can be retrieved from a view the same way it can be retrieved from a table. However, whether or not a view can be used in insert, update, and delete operations depends upon how it was defined—views can be defined as being insertable, updatable, deletable, and read-only.

Although views look similar to base tables, they do not contain real data. Instead, views refer to data stored in other base tables. Only the view definition itself is actually stored in the database. (In fact, when changes are made to the data presented in a view, the changes are actually made to the data stored in the base table(s) the view references.) Figure 4–13 shows the structure of a simple view, along with its relationship to a base table.

Because views allow different users to see different presentations of the same data, they are often used to control access to data. For example, suppose you had a table that contained information about all employees that worked for a particular company. Managers could be given access to this table using a view that only allows them to see information about the employees that work in their department. Members of the payroll department, on the other hand, could be given access to the table using a view that only allows them to see the information needed to generate employee paychecks. Both sets of users

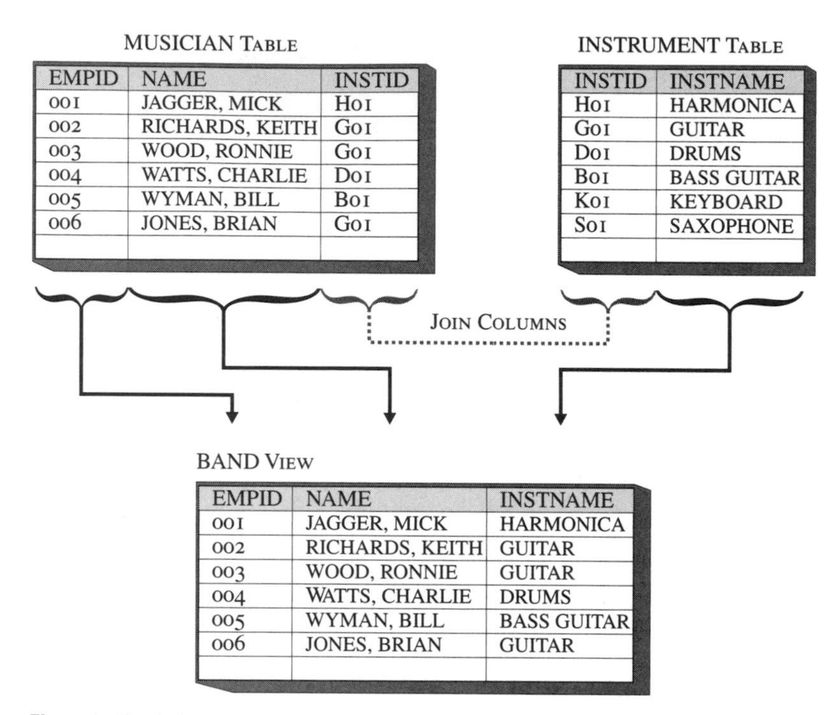

MUSICIAN TABLE
EMPID NAME INSTID
001 JAGGER, MICK H01
002 RICHARDS, KEITH G01
003 WOOD, RONNIE G01
004 WATTS, CHARLIE D01
005 WYMAN, BILL B01
006 JONES, BRIAN G01
INSTRUMENT TABLE
INSTID INSTNAME
H01 HARMONICA
G01 GUITAR
D01 DRUMS
B01 BASS GUITAR
K01 KEYBOARD
S01 SAXOPHONE
JOIN COLUMNS
BAND VIEW
EMPID NAME INSTNAME
001 JAGGER, MICK HARMONICA
002 RICHARDS, KEITH GUITAR
003 WOOD, RONNIE GUITAR
004 WATTS, CHARLIE DRUMS
005 WYMAN, BILL BASS GUITAR
006 JONES, BRIAN GUITAR

Figure 4–13 A simple view that references a base table.

are given access to the same table; however, because each user works with a different view, it appears that they are working with their own tables.

Because there is no way to grant SELECT privileges on specific columns within a table, the only way to prevent users from accessing every column in a table is by creating a result, summary, or declared temporary table that holds only the data a particular user needs, or by creating a view that only contains the table columns a user is allowed to access. Of these two methods, the view is easier to implement and manage.

Aliases

An alias is an alternate name for a table or view. (Aliases can also be created for *nicknames* that refer to data tables or views located on federated systems.) Aliases can be used to reference any table or view that can be referenced by its primary name. However, an alias cannot be used in every context that a primary table or view name can. For example, an alias cannot be used in the check condition of a check constraint, nor can it be used to reference a user-defined temporary table.

Like tables and views, an alias can be created, dropped, and have comments associated with it. However, unlike tables (but similar to views), aliases can refer to other aliases, using a process known as *chaining*.

Aliases are publicly referenced names, so no special authority or privilege is required to use them. However, access to the table or view that is referred to by an alias still has the authorization requirements associated with these types of objects.

So why would you want use an alias instead of the actual table/view name? Suppose you needed to develop an application that interacts with a table named EMPLOYEES that resides in your company's payroll database. During the development process, you would like to run the application against a test EMPLOYEES table; then when development is complete, the application will need to run against the production EMPLOYEES table. By using an alias instead of a base table name in all table references made by the application, you can quickly change the application so that it works with the production EMPLOYEES table instead of the test EMPLOYEES table simply by changing table name the alias refers to.

Schemas

Schemas are objects that are used to logically classify and group other objects in the database. Because schemas are objects themselves, they have privileges associated with them that allow the schema owner to control which users can create, alter, and drop objects within them.

Most objects in a database are named using a two-part naming convention. The first (leftmost) part of the name is called the *schema name* or *qualifier*, and the second (rightmost) part is called the *object name*. Syntactically, these two parts are concatenated and delimited with a period (for example, HR.EMPLOYEE). Each time an object that can be qualified by a schema name is created, it is assigned to the schema that is provided with its name. (If no schema name is provided, the object is assigned to the default schema, which is usually the user ID of the individual that created the object.) Some schema names, such as the names assigned to the four schemas implicitly created when a database is created (SYSIBM, SYSCAT, SYSSTAT, and SYSFUN), are reserved and cannot be used.

Schemas are usually created implicitly when other objects are created. (When a new database is created, all users are granted IMPLICIT_SCHEMA privileges. This allows any user to create objects in any schema not already in existence.) However, schemas can be created explicitly as well.

Triggers

A trigger is used to define a set of actions that are to be executed whenever an insert, update, or delete operation is performed on a specified table. Triggers can be used, along with referential constraints and check constraints, to enforce data integrity rules and business rules. (A data integrity rule might be that whenever the record for an employee is deleted from the table that holds employee information, the corresponding record will be deleted from the table that holds payroll information. A business rule might be that an employee's salary cannot be increased by more than 10 percent.) Triggers can also be used to update other tables, automatically generate or transform values for inserted and/or updated rows, or invoke functions to perform special tasks.

By using triggers, the logic needed to enforce such business rules can be placed directly in the database, and applications that work with the database can concentrate solely on data storage, data management, and data retrieval. And by storing the logic needed to enforce data integrity rules and business rules directly in the database, it can be modified as data integrity rules and business rules change without requiring applications to be recoded and recompiled.

Before a trigger can be created, several criteria must be identified:

Subject table. The table that the trigger is to interact with.

Trigger event. An SQL operation that causes the trigger to be activated whenever it is performed against the subject table. This operation can be an insert operation, an update operation, or a delete operation.

Trigger activation time. Indicates whether the trigger should be activated before or after the trigger event occurs. A *before* trigger will be activated before the trigger event occurs; therefore, it will be able to see new data values before they are inserted into the subject table. An *after* trigger will be activated after the trigger event occurs; therefore, it can only see data values that have already been inserted into the subject table.

Set of affected rows. The rows of the subject table that are being inserted, updated, or deleted.

Trigger granularity. Specifies whether the actions the trigger will perform are to be performed once for the entire insert, update, or delete operation or once for every row affected by the insert, update, or delete operation.

Triggered action. An optional search condition and a set of SQL statements that are to be executed whenever the trigger is activated. (If a search condition is specified, the SQL statements will only be executed if the search condition evaluates to true.) If the trigger is a before trigger, the triggered action can include statements that retrieve data, set transition variables, or signal SQL states. If the trigger is an after trigger, the triggered action can include statements that retrieve data, insert records, update records, delete records, or signal SQL states.

Triggered actions can refer to the values in the set of affected rows using what are known as *transition variables*. Transition variables use the names of the columns in the subject table, qualified by a specified name that indicates whether the reference is to the original value (before the insert, update, or delete operation is performed) or the new value (after the insert, update, or delete operation is performed). Another means of referring to values in the set of affected rows is through the use of *transition tables*. Transition tables also use the names of the columns in the subject table, but they allow the complete set of affected rows to be treated as a table. Unfortunately, transition tables can only be used in after triggers.

The activation of one trigger may cause the activation of other triggers, or even the reactivation of the same trigger. This event is known as *trigger cascading*, and because trigger cascading can occur, a significant change can be made to a database as the result of a single `INSERT`, `UPDATE`, or `DELETE` statement.

User-Defined Data Types

As the name implies, user-defined data types (UDTs) are data types that are created (and named) by a database user. A user-defined data type can be a distinct data type that shares a common representation with one of the built-in data types provided with DB2 UDB, or it can be a structured type that consists of a sequence of named attributes, each of which has its own data type. Structured data types can also be created as subtypes of other structured types, thereby defining a type hierarchy.

User-defined data types support strong data typing, which means that even though they may share the same representation as other built-in or user-defined data types, the value of one user-defined data type is only compatible with values of that same type (or of other user-defined data types within the same data type hierarchy). As a result, user-defined data types cannot be used as arguments for most of the built-in functions available. Instead, user-defined functions (or methods) that provide similar functionality must be developed whenever that kind of capability is needed.

User-Defined Functions (or Methods)

User-defined functions (UDFs) are special objects used to extend and enhance the support provided by the built-in functions available with DB2 UDB. Like user-defined data types, user-defined functions (or methods) are created and named by a database user. A user-defined function can be an external function written in a high-level programming language, or a sourced function whose implementation is inherited from some other function that already exists.

Like all built-in functions, user-defined functions are classified as being *scalar*, *column* (or aggregate), or *table* in nature. Scalar functions return a single value and can be specified in an SQL statement wherever a regular expression can be used. (The built-in function `SUBSTR()` is an example of a scalar function.) Column functions return a single-valued answer from a set of like values (a column) and can also be specified in an SQL statement wherever a regular expression can be used. (The built-in function `AVG()` is an example of a column function.) Table functions return a table to the SQL statement that references it and can only be specified in the `FROM` clause of a `SELECT` statement. Table functions are used to work with data that does not reside in a DB2 UDB database and/or to convert such data into a format that resembles that of a DB2 table. (The built-in function `SNAPSHOT_TABLE` is an example of a table function.)

Sequences

A sequence is an object that is used to automatically generate data values. Unlike an identity column, which is used to generate data values for a specific column in a table, a sequence is not tied to any specific column or any specific table. Instead, a sequence behaves like a unique counter that resides outside the database, with the exception that it does not present the same concurrency and performance problems that can occur when external counters are used.

All sequences have the following characteristics:

- Values generated can be any exact numeric data type that has a scale of zero (SMALLINT, BIGINT, INTEGER, and DECIMAL).

- Consecutive values can differ by any specified increment value. The default increment value is 1.
- Counter values are recoverable. (Counter values are reconstructed from logs when recovery is required.)
- Values generated can be cached to improve performance.

In addition, sequences generate values in one of three ways:

- Incrementing or decrementing by a specified amount, without bounds
- Incrementing or decrementing by a specified amount to a user-defined limit and stop
- Incrementing or decrementing by a specified amount to a user-defined limit, then cycle back to the beginning and start again

To facilitate the use of sequences in SQL operations, two expressions are available: `PREVVAL` and `NEXTVAL`. The `PREVVAL` expression returns the most recently generated value for the specified sequence, and the `NEXTVAL` expression returns the next value for the specified sequence.

Sequences can only be used in nonpartitioned database environments.

Practice Questions

Question 1

When attempting to connect to a database stored on a AIX server from a client workstation, the following message is displayed:

SQL1013N The database alias name or database name "TEST_DB" could not be found.

Which of the following is NOT a valid reason why this message was generated?

❍ A. The server's database directory does not contain an entry for the database TEST_DB

❍ B. The client's database directory does not contain an entry for the database TEST_DB

❍ C. The client's node directory does not contain an entry for the server

❍ D. The client's DB2 version is not compatible with the server's DB2 version

Question 2

Given the following command:

CREATE DATABASE TEST_DB ON /home/db2data/db_dir USER TABLESPACE MANAGED BY DATABASE USING (FILE '/home/db2data/user' 16777215)

How many SMS tablespaces are created?

❍ A. 1

❍ B. 2

❍ C. 3

❍ D. 4

Question 3

Which of the following are NOT stored in the system catalog tables?

❍ A. SQL statements used to create views

❍ B. SQL statements used to create triggers

❍ C. SQL statements used to create constraints

❍ D. Table names

Question 4

Given the following table:

TABLE1

C1 (INTEGER)	C2 (INTEGER)
1	2
2	3

Which two of the following could be used to automatically increment the value of C1 whenever a new row is added to table TABLE1?

- ❑ A. A sequence
- ❑ B. An index
- ❑ C. A view
- ❑ D. A trigger
- ❑ E. A transition variable

Question 5

Which of the following would NOT provide access to data stored in table TABLE1 using the name T1?

- ❍ A. An alias named T1 that references table TABLE1
- ❍ B. A view named T1 that references table TABLE1
- ❍ C. A schema named T1 that references table TABLE1
- ❍ D. An alias named T1 that references view V1 that references table TABLE1

Question 6

Communications is being manually established between a Windows 2000 client and a Solaris server. Which of the following pieces of information is needed?

- ❍ A. The system administrator's user ID and password
- ❍ B. The client workstation name
- ❍ C. The server's operating system version
- ❍ D. The hostname

Question 7

Database MY_DB has just been created on a Windows 2000 server. Which of the following statements is accurate?

❍ A. Containers used by USERSPACE1 cannot be used by other tablespaces.

❍ B. Buffer pool IBMDEFAULTBP can hold up to 2000 4k pages.

❍ C. The system catalog must be manually created before the database can be used.

❍ D. Sequences can now be created in the SYSFUN schema.

Question 8

Given the following information:

Protocol: TCP/IP
Port Number: 5000
Host Name: DB_SERVER
Database Name: TEST_DB
Database Server Platform: Linux

Which of the following will allow a client to access the database stored on the server?

❍ A. CATALOG DATABASE test_db AS test_db REMOTE TCPIP SERVER db_server PORT 5000 OSTYPE LINUX

❍ B. CATALOG TCPIP NODE 5000 REMOTE SERVER db_server OSTYPE LINUX

CATALOG DATABASE test_db AS test_db AT NODE db_server AUTHENTICATION SERVER

❍ C. CATALOG TCPIP NODE db_server REMOTE db_server SERVER 5000 OSTYPE LINUX

CATALOG DATABASE test_db AS test_db AT NODE db_server AUTHENTICATION SERVER

❍ D. CATALOG TCPIP NODE db_server REMOTE db_server PORT 5000 OSTYPE LINUX

CATALOG DATABASE test_db AS test_db AT NODE db_server AUTHENTICATION SERVER

Question 9

Assuming DB2 UDB is installed on an AIX system, which of the following commands provides the information needed to connect to a local database?

❍ A. CATALOG NODE

❍ B. CATALOG DCS

❍ C. CATALOG DATABASE

❍ D. CATALOG ODBC DATA SOURCE

Question 10

Which of the following events will NOT cause a trigger to be activated?

❍ A. A select operation

❍ B. An insert operation

❍ C. An update operation

❍ D. A delete operation

Answers

Question 1

The correct answer is **D.** In order to access a remote database from a client workstation, the database must be cataloged in the system database directory of both the client and the server, AND the server workstation must be cataloged in the client's node directory. (The entry in the node directory tells the DB2 Database Manager how to connect to the server to get access to the database stored there.)

Question 2

The correct answer is **B.** By default, when a database is created, three SMS tablespaces are created and assigned the names SYSCATSPACE, USERSPACE1, and TEMPSPACE1. This particular CREATE DATABASE statement overrides this default behavior and makes the USERSPACE1 tablespace a DMS tablespace; therefore, this database will have 2 SMS tablespaces and 1 DMS tablespace.

Question 3

The correct answer is **A.** The system catalog tables are used to keep track of information like database object definitions, database object dependencies, database object privileges, column data types, and table constraints. In most cases, the complete characteristics of a database object are stored in one or more system catalog tables when the object is created. However in some cases, such as when triggers and constraints are defined, the actual SQL used to create the object is stored instead. Characteristics of views, not the SQL used to create them, are stored in the system catalog tables.

Question 4

The correct answers are **A** and **D.** Sequences, identity columns, and triggers can be used to automatically generate values for columns. The following SQL could be used to create such a trigger:

```
CREATE TRIGGER DEMO.PARTID_AUTOINC
NO CASCADE BEFORE
INSERT ON DEMO.PARTS
REFERENCING NEW AS N
FOR EACH ROW
MODE DB2SQL
BEGIN ATOMIC
    SET N.PART_ID = (SELECT MAX(PART_ID) FROM DEMO.PARTS);
    SET N.PART_ID = VALUE(N.PART_ID + 1, 1);
END:
```

Question 5

The correct answer is **C.** An alias is an alternate name for a table or view; therefore, it is possible to create the alias T1 for the table TABLE1, and it is possible to create the alias T1 for the view V1. Views are used to provide a different way of looking at the data stored in one or more base tables. Schemas, on the other hand, are used to logically group data; therefore, a schema named T1 could be used to group aliases and views that reference table TABLE1 together, but it could not be used to provide access to the data stored in table TABLE1.

Question 6

The correct answer is **D.** When cataloging a node, the hostname is required, but the system administrator's user ID and password, the client workstation name, and the server's operating system version are not. (You must have proper authority on the client workstation in order to catalog the node, but you do not have to use the system administrator's account; you are cataloging the node on the client workstation, so you don't have to provide information about the client; and the type of operating system being used on the server can be specified, but the version of that operating system is not needed.)

Question 7

The correct answer is **A.** A single tablespace—in this case tablespace USERSPACE1—can span many containers, but each container can only belong to one tablespace. (When a database is first created on a Windows platform, the buffer pool IBMDEFAULTBP is 250 4K pages in size; the system catalog is created automatically as part of the database creation process; and because the schemas SYSIBM, SYSCAT, SYSSTAT, and SYSFUN are reserved schemas, data objects cannot be created in them.)

Question 8

The correct answer is **C.** In this case, both the node and the database must be cataloged by executing the CATALOG ... NODE and CATALOG DATABASE commands. Answer C is the only answer that uses the correct syntax for these two commands.

Question 9

The correct answer is **C.** In order to connect to a local database, that database must be cataloged in the system database directory. Databases are implicitly cataloged when they are created; databases can be explicitly cataloged using the Control Center or the CATALOG DATABASE command; and because the database is local, entries do not have to be made in the node directory or the DCS directory.

Question 10

The correct answer is **A.** A trigger can be activated whenever an insert, update, or delete operation is performed against the subject table of the trigger.

Working with DB2 UDB Data

Thirty-one percent (31%) of the DB2 UDB V8.1 Family Fundamentals certification exam (Exam 700) is designed to test your knowledge of the various Structured Query Language (SQL) statements that are commonly used to create database objects and manipulate data. The questions that make up this portion of the exam are intended to evaluate the following:

- Your ability to identify the Data Control Language (DCL) statements available with DB2 UDB.
- Your ability to identify the Data Definition Language (DDL) statements available with DB2 UDB.
- Your ability to identify the Data Manipulation Language (DML) statements available with DB2 UDB.
- Your ability to perform insert, update, and delete operations against a database.
- Your ability to retrieve and format data using various forms of the `SELECT` statement.
- Your ability to create and invoke a stored procedure.
- Your knowledge of what transactions are, as well as how transactions are initiated and terminated.

This chapter is designed to introduce you to the Structured Query Language (SQL) statements that you need to be familiar with in order to create database objects, and access and manipulate data. In this chapter, you will also learn what transactions are and how to terminate a transaction in such a way that all operations performed within that transaction are either applied to the database and made permanent (committed) or backed out (rolled back).

Terms you will learn:

Structured Query Language (SQL)
Embedded SQL Application Construct Statements
Data Control Language (DCL) Statements
Data Definition Language (DDL) Statements
Data Manipulation Language (DML) Statements
Transaction Management Statements
The `CONNECT` Statement
The `GRANT` Statement
The `REVOKE` Statement
The `CREATE BUFFERPOOL` Statement
The `CREATE TABLESPACE` Statement
System Managed Space (SMS) tablespace
Database Managed Space (DMS) tablespace
Prefetching
The `ALTER TABLESPACE` Statement
The `CREATE TABLE` Statement
Data Types
The `ALTER TABLE` Statement
The `CREATE INDEX` Statement
Clustered Index
The `CREATE VIEW` Statement
`WITH CHECK OPTION`
The `CREATE ALIAS` Statement
The `CREATE SCHEMA` Statement
The `CREATE TRIGGER` Statement
Trigger Subject Table
Trigger Event
Trigger Activation Time
Set of Affected Rows

Trigger Granularity
Triggered Action
Before Trigger
After Trigger
The DROP Statement
The INSERT Statement
Subselect
The UPDATE Statement
Cursor
The DELETE Statement
The SELECT Statement
Query
The DISTINCT Clause
The FROM Clause
The WHERE Clause
Relational Predicates
The BETWEEN Predicate
The LIKE Predicate
Wild Card Characters
The IN Predicate
Subquery
The EXISTS Predicate
The NULL Predicate
The GROUP BY Clause
GROUP BY ROLLUP
GROUP BY CUBE
The HAVING Clause
The ORDER BY Clause
The FETCH FIRST Clause
Cartesian Product
Inner Join
Left Outer Join
Right Outer Join
Full Outer Join

Set Operator

The UNION Set Operator

The UNION ALL Set Operator

The EXCEPT Set Operator

The EXCEPT ALL Set Operator

The INTERSECT Set Operator

The INTERSECT ALL Set Operator

SQL Functions

The DECLARE CURSOR Statement

The OPEN Statement

The FETCH Statement

The CLOSE Statement

Transaction

The COMMIT Statement

The ROLLBACK Statement

Stored Procedure

External Procedure

SQL Procedure

The CREATE PROCEDURE statement

The CALL Statement

Techniques you will master:

Recognizing the various Data Control Language (DCL) statements available, and understanding how each is used.

Recognizing the various Data Definition Language (DDL) statements available, and understanding how each is used.

Recognizing the various Data Manipulation Language (DML) statements available, and understanding how each is used.

Understanding how to add data to a table using the INSERT SQL statement.

Understanding how to modify data stored in a table using the UPDATE SQL statement.

Understanding how to remove data from a table using the DELETE SQL statement.

Knowing how to construct simple and complex queries using the SELECT SQL statement and its clauses.

Understanding how transactions are initiated and terminated.

Understanding how stored procedures are created and invoked.

Structured Query Language (SQL)

Structured Query Language (SQL) is a standardized language used to work with database objects and the data they contain. Using SQL, you can define, alter, and remove database objects, as well as add, update, delete, and retrieve data values. One of the strengths of SQL is that it can be used in a variety of ways: SQL statements can be executed interactively using tools such as the Command Center and the Command Line Processor, they can be placed directly in UNIX shell scripts or Windows batch files, and they can be embedded in high-level programming language source code files that are precompiled/compiled to create a database application. (Because SQL is nonprocedural by design, it is not an actual programming language; therefore, most embedded SQL applications are built by combining the decision and sequence control of a high-level programming language with the data storage, manipulation, and retrieval capabilities of SQL).

Like most other languages, SQL has a defined syntax and a set of language elements. Most SQL statements can be categorized according to the function they have been designed to perform; SQL statements typically fall under one of the following categories:

Embedded SQL Application Construct Statements. SQL statements used for the sole purpose of constructing embedded SQL applications.

Data Control Language (DCL) Statements. SQL statements used to grant and revoke authorities and privileges.

Data Definition Language (DDL) Statements. SQL statements used to create, alter, and delete database objects.

Data Manipulation Language (DML) Statements. SQL statements used to store data in and retrieve or remove data from database objects.

Transaction Management Statements. SQL statements used to establish and terminate database connections and active transactions.

You do not have to be familiar with the Embedded SQL Application Construct Statements in order to pass the DB2 UDB V8.1 Family Fundamentals certification exam (Exam 700). However, you must know how the more common DCL, DDL, and DML statements are used, and you must be familiar with the Transaction Management Statements available. With that in mind, this chapter will focus on introducing you to the most common SQL statements used to create database objects and manipulate data.

Although basic syntax is presented for most of the SQL statements covered in this chapter, the actual syntax supported may be much more complex. To view the complete syntax for a specific SQL statement or to obtain more information about a particular statement, refer to the *IBM DB2 Universal Database, Version 8 SQL Reference Volume 2* product documentation.

Data Control Language (DCL) Statements

You may recall that in Chapter 3, "Security," we saw that authorities and privileges are used to control access to the DB2 Database Manager for an instance, to one or more databases running under that instance's control, and to a particular database's objects. Users are only allowed to work with those objects for which they have been given the appropriate authority or privilege; the authorities and privileges they possess also determine what they can and cannot do with the objects they have access to. Authorities and privileges are given using the `GRANT` SQL statement. Likewise, authorities and privileges are revoked using the `REVOKE` SQL statement. The `GRANT` statement and the `REVOKE` statement, along with the `CONNECT` SQL statement, make up the bulk of the Data Control Language (DCL) statements available with DB2 UDB.

The `CONNECT` statement

Before a user can access data stored in a DB2 UDB database (or do anything else with a database for that matter), they must first establish a connection to that database. In some cases, a database connection can be established using the Control Center; however, in most cases, a database connection is established by executing the `CONNECT` SQL statement. The basic syntax for this statement is:

```
CONNECT TO [DatabaseName]
<USER [UserID] USING [Password]>
```

where:

DatabaseName	Identifies the name assigned to the database a connection is to be established with.
UserID	Identifies the authentication ID (or user ID) assigned to the user attempting to establish the database connection.
Password	Identifies the password assigned to the user trying to establish the database connection.

Thus, in order for a user whose authentication ID is "db2user" and whose password is "ibmdb2" to establish a connection to a database named SAMPLE, a CONNECT statement that looks something like this would need to be executed:

```
CONNECT TO SAMPLE USER db2user USING ibmdb2
```

And as soon as the CONNECT statement is successfully executed, you might see a message that looks something like this:

```
Database Connection Information

Database server          = DB2/NT 8
SQL authorization ID     = DB2USER
Local database alias     = SAMPLE
```

The CONNECT statement can be executed without specifying a user ID and password (since these are optional parameters). When the CONNECT statement is executed without this information, the DB2 Database Manager will either attempt to use the user ID and password you provided to gain access to the system or prompt you for this information. (Such a connect operation is called an *implicit connect,* as it is implied that the credentials of the current user are to be used; on the other hand, when a user ID and password are specified, the connect operation is called an *explicit connect,* because the required user credentials have been explicitly provided.

Once a database connection has been established, it will remain in effect until it is explicitly terminated or until the application that established the connection ends. Database connections can be explicitly terminated at any time by executing a special form of the CONNECT statement. The syntax for this form of the CONNECT statement is:

```
CONNECT RESET
```

The GRANT statement (revisited)

In Chapter 3, "Security," we saw that authorities and privileges can be explicitly granted to an individual user or a group of users by executing the GRANT SQL statement. Several flavors of the GRANT statement are available, and the appropriate form to use is determined by the database object for which authorities and privileges are to be granted. (Objects for which authorities and privileges can be granted include databases, schemas, tablespaces, tables, indexes, views, packages, routines, sequences, servers, and nicknames.) In general, the basic syntax for the GRANT statement looks something like this:

```
GRANT [Privilege] ON [ObjectType] [ObjectName]
TO [Recipient, ...]
<WITH GRANT OPTION>
```

where:

Privilege	Identifies one or more authorities or privileges to be given to one or more users and/or groups.
ObjectType	Identifies the type of object one or more authorities or privileges are to be granted for.
ObjectName	Identifies the name assigned to the object one or more authorities or privileges are to be granted for.
Recipient	Identifies the name of the user(s) and/or group(s) that are to receive the object privileges specified. The value specified for the this parameter can be any combination of the following:

`USER` [*UserName*]	Identifies a specific user that the privileges specified are to be given to.
`GROUP` [*GroupName*]	Identifies a specific group that the privileges specified are to be given to.
`PUBLIC`	Indicates that the specified privilege(s) are to be given to the special group PUBLIC. (All users are a member of the group PUBLIC).

If the `WITH GRANT OPTION` clause is specified with the `GRANT` statement, the user and/or group receiving the specified privileges is given the ability to grant the newly received privileges (except for the CONTROL privilege) to other users.

For more information about available authorities and privileges, and for examples of how the `GRANT` SQL statement can be used, refer to Chapter 3, "Security."

The `REVOKE` statement (revisited)

Authorities and privileges can be explicitly revoked from an individual user or a group of users by executing the `REVOKE` SQL statement. As with the `GRANT` SQL statement, several flavors of the `REVOKE` statement are available, and the appropriate form to use is determined by the database object for which authorities and privileges are to be revoked. In general, the basic syntax for the `REVOKE` statement looks something like this:

```
REVOKE [Privilege] ON [ObjectType] [ObjectName]
FROM [Forfeiter, ...]
<BY ALL>
```

where:

Privilege	Identifies one or more authorities or privileges to be taken from one or more users and/or groups.
ObjectType	Identifies the type of object one or more authorities or privileges are to be revoked for.
ObjectName	Identifies the name assigned to the object one or more authorities or privileges are to be revoked for.
Forfeiter	Identifies the name of the user(s) and/or group(s) that are to lose DBADM authority or the privileges specified. As with the GRANT statement, the value specified for this parameter can be any combination of the following:

USER [*UserName*]	Identifies a specific user that the privileges specified are to be taken from.
GROUP [*GroupName*]	Identifies a specific group that the privileges specified are to be taken from.
PUBLIC	Indicates that the specified privilege(s) are to be taken from the special group PUBLIC. (All users are a member of the group PUBLIC.)

The BY ALL clause is optional and is provided as a courtesy for administrators who are familiar with the syntax of the DB2 for OS/390 REVOKE SQL statement. Whether it is included or not, the results will always be the same—the privilege(s) specified will be revoked from all users and/or groups specified, regardless of who granted it originally.

Again, for more information about the authorities and privileges available, and for examples of how the REVOKE statement can be used, refer to Chapter 3, "Security."

Data Definition Language (DDL) Statements

When a database is first created, it cannot be used to store data because, aside from the read-only system catalog tables and views that get created by default, no other data objects exist. That's where the Data Definition Language (DDL) statements come into play. The Data Definition Language statements are a set of SQL statements that are used to define and create objects in a database that will be used both to store user data and to improve data access performance. Various forms of CREATE statements and ALTER statements, along with the DROP statement, make up the set of Data Definition Language (DDL) statements available with DB2 UDB.

The CREATE BUFFERPOOL statement

Earlier, we saw that a buffer pool is an area of main memory that has been allocated to the DB2 Database Manager for the purpose of caching table and index data pages as they are read from disk. By default, one buffer pool (named IBMDEFAULTBP) is created for a particular database when that database is first created. On Linux and UNIX platforms, this buffer pool is 1,000 4K (kilobyte) pages in size; on Windows platforms, this buffer pool is 250 4K pages in size. Additional buffer pools can be created by executing the `CREATE BUFFERPOOL` SQL statement. The basic syntax for this statement is:

```
CREATE BUFFERPOOL [BufferPoolName]
<IMMEDIATE | DEFERRED>
SIZE [Size]
<PAGESIZE [PageSize] <K>>
<NOT EXTENDED STORAGE | EXTENDED STORAGE>
```

where:

BufferPoolName	Identifies the name to be assigned to the buffer pool to be created.
Size	Identifies the number of pages (of *PageSize* size) to be allocated for the buffer pool to be created.
PageSize	Specifies the size that each page used by the buffer pool being created is to be. (Valid values include 4096, 8192, 16384, or 32768 bytes—if the suffix K (for kilobytes) is provided, this parameter must be set to 4, 8, 16, or 32.) Unless otherwise specified, pages used by buffer pools are 4K in size. (It is important to note that the page size used by a buffer pool determines what tablespaces can be used with it; a buffer pool can only be used by a tablespace that has a corresponding page size.)

If the `IMMEDIATE` clause is specified with the `CREATE BUFFERPOOL` statement, the buffer pool will be created immediately unless the amount of memory required is not available, in which case a warning message will be generated and the buffer pool creation process will behave as if the `DEFERRED` clause were specified. If the `DEFERRED` clause is specified, the buffer pool will not be created until all connections to the database the buffer pool is to be created for have been terminated. If neither clause is specified, the buffer pool will not be created until all connections to the database the buffer pool is to be created for have been terminated.

So, if you wanted to create a buffer pool that has the name TEMP_BP, consists of 100 pages that are 8 kilobytes in size, and is to be created immediately if enough free memory is available, you could do so by executing a `CREATE BUFFERPOOL` SQL statement that looks something like this:

```
CREATE BUFFERPOOL TEMP_BP
IMMEDIATE
SIZE 100
PAGESIZE 8 K
```

Buffer pools can also be created using the Create Buffer Pool dialog, which can be activated by selecting the appropriate action from the *Buffer Pools* menu found in the Control Center. Figure 5–1 shows the Control Center menu items that must be selected to activate the Create Buffer Pool dialog; Figure 5–2 shows how the Create Buffer Pool dialog might look after its input fields have been populated.

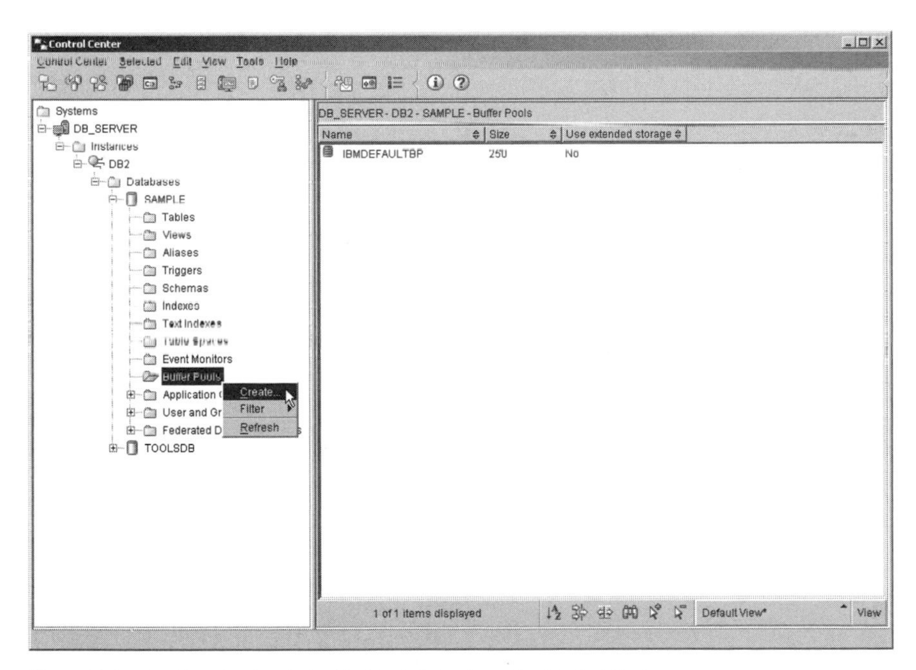

Figure 5–1 Invoking the Create Buffer Pool dialog from the Control Center.

The `CREATE TABLESPACE` statement

As mentioned earlier, tablespaces are used to control where data is physically stored and to provide a layer of indirection between database objects and the directories, files, or raw devices (referred to as containers) in which the data physically resides. Depending upon how it is defined, a tablespace can be

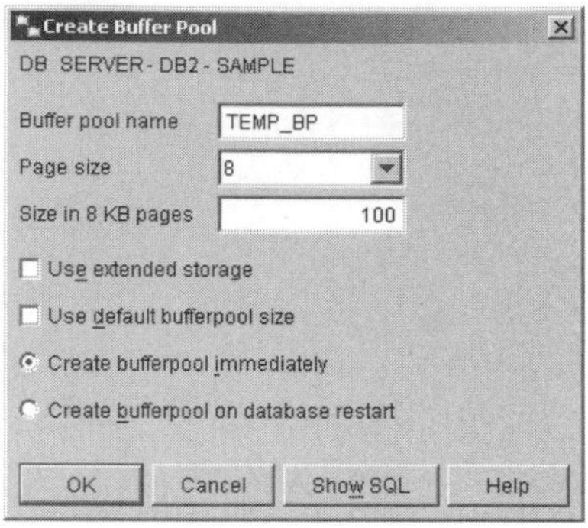

Figure 5–2 The Create Buffer Pool dialog.

either a System Managed Space (SMS) tablespace or a Database Managed Space (DMS) tablespace. With SMS tablespaces, each container used must be a directory that resides within the file space of the operating system, and the operating system's file manager is responsible for managing data storage. With DMS tablespaces, each container used must be either a fixed-size pre-allocated file or a raw device, and the DB2 Database Manager is responsible for managing data storage. By default, three tablespaces (named SYSCAT-SPACE, USERSPACE1, and TEMPSPACE1) are created for a database as part of the database creation process. Additional tablespaces can be created by executing the `CREATE TABLESPACE` SQL statement. The basic syntax for this statement is:

```
CREATE TABLESPACE [TablespaceName]
<PAGESIZE [PageSize] <K>>
MANAGED BY SYSTEM USING
    ( '[Container]' ,... )
<EXTENTSIZE [ExtentPages | ExtentSize <K | M | G>]>
<PREFETCHSIZE [PrefetchPages | PrefetchSize <K | M |
    G>]>
<BUFFERPOOL [BufferPoolName]>
```

or

```
CREATE TABLESPACE [TablespaceName]
<PAGESIZE [PageSize] <K>>
MANAGED BY DATABASE USING
    ( [FILE | DEVICE] '[Container]' [ContainerSize]
,... )
<EXTENTSIZE [ExtentPages | ExtentSize <K | M | G>]>
<PREFETCHSIZE [PrefetchPages | PrefetchSize <K | M |
    G>]>
<BUFFERPOOL [BufferPoolName]>
```

where:

TablespaceName	Identifies the name to be assigned to the tablespace to be created.
PageSize	Specifies the size that each page used by the tablespace being created is to be. (Valid values include 4096, 8192, 16384, or 32768 bytes—if the suffix K (for kilobytes) is provided, this parameter must be set to 4, 8, 16, or 32.) Unless otherwise specified, pages used by tablespaces are 4K in size.
Container	Identifies one or more containers that are to be used to store the data associated with the tablespace to be created. (If multiple containers are used, data is written to each in a round-robin fashion, one extent at a time.)
ContainerSize	Identifies the number of pages (of *PageSize* size) to be stored in the tablespace container specified.
ExtentPages	Identifies the number of pages of data to be written to a single tablespace container before another container will be used.
ExtentSize	Identifies the amount of data to be written to a single tablespace container before another container will be used. The value specified for this parameter is treated as the total number of bytes, unless the letter K (for kilobytes), M (for megabytes), or G (for gigabytes) is also specified. (If an *ExtentSize* value is specified, it is converted to an *ExtentPages* value using the *PageSize* value provided.)
PrefetchPages	Identifies the number of pages of data to be read from the tablespace when data prefetching is performed (prefetching allows data needed by a query to be read before it is referenced so that the query spends less time waiting for I/O).
PrefetchSize	Identifies the amount of data to be read from the tablespace when data prefetching is performed. The value specified for this parameter is treated as the total number of bytes, unless the letter K (for kilobytes), M (for megabytes), or G (for gigabytes) is also specified. (If a *PrefetchSize* value is specified, it is converted to a *PrefetchPages* value using the *PageSize* value provided.)

BufferPoolName	Identifies the name of the buffer pool to be used by the tablespace to be created. (The page size of the buffer pool specified must match the page size of the tablespace to be created, or the CREATE TABLESPACE statement will fail.)

If the MANAGED BY SYSTEM version of this statement is executed, the resulting tablespace will be an SMS tablespace. On the other hand, if the MANAGED BY DATABASE version is executed, the resulting tablespace will be a DMS tablespace. Furthermore, if an SMS tablespace is to be created, only existing directories can be used as that tablespace's storage container(s), and if a DMS tablespace is to be created, only fixed-size preallocated files or physical raw devices can be used as that tablespace's storage container(s).

The size of each container assigned to a single tablespace can differ; however, optimal performance is achieved when all containers used are the same size.

Thus, if you wanted to create a DMS tablespace that has the name PAYROLL_TS, consists of pages that are 8 kilobytes in size, uses the file DMS_TBS, which is 1000 megabytes in size and resides in the directory C:\TABLESPACES as its storage container, and uses the buffer pool PAYROLL_BP, you could do so by executing a CREATE TABLESPACE SQL statement that looks something like this:

```
CREATE TABLESPACE PAYROLL_TS
PAGESIZE 8K
MANAGED BY DATABASE USING
   (FILE 'C:\TABLESPACES\DMS_TBSP.TSF', 100 M)
BUFFERPOOL PAYROLL_BP
```

Tablespaces can also be created using the Create Table Space Wizard, which can be activated by selecting the appropriate action from the *Table Spaces* menu found in the Control Center. Figure 5–3 shows the Control Center menu items that must be selected to activate the Create Table Space Wizard; Figure 5–4 shows how the first page of the Create Table Space Wizard might look after its input fields have been populated.

The ALTER TABLESPACE statement

Because SMS tablespaces rely on the operating system for physical storage space management, they rarely need to be modified after they have been successfully created. DMS tablespaces, on the other hand, have to be monitored closely to ensure that the fixed-size preallocated file(s) or physical raw device(s) that they

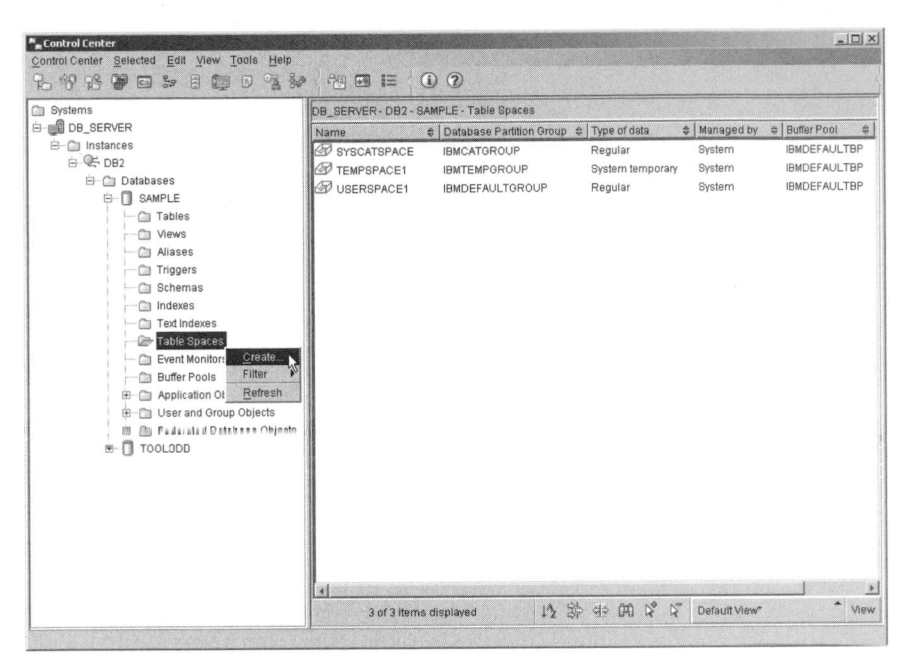

Figure 5–3 Invoking the Create Table Space Wizard from the Control Center.

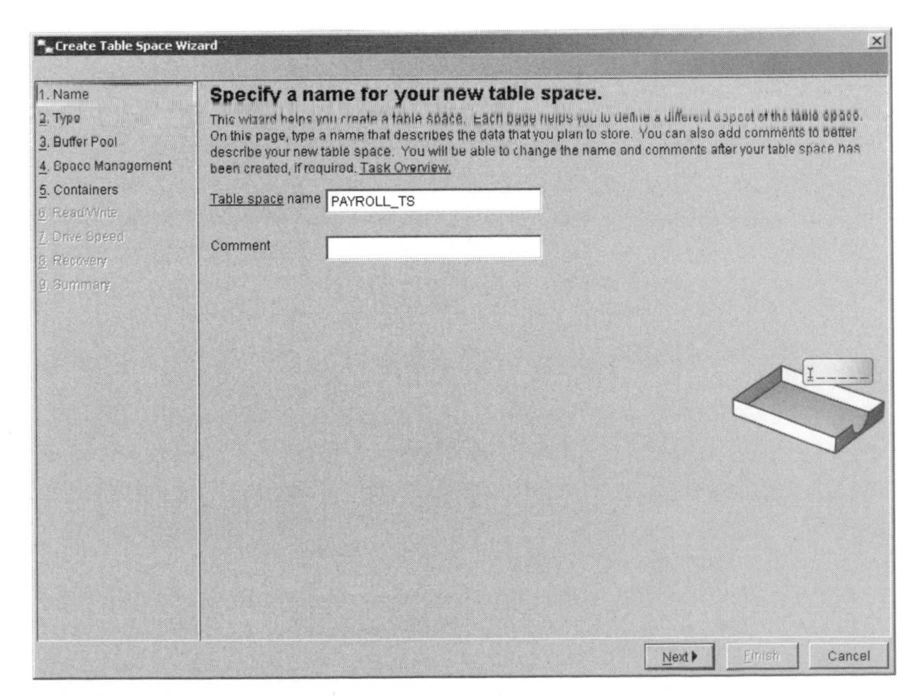

Figure 5–4 The first page of the Create Table Space Wizard.

use for storage always have enough free space available to meet the database's needs. When the amount of free storage space available to a DMS tablespace becomes dangerously low (typically less than 10 percent), more free space can be added either by increasing the size of one or more of its containers or by making one or more new containers available to it. Existing tablespace containers can be resized, new containers can be made available to an existing tablespace, and an existing tablespace's properties can be altered by executing the ALTER TABLESPACE SQL statement. The basic syntax for this statement is:

```
ALTER TABLESPACE [TablespaceName]
ADD ( [FILE | DEVICE] '[Container]' [ContainerSize]
   ,... )
```

or

```
ALTER TABLESPACE [TablespaceName]
DROP ( [FILE | DEVICE] '[Container]' ,... )
```

or

```
ALTER TABLESPACE [TablespaceName]
[EXTEND | REDUCE | RESIZE]
   ( [FILE | DEVICE] '[Container]' ,... )
```

or

```
ALTER TABLESPACE [TablespaceName]
<PREFETCHSIZE [PrefetchPages | PrefetchSize <K | M |
   G>]>
<BUFFERPOOL [BufferPoolName]>
<DROPPED TABLE RECOVERY [ON | OFF]>
```

where:

TablespaceName	Identifies the name assigned to the tablespace to be altered.
Container	Identifies one or more containers that are to be used to store the data associated with the tablespace to be altered.
ContainerSize	Identifies the number of pages to be stored in the tablespace container specified.
PrefetchPages	Identifies the number of pages of data to be read from the tablespace when data prefetching is performed.
PrefetchSize	Identifies the amount of data to be read from the tablespace when data prefetching is performed. The value specified for this parameter is treated as the total number of bytes, unless the letter K (for

kilobytes), M (for megabytes), or G (for gigabytes) is also specified. (If a *PrefetchSize* value is specified, it is converted to a *PrefetchPages* value using the page size of the tablespace being altered.)

BufferPoolName — Identifies the name of the buffer pool to be used by the tablespace to be altered. (The page size of the buffer pool specified must match the page size used by the tablespace to be altered.)

Thus, if you wanted a fixed-size preallocated file named NEWFILE.TSF, which is 1000 megabytes in size and resides in the directory C:\TABLESPACES, to be used as a new storage container for an existing DMS tablespace named PAYROLL_TS, you could make the PAYROLL_TS tablespace use this file as a new storage container by executing an `ALTER TABLESPACE` SQL statement that looks like this:

```
ALTER TABLESPACE PAYROLL_TS
ADD (FILE 'C:\TABLESPACES\NEWFILE.TSF', 100 M)
```

Tablespaces can also be altered using the Alter Table Space dialog, which can be activated by selecting the appropriate action from the *Table Spaces* menu found in the Control Center. Figure 5–5 shows the Control Center menu items that must be selected in order to activate the Alter Table Space dialog; Figure 5–6 shows how the first page of the Alter Table Space dialog might look after its input fields have been populated.

The CREATE TABLE statement

Earlier, we saw that a table is a logical structure used to present data as a collection of unordered rows with a fixed number of columns. Each column contains a set of values of the same data type, and each row contains the actual table data. Because tables are the basic data objects used to store information, many are often created for a single database. Tables are created by executing the `CREATE TABLE` SQL statement. In its simplest form, the syntax for this statement is:

```
CREATE TABLE [TableName]
([ColumnName] [DataType] ,...)
```

where:

TableName — Identifies the name to be assigned to the table to be created. (A table name must be unique within the schema the table is to be defined in.)

ColumnName — Identifies the unique name (within the table definition) to be assigned to the column that is to be created.

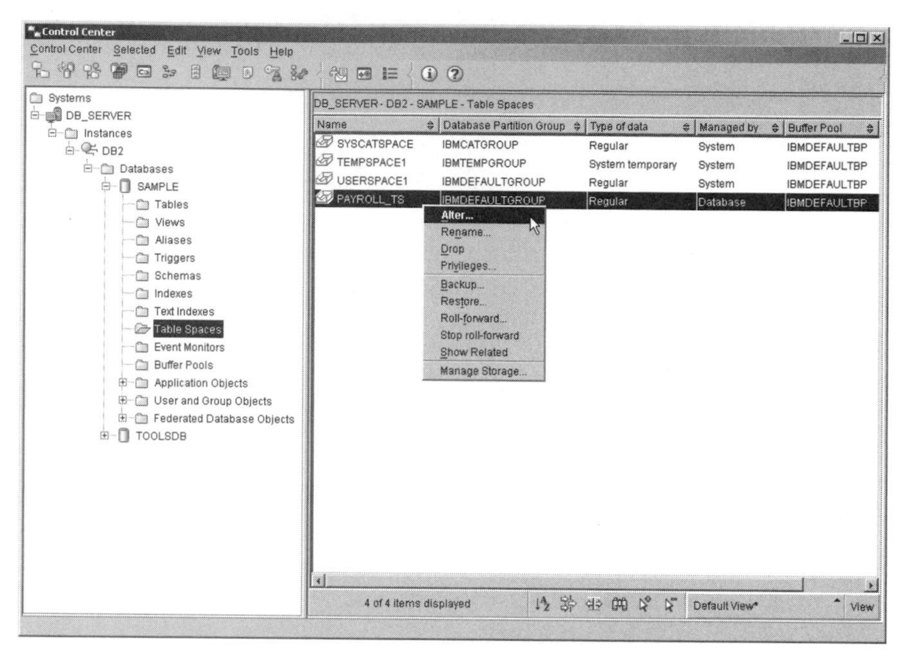

Figure 5–5 Invoking the Alter Table Space dialog from the Control Center.

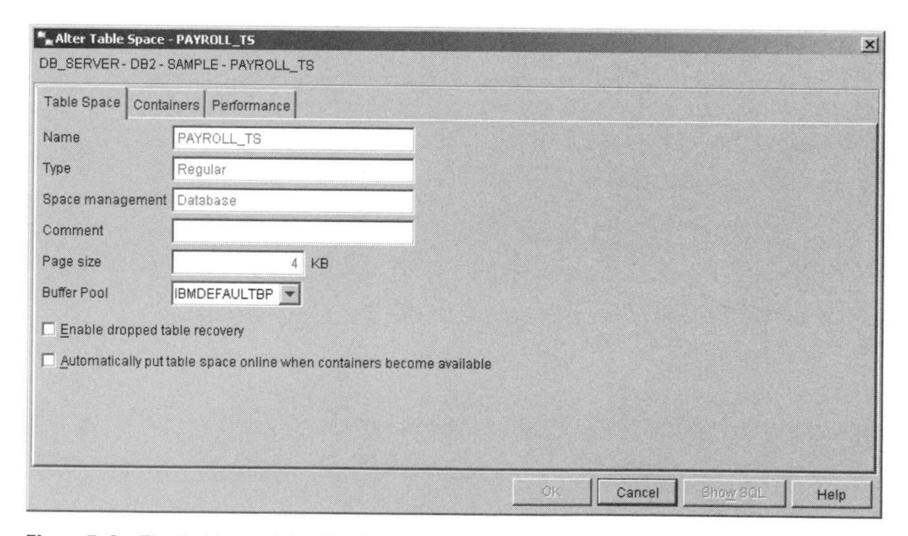

Figure 5–6 The first page of the Alter Table Space dialog.

DataType	Identifies the data type (built-in or user-defined) to be assigned to the column to be created; the data type specified determines the kind of data values that can be stored in the column. (Table 5–1 contains a list of valid data type definitions.)

Table 5–1 Data Type Definitions That Can Be Used with the CREATE TABLE Statement

Definition(s)	Data Type
SMALLINT	Numeric
INTEGER INT	Numeric
BIGINT	Numeric
DECIMAL(*Precision, Scale*) DEC(*Precision, Scale*) NUMERIC(*Precision, Scale*) NUM(*Precision, Scale*) where *Precision* is any number between 1 and 31; *Scale* is any number between 0 and *Precision*	Numeric
REAL FLOAT(*Precision*) where *Precision* is any number between 1 and 24	Numeric
DOUBLE FLOAT(*Precision*) where *Precision* is any number between 25 and 53	Numeric
CHARACTER(*Length*) <FOR BIT DATA>* CHAR(*Length*) <FOR BIT DATA>* where *Length* is any number between 1 and 254	Character/Character string
CHARACTER VARYING(*MaxLength*) <FOR BIT DATA>* CHAR VARYING(*MaxLength*) <FOR BIT DATA>* VARCHAR(*MaxLength*) <FOR BIT DATA>* where *MaxLength* is any number between 1 and 32,672	Character string
LONG VARCHAR	Character string
GRAPHIC(*Length*) where *Length* is any number between 1 and 127	Double-byte character string
VARGRAPHIC(*MaxLength*) where *MaxLength* is any number between 1 and 16,336	Double-byte character string
LONG VARGRAPHIC	Double-byte character string
DATE	Date
TIME	Time
TIMESTAMP	Date and time

(*continued*)

Table 5–1 Data Type Definitions That Can Be Used with the CREATE TABLE Statement *(Continued)*

<table>
<tr><th>Definition(s)</th><th>Data Type</th></tr>
<tr><td>BINARY LARGE OBJECT(Size <K | M | G>)
BLOB(Size <K | M | G>)
where Length is any number between 1 and 2,147,483,647; if K (for kilobyte) is specified, Length is any number between 1 and 2,097,152; if M (for megabyte) is specified, Length is any number between 1 and 2,048; if G (for gigabyte) is specified, Length is any number between 1 and 2.</td><td>Binary</td></tr>
<tr><td>CHARACTER LARGE OBJECT(Size <K | M | G>)
CHAR LARGE OBJECT(Size <K | M | G>)
CLOB(Size <K | M | G>)
where Length is any number between 1 and 2,147,483,647; if K (for kilobyte) is specified, Length is any number between 1 and 2,097,152; if M (for megabyte) is specified, Length is any number between 1 and 2,048; if G (for gigabyte) is specified, Length is any number between 1 and 2.</td><td>Character string</td></tr>
<tr><td>DBCLOB(Size <K | M | G>)
where Length is any number between 1 and 1,073,741,823; if K (for kilobyte) is specified, Length is any number between 1 and 1,048,576; if M (for megabyte) is specified, Length is any number between 1 and 1,024; if G (for gigabyte) is specified, Length is must be 1.</td><td>Double-byte character string</td></tr>
<tr><td colspan="2">*If the FOR BIT DATA option is used with any character string data type definition, the contents of the column the data type is assigned to are treated as binary data.</td></tr>
</table>

Thus, if you wanted to create a table that had three columns in it, two of which are used to store numeric values and one that is used to store character string values, you could do so by executing a CREATE TABLE SQL statement that looks something like this:

```
CREATE TABLE EMPLOYEES
    (EMPID   INTEGER,
     NAME    CHAR(50),
     DEPT    INTEGER)
```

It is important to note that this is an example of a relatively simple table. Table definitions can be quite complex, and as a result, the CREATE TABLE statement has several different permutations. Because the definition for a table object can be so complex, and because the syntax for the CREATE TABLE SQL statement can be complex as well, both are covered in much more detail in Chapter 6, "Working With DB2 UDB Objects." (A detailed description of available data types is presented in Chapter 6 as well.)

Like many of the other database objects available, tables can be created using a GUI tool that is accessible from the Control Center. In this case, the tool is the Create Table Wizard, and it can be activated by selecting the appropriate action from the *Tables* menu found in the Control Center. Figure 5–7 shows the Control Center menu items that must be selected to activate the Create Table Wizard; Figure 5–8 shows how the first page of the Create Table Wizard might look after its input fields have been populated.

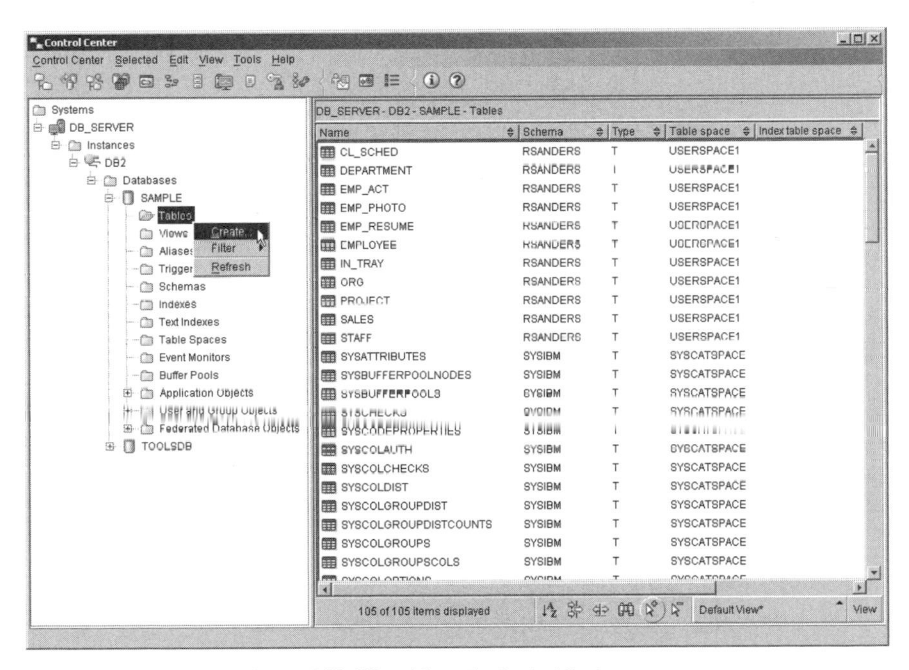

Figure 5–7 Invoking the Create Table Wizard from the Control Center.

The ALTER TABLE statement

Over time, a table may be required to hold additional data values that did not exist or were not considered at the time the table was created. Or character data that was originally thought to be one size may have turned out to be larger than was anticipated. These are just a couple of reasons why it can become necessary to modify an existing table's definition. When the amount of data stored in a table is relatively small, and when the table has few or no

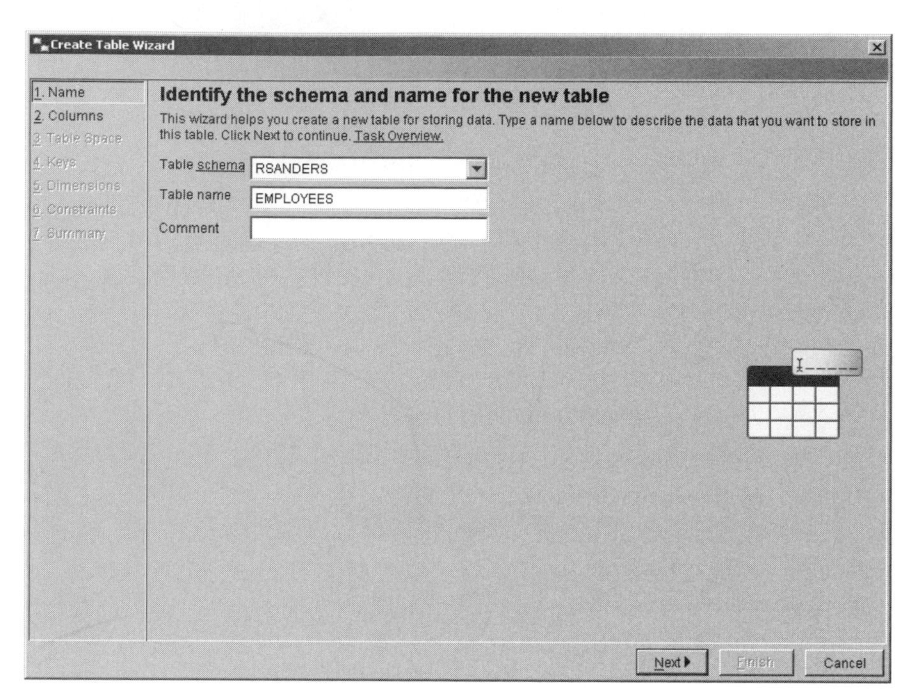

Figure 5–8 The first page of the Create Table Wizard.

dependencies, it is relatively easy to save the associated data, drop the existing table, create a new table incorporating the appropriate modifications, load the previously saved data into the new table, and redefine all appropriate dependencies. But how can you make such modifications to a table that holds a large volume of data or has numerous dependency relationships?

Certain properties of an existing table can be changed, additional columns and constraints can be added (constraints are covered in detail in Chapter 6, "Working with DB2 UDB Objects"), existing constraints can be removed, and the length of varying-length character data type values allowed for a particular column can be increased by executing the `ALTER TABLE` SQL statement. Like the `CREATE TABLE` statement, the `ALTER TABLE` statement can be quite complex. However, in its simplest form, the syntax for the `ALTER TABLE` statement is:

```
ALTER TABLE [TableName] ADD [Element ,...]
```

or

```
ALTER TABLE [TableName]
ALTER COLUMN [ColumnName]
SET DATA TYPE
    [VARCHAR | CHARACTER VARYING | CHAR VARYING] ([Length])
```

or

```
ALTER TABLE [TableName]
DROP [PRIMARY KEY |
      FOREIGN KEY [ConstraintName] |
      UNIQUE [ConstraintName] |
      CHECK [ConstraintName] |
      CONSTRAINT [ConstraintName]]
```

where:

TableName — Identifies the name assigned to the table whose definition is to be modified.

Element — Identifies one or more columns, unique/primary key constraints, referential constraints, and/or check constraints that are to be added to the existing table's definition. The syntax used for defining each of these elements varies according to the element being defined.

ColumnName — Identifies an existing varying-length character column in the table whose size is to be altered.

Length — Identifies the new maximum length that data values can be for the varying-length character column specified. (The new length value provided must be larger than the current length of the column.)

ConstraintName — Identifies an existing unique, foreign key, or check constraint that is to be removed from the table definition.

The basic syntax used to add a new column is:

```
<COLUMN> [ColumnName] [DataType]
<NOT NULL WITH DEFAULT <[DefaultValue] | CURRENT DATE |
    CURRENT TIME | CURRENT TIMESTAMP>>
<UniqueConstraint>
<CheckConstraint>
<ReferentialConstraint>
```

where:

ColumnName — Identifies the unique name to be assigned to the column to be created.

DataType — Identifies the data type (built-in or user-defined) to be assigned to the column to be

	created; the data type specified determines the kind of data values that can be stored in the column. (Table 5–1 contains a list of valid data type definitions).
DefaultValue	Identifies the value to be provided for the column in the event no value is supplied for the column when an insert or update operation is performed against the table.
UniqueConstraint	Identifies a unique or primary key constraint that is to be associated with the column.
CheckConstraint	Identifies a check constraint that is to be associated with the column.
ReferentialConstraint	Identifies a referential constraint that is to be associated with the column.

The ALTER TABLE statement syntax used to add a unique or primary key constraint, a check constraint, and/or a referential constraint as part of a column definition is the same as the syntax used with the more advanced form of the CREATE TABLE statement. This syntax, along with details on how each of these constraints is used, is covered in Chapter 6, "Working with DB2 UDB Objects."

So if you wanted to add two new columns that use a date data type to an existing table named EMPLOYEES, you could do so by executing an ALTER TABLE SQL statement that looks something like this:

```
ALTER TABLE EMPLOYEES
     ADD COLUMN BIRTHDAY  DATE
     ADD COLUMN HIREDATE  DATE
```

On the other hand, if you wanted to change the maximum length of the data value allowed for a varying-length character data type column named DEPTNAME found in a table named DEPARTMENT from 50 to 100, you could do so by executing an ALTER TABLE statement that looks something like this:

```
ALTER TABLE DEPARTMENT
     ALTER COLUMN DEPTNAME SET DATA TYPE VARCHAR(100)
```

As you might imagine, existing tables can also be modified using the Alter Table dialog, which can be activated by selecting the appropriate action from the *Tables* menu found in the Control Center. Figure 5–9 shows the Control Center menu items that must be selected in order to activate the Alter Table dialog; Figure 5–10 shows how the Alter Table dialog might look after its input fields have been populated.

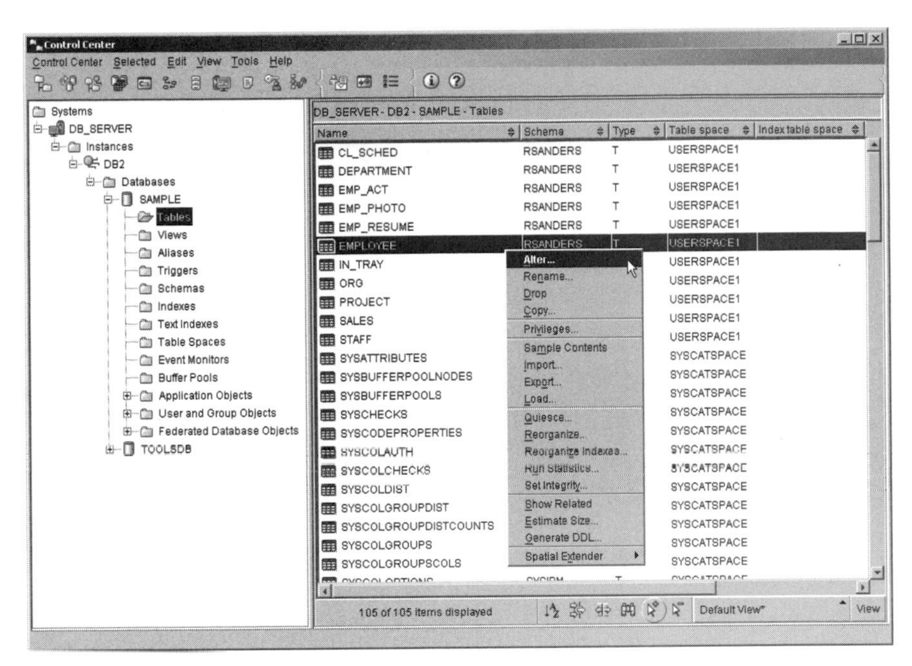

Figure 5–9 Invoking the Alter Table dialog from the Control Center.

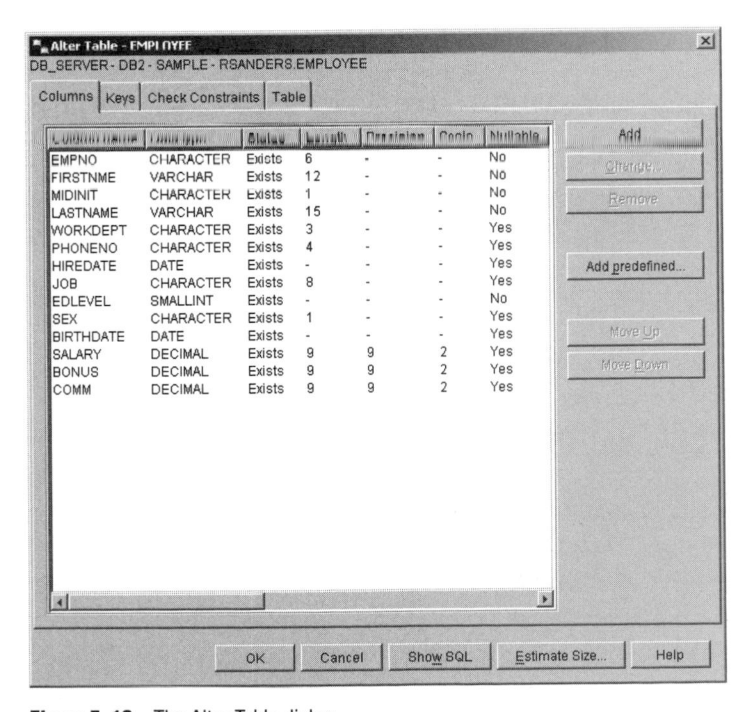

Figure 5–10 The Alter Table dialog.

The `CREATE INDEX` statement

It was mentioned earlier that an index is an object that contains an ordered set of pointers that refer to records stored in a base table. Indexes are important because they:

- Provide a fast, efficient method for locating specific rows of data in very large tables. (In some cases, all the information needed to resolve a query may be found in the index itself, in which case the actual table data does not have to be accessed.)
- Provide a logical ordering of the rows of a table. (When indexes are used, the values of one or more columns can be sorted in ascending or descending order; this property is very beneficial when processing queries that contain `ORDER BY` and `GROUP BY` clauses.)
- Can enforce the uniqueness of records stored in a table.
- Can require a table to use *clustering* storage, which causes the rows of a table to be physically arranged according to the ordering of their index column values. (Although all indexes provide a logical ordering of data, only a clustering index provides a physical ordering of data.)

A clustering index usually increases performance by decreasing the amount of I/O required to access data: When a logical set of rows are physically stored close together, a read operation on the set of rows will require less I/O, because adjacent rows are more likely to be found within the same extent (remember, data pages are written in batches called extents) instead of being widely distributed across multiple extents.

While some indexes are created implicitly to provide support for a table's definition (for example to provide support for a primary key), indexes are typically created explicitly, using the tools provided with DB2 UDB. Indexes can be created by executing the `CREATE INDEX` SQL statement. The basic syntax for this statement is:

```
CREATE <UNIQUE> INDEX [IndexName]
ON [TableName] ( [PriColumnName] <ASC | DESC> ,... )
<INCLUDE ( [SecColumnName] ,... )>
<CLUSTER>
<DISALLOW REVERSE SCANS | ALLOW REVERSE SCANS>
```

where:

IndexName Identifies the name to be assigned to the index to be created.

TableName Identifies the name assigned to the base table that the index to be created is to be associated with.

PriColumnName	Identifies one or more primary columns that are to be part of the index's key. (The combined values of each primary column specified will be used to enforce data uniqueness in the associated base table.)
SecColumnName	Identifies one or more secondary columns whose values are to be stored with the values of the primary columns specified, but are not to be used to enforce data uniqueness.

If the `UNIQUE` clause is specified when the `CREATE INDEX` statement is executed, rows in the table associated with the index to be created must not have two or more occurrences of the same values in the set of columns that make up the index key. If the base table the index is to be created for contains data, this uniqueness is checked when the DB2 Database Manager attempts to create the index specified; once the index has been created, this uniqueness is enforced each time an insert or update operation is performed against the table. In both cases, if the uniqueness of the index key is compromised, the index creation, insert, or update operation will fail, and an error will be generated. It is important to keep in mind that when the `UNIQUE` clause is used, it is possible to have an index key that contains one (and only one) NULL value.

So, if you wanted to create a unique index for a base table named EMPLOYEES that has the following characteristics:

Column Name	Data Type
EMPNO	INTEGER
FNAME	CHAR(20)
LNAME	CHAR(30)
TITLE	CHAR(10)
DEPARTMENT	CHAR(20)
SALARY	DECIMAL(6,2)

such that the index key consists of the column named EMPNO, you could do so by executing a `CREATE INDEX` statement that looks something like this:

```
CREATE INDEX EMPNO_INDX
ON EMPLOYEES (EMPNO)
```

Indexes can also be created using the Create Index dialog, which can be activated by selecting the appropriate action from the *Indexes* menu found in the

Control Center. Figure 5–11 shows the Control Center menu items that must be selected to activate the Create Indexes dialog; Figure 5–12 shows how the Create Indexes dialog might look after its input fields have been populated.

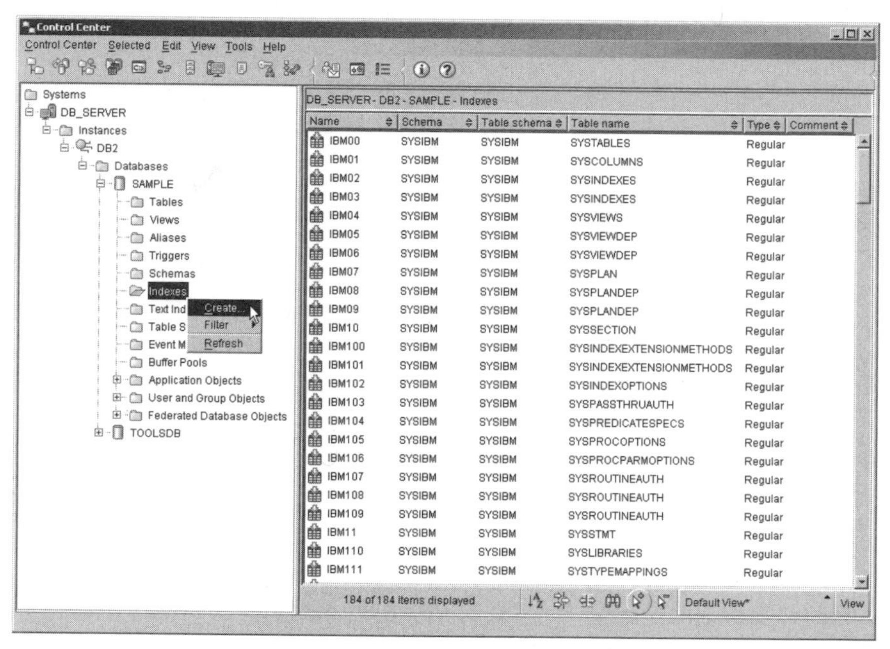

Figure 5–11 Invoking the Create Index dialog from the Control Center.

If an index is created for an empty table, that index will not have any entries stored in it until the table the index is associated with is populated. On the other hand, if an index is created for a table that already contains data, index entries will be generated for the existing data and added to the index as soon as it is created. Any number of indexes can be created for a table, using a wide variety of combinations of columns. However each index comes at a price in both storage requirements and performance: Since each index replicates its key values, and this replication requires additional storage space, and each modification to a table results in a similar modification to all indexes defined on the table, performance can decrease when insert, update, and delete operations are performed. In fact, if a large number of indexes are created for a table that is modified frequently, overall performance will decrease, rather than increase for all operations *except* data retrieval. Tables that are used for data mining, business intelligence, business warehousing, and other applications that execute many (and often complex) queries while rarely modifying data are prime targets for multiple indexes. On the other hand, tables that are

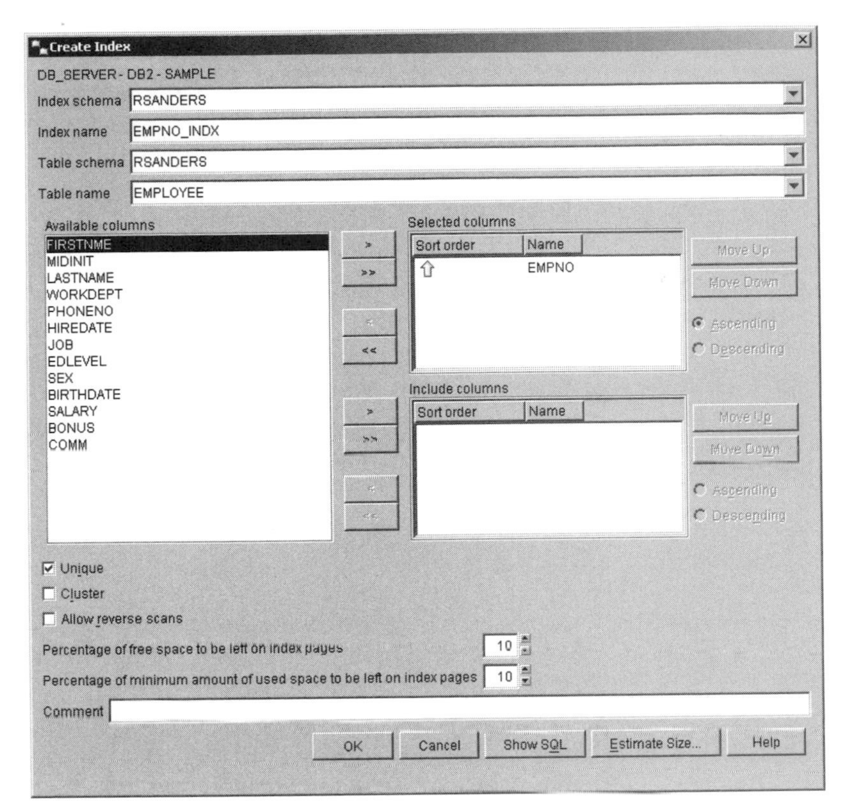

Figure 5–12 The Create Index dialog.

used in OLTP (On-Line Transactional Processing) environments or other environments where data throughput is high should use indexes sparingly.

The `CREATE VIEW` statement

We saw earlier that a view is an object that acts as a named specification of a result data set that is produced each time the view is referenced. A view can be thought of as having columns and rows, just like base tables, and in most cases, data can be retrieved directly from a view in the same way that it can be retrieved from a base table. However, whether a view can be used to insert, update, or delete data depends on how it is defined. (In general, a view can be used in an insert, update, or delete operation if each row in the view can be uniquely mapped onto a single row of a base table.)

Although views look (and often behave) like base tables, they do not have their own physical storage (contrary to indexes, which are also based on base tables); therefore, they do not contain data. Instead, views refer to data that is physically stored in other base tables. And because a view can reference the data stored in any number of columns found in the base table it refers to, views can be used, together with view privileges, to control what data a user can and cannot see. For example, suppose a company has a database that contains a table that has been populated with information about each employee of that company. Managers might work with a view that only allow them to see information about employees they manage, while users in Corporate Communications might work with a view that only allows them to see contact information about each employee, and users in Payroll might work with a view that allows them to see both contact information and salary information. By creating views and coupling them with the view privileges available, a database administrator can have greater control over how individual users access specific pieces of data.

Views can be created by executing the `CREATE VIEW` SQL statement. The basic syntax for this statement is:

```
CREATE VIEW [ViewName]
<( [ColumnName] ,... )>
AS [SELECTStatement]
<WITH CHECK OPTION>
```

where:

ViewName — Identifies the name to be assigned to the view to be created.

ColumnName — Identifies the names of one or more columns that are to be included in the view to be created. If a list of column names is specified, the number of column names provided must match the number of columns that will be returned by the `SELECT` statement used to create the view. (If a list of column names is not provided, the columns of the view will inherit the names that are assigned to the columns returned by the `SELECT` statement used to create the view.)

SELECTStatement — Identifies a `SELECT` SQL statement that, when executed, will produce data that can be seen using the view to be created.

Thus, if you wanted to create a view that references all data stored in a table named DEPARTMENT and assign it the name DEPT_VIEW, you could do so by executing a `CREATE VIEW` SQL statement that looks something like this:

```
CREATE VIEW DEPT_VIEW
AS SELECT * FROM DEPARTMENT
```

On the other hand, if you wanted to create a view that references specific data values stored in the table named DEPARTMENT and assign it the name ADV_DEPT_VIEW, you could do so by executing a `CREATE VIEW` SQL statement that looks something like this:

```
CREATE VIEW ADV_DEPT_VIEW
AS SELECT (DEPT_NO, DEPT_NAME, DEPT_SIZE) FROM DEPARTMENT
WHERE DEPT_SIZE > 25
```

The view created by this statement would only contain department number, department name, and department size information for each department that has more than 25 people in it.

Views can also be created using the Create View dialog, which can be activated by selecting the appropriate action from the *Views* menu found in the Control Center. Figure 5–13 shows the Control Center menu items that must be selected to activate the Create View dialog; Figure 5–14 shows how the Create View dialog might look after its input fields have been populated.

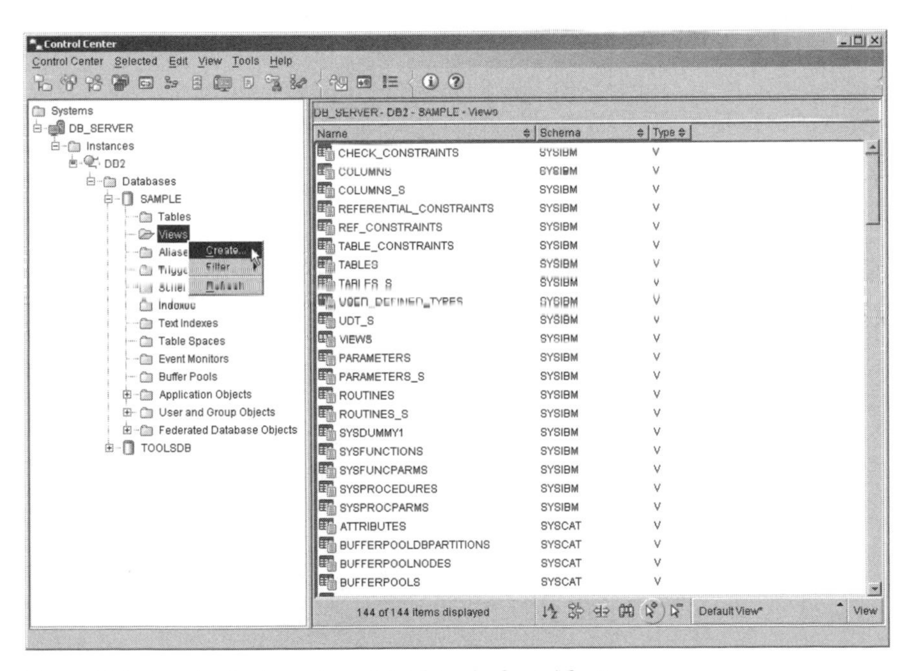

Figure 5–13 Invoking the Create View dialog from the Control Center.

If the `WITH CHECK OPTION` clause of with the `CREATE VIEW` SQL statement is specified, insert and update operations performed against the view that is created are validated to ensure that all rows being inserted into or updated in the base table the view refers to conform to the view's definition

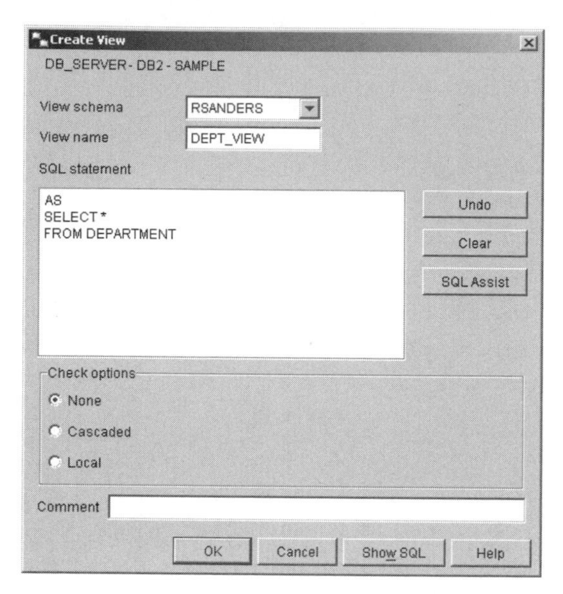

Figure 5–14 The Create View dialog.

(otherwise, the insert/update operation will fail). So what exactly does this mean? Suppose a view was created using the following `CREATE VIEW` statement:

```
CREATE VIEW PRIORITY_ORDERS
AS SELECT * FROM ORDERS WHERE RESPONSE_TIME < 4
WITH CHECK OPTION
```

Now, suppose a user tries to insert a record into this view that has a RESPONSE_TIME value of 6. The insert operation will fail because the record violates the view's definition. Had the view not been created with the `WITH CHECK OPTION` clause, the insert operation would have been successful, even though the new record would not be visible to the view that was used to add it. Figure 5–15 illustrates how the `WITH CHECK OPTION` works.

Views created with the `WITH CHECK OPTION` clause specified are referred to as *symmetric views,* because every record that can be inserted into them can also be retrieved from them.

The `CREATE ALIAS` statement

We saw earlier that an alias is simply an alternate name for a table or view and that once created, aliases can be referenced the same way tables or views can be referenced. By using aliases, SQL statements can be constructed such that they

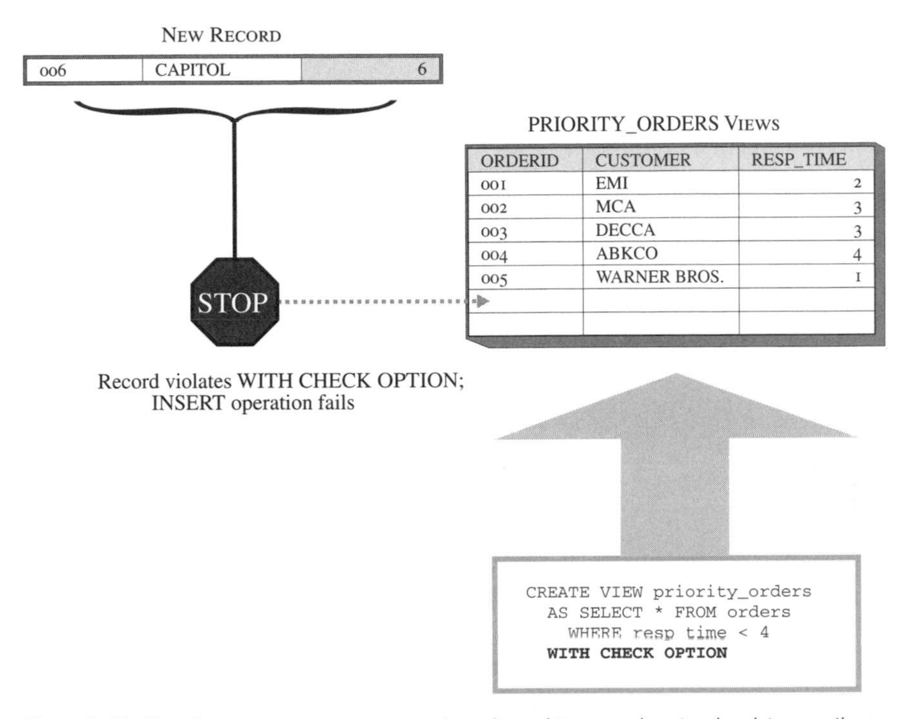

Figure 5–15 How the `WITH CHECK OPTION` clause is used to ensure insert and update operations conform to a view's definition.

are independent of the qualified names that identify the base tables or views they reference. Whenever an alias is used in an SQL statement, the behavior is the same as when the target (source table or view) of the alias is used instead. Therefore, any application that uses an alias to access data can easily be made to work with many different targets. That's because when the target of an alias is changed, no changes to applications that use the alias are necessary.

Aliases can be created by executing the `CREATE ALIAS` SQL statement. The basic syntax for this statement is:

```
CREATE [ALIAS | SYNONYM] [AliasName]
FOR [TableName | ViewName | ExistingAlias]
```

where:

AliasName	Identifies the name to be assigned to the alias to be created.
TableName	Identifies the name assigned to the table the alias to be created is to reference.
ViewName	Identifies the name assigned to the view the alias to be created is to reference.

ExistingAlias Identifies the name assigned to the alias the alias to be created is to reference.

Thus, if you wanted to create an alias that references a table named EMPLOYEES and you wanted to assign it the name EMPINFO, you could do so by executing a `CREATE ALIAS` SQL statement that looks something like this:

```
CREATE ALIAS EMPINFO FOR EMPLOYEES
```

Aliases can also be created using the Create Alias dialog, which can be activated by selecting the appropriate action from the *Alias* menu found in the Control Center. Figure 5–16 shows the Control Center menu items that must be selected to activate the Create Alias dialog; Figure 5–17 shows how the Create Alias dialog might look after its input fields have been populated.

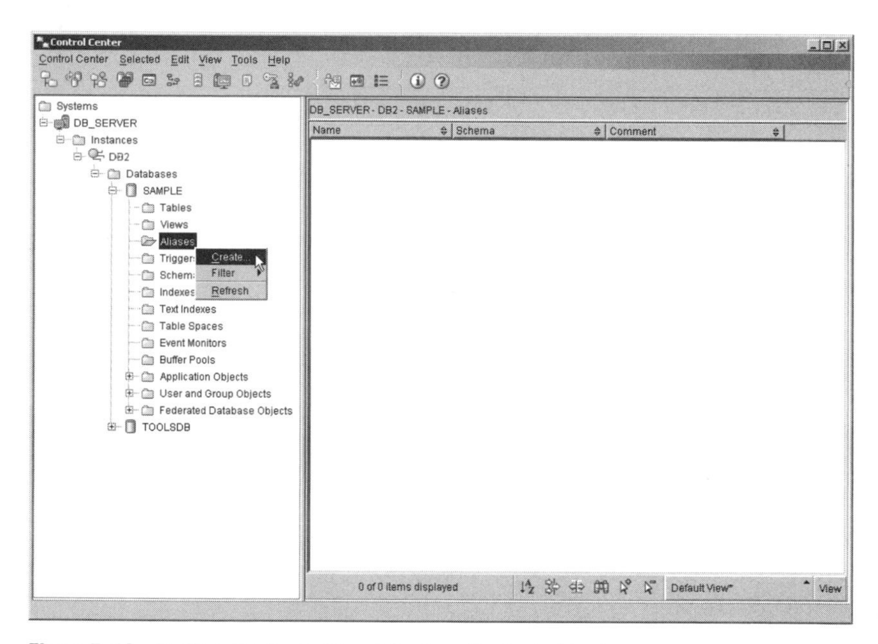

Figure 5–16 Invoking the Create Alias dialog from the Control Center.

Create Alias
DB SERVER - DB2 - SAMPLE
Alias schema RSANDERS
Alias name EMPINFO
Object schema RSANDERS
Object name EMPLOYEES
Comment
OK Cancel Show SQL Help

Figure 5–17 The Create Alias dialog.

The CREATE SCHEMA statement

Earlier, we saw that a schema is an identifier that helps provide a means of classifying or grouping objects stored in a database. And because a schema is an object itself, it can be owned by an individual, who can control access to both the data and the objects that reside within it. Whenever a data object, such as a table, view, or index, is created, it is always assigned, either implicitly or explicitly, to a schema.

Schemas are implicitly created whenever a data object that has been assigned a qualifier name that is different from existing schema names found in the database is created—provided the user creating the object holds IMPLICIT_SCHEMA authority. (If a qualifier is not included as part of the name assigned to an object during the creation process, the authorization ID of the user creating the object is used as the schema, by default.) Schemas can be explicitly created by executing the `CREATE SCHEMA` SQL statement. The basic syntax for this statement is:

```
CREATE SCHEMA [SchemaName]
<SQLStatement ,...>
```

or

```
CREATE SCHEMA AUTHORIZATION [AuthorizationName]
<SQLStatement ,...>
```

or

```
CREATE SCHEMA [SchemaName]
AUTHORIZATION [AuthorizationName]
<SQLStatement ,...>
```

where:

SchemaName	Identifies the name to be assigned to the schema to be created.
AuthorizationName	Identifies the user to be given ownership of the schema to be created.
SQLStatement	Specifies one or more SQL statements that are to be executed together with the `CREATE SCHEMA` statement. (Only the following SQL statements are valid: `CREATE TABLE`, `CREATE VIEW`, `CREATE INDEX`, `COMMENT ON`, and `GRANT`).

If a schema name is specified, but no authorization name is provided, the authorization ID of the user that issued the `CREATE SCHEMA` statement is given ownership of the new schema when it is created; if an authorization name is specified but no schema name is provided, the new schema is assigned the same name as the authorization name used.

So, if you wanted to explicitly create a schema named INVENTORY, along with a table named PARTS that is associated with the schema named INVENTORY, you could do so by executing a `CREATE SCHEMA` SQL statement that looks something like this:

```
CREATE SCHEMA INVENTORY
CREATE TABLE PARTS (PARTNO        INTEGER NOT NULL,
                    DESCRIPTION   VARCHAR(50),
                    QUANTITY      SMALLINT)
```

Schemas can also be created using the Create Schema dialog, which can be activated by selecting the appropriate action from the *Schemas* menu found in the Control Center. Figure 5–18 shows the Control Center menu items that must be selected to activate the Create Schema dialog; Figure 5–19 shows how the Create Schema dialog might look after its input fields have been populated.

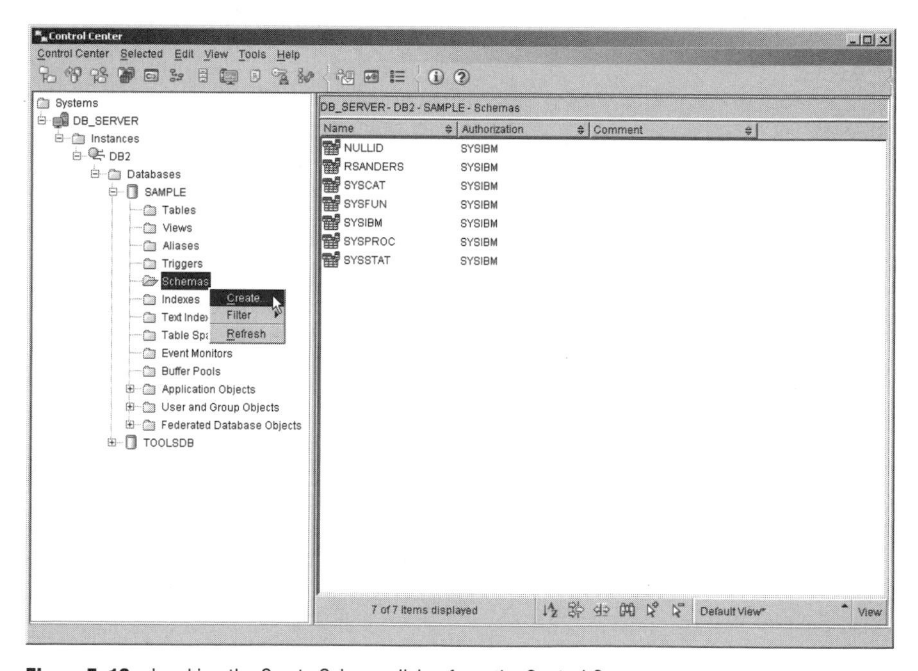

Figure 5–18 Invoking the Create Schema dialog from the Control Center.

Since schemas can be implicitly created by creating an object with a new schema name, you may be wondering why anyone would want to explicitly cre-

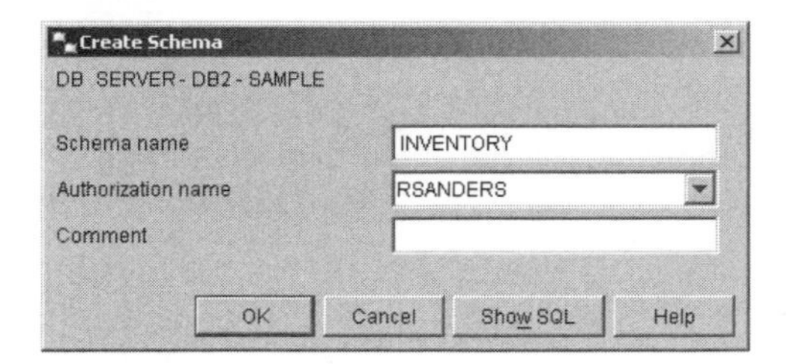

Figure 5–19 The Create Schema dialog.

ate a schema using the CREATE SCHEMA statement or the Create Schema dialog. The primary reason for explicitly creating a schema has to do with access control. An explicitly created schema has an owner, identified either by the authorization ID of the user who executed the CREATE SCHEMA statement or by the authorization ID provided to identify the owner when the schema was created. A schema owner has the authority to create, alter, and drop any object stored in the schema; to drop the schema itself; and to grant these privileges to other users. On the other hand, implicitly created schemas are considered to be owned by the user "SYSIBM." Any user can create an object in an implicitly created schema, and each object in the schema is controlled by the user who created it. Furthermore, only users with System Administrator (SYSADM) or Database Administrator (DBADM) authority are allowed to drop implicitly created schemas. Thus, in order for a user other than a system administrator or database administrator to have complete control over a schema, as well as all data objects stored in it, the schema must be created explicitly.

The CREATE TRIGGER statement

We saw earlier that a trigger is a group of actions that are automatically executed (or "triggered") whenever an insert, update, or delete operation is performed against a particular table. Triggers are often used in conjunction with constraints to enforce data integrity rules. However, triggers can also be used to automatically perform operations on other tables, to automatically generate and/or transform values for new or existing rows, to generate audit trails, and to detect exception conditions. By using triggers, the logic needed to enforce business rules can be placed directly in the database instead of in one or more applications; and by requiring the database to enforce business rules, the need to recode and recompile database applications each time business rules change is eliminated.

Before a trigger can be created, the following components must be identified:

Subject table. The table the trigger is to interact with.

Trigger event. An SQL operation that causes the trigger to be activated whenever it is performed against the subject table. This operation can be an insert operation, an update operation, or a delete operation.

Trigger activation time. Indicates whether the trigger should be activated before or after the trigger event occurs. A *before* trigger will be activated before the trigger event occurs; therefore, it will be able to see new data values before they are inserted into the subject table. An *after* trigger will be activated after the trigger event occurs; therefore, it can only see data values that have already been inserted into the subject table. (A before trigger might be used to trap and process unwanted values, while an after trigger could be used to copy data values entered to other tables or views.)

Set of affected rows. The rows of the subject table that are being inserted, updated, or deleted.

Trigger granularity. Specifies whether the actions the trigger will perform are to be performed once for the entire insert, update, or delete operation or once for every row affected by the insert, update, or delete operation.

Triggered action. An optional search condition and a set of SQL statements that are to be executed whenever the trigger is activated. (If a search condition is specified, the SQL statements will only be executed if the search condition evaluates to true.) If the trigger is a before trigger, the triggered action can include statements that retrieve data, set transition variables, or signal SQL states. If the trigger is an after trigger, the triggered action can include statements that retrieve data, insert records, update records, delete records, or signal SQL states.

Triggered actions can refer to the values in the set of affected rows using what are known as *transition variables.* Transition variables use the names of the columns in the subject table, qualified by a specified name that indicates whether the reference is to the original value (before the insert, update, or delete operation is performed) or the new value (after the insert, update, or delete operation is performed). Another means of referring to values in the set of affected rows is through the use of *transition tables.* Transition tables also use the names of the columns in the subject table, but they allow the complete set of affected rows to be treated as a table. Unfortunately, transition tables can only be used in after triggers.

Once the appropriate trigger components have been identified, a trigger can be created by executing the `CREATE TRIGGER` SQL statement. The basic syntax for this statement is:

```
CREATE TRIGGER [TriggerName]
[NO CASCADE BEFORE | AFTER]
```

```
[INSERT | DELETE | UPDATE <OF [ColumnName], ... >]
ON [TableName]
<REFERENCING [Reference]>
[FOR EACH ROW | FOR EACH STATEMENT]
MODE DB2SQL
<WHEN ( [SearchCondition] )>
[TriggeredAction]
```

where:

TriggerName Identifies the name to be assigned to the trigger to be created.

ColumnName Identifies one or more columns in the subject table of the trigger whose values must be updated before the trigger's triggered action (*TriggeredAction*) will be executed.

Reference Identifies one or more transition variables and/or transition tables that are to be used by the trigger's triggered action (*TriggeredAction*). The syntax used to create transition variables and/or transition tables that are to be used by the trigger's triggered action is:

```
<OLD <AS> [CorrelationName]>
<NEW <AS> [CorrelationName]>
<OLD TABLE <AS> [Identifier]>
<NEW TABLE <AS> [Identifier]>
```

where:

CorrelationName Identifies a name to be used to identify a specific row in the subject table of the trigger, either before it was modified by the trigger's triggered action (`OLD <AS>`) or after it has been modified by the trigger's triggered action (`NEW <AS>`).

Identifier Identifies a name that is to be used to identify a temporary table that contains a set of rows found in the subject table of the trigger, either before they were modified by the trigger's triggered action (`OLD TABLE <AS>`) or after they have been modified by the trigger's triggered action (`NEW TABLE <AS>`).

Each column affected by an activation event (insert, update, or delete operation) can be made

	available to the trigger's triggered action by qualifying the column's name with the appropriate correlation name or table identifier.
SearchCondition	Specifies a search condition that, when evaluated, will return either TRUE, FALSE, or Unknown. This condition is used to determine whether or not the trigger's triggered action (*TriggeredAction*) is to be performed.
TriggeredAction	Identifies the action to be performed when the trigger is activated. The triggered action must consist of one or more SQL statements; when multiple statements are specified, the first statement must be preceded by the keywords `BEGIN ATOMIC`, the last statement must be followed by the keyword `END`, and every statement between these keywords must be terminated with a semicolon (;).

Thus, if you wanted to create a trigger for a base table named EMPLOYEES that has the following characteristics:

Column Name	Data Type
EMPNO	INTEGER
FNAME	CHAR(20)
LNAME	CHAR(30)
TITLE	CHAR(10)
DEPARTMENT	CHAR(20)
SALARY	DECIMAL(6,2)

that will cause the value for the column named EMPNO to be incremented each time a row is added to the table, you could do so by executing a `CREATE TRIGGER` statement that looks something like this:

```
CREATE TRIGGER EMPNO_INC
AFTER INSERT ON EMPLOYEES
FOR EACH ROW
MODE DB2SQL
UPDATE EMPNO SET EMPNO = EMPNO + 1
```

Triggers can also be created using the Create Trigger dialog, which can be activated by selecting the appropriate action from the *Triggers* menu found in the Control Center. Figure 5–20 shows the Control Center menu items that must be selected to activate the Create Trigger dialog; Figure 5–21 shows how the Create Trigger dialog might look after its input fields have been populated.

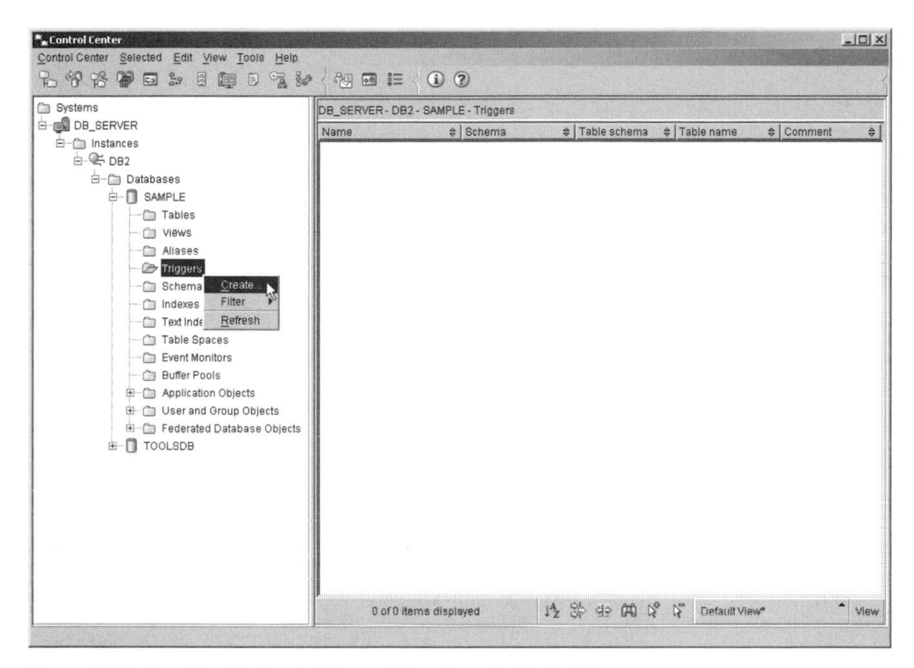

Figure 5–20 Invoking the Create Trigger dialog from the Control Center.

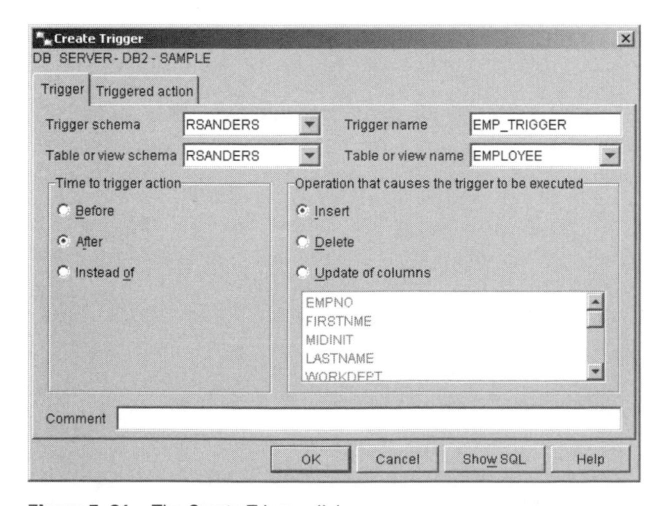

Figure 5–21 The Create Trigger dialog.

The DROP statement

Just as it is important to be able to create and modify objects, it is important to be able to delete an existing object when it is no longer needed. Existing objects can be removed from a database by executing the `DROP` SQL statement. The basic syntax for this statement is:

```
DROP [ObjectType] [ObjectName]
```

where:

ObjectType	Identifies the type of object to be deleted (dropped). (Valid values include: BUFFERPOOL, TABLESPACE, TABLE, INDEX, VIEW, ALIAS, SCHEMA, and TRIGGER.)
ObjectName	Identifies the name assigned to the object to be deleted.

So, if you wanted to delete a table that has been assigned the name SALES, you could do so by executing a `DROP` SQL statement that looks something like this:

```
DROP TABLE SALES
```

Database objects can also be dropped from the Control Center by highlighting the appropriate object and selecting the appropriate action from any object menu found. Figure 5–22 shows the Control Center menu items that must be selected in order to drop a particular object (in this case, a tablespace object).

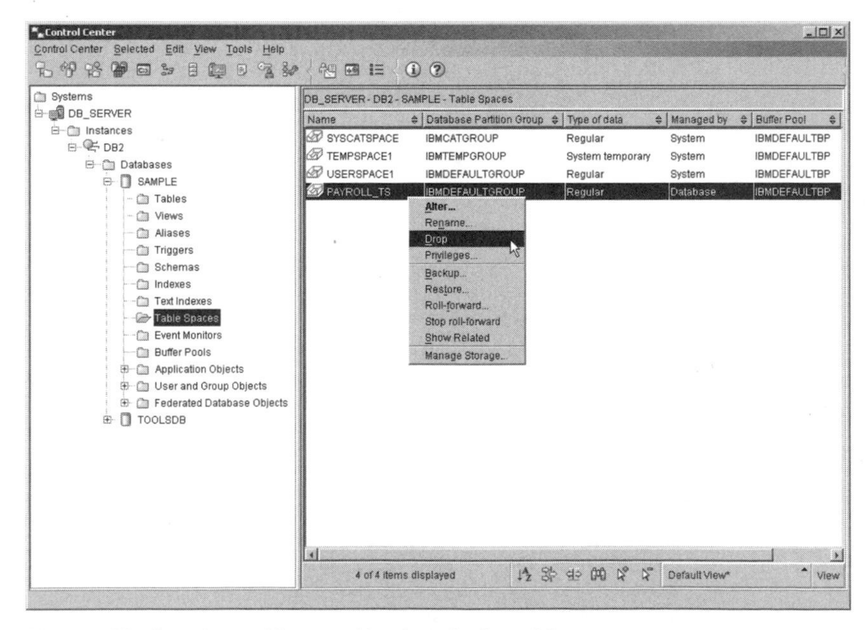

Figure 5–22 Dropping a tablespace object from the Control Center.

It is important to keep in mind that when an object is dropped, its removal may affect other objects that depend upon its existence. In some cases, when an object is dropped, all objects dependent upon that object are dropped as well (for example, if a tablespace containing one or more tables is dropped, all tables that resided in that tablespace, along with their corresponding data, are also dropped). In other cases, an object cannot be dropped if other objects are dependent upon its existence (for example, a schema can only be dropped after all objects that were in that schema have been dropped). And it goes without saying that built-in objects, such as the system catalog tables and views, cannot be dropped.

The rules that govern how objects can be dropped as well as the rules that determine how dependent objects are affected when an object is dropped can be found in the *IBM DB2 Universal Database, Version 8 SQL Reference Volume 2* product documentation.

Data Manipulation Language (DML) Statements

Once the appropriate data objects have been created for a particular database, they can be used to store data values. And just as there is a set of SQL statements that is used to define and create objects, there is a set of SQL statements that is used exclusively to store, modify, remove, and retrieve data values. This set of statements is referred to as Data Manipulation Language (DML) statements. There are four Data Manipulation Language statements available: the `INSERT` statement, the `UPDATE` statement, the `DELETE` statement, and the `SELECT` statement.

The `INSERT` statement

As you might expect, when a table is first created, it is empty. But once a table is created, it can be populated in a variety of ways: It can be bulk-loaded using the LOAD utility, it can be bulk-loaded using the IMPORT utility, or one or more rows can be added to it by executing the `INSERT` SQL statement. Of the three, the `INSERT` statement is the method most commonly used. And it can work directly with the table to be populated or it can work with an updatable view that references the table to be populated. The basic syntax for the `INSERT` statement is:

```
INSERT INTO [TableName | ViewName]
< ( [ColumnName] ,... ) >
VALUES ( [Value] ,...)
```

or

```
INSERT INTO [TableName | ViewName]
< ( [ColumnName] ,... ) >
[SELECTStatement]
```

where:

TableName	Identifies the name assigned to the table data is to be added to.
ViewName	Identifies the name assigned to the updatable view data is to be added to.
ColumnName	Identifies the name of one or more columns that data values being added to the table/view are to be assigned to. Each name provided must identify an existing column in the table or updatable view specified.
Value	Identifies one or more data values that are to be added to the column(s), table, or updatable view specified.
SELECTStatement	Identifies a `SELECT` SQL statement that, when executed, will produce the data values to be added to the column(s), table, or updatable view specified (by retrieving data from other tables and/or views).

So, if you wanted to add a record to a base table named DEPARTMENT that has the following characteristics:

Column Name	Data Type
DEPTNO	INTEGER
DEPTNAME	CHAR(20)
MGRID	INTEGER

you could do so by executing an `INSERT` statement that looks something like this:

```
INSERT INTO DEPARTMENT (DEPTNO, DEPTNAME, MGRID)
VALUES (001, 'SALES', 1001)
```

It is important to note that the number of values provided in the VALUES clause must be equal to the number of column names provided in the column name list. Furthermore, the values provided will be assigned to the columns specified based upon the order in which they appear—in other words, the first value provided will be assigned to the first column identified in the column name list, the second value provided will be assigned to the second column identified, and so on. Each value provided must also be compatible with the data type of the column the value is to be assigned to.

If values are provided for every column found in the table (in the VALUES clause), the column name list can be omitted. In this case, the first value provided will be assigned to the first column found in the table, the second value provided will be assigned to the second column found, and so on. Thus, the row of data that was added to the DEPARTMENT table in the previous example could just as well have been added by executing the following INSERT statement:

```
INSERT INTO DEPARTMENT VALUES (001, 'SALES', 1001)
```

Along with literal values, two special tokens can be used to designate values that are to be assigned to base table columns. The first of these is the DEFAULT token, which is used to assign a system or user-supplied default value to a column defined with the WITH DEFAULT constraint. The second is the NULL token, which is used to assign a NULL value to any column that was not defined with the NOT NULL constraint. (Both of these constraints are covered in detail in Chapter 6, "Working With DB2 UDB Objects.") Thus, you could add a record that contains a NULL value for the MGRID column to the DEPARTMENT table we looked at earlier by executing an INSERT statement that looks something like this:

```
INSERT INTO DEPARTMENT VALUES (001, 'SALES', NULL)
```

By using a special form of the INSERT SQL statement, the results of a query can also be used to provide values for one or more columns in a base table. With this form of the INSERT statement, a SELECT statement (known as a *subselect*) is provided in place of the VALUES clause (we'll look at the SELECT statement shortly), and the results of the SELECT statement are assigned to the appropriate columns. (This form of the INSERT statement creates a type of "cut and paste" action where values are retrieved from one base table or view and inserted into another.) As you might imagine, the number of values returned by the subselect must match the number of columns provided in the column name list (or the number of columns found in the table if no column name list is provided), and the order of assignment is the same as that used when literal values are provided in a VALUES clause. Therefore, you could add a record to the DEPARTMENT table we looked at earlier, using the results of a query, by executing an INSERT statement that looks something like this:

```
INSERT INTO DEPARTMENT (DEPTNO, DEPTNAME)
SELECT DEPTNO, DEPTNAME FROM OLD_DEPARTMENT
```

You may have noticed that the `INSERT` statement used in the last example did not provide values for every column found in the DEPARTMENT table. Just as there are times you may want to insert complete records into a table, there may be times when you wish to insert partial records into a table. Such operations can be performed by listing just the columns you have data values for in the column names list and providing the corresponding values using either the `VALUES` clause or a subselect. However, in order for such an `INSERT` statement to execute correctly, all columns in the table the record is being inserted into that do not appear in the column name list provided must either accept null values or have a default value constraint defined. Otherwise the `INSERT` statement will fail.

The `UPDATE` statement

Data stored in a database is rarely static; over time, the need to modify (or even remove) one or more values residing in a database can arise. In such situations, specific data values can be changed by executing the `UPDATE` SQL statement. The basic syntax for this statement is:

```
UPDATE [TableName | ViewName]
SET [[ColumnName] = [Value] | NULL | DEFAULT ,... ]
<WHERE [Condition]>
```

or

```
UPDATE [TableName | ViewName]
SET ([ColumnName] ,... ) =
    ([Value] | NULL | DEFAULT ,... )
<WHERE [Condition]>
```

or

```
UPDATE [TableName | ViewName]
SET ([ColumnName] ,... ) = ( [SELECTStatement] )
<WHERE [Condition]>
```

where:

TableName — Identifies the name assigned to the table that contains the data to be modified.

ViewName — Identifies the name assigned to the updatable view that contains the data to be modified.

ColumnName — Identifies the name of one or more columns that contain data values to be modified. Each

	name provided must identify an existing column in the table or updatable view specified.
Value	Identifies one or more data values that are to be used to replace existing values found in the column(s) specified.
SELECTStatement	Identifies a SELECT SQL statement that, when executed, will produce the data values to be used to replace existing values found in the column(s) specified (by retrieving data from other tables and/or views).
Condition	Identifies the search criterion that is to be used to locate one or more specific rows whose data values are to be modified. (This condition is coded like the WHERE clause that can be used with a SELECT SQL statement; we will look at the WHERE clause and its predicates later.) If no condition is specified, the update operation will be performed on every row found in the table or updatable view specified.

So, if you wanted to modify the records stored in a base table named EMPLOYEES that has the following characteristics:

Column Name	Data Type
EMPNO	INTEGER
FNAME	CHAR(20)
LNAME	CHAR(30)
TITLE	CHAR(10)
DEPARTMENT	CHAR(20)
SALARY	DECIMAL(6,2)

such that the salary of every employee that has the title of DBA is increased by 10%, you could do so by executing an UPDATE statement that looks something like this:

```
UPDATE EMPLOYEES SET SALARY = SALARY * 1.10
WHERE TITLE = 'DBA'
```

The UPDATE statement can also be used to remove values from nullable columns. This is done by changing the column's current value to NULL. Thus, the value assigned to the DEPARTMENT column of the EMPLOYEES table shown in the previous example could be removed by executing the following UPDATE statement:

```
UPDATE EMPLOYEES SET SALARY = NULL
```

Like the INSERT statement, the UPDATE statement can either work directly with the table that contains the values to be modified or it can work with an updatable view that references the table containing the values to be modified. Similarly, the results of a query, or subselect, can be used to provide values for one or more columns identified in the column name list provided. (This form of the UPDATE statement creates a type of "cut and paste" action where values retrieved from one base table or view are used to modify values stored in another.) As you might imagine, the number of values returned by the subselect must match the number of columns provided in the column name list specified. Thus, you could change the value assigned to the DEPARTMENT columns of each record found in the EMPLOYEES table we looked at earlier, using the results of a query, by executing an UPDATE statement that looks something like this:

```
UPDATE EMPLOYEES SET (DEPARTMENT) =
  (SELECT DEPTNAME FROM DEPARTMENT WHERE DEPTNO = 1)
```

It is important to note that update operations can be conducted in one of two ways: by performing a *searched update* operation or by performing a *positioned update* operation. So far, all of the examples we have looked at have been searched update operations. To perform a positioned update, a cursor must first be created, opened, and positioned on the row that is to be updated. Then, the UPDATE statement that is to be used to modify one or more data values must contain a WHERE CURRENT OF [*CursorName*] clause (*CursorName* identifies the cursor being used—we'll look at cursors shortly). Because of their added complexity, positioned update operations are typically performed by embedded SQL applications.

It is very important that you provide the proper WHERE clause whenever the UPDATE statement is used. Failure to do so will cause an update operation to be performed on every row found in the table or updatable view specified.

The DELETE statement

Although the UPDATE statement can be used to delete individual values from a base table (by setting those values to NULL), it cannot be used to remove entire rows. When one or more rows of data need to be removed from a base table, the DELETE SQL statement must be used instead. As with the INSERT statement and the UPDATE statement, the DELETE statement can either work directly with the table that rows are to be removed from or it can work with an updatable view that references the table that rows are to be removed from. The basic syntax for the `DELETE` statement is:

```
DELETE FROM [TableName | ViewName]
<WHERE [Condition]>
```

where:

TableName — Identifies the name assigned to the table data is to be removed from.

ViewName — Identifies the name assigned to the updatable view data is to be removed from.

Condition — Identifies the search criterion to be used to locate one or more specific rows that are to be removed. (This condition is coded like the `WHERE` clause used with a `SELECT` SQL statement; we will look at the `WHERE` clause and its predicates later.) If no condition is specified, the delete operation will be performed on every row found in the table or updatable view specified.

Therefore, if you wanted to remove every record for company XYZ from a base table named SALES that has the following characteristics:

Column Name	Data Type
PONUMBER	CHAR(10)
COMPANY	CHAR(20)
PURCHASEDATE	DATE
SALESPERSON	INTEGER

you could do so by executing a `DELETE` statement that looks something like this:

```
DELETE FROM SALES
WHERE COMPANY = 'XYZ'
```

Like update operations, delete operations can be conducted in one of two ways: as *searched delete* operations or as a *positioned delete* operations. To perform a positioned delete, a cursor must first be created, opened, and positioned on the row to be deleted. Then, the `DELETE` statement used to remove the row must contain a `WHERE CURRENT OF` [*CursorName*] clause (*CursorName* identifies the cursor being used). Because of their added complexity, positioned delete operations are typically performed by embedded SQL applications.

Because omitting the `WHERE` clause in a `DELETE` SQL statement causes the delete operation to be applied to all rows in the table or view specified, it is important to always provide a `WHERE` clause with a `DELETE` statement unless you explicitly want to erase all data stored in a table.

The `SELECT` statement

Although the primary function of a database is to act as a data repository, a database serves another, equally important purpose. Sooner or later, almost all database users and/or applications have the need to retrieve specific pieces of information (data) from the database they are interacting with. The operation used to retrieve data from a database is called a *query* (because it searches the database to find the answer to some question), and the results returned by a query are typically expressed in one of two forms: either as a single row of data values or as a set of rows of data values, otherwise known as a result data set (or result set). (If no data values that correspond to the query specification provided can be found in the database, an empty result data set will be returned.)

All queries begin with the `SELECT` SQL statement, which is an extremely powerful statement used to construct a wide variety of queries containing an infinite number of variations (using a finite set of rules). And because the `SELECT` statement is recursive, a single `SELECT` statement can derive its output from a successive number of nested `SELECT` statements (which are known as *subqueries*). (We have already seen how `SELECT` statements can be used to provide input to `INSERT` and `UPDATE` statements; `SELECT` statements can be used to provide input to other `SELECT` statements in a similar manner.)

In its simplest form, the syntax for the `SELECT` statement is:

```
SELECT * FROM [ [TableName] | [ViewName] ]
```

where:

TableName	Identifies the name assigned to the table data is to be retrieved from.
ViewName	Identifies the name assigned to the view data is to be retrieved from.

Consequently, if you wanted to retrieve all values stored in a base table named DEPARTMENT, you could do so by executing a `SELECT` statement that looks something like this:

```
SELECT * FROM DEPARTMENT
```

The SELECT Statement and Its Clauses

We just saw that, if you wanted to retrieve all values stored in a base table, you could do so by executing a SELECT statement that looks something like this:

```
SELECT * FROM [TableName]
```

But what if you only wanted to see the values stored in two columns of a table? Or what if you wanted the data retrieved to be ordered alphabetically in ascending order (data is stored in a table in no particular order, and unless otherwise specified, a query only returns data in the order in which it is found)? How do you construct a query using a SELECT SQL statement that only retrieves certain data values and returns those values in a very specific format? You do so by using a more advanced form of the SELECT SQL statement to construct your query. The syntax used to construct more advanced forms of the SELECT SQL statement is:

```
SELECT <DISTINCT>
[* | [Expression] <<AS> [NewColumnName]> ,...]
FROM [[TableName] | [ViewName]
   <<AS> [CorrelationName]> ,...]
<WhereClause>
<GroupByClause>
<HavingClause>
<OrderByClause>
<FetchFirstClause>
```

where:

Expression	Identifies one or more columns values are to be returned for when the SELECT statement is executed. The value specified for this option can be any valid SQL language element; however, corresponding table or view column names are commonly used.
NewColumnName	Identifies a new column name to be used in place of the corresponding table or view column name specified in the result data set returned by the SELECT statement.
TableName	Identifies the name(s) assigned to one or more tables data is to be retrieved from.
ViewName	Identifies the name(s) assigned to one or more views data is to be retrieved from.

CorrelationName	Identifies a shorthand name that can be used when referencing the table or view the correlation name is associated with in any of the SELECT statement clauses.
WhereClause	Identifies a WHERE clause that is to be used with the SELECT statement.
GroupByClause	Identifies a GROUP BY clause that is to be used with the SELECT statement.
HavingClause	Identifies a HAVING clause that is to be used with the SELECT statement.
OrderByClause	Identifies an ORDER BY clause that is to be used with the SELECT statement.
FetchFirstClause	Identifies a FETCH FIRST clause that is to be used with the SELECT statement.

If the DISTINCT clause is specified with the SELECT statement, duplicate rows are removed from the final result data set returned. (Two rows are only considered to be duplicates of one another if each value in the first row is identical to the corresponding value of the second row. For the purpose of determining whether or not two rows are identical, null values are considered equal.) However, if the DISTINCT clause is used, the result data set produced must not contain columns that hold LONG VARCHAR, LONG VARGRAPHIC, DATALINK, BLOB, CLOB, or DBCLOB data.

So if you wanted to retrieve all values for the columns named WORKDEPT and JOB from a table named EMPLOYEES, you could do so by executing a SELECT statement that looks something like this:

```
SELECT WORKDEPT, JOB FROM EMPLOYEES
```

And when this SELECT statement is executed, you might see a result data set that looks something like this:

```
WORKDEPT JOB
-------- --------
A00       PRES
B01       MANAGER
C01       MANAGER
E01       MANAGER
D11       MANAGER
D21       MANAGER
E11       MANAGER
E21       MANAGER
A00       SALESREP
```

```
A00         CLERK
C01         ANALYST
C01         ANALYST
D11         DESIGNER
D11         DESIGNER
D11         DESIGNER
D11         DESIGNER
D11         DESIGNER
D11         DESIGNER
D11         DESIGNER
D11         DESIGNER
D21         CLERK
D21         CLERK
D21         CLERK
D21         CLERK
D21         CLERK
E11         OPERATOR
E11         OPERATOR
E11         OPERATOR
E11         OPERATOR
E21         FIELDREP
E21         FIELDREP
E21         FIELDREP

  32 record(s) selected.
```

On the other hand, if you wanted to retrieve the same data values, but remove all duplicate records found, you could do so by executing the same SELECT statement using the DISTINCT clause. The resulting SELECT statement would look something like this:

```
SELECT DISTINCT WORKDEPT, JOB FROM EMPLOYEES
```

This time, when the SELECT statement is executed you should see a result data set that looks something like this:

```
WORKDEPT JOB
-------- --------
C01       ANALYST
A00       CLERK
D21       CLERK
D11       DESIGNER
E21       FIELDREP
B01       MANAGER
C01       MANAGER
```

```
D11         MANAGER
D21         MANAGER
E01         MANAGER
E11         MANAGER
E21         MANAGER
E11         OPERATOR
A00         PRES
A00         SALESREP

  15 record(s) selected.
```

Now suppose you wanted to retrieve all unique values (no duplicates) for the column named JOB from a table named EMPLOYEES, and you wanted to change the name of the JOB column in the result data set produced to TITLES. You could do so by executing a `SELECT` statement that looks something like this:

```
SELECT DISTINCT JOB AS TITLE FROM EMPLOYEES
```

When this `SELECT` statement is executed, you should see a result set that looks something like this:

```
TITLE
--------
ANALYST
CLERK
DESIGNER
FIELDREP
MANAGER
OPERATOR
PRES
SALESREP

  8 record(s) selected.
```

You could also produce the same result data set by executing the same `SELECT` SQL statement, using the correlation name "EMP" for the table named EMPLOYEES. The only difference is that, the `SELECT` statement would look something like this:

```
SELECT DISTINCT EMP.JOB AS TITLE FROM EMPLOYEES AS EMP
```

Notice that the column named JOB is qualified with the same correlation name assigned to the table named EMPLOYEES. For this example, this is not really necessary, since data is only being retrieved from one table and no two columns in a table can have the same name. However, if data was being retrieved from two or more tables and if columns in different tables had the same name, the qualifier would be needed to tell the DB2 Database Manager which table to retrieve data for that particular column from.

If you were counting when we examined the syntax for the `SELECT` statement earlier, you may have noticed that a single `SELECT` statement can contain up to seven different clauses. These clauses are:

- The `DISTINCT` clause
- The `FROM` clause
- The `WHERE` clause
- The `GROUP BY` clause
- The `HAVING` clause
- The `ORDER BY` clause
- The `FETCH FIRST` clause

(Incidentally, these clauses are processed in the order shown.) We have already seen how the `DISTINCT` clause and the `FROM` clause are used, in the previous `SELECT` statement examples provided. Now let's turn our attention to the other clauses the `SELECT` statement recognizes.

The `WHERE` Clause

The `WHERE` clause is used to tell the DB2 Database Manager how to select the rows that are to be returned in the result data set produced in response to a query. When specified, the `WHERE` clause is followed by a *search condition* which is essentially a simple test that, when applied to a row of data, will evaluate to TRUE, FALSE, or Unknown. If this test evaluates to TRUE, the row is to be returned in the result data set produced; if the test evaluates to FALSE or Unknown, the row is skipped.

The search condition of a `WHERE` clause is made up of one or more predicates that are used to compare the contents of a column with a constant value, the contents of a column with the contents of another column from the same table, or the contents of a column in one table with the contents of a column from another table (just to name a few). DB2 UDB recognizes six common types of `WHERE` clause predicates. They are:

- Relational Predicates (Comparisons)
- `BETWEEN`
- `LIKE`
- `IN`

- EXISTS
- NULL

Each of these predicates can be used alone, or one or more can be combined by using parentheses or Boolean operators such as AND, OR, and NOT.

Relational predicates

The *relational predicates* (or *comparison operators*) consist of a set of special operators used to define a comparison relationship between the contents of a column and a constant value, the contents of two columns from the same table, or the contents of a column in one table with the contents of a column from another table. The following comparison operators are available:

- < (Less than)
- > (Greater than)
- <= (Less than or equal to)
- >= (Greater than or equal to)
- = (Equal to)
- <> (Not equal to)
- NOT (Negation)

Typically, relational predicates are used to include or exclude specific rows from the final result data set produced in response to a query. Thus, if you wanted to retrieve values for the columns named EMPNO and SALARY in a table named EMPLOYEES where the value for the SALARY column is greater than or equal to $40,000.00, you could do so by executing a `SELECT` statement that looks something like this:

```
SELECT EMPNO, SALARY FROM EMPLOYEES
WHERE SALARY >= 40000.00
```

When this `SELECT` statement is executed, you might see a result data set that looks something like this:

```
EMPNO      SALARY
------     -----------
000010     52750.00
000020     41250.00
000050     40175.00
000110     46500.00

  4 record(s) selected.
```

It is important to note that the data types of all items involved in a relational predicate comparison must be compatible or the comparison will fail. If necessary, scalar functions can be used (to make the necessary conversions) in conjunction with the relational predicate to meet this requirement.

The BETWEEN predicate

The `BETWEEN` predicate is used to define a comparison relationship in which contents of a column are checked to see whether or not they fall within a range of values. As with relational predicates, the `BETWEEN` predicate is used to include or exclude specific rows from the result data set produced in response to a query.

So, if you wanted to retrieve values for the columns named EMPNO and SALARY in a table named EMPLOYEES where the value for the SALARY column is greater than or equal to $10,000.00 and less than or equal to $20,000.00, you could do so by executing a `SELECT` statement that looks something like this:

```
SELECT EMPNO, SALARY FROM EMPLOYEES
WHERE SALARY BETWEEN 10000.00 AND 20000.00
```

When this `SELECT` statement is executed, you might see a result data set that looks something like this:

```
EMPNO      SALARY
------     -----------
000210     18270.00
000250     19180.00
000260     17250.00
000290     15340.00
000300     17750.00
000310     15900.00
000320     19950.00

  7 record(s) selected.
```

If the NOT (negation) operator is used in conjunction with the `BETWEEN` predicate (or with any other predicate, for that matter), the meaning of the predicate is reversed. (In the case of the `BETWEEN` predicate, contents of a column are checked, and only values that fall outside the range of values specified are returned to the final result data set produced.) Thus, if you wanted to retrieve values for the columns named EMPNO and SALARY in a table named EMPLOYEES where the value for the SALARY column is less than $10,000.00 and more than $30,000.00, you could do so by executing a `SELECT` statement that looks something like this:

```
SELECT EMPNO, SALARY FROM EMPLOYEES
WHERE SALARY NOT BETWEEN 10000.00 AND 30000.00
```

When this SELECT statement is executed, you might see a result data set that looks something like this:

```
EMPNO      SALARY
------     -----------
000010     52750.00
000020     41250.00
000030     38250.00
000050     40175.00
000060     32250.00
000070     36170.00
000110     46500.00

  7 record(s) selected.
```

The LIKE predicate

The LIKE predicate is used to define a comparison relationship in which a character value is checked to see whether or not it contains a specific pattern of characters. The pattern of characters specified can consist of regular alphanumeric characters and/or special metacharacters that DB2 UDB recognizes, which are interpreted as follows:

- The underscore character (_) is treated as a wild card character that stands for any single alphanumeric character.
- The percent character (%) is treated as a wild card character that stands for any sequence of alphanumeric characters.

Thus, if you wanted to retrieve values for the columns named EMPNO and LASTNAME in a table named EMPLOYEES where the value for the LASTNAME column begins with the letter "S", you could do so by executing a SELECT statement that looks something like this:

```
SELECT EMPNO, LASTNAME FROM EMPLOYEES
WHERE LASTNAME LIKE 'S%'
```

And when this SELECT statement is executed, you might see a result data set that looks something like this:

```
EMPNO  LASTNAME
------ ---------------
000060 STERN
000100 SPENSER
000180 SCOUTTEN
```

```
000250 SMITH
000280 SCHNEIDER
000300 SMITH
000310 SETRIGHT

  7 record(s) selected.
```

When using wild card characters, care must be taken to ensure that they are placed in the appropriate location in the pattern string specified. Note that in the previous example, only records for employees whose last name begins with the letter "S" are returned. If the character string pattern specified had been "%S%", records for employees whose last name contains the character "S" (anywhere in the name) would have been returned and the result data set produced might have looked something like this instead:

```
EMPNO  LASTNAME
------ ---------------
000010 HAAS
000020 THOMPSON
000060 STERN
000070 PULASKI
000090 HENDERSON
000100 SPENSER
000110 LUCCHESSI
000140 NICHOLLS
000150 ADAMSON
000170 YOSHIMURA
000180 SCOUTTEN
000210 JONES
000230 JEFFERSON
000250 SMITH
000260 JOHNSON
000280 SCHNEIDER
000300 SMITH
000310 SETRIGHT

  18 record(s) selected.
```

Likewise, you must also be careful about using uppercase and lowercase characters in pattern strings; if the data being examined is stored in a case-sensitive manner, the characters used in a pattern string must match the case that was used to store the data in the column being searched, or no corresponding records will be found.

Although the `LIKE` predicate provides a relatively easy way to search for data values, it should be used with caution; the overhead involved in processing a `LIKE` predicate is very high and can be extremely resource-intensive.

The `IN` predicate

The `IN` predicate is used to define a comparison relationship in which a value is checked to see whether or not it matches a value in a finite set of values. This finite set of values can consist of one or more literal values that are coded directly in the `SELECT` statement, or it can be composed of the non-null values found in the result data set generated by a second `SELECT` statement (otherwise known as a *subquery*).

Subqueries usually appear within the search condition of a `WHERE` clause or a `HAVING` clause (subqueries can also be used with insert, update, and delete operations). A subquery may include search conditions of its own, and these search conditions may in turn include their own subqueries. When such "nested" subqueries are processed, the DB2 Database Manager executes the innermost query first and uses the results to execute the next outer query, and so on until all nested queries have been processed.

Thus, if you wanted to retrieve values for the columns named EMPNO and WORKDEPT in a table named EMPLOYEES where the value for the WORKDEPT column matches a value in a list of department codes, you could do so by executing a `SELECT` statement that looks something like this:

```
SELECT LASTNAME, WORKDEPT FROM EMPLOYEES
WHERE WORKDEPT IN ('E11', 'E21')
```

When this `SELECT` statement is executed, you might see a result data set that looks something like this:

```
LASTNAME        WORKDEPT
--------------- --------
HENDERSON       E11
SPENSER         E21
SCHNEIDER       E11
PARKER          E11
SMITH           E11
SETRIGHT        E11
MEHTA           E21
LEE             E21
GOUNOT          E21

  9 record(s) selected.
```

Assuming we don't know that the values 'E11' and 'E21' have been assigned to the departments named "OPERATIONS" and "SOFTWARE SUPPORT" but we do know that department names and numbers are stored in a table named DEPARTMENTS (for normalization) that has two columns named DEPNO and DEPNAME, we could produce the same result data set by executing a `SELECT` statement that looks like this:

```
SELECT LASTNAME, WORKDEPT FROM EMPLOYEES
WHERE WORKDEPT IN (SELECT DEPTNO FROM DEPARTMENTS
                   WHERE DEPTNAME = 'OPERATIONS' OR
                   DEPTNO = 'SOFTWARE SUPPORT')
```

In this case, the subquery `SELECT DEPTNO FROM DEPARTMENTS WHERE DEPTNAME = 'OPERATIONS' OR DEPTNO = 'SOFTWARE SUPPORT'` produces a result data set that contains the values 'E11' and 'E21', and the main query evaluates each value found in the WORKDEPT column of the EMPLOYEES table to determine whether or not it matches one of the values in the result data set produced by the subquery.

The `EXISTS` predicate

The `EXISTS` predicate is used to determine whether or not a particular value exists in a given table. The `EXISTS` predicate is always followed by a subquery, and it returns either TRUE or FALSE to indicate whether a specific value is found in the result data set produced by the subquery. Thus, if you wanted to find out which values found in the column named DEPTNO in a table named DEPARTMENT are used in the column named WORKDEPT found in a table named EMPLOYEES, you could do so by executing a `SELECT` statement that looks something like this:

```
SELECT DEPTNO, DEPTNAME FROM DEPARTMENT
WHERE EXISTS
     (SELECT WORKDEPT FROM EMPLOYEES
      WHERE WORKDEPT = DEPTNO)
```

When this `SELECT` statement is executed, you might see a result data set that looks something like this:

```
DEPTNO DEPTNAME
------ -----------------------------
A00    SPIFFY COMPUTER SERVICE DIV.
B01    PLANNING
C01    INFORMATION CENTER
D11    MANUFACTURING SYSTEMS
D21    ADMINISTRATION SYSTEMS
E01    SUPPORT SERVICES
```

```
E11      OPERATIONS
E21      SOFTWARE SUPPORT

  8 record(s) selected.
```

In most situations, EXISTS predicates are AND-ed with other predicates to determine final row selection.

The NULL predicate

The NULL predicate is used to determine whether or not a particular value is a NULL value. Therefore, if you wanted to retrieve values for the columns named FIRSTNAME, MIDINIT, and LASTNAME in a table named EMPLOYEES where the value for the MIDINIT column is a NULL value, you could do so by executing a SELECT statement that looks something like this:

```
SELECT FIRSTNME, MIDINIT, LASTNAME FROM EMPLOYEES
WHERE MIDINIT IS NULL
```

When this SELECT statement is executed, you might see a result data set that looks something like this:

```
FIRSTNME     MIDINIT LASTNAME
------------ ------- ---------------
SEAN            -      O'CONNELL
BRUCE           -      ADAMSON
DAVID           -      BROWN
WING            -      LEE

  4 record(s) selected.
```

When using the NULL predicate, it is important to keep in mind that NULL, zero (0), and blank (" ") are not the same value. NULL is a special marker that is used to represent missing information, while zero and blank (empty string) are actual values that can be stored in a column to indicate a specific value (or lack thereof). Furthermore, some columns accept NULL values, while other columns do not, depending upon their definition. So, before writing SQL statements that check for NULL values, make sure that the NULL value is supported by the column(s) being specified.

The GROUP BY Clause

The GROUP BY clause is used to tell the DB2 Database Manager how to organize the rows of data returned in the result data set produced in response to a query. In its simplest form, the GROUP BY clause is followed by a grouping expression that is usually one or more column names (that correspond to column names found in the result data set to be organized by the GROUP BY clause). The GROUP BY clause is also used to specify what columns are to be grouped together to provide input to aggregate functions such as SUM() and AVG().

Thus, if you wanted to obtain the average salary for all departments found in the column named DEPTNAME in a table named DEPARTMENTS using salary information stored in a table named EMPLOYEES, and you wanted to organize the data retrieved by department, you could do so by executing a SELECT statement that looks something like this:

```
SELECT DEPTNAME, AVG(SALARY) AS AVG_SALARY
FROM DEPARTMENT D, EMPLOYEES E
WHERE E.WORKDEPT = D.DEPTNO
GROUP BY DEPTNAME
```

When this SELECT statement is executed, you might see a result data set that looks something like this:

```
DEPTNAME                              AVG_SALARY
------------------------------       -----------
ADMINISTRATION SYSTEMS                 25153.33
INFORMATION CENTER                     30156.66
MANUFACTURING SYSTEMS                  24677.77
OPERATIONS                             20998.00
PLANNING                               41250.00
SOFTWARE SUPPORT                       23027.50
SPIFFY COMPUTER SERVICE DIV.           42833.33
SUPPORT SERVICES                       40175.00

  8 record(s) selected.
```

In this example, each row in the result data set produced contains the department name and the average salary for individuals who work in that department.

A common mistake that is often made when using the GROUP BY clause is the addition of nonaggregate columns to the list of columns that follow the GROUP BY clause. Since grouping is performed by combining all of the nonaggregate columns together into a single concatenated key and breaking whenever that key value changes, extraneous columns can cause unexpected breaks to occur.

The GROUP BY ROLLUP clause

The GROUP BY ROLLUP clause is used to analyze a collection of data in a single (hierarchal) dimension, but at more than one level of detail. For example you could group data by successively larger organizational units, such as team, department, and division, or by successively larger geographical units, such as city, county, state or province, country, and continent. Thus, if you were to execute a SELECT statement that looks something like this:

```
SELECT WORKDEPT AS DEPARTMENT, AVG(SALARY) AS
AVG_SALARY FROM EMPLOYEES
GROUP BY ROLLUP (WORKDEPT)
```

you might see a result data set that looks something like this:

```
DEPARTMENT AVERAGE_SALARY
---------- --------------
-                27303.59
A00              42833.33
B01              41250.00
C01              30156.66
D11              24677.77
D21              25153.33
E01              40175.00
E11              20998.00
E21              23827.50

  9 record(s) selected.
```

This result data set contains average salary information for all employees found in the table named EMPLOYEES regardless of which department they work in (the first line in the result data set returned), as well as average salary information for each department available (the remaining lines in the result data set returned).

In this example, only one expression (known as the *grouping expression*) is specified in the GROUP BY ROLLUP clause (in this case, the grouping expression is WORKDEPT). However, one or more grouping expressions can be specified in a single GROUP BY ROLLUP clause (for example, GROUP BY ROLLUP (WORKDEPT, DIVISION)). When multiple grouping expressions are specified, the DB2 Database Manager groups the data by all grouping expressions used, then by all but the last grouping expression used, and so on. Then, it makes one final grouping that consists of the entire contents of the specified table. In addition, when specifying multiple grouping expressions, it is important to ensure that they are listed in the appropriate order—if one kind of group is logically contained inside another (for example departments within a division), then that group should be listed after the group that it is contained in (i.e., GROUP BY ROLLUP (DEPARTMENTS, DIVISION)), never before.

The GROUP BY CUBE clause

The GROUP BY CUBE clause is used to analyze a collection of data by organizing it into groups in multiple dimensions. Thus, if you were to execute a SELECT statement that looks something like this:

```
SELECT SEX, WORKDEPT, AVG(SALARY) AS AVG_SALARY
FROM EMPLOYEES
GROUP BY CUBE (SEX, WORKDEPT)
```

you might see a result data set that looks something like this:

```
SEX WORKDEPT AVG_SALARY
--- -------- -----------
-   A00       42833.33
-   B01       41250.00
-   C01       30156.66
-   D11       24677.77
-   D21       25153.33
-   E01       40175.00
-   E11       20998.00
-   E21       23827.50
-   -         27303.59
F   -         28411.53
M   -         26545.52
F   A00       52750.00
F   C01       30156.66
F   D11       24476.66
F   D21       26933.33
F   E11       23966.66
M   A00       37875.00
M   B01       41250.00
M   D11       24778.33
M   D21       23373.33
M   E01       40175.00
M   E11       16545.00
M   E21       23827.50

  23 record(s) selected.
```

This result set contains average salary information for each department found in the table named EMPLOYEES (the lines that contain a null value in the SEX column and a value in the WORKDEPT column of the result data set returned), average salary information for all employees found in the table named EMPLOYEES regardless of which department they work in (the line that contains a NULL value for both the SEX and the WORKDEPT column of the result data set returned), average salary information for each sex (the lines that contain a value in the SEX column and a NULL value in the WORKDEPT column of the result data set returned), and average salary information for each sex in each department available (the remaining lines in the result data set returned).

In other words, the data in the result data set produced is grouped:

- By department only
- By sex only
- By sex and department
- As a single group that contains all sexes and all departments.

The term CUBE is intended to suggest that data is being analyzed in more than one dimension. And as you can see in the previous example, data analysis was actually performed in two dimensions, which resulted in four types of groupings. If the `SELECT` statement:

```
SELECT SEX, WORKDEPT, JOB, AVG(SALARY) AS AVG_SALARY
FROM EMPLOYEES
GROUP BY CUBE (SEX, WORKDEPT, JOB)
```

had been used instead, data analysis would have been performed in three dimensions, and the data would have been broken into eight types of groupings. Thus, the number of types of groups produced by a CUBE operation can be determined by the formula: 2^n where n is the number of expressions used in the `GROUP BY CUBE` clause.

The `HAVING` Clause

The `HAVING` clause is used to apply further selection criteria to columns referenced in a `GROUP BY` clause. This clause behaves like the `WHERE` clause, except that it refers to data that has already been grouped by a `GROUP BY` clause (the `HAVING` clause is used to tell the DB2 Database Manager how to select the rows to be returned in a result data set from rows that have already been grouped). And like the `WHERE` clause, the `HAVING` clause is followed by a search condition that acts as a simple test that, when applied to a row of data, will evaluate to TRUE, FALSE, or Unknown. If this test evaluates to TRUE, the row is to be returned in the result data set produced; if the test evaluates to FALSE or Unknown, the row is skipped. In addition, the search condition of a HAVING clause can consist of the same predicates that are recognized by the WHERE clause.

Thus, if you wanted to obtain the average salary for all departments found in the column named DEPTNAME in a table named DEPARTMENTS using salary information stored in a table named EMPLOYEES, and you wanted to organize the data retrieved by department, but you are only interested in departments whose average salary is greater than $30,000.00, you could do so by executing a SELECT statement that looks something like this:

```
SELECT DEPTNAME, AVG(SALARY) AS AVG_SALARY
FROM DEPARTMENT D, EMPLOYEES E
WHERE E.WORKDEPT = D.DEPTNO
GROUP BY DEPTNAME
HAVING AVG(SALARY) > 30000.00
```

When this SELECT statement is executed, you might see a result data set that looks something like this:

```
DEPTNAME                       AVG_SALARY
----------------------------- -----------
INFORMATION CENTER             30156.66
PLANNING                       41250.00
SPIFFY COMPUTER SERVICE DIV.   42833.33
SUPPORT SERVICES               40175.00

  4 record(s) selected.
```

In this example, each row in the result data set produced contains the department name for every department whose average salary for individuals working in that department is greater than $30,000.00, along with the actual average salary for each department.

The ORDER BY Clause

The ORDER BY clause is used to tell the DB2 Database Manager how to sort and order the rows that are to be returned in a result data set produced in response to a query. When specified, the ORDER BY clause is followed by the name of the column(s) whose data values are to be sorted. Multiple columns can be used for sorting, and each column used can be ordered in either ascending or descending order. If the keyword ASC follows the column's name, ascending order is used, and if the keyword DESC follows the column name, descending order is used. Furthermore, when more than one column is identified in an ORDER BY clause, the corresponding result data set is sorted by the first column specified (the primary sort), then the sorted data is sorted again by the next column specified, and so on until the data has been sorted by each column specified.

Thus, if you wanted to retrieve values for the columns named LASTNAME, FIRSTNME, and EMPNO in a table named EMPLOYEES where the value for the EMPNO column is greater than '000200', and you wanted the information sorted by LASTNAME followed by FIRSTNME, you could do so by executing a SELECT statement that looks something like this:

```
SELECT LASTNAME, FIRSTNME, EMPNO
FROM EMPLOYEES
WHERE EMPNO > '000200'
ORDER BY LASTNAME ASC, FIRSTNME ASC
```

When this SELECT statement is executed, you might see a result data set that looks something like this:

```
LASTNAME         FIRSTNME     EMPNO
---------------  ------------ ------
GOUNOT           JASON        000340
JEFFERSON        JAMES        000230
JOHNSON          SYBIL        000260
JONES            WILLIAM      000210
LEE              WING         000330
LUTZ             JENNIFER     000220
MARINO           SALVATORE    000240
MEHTA            RAMLAL       000320
PARKER           JOHN         000290
PEREZ            MARIA        000270
SCHNEIDER        ETHEL        000280
SETRIGHT         MAUDE        000310
SMITH            DANIEL       000250
SMITH            PHILIP       000300

  14 record(s) selected.
```

As you can see, the data returned is ordered by employee last names and employee first names (the LASTNAME values are placed in ascending alphabetical order, and the FIRSTNME values are also placed in ascending alphabetical order).

Using the ORDER BY clause is easy if the result data set is comprised entirely of named columns. But what happens if the result data set produced needs to be ordered by a summary column or a result column that cannot be specified by name? Because these types of situations can exist, an integer value that corresponds to a particular column's number can be used in place of the column name with the ORDER BY clause. When integer values are used, the first or leftmost column in the result data set produced is treated as column 1, the next is column 2, and so on. Therefore, you could have produced the same result data set generated earlier by executing a SELECT statement that looks like this:

```
SELECT LASTNAME, FIRSTNME, EMPNO
FROM EMPLOYEES
WHERE EMPNO > '000200'
ORDER BY 1 ASC, 2 ASC
```

It is important to note that even though integer values are primarily used in the ORDER BY clause to specify columns that cannot be specified by name, they can be used in place of any valid column name as well.

The FETCH FIRST Clause

The FETCH FIRST clause is used to limit the number of rows returned to the result data set produced in response to a query. When used, the FETCH FIRST clause is followed by a positive integer value and the words ROWS ONLY. This tells the DB2 Database Manager that the user/application executing the query does not want to see more than *n* number of rows, regardless of how many rows might exist in the result data set that would be produced were the FETCH FIRST clause not specified.

Thus, if you wanted to retrieve the first 10 values for the columns named WORKDEPT and JOB from a table named EMPLOYEES, you could do so by executing a SELECT statement that looks something like this:

```
SELECT WORKDEPT, JOB FROM EMPLOYEES
FETCH FIRST 10 ROWS ONLY
```

And when this SELECT statement is executed, you might see a result data set that looks something like this:

```
WORKDEPT JOB
-------- --------
A00       PRES
B01       MANAGER
C01       MANAGER
```

```
E01         MANAGER
D11         MANAGER
D21         MANAGER
E11         MANAGER
E21         MANAGER
A00         SALESREP
A00         CLERK

  10 record(s) selected.
```

Joining Tables

Most of the examples we have looked at so far have involved only one table. However, one of the more powerful features of the SELECT statement (and the element that makes data normalization possible) is the ability to retrieve data from two or more tables by performing what is known as a join operation. (If you go back through the examples that have been presented so far, you will see an occasional "sneak preview" of a join operation—particularly in the examples provided for the IN predicate and the HAVING and GROUP BY clauses.)

In its simplest form, the syntax for a SELECT statement that performs a join operation is:

```
SELECT * FROM [ [TableName] | [ViewName] ,...]
```

where:

TableName Identifies the name(s) assigned to one or more tables that data is to be retrieved from.

ViewName Identifies the name(s) assigned to one or more views that data is to be retrieved from.

Consequently, if you wanted to retrieve all values stored in a base table named DEPARTMENT and all values stored in a base table named ORG, you could do so by executing a SELECT statement that looks something like this:

```
SELECT * FROM DEPARTMENT, ORG
```

When such a SELECT statement is executed, the result data set produced will contain all possible combinations of the rows found in each table specified (otherwise known as the Cartesian product). Every row in the result data set produced is a row from the first table referenced concatenated with a row from the second table referenced, concatenated in turn with a row from the third table referenced, and so on. The total number of rows found in the result data set produced is the product of the number of rows in all the individual table-references. Thus, if the table named DEPARTMENT in our previous example contains five rows and the table named ORG contains two rows, the result data set produced by the statement `SELECT * FROM DEPARTMENT, ORG` will consist of 10 rows (2 x 5 = 10).

A more common join operation involves collecting data from two or more tables that have one specific column in common and combining the results to create an intermediate result table that contains the values needed to resolve a query. The syntax for a `SELECT` statement that performs this type of join operation is:

```
SELECT
[* | [Expression] <<AS> [NewColumnName]> ,...]
FROM [[TableName] <<AS> [CorrelationName]> ,...]
[JoinCondition]
```

where:

Expression	Identifies one or more columns whose values are to be returned when the `SELECT` statement is executed. The value specified for this option can be any valid SQL language element; however, corresponding table or view column names are commonly used.
NewColumnName	Identifies a new column name that is to be used in place of the corresponding table or view column name specified in the result data set returned by the `SELECT` statement.
TableName	Identifies the name(s) assigned to one or more tables that data is to be retrieved from.
CorrelationName	Identifies a shorthand name that can be used when referencing the table name specified in the *TableName* parameter.
JoinCondition	Identifies the condition to be used to join the tables specified. Typically, this is a `WHERE` clause in which the values of a column in one table are compared with the values of a similar column in another table.

Thus, a simple join operation could be conducted by executing a `SELECT` statement that looks something like this:

```
SELECT LASTNAME, DEPTNAME
FROM EMPLOYEES E, DEPARTMENT D
WHERE E.WORKDEPT = D.DEPTNO
```

And when this SELECT statement is executed, you might see a result data set that looks something like this:

```
LASTNAME        DEPTNAME
--------------- -----------------------------
HAAS            SPIFFY COMPUTER SERVICE DIV.
THOMPSON        PLANNING
KWAN            INFORMATION CENTER
GEYER           SUPPORT SERVICES
STERN           MANUFACTURING SYSTEMS
PULASKI         ADMINISTRATION SYSTEMS
HENDERSON       OPERATIONS
SPENSER         SOFTWARE SUPPORT
LUCCHESSI       SPIFFY COMPUTER SERVICE DIV.
O'CONNELL       SPIFFY COMPUTER SERVICE DIV.
QUINTANA        INFORMATION CENTER
NICHOLLS        INFORMATION CENTER
ADAMSON         MANUFACTURING SYSTEMS
LUTZ            MANUFACTURING SYSTEMS
SMITH           ADMINISTRATION SYSTEMS
PEREZ           ADMINISTRATION SYSTEMS
SCHNEIDER       OPERATIONS
PARKER          OPERATIONS
SETRIGHT        OPERATIONS
MEHTA           SOFTWARE SUPPORT
GOUNOT          SOFTWARE SUPPORT

  21 record(s) selected.
```

This type of join is referred to as an *inner join*. Aside from a Cartesian product, only two types of joins can exist: inner joins and *outer joins*. And as you might imagine, there is a significant difference between the two.

DB2 UDB allows up to 15 tables to be joined by a single SELECT statement.

Inner joins

An inner join is the simplest type of join operation that can be performed. An inner join can be thought of as the cross product of two tables, in which every row in one table that has a corresponding row in another table is combined with that row to produce a new record. This type of join works well as long as every row in the first table has a corresponding row in the second table. However, if this is not the case, the result table produced may be missing rows found in either or both of the tables that were joined. Earlier, we saw the most common `SELECT` statement syntax used to perform an inner join operation. The following syntax can also be used to create a `SELECT` statement that performs an inner join operation:

```
SELECT
[* | [Expression] <<AS> [NewColumnName]> ,...]
FROM [[TableName1] <<AS> [CorrelationName1]>]
<INNER> JOIN
[[TableName2] <<AS> [CorrelationName2]>]
ON [JoinCondition]
```

where:

Expression	Identifies one or more columns whose values are to be returned when the `SELECT` statement is executed. The value specified for this option can be any valid SQL language element; however, corresponding table or view column names are commonly used.
NewColumnName	Identifies a new column name to be used in place of the corresponding table or view column name specified in the result data set returned by the `SELECT` statement.
TableName1	Identifies the name assigned to the first table data is to be retrieved from.
CorrelationName1	Identifies a shorthand name that can be used when referencing the leftmost table of the join operation.
TableName2	Identifies the name assigned to the second table data is to be retrieved from.
CorrelationName2	Identifies a shorthand name that can be used when referencing the rightmost table of the join operation.
JoinCondition	Identifies the condition to be used to join the two specified tables.

Consequently, the same inner join operation we looked at earlier could be conducted by executing a `SELECT` statement that looks something like this:

```
SELECT LASTNAME, DEPTNAME
FROM EMPLOYEES E INNER JOIN DEPARTMENT D
ON E.WORKDEPT = D.DEPTNO
```

Figure 5–23 illustrates how such an inner join operation would work.

EMPLOYEES TABLE

EMPNO	LASTNAME	WORKDEPT
001	JAGGER	A01
002	RICHARDS	M01
003	WOOD	M01
004	WATTS	C01
005	WYMAN	-
006	JONES	S01

DEPARTMENT TABLE

DEPTNO	DEPTNAME
A01	ADMINISTRATIVE
E01	ENGINEERING
M01	MANUFACTURING
S01	MARKETING
S02	SALES
C01	CUSTOMER SUPPORT

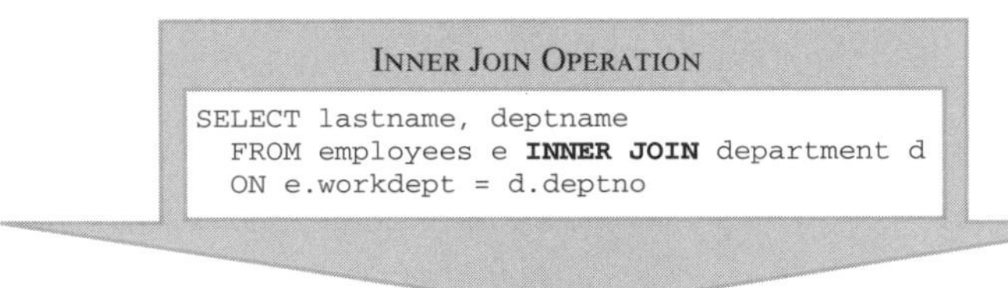
INNER JOIN OPERATION
SELECT lastname, deptname
FROM employees e INNER JOIN department d
ON e.workdept = d.deptno

RESULT DATA SET

LASTNAME	DEPTNAME
JAGGER	ADMINISTRATIVE
RICHARDS	MANUFACTURING
WOOD	MANUFACTURING
WATTS	CUSTOMER SUPPORT
JONES	MARKETING

Record for WYMAN is not in the result data set produced because it has no corresponding DEPTNO value; likewise, records for ENGINEERING and SALES are not in the result data set produced because they have no corresponding WORKDEPT value

Figure 5–23 A simple inner join operation.

Outer joins

Outer joins operations are used when a join operation is needed and any rows that would normally be eliminated by an inner join operation need to be preserved. With DB2 UDB, three types of outer joins are available:

Left outer join. When a left outer join operation is performed, rows that would have been returned by an inner join operation, together with all rows stored in the leftmost table of the join operation (i.e., the table listed first in the OUTER JOIN clause) that would have been eliminated by the inner join operation, are returned in the result data set produced.

Right outer join. When a right outer join operation is performed, rows that would have been returned by an inner join operation, together with all rows stored in the rightmost table of the join operation (i.e., the table listed last in the OUTER JOIN clause) that would have been eliminated by the inner join operation, are returned in the result data set produced.

Full outer join. When a full outer join operation is performed, rows that would have been returned by an inner join operation and all rows stored in both tables of the join operation that would have been eliminated by the inner join operation are returned in the result data set produced.

To understand the basic principles behind an outer join operation, it helps to look at an example. Suppose Table A and Table B are joined by an ordinary inner join operation. Any row in either Table A or Table B that does not have a matching row in the other table (according to the rules of the join condition) is eliminated from the final result data set produced. By contrast, if Table A and Table B are joined by an outer join, any row in either Table A or Table B that does not contain a matching row in the other table is included in the result data set (exactly once), and columns in that row that would have contained matching values from the other table are empty. Thus, an outer join operation adds nonmatching rows to the final result data set produced where an inner join operation excludes them. A left outer join of Table A with Table B preserves all nonmatching rows found in Table A, a right outer join of Table A with Table B preserves all nonmatching rows found in Table B, and a full outer join preserves nonmatching rows found in both Table A and Table B.

The basic syntax for a SELECT statement used to perform an outer join operation is:

```
SELECT
[* | [Expression] <<AS> [NewColumnName]> ,...]
FROM [[TableName1] <<AS> [CorrelationName1]>]
[LEFT | RIGHT | FULL] OUTER JOIN
[[TableName2] <<AS> [CorrelationName2]>]
ON [JoinCondition]
```

where:

Expression	Identifies one or more columns whose values are to be returned when the SELECT statement is executed. The value specified for this option can be any valid SQL language element; however, corresponding table or view column names are commonly used.
NewColumnName	Identifies a new column name that is to be used in place of the corresponding table or view column name specified in the result data set returned by the SELECT statement.
TableName1	Identifies the name assigned to the first table data is to be retrieved from. This table is considered the "left" table in an outer join.
CorrelationName1	Identifies a shorthand name that can be used when referencing the leftmost table of the join operation.
TableName2	Identifies the name assigned to the second table data is to be retrieved from. This table is considered the "right" table in an outer join.
CorrelationName2	Identifies a shorthand name that can be used when referencing the rightmost table of the join operation.
JoinCondition	Identifies the condition to be used to join the two tables specified.

Thus, a simple left outer join operation could be conducted by executing a SELECT statement that looks something like this:

```
SELECT LASTNAME, DEPTNAME
FROM EMPLOYEES E LEFT OUTER JOIN DEPARTMENT D
ON E.WORKDEPT = D.DEPTNO
```

The same query could be used to perform a right outer join operation or a full outer join operation by substituting the keyword RIGHT or FULL for the keyword LEFT. Figure 5–24 illustrates how such a left outer join operation would work; Figure 5–25 illustrates how such a right outer join operation would work; and Figure 5–26 illustrates how such a full join operation would work.

EMPLOYEES TABLE

(Left Table)

EMPNO	LASTNAME	WORKDEPT
001	JAGGER	A01
002	RICHARDS	M01
003	WOOD	M01
004	WATTS	C01
005	WYMAN	-
006	JONES	S01

DEPARTMENT TABLE

(Right Table)

DEPTNO	DEPTNAME
A01	ADMINISTRATIVE
E01	ENGINEERING
M01	MANUFACTURING
S01	MARKETING
S02	SALES
C01	CUSTOMER SUPPORT

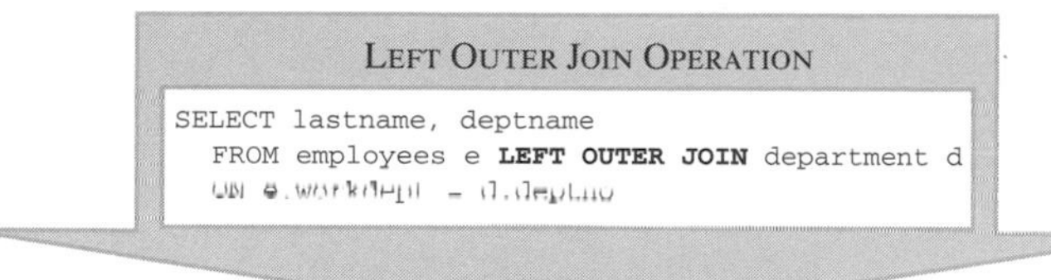
LEFT OUTER JOIN OPERATION
SELECT lastname, deptname
FROM employees e LEFT OUTER JOIN department d
ON e.workdept = d.deptno

RESULT DATA SET

LASTNAME	DEPTNAME
JAGGER	ADMINISTRATIVE
RICHARDS	MANUFACTURING
WOOD	MANUFACTURING
WATTS	CUSTOMER SUPPORT
WYMAN	-
JONES	MARKETING

Record for WYMAN is included in the result data set produced even though it has no corresponding DEPTNO value; however, records for ENGINEERING and SALES are not in the result data set produced because they have no corresponding WORKDEPT value.

Figure 5–24 A simple left outer join operation.

Combining Two or More Queries with a Set Operator

With DB2 UDB, it is possible to combine two or more queries into a single query by using a special operator known as a *set operator*. When a set operator is used, the results of each query executed are combined in a specific manner to produce a single result data set. The following set operators are available:

> **UNION.** When the `UNION` set operator is used, the result data sets produced by each individual query are combined and all duplicate rows are eliminated.

EMPLOYEES TABLE

EMPNO	LASTNAME	WORKDEPT
001	JAGGER	A01
002	RICHARDS	M01
003	WOOD	M01
004	WATTS	C01
005	WYMAN	-
006	JONES	S01

(Left Table)

DEPARTMENT TABLE

DEPTNO	DEPTNAME
A01	ADMINISTRATIVE
E01	ENGINEERING
M01	MANUFACTURING
S01	MARKETING
S02	SALES
C01	CUSTOMER SUPPORT

(Right Table)

RIGHT OUTER JOIN OPERATION

```
SELECT lastname, deptname
 FROM employees e RIGHT OUTER JOIN department d
 ON e.workdept = d.deptno
```

RESULT DATA SET

LASTNAME	DEPTNAME
JAGGER	ADMINISTRATIVE
-	ENGINEERING
RICHARDS	MANUFACTURING
WOOD	MANUFACTURING
JONES	MARKETING
-	SALES
WATTS	CUSTOMER SUPPORT

Record for WYMAN is NOT in the result data set produced because it has no corresponding DEPTNO value; however, records for ENGINEERING and SALES are included in the result data set produced even though they have no corresponding WORKDEPT value

Figure 5–25 A simple right outer join operation.

UNION ALL. When the `UNION ALL` set operator is used, the result data sets produced by each individual query are combined and any duplicate rows found are retained.

EXCEPT. When the `EXCEPT` set operator is used, all duplicate rows found in each result data set produced are eliminated from the result data set of the first query and this modified result data set is returned.

EXCEPT ALL. When the `EXCEPT ALL` set operator is used, all rows found in the first result data set produced that do not have a matching row in the second result data set are returned.

INTERSECT. When the `INTERSECT` set operator is used, the result data sets produced by each individual query are compared, and every record that is found in both result data sets is copied to a new

EMPLOYEES TABLE

EMPNO	LASTNAME	WORKDEPT
001	JAGGER	A01
002	RICHARDS	M01
003	WOOD	M01
004	WATTS	C01
005	WYMAN	-
006	JONES	S01

(Left Table)

DEPARTMENT TABLE

DEPTNO	DEPTNAME
A01	ADMINISTRATIVE
E01	ENGINEERING
M01	MANUFACTURING
S01	MARKETING
S02	SALES
C01	CUSTOMER SUPPORT

(Right Table)

FULL OUTER JOIN OPERATION

```
SELECT lastname, deptname
  FROM employees e FULL OUTER JOIN department d
  ON e.workdept = d.deptno
```

RESULT DATA SET

LASTNAME	DEPTNAME
JAGGER	ADMINISTRATIVE
RICHARDS	MANUFACTURING
WOOD	MANUFACTURING
WATT	CUSTOMER SUPPORT
WYMAN	-
JONES	MARKETING
-	ENGINEERING
-	SALES

Record for WYMAN is included in the result data set produced even though it has no corresponding DEPTNO value; likewise, records for ENGINEERING and SALES are included in the result data set produced even though they have no corresponding WORKDEPT value

Figure 5–26 A simple full outer join operation.

result data set, all duplicate rows in this new result data set are eliminated, and the new result data set is returned.

INTERSECT ALL. When the `INTERSECT ALL` set operator is used, the result data sets produced by each individual query are compared and each record that is found in both result data sets is copied to a new result data set; all duplicate rows found in this new result data set are retained.

In order for two result data sets to be combined with a set operator, both must have the same number of columns, and each of those columns must have the exact same data types assigned to them. So when would you want to combine the results of two queries using a set operator? Suppose your company keeps individual employee expense account information in a table whose contents are archived at the end of each fiscal year. When a new fiscal year begins, expenditures for that year are essentially recorded in a new table. Now suppose, for tax purposes, you need a record of all employees' expenses for the last two years. To obtain this information, each archived table must be queried, and the results must then be combined. Rather than do this by running individual queries against the archived tables and storing the results in some kind of temporary table, this operation could be performed simply by using the `UNION` set operator, along with two `SELECT` SQL statements. Such a set of `SELECT` statements might look something like this:

```
SELECT * FROM EMP_EXP_02
UNION
SELECT * FROM EMP_EXP_01
ORDER BY EXPENSES DESC
```

Figure 5–27 illustrates how such a set operation would work.

The same set of queries could be combined using the `UNION ALL`, `EXCEPT`, `EXCEPT ALL`, `INTERSECT`, or `INTERSECT ALL` set operator simply by substituting the appropriate keyword for the keyword `UNION`. However, the results of each operation would be significantly different.

Using SQL Functions to Transform Data

Along with a rich set of SQL statements, DB2 UDB comes with a set of built-in functions that can return a single result value or convert data values from one data type to another. (A function is an operation denoted by a function name followed by a pair of parentheses enclosing zero or more arguments.) Most of the built-in functions provided by DB2 UDB are classified as being either *aggregate*, or *columnar* (because they work on all values of a column), or *scalar* (because they work on a single value in a table or view).

The argument of a columnar function is a collection of like values. A columnar function returns a single value (possibly null), and can be specified in an SQL statement wherever an expression can be used. Some of the more common columnar functions include:

SUM(*Column*). Returns the sum of the values in the column specified.

AVG(*Column*). Returns the sum of the values in the column specified divided by the number of values found in that column (the average).

MIN(*Column*). Returns the smallest value found in the column specified.

EMP_EXP_02 TABLE

EMPNO	LASTNAME	EXPENSES
001	JAGGER	5210.00
002	RICHARDS	3947.50
006	WOOD	4825.00
007	WYMAN	4274.50
008	KEYS	3892.50

EMP_EXP_01 TABLE

EMPNO	LASTNAME	EXPENSES
001	JAGGER	5210.00
002	RICHARDS	5822.00
003	WYMAN	3684.25
004	JONES	3421.50
005	STEWART	4976.00

UNION SET OPERATION

```
SELECT * FROM emp_exp_02
UNION
SELECT * FROM emp_exp_01
ORDER BY EXPENSES DESC
```

RESULT DATA SET

EMPNO	LASTNAME	EXPENSES
002	RICHARDS	5822.00
001	JAGGER	5210.00
005	STEWART	4976.00
006	WOOD	4825.00
007	WATTS	4274.50
002	RICHARDS	3947.50
008	KEYS	3892.50
003	WYMAN	3684.25
004	JONES	3421.50

Because the record for JAGGER is identical in both tables, it occus only once in the result data set produced; had the UNION ALL set operator been used instead of the UNION set operator, both records for JAGGER would have appeared in the result data produced

Figure 5–27 A simple UNION set operation.

MAX(*Column*). Returns the largest value found in the column specified.

COUNT(*Column*). Returns the total number of non-null values found in the column specified.

The arguments of a scalar function are individual scalar values, which can be of different data types and can have different meanings. A scalar function returns a single value (possibly null) and can be specified in an SQL statement wherever an expression can be used. Some of the more common scalar functions include:

ABS(*Value*). Returns the absolute value of the value specified.

LENGTH('*CharacterString*'). Returns the number of bytes found in the character string value specified.

LCASE('*CharacterString*') or **LOWER('*CharacterString*').** Returns a character string in which all of the characters in the character string value specified are converted to lowercase characters.

UCASE('*CharacterString*') or **UPPER('*CharacterString*').** Returns a character string in which all of the characters in the character string value specified are converted to uppercase characters.

MONTH('*DataValue*'). Returns the month portion of the date value specified.

DAY('*DateValue*'). Returns the day portion of the date value specified.

YEAR('*DateValue*'). Returns the year portion of the date value specified.

To view the complete set of columnar and scalar functions available with DB2 UDB, or to obtain more information about a particular function, refer to the *IBM DB2 Universal Database, Version 8 SQL Reference Volume 1* product documentation.

Retrieving Rows from a Result Data Set Using a Cursor

When a query is executed from within an application, DB2 UDB uses a mechanism known as a *cursor* to retrieve data values from the result data set produced. The name cursor probably originated from the blinking cursor found on early computer screens, and just as that cursor indicated the current position on the screen and identified where typed words would appear next, a DB2 UDB cursor indicates the current position in the result data set (i.e. the current row) and identifies which row of data will be returned to the application next.

The steps involved in using a cursor in an application program are as follows:

1. Define a cursor by executing the `DECLARE CURSOR` SQL statement, using the appropriate `SELECT` statement to construct the query desired.
2. Execute the query and generate a result data set by executing the `OPEN` SQL statement. (If the cursor was declared with the `WITH HOLD` option specified—for example, `DECLARE c1 CURSOR WITH HOLD` ...—, it will remain open across transaction boundaries until it is explicitly closed;

otherwise, it will be implicitly closed when the transaction that opens it is terminated.)

3. Retrieve each row in the result data set, one by one, until an end of data condition occurs, by executing the `FETCH` SQL statement—each time the `FETCH` statement is executed, the cursor is automatically moved to the next row in the result data set.

4. If appropriate, modify or delete the current row with either the `UPDATE ... WHERE CURRENT OF` or the `DELETE ... WHERE CURRENT OF` SQL statement (provided the cursor is an updatable cursor).

5. Shut down the cursor and delete the result data set produced by the query, by executing the `CLOSE` SQL statement.

For example, an application written in the C programming language designed to retrieve data from a table using a cursor might look something like this:

```
#include <stdio.h>
#include <stdlib.h>
#include <sql.h>

void main()
{
     /* Include The SQLCA Data Structure Variable */
     EXEC SQL INCLUDE SQLCA;

     /* Declare The SQL Host Memory Variables */
     EXEC SQL BEGIN DECLARE SECTION;
          char       EmployeeNo[7];
          char       LastName[16];
     EXEC SQL END DECLARE SECTION;

     /* Connect To The SAMPLE Database */
     EXEC SQL CONNECT TO SAMPLE USER;

     /* Declare A Cursor */
     EXEC SQL DECLARE C1 CURSOR FOR
          SELECT EMPNO, LASTNAME
          FROM EMPLOYEE
          WHERE JOB = 'DESIGNER';
```

```
    /* Open The Cursor */
    EXEC SQL OPEN C1;

    /* Fetch The Records */
    while (sqlca.sqlcode == SQL_RC_OK)
    {
        /* Retrieve A Record */
        EXEC SQL FETCH C1
            INTO :EmployeeNo, :LastName

        /* Print The Information Retrieved */
        if (sqlca.sqlcode == SQL_RC_OK)
            printf("%s, %s\n", EmployeeNo, LastName);
    }

    /* Close The Cursor */
    EXEC SQL CLOSE C1;

    /* Issue A COMMIT To Free All Locks */
    EXEC SQL COMMIT;

    /* Disconnect From The SAMPLE Database */
    EXEC SQL DISCONNECT CURRENT;
}
```

An application can use several cursors concurrently; however, each cursor must have its own unique name and its own set of `DECLARE CURSOR`, `OPEN`, `FETCH`, and `CLOSE` SQL statements.

Transactions

A *transaction* (also known as a *unit of work*) is a sequence of one or more SQL operations grouped together as a single unit, usually within an application process. Such a unit is called "atomic" because, like atoms (before fission and fusion were discovered), it is indivisible—either all of its work is carried out or none of its work is carried out. A given transaction can perform any number of SQL operations—from a single operation to many hundreds or even thousands, depending upon what is considered a "single step" within your business logic. (It is important to note that the longer a transaction is, the more database concurrency decreases and the more resource locks are acquired; this is usually considered the sign of a poorly written application.)

The initiation and termination of a single transaction defines points of data consistency within a database (we'll take a closer look at data consistency in Chapter 7, "Database Concurrency"); either the effects of all operations performed within a transaction are applied to the database and made permanent (committed), or the effects of all operations performed are backed out (rolled back) and the database is returned to the state it was in before the transaction was initiated.

In most cases, transactions are initiated the first time an executable SQL statement is executed after a connection to a database has been made or immediately after a pre-existing transaction has been terminated. Once initiated, transactions can be implicitly terminated, using a feature known as "automatic commit" (in which case, each executable SQL statement is treated as a single transaction, and any changes made by that statement are applied to the database if the statement executes successfully or discarded if the statement fails) or they can be explicitly terminated by executing the `COMMIT` or the `ROLLBACK` SQL statement. The basic syntax for these two statements is:

```
COMMIT <WORK>
```

and

```
ROLLBACK <WORK>
```

When the `COMMIT` statement is used to terminate a transaction, all changes made to the database since the transaction began are made permanent. On the other hand, when the `ROLLBACK` statement is used, all changes made are backed out and the database is returned to the state it was in just before the transaction began. Figure 5–28 shows the effects of a transaction that was terminated with a `COMMIT` statement; Figure 5–29 shows the effects of a transaction that was terminated with a `ROLLBACK` statement.

It is important to remember that commit and rollback operations only have an effect on changes that have been made within the transaction they terminate. So in order to evaluate the effects of a series of transactions, you must be able to identify where each transaction begins, as well as when and how each transaction is terminated. Figure 5–30 shows how the effects of a series of transactions can be evaluated.

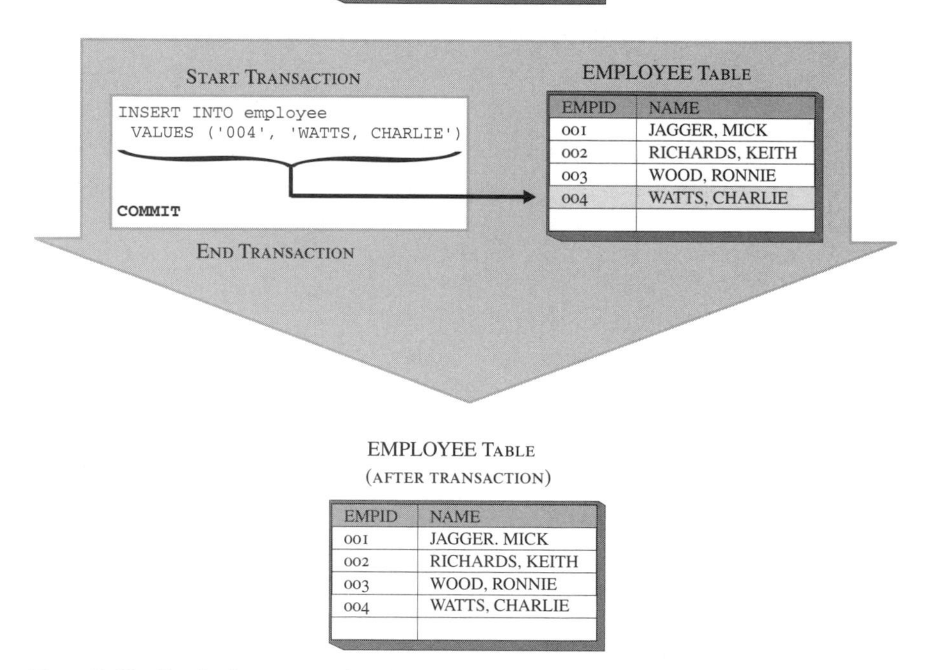

Figure 5–28 Terminating a transaction with the `COMMIT` SQL statement.

Changes made by a transaction that have not been committed are usually inaccessible to other users and applications (there are exceptions which we will look at in Chapter 7, "Database Concurrency," when we look at "dirty reads" and the Uncommitted Read isolation level), and can be backed out with a rollback operation. However, once changes made by a transaction have been committed, they become accessible to all other users and/or applications and can only be removed by executing new SQL statements (within a new transaction). So what happens if a system failure occurs before a transaction's changes can be committed? If only the user/application is disconnected (for example, because of a network failure), the DB2 Database Manager backs out all uncommitted changes (by replaying information

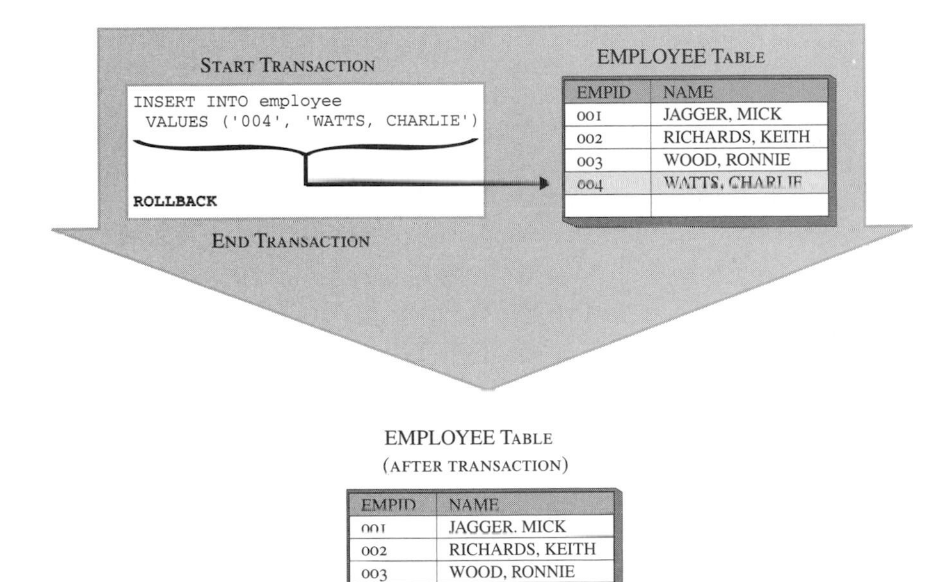

Figure 6–20 Terminating a transaction with the ROLLBACK SQL statement.

stored in the transaction log files), and the database is returned to the state it was in just before the transaction that was terminated unexpectedly began. On the other hand, if the database or the DB2 Database Manager is terminated (for example, because of a hard disk failure or a loss of power), the DB2 Database Manager will try to roll back all open transactions it finds in the transaction log file the next time the database is restarted (which will take place automatically the next time a user attempts to connect to the database if the database configuration parameter *autorestart* has been set accordingly). Only after this succeeds will the database be placed online again (i.e., made accessible to users and applications).

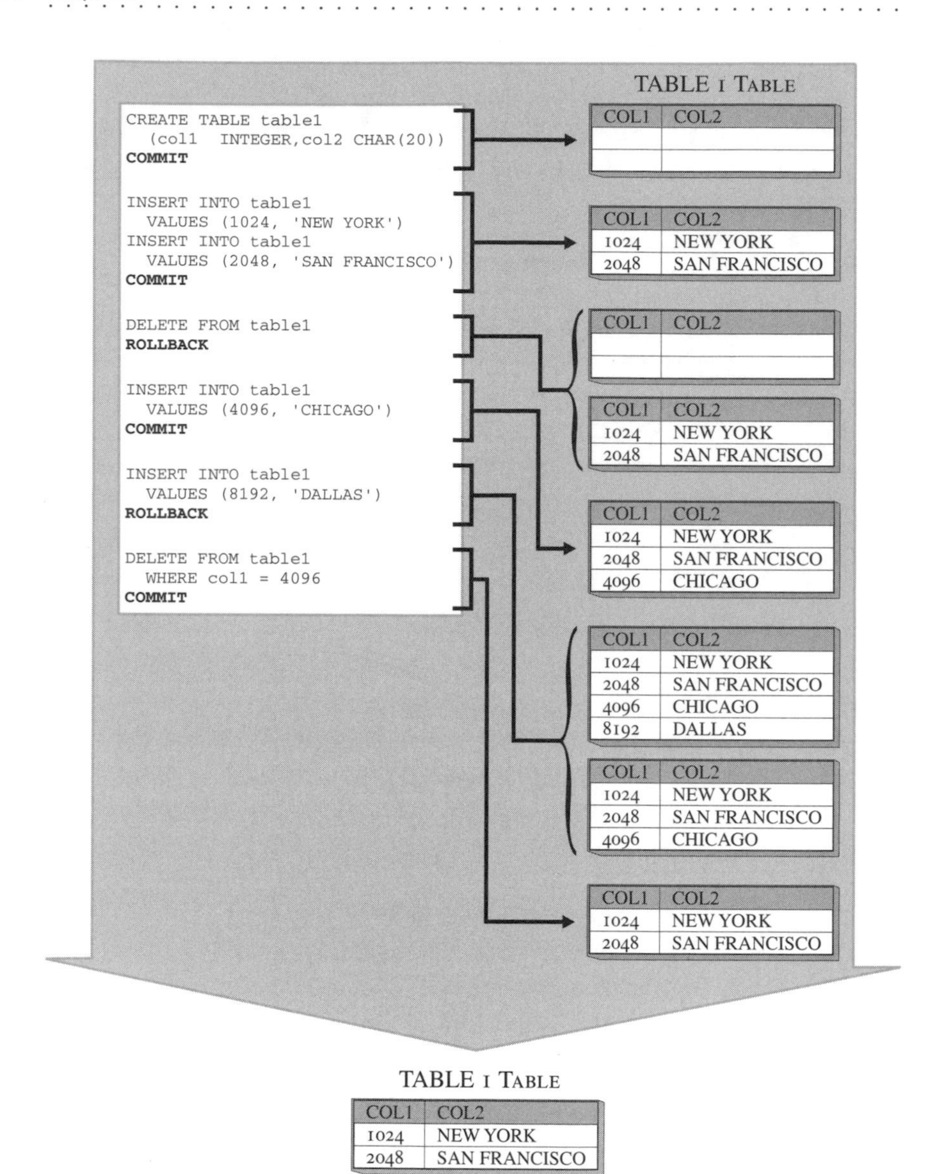

Figure 5–30 Evaluating the effects of a series of transactions.

SQL Procedures

When you set up a remote DB2 UDB database server and access it from one or more DB2 UDB client workstations, you have, in essence, established a basic DB2 UDB client/server environment. In this environment, each time an SQL statement is executed against the database on the remote server, the statement itself is sent, through a network, from the client workstation to the database server. The database server then processes the statement, and the results are sent back, again through the network, to the client workstation. (This means that two messages must go through the network for every SQL statement that is executed.)

If you have an application that contains one or more transactions that perform a relatively large amount of database activity with little or no user interaction, each transaction can be stored on the database server as what is known as a stored procedure. By using an SQL procedure (also known as a stored procedure), all database processing done by the transaction can be performed directly at the server workstation. And, because a stored procedure is invoked by a single SQL statement, fewer messages have to be transmitted across the network—only the data that is actually needed at the client workstation has to be sent across. This architecture allows the code that interacts directly with a database to reside on a high-performance PC or minicomputer where computing power and centralized control can be used to provide quick, coordinated data access. At the same time, the application logic can reside on one or more smaller (client) workstations so that it can make effective use of all the resources the client workstation has to offer. Thus, the resources of both the client workstation and the server workstation are utilized to their fullest potential.

Creating a Stored Procedure

Two different types of stored procedures can be created and used with a DB2 UDB database. They are:

> **External.** The body of the stored procedure is written using a high-level programming language (C, C++, Java, or COBOL).
>
> **SQL.** The body of the stored procedure is written in SQL.

Regardless of whether a stored procedure is an external procedure or an SQL procedure, all procedures must be structured such that they performs three distinct tasks:

- First, they must accept input parameter values, if any, from the client application.
- Next, they must perform whatever processing is appropriate.
- Finally, they must return output data, if any, to the client application. At the very least, a stored procedure should always return a value that indicates success or failure.

Before the source code for an external procedure actually becomes a usable stored procedure, unless the procedure was written with JDBC or DB2 CLI, the source code must be precompiled with the DB2 SQL Precompiler, then the precompiled source code must be compiled and linked to produce a library, and finally the library must be bound to the database. Typically, this binding takes place when the source code is precompiled. Once a library containing the stored procedure has been created, that library must be physically stored on the server workstation. (By default, the DB2 Database Manager looks for stored procedures in the *\sqllib\function* and *\sqllib\function\unfenced* subdirectories.) Additionally, the system permissions for the library file containing the stored procedure must be modified so that all users can execute it. For example, in a UNIX environment, the `chmod` command is used to make a file executable; in a Windows environment, the `attrib` command is used to make a file executable.

Both external procedures and SQL procedures must be registered with the database they are designed to interact with. This is done by executing the appropriate form of the `CREATE PROCEDURE` SQL statement. The basic syntax for this statement is:

```
CREATE PROCEDURE [ProcedureName]
( [ParamType] [ParamName] [DataType] ,...)
<SPECIFIC [SpecificName]>
<DYNAMIC RESULT SETS [NumResultSets]>
<NO SQL | CONTAINS SQL | READS SQL DATA>
<DETERMINISTIC | NOT DETERMINISTIC>
<CALLED ON NULL INPUT>
<FEDERATED | NOT FEDERATED>
<LANGUAGE SQL>
[SQLStatements]
```

or

```
CREATE PROCEDURE [ProcedureName]
( [ParamType] [ParamName] [DataType] ,...)
<SPECIFIC [SpecificName]>
<DYNAMIC RESULT SETS [NumResultSets]>
<NO SQL | CONTAINS SQL | READS SQL DATA>
<DETERMINISTIC | NOT DETERMINISTIC>
<CALLED ON NULL INPUT>
LANGUAGE [C | JAVA | COBOL | OLE]
EXTERNAL <NAME [ExternalName] | [Identifier]>
<FENCED <THREADSAFE | NOT THREADSAFE> |
    NOT FENCED <THREADSAFE>>
```

```
PARAMETER STYLE [DB2GENERAL | DB2SQL | GENERAL |
    GENERAL WITH NULLS | JAVA | SQL]
<PROGRAM TYPE [SUB | MAIN]>
<DBINFO | NO DBINFO>
```

where:

ProcedureName	Identifies the name to be assigned to the procedure to be created.
ParamType	Indicates whether the parameter identified by *ParamName* is an input parameter (IN), an output parameter (OUT), or both an input parameter and an output parameter (INOUT). (Valid values include IN, OUT, and INOUT.)
ParamName	Identifies the name to be assigned to a procedure parameter.
DataType	Identifies the type of data the procedure expects to receive/send for the parameter identified by *ParamName*.
SpecificName	Identifies the specific name to be assigned to the stored procedure. This name can be used later to comment on the stored procedure or to drop the stored procedure; however, it cannot be used to invoke the stored procedure.
NumResultSets	Identifies whether or not the stored procedure being registered returns result data sets, and if so how many.
SQLStatements	Specifies one or more SQL statements that are to be executed when the stored procedure is invoked. These statements make up the body of an SQL procedure.
ExternalName	Identifies the name of the library, along with the name of the function in the library, that contains the executable code of the stored procedure being registered.
Identifier	Identifies the name of the library that contains the executable code of the stored procedure being registered, but only if the procedure was written using C or C++. The DB2 Database Manager will look for a function that has the same name as the library name specified.

Thus, a simple SQL procedure could be created by executing a CREATE PROCEDURE statement that looks something like this:

```
CREATE PROCEDURE GET_SALES
(IN QUOTA INTEGER, OUT RETCODE CHAR(5))
DYNAMIC RESULT SETS 1
LANGUAGE SQL
BEGIN
    DECLARE RETCODE CHAR(5);
    DECLARE SALES_RESULTS CURSOR WITH RETURN FOR
       SELECT SALES_PERSON, SUM(SALES) AS
    TOTAL_SALES FROM SALES
       GROUP BY SALES_PERSON
       HAVING SUM(SALES) > QUOTA;
    OPEN SALES_RESULTS;
    SET RETCODE = SQLSTATE;
END
```

The resulting SQL procedure, called GET_SALES, accepts an integer input value (in an input parameter called QUOTA) and returns a character value (in an output parameter called RETCODE) that reports the success or failure of the SQL procedure. The procedure body consists of a single SELECT statement that returns the name and the total sales figures for each salesperson whose total sales exceed the quota specified. This procedure also returns one result data set. This is done by:

1. Indicating the SQL procedure is to return a result data set by specifying the DYNAMIC RESULT SETS clause of the CREATE PROCEDURE statement and assigning it the value 1.

2. Declaring a cursor within the procedure body (using the WITH RETURN FOR clause) for the result data set that is to be returned. (Earlier, we saw that a cursor is a named control structure that points to a specific row within a set of rows and is used by an application program to retrieve values form this set of rows.)

3. Opening the cursor, which produces the result data set that is to be returned.

4. Leaving the cursor open when the SQL procedure ends. (It is up to the calling application to close the open cursor when it is no longer needed.)

Calling an SQL Procedure

Once a stored procedure has been registered with a database (by executing the `CREATE PROCEDURE` SQL statement), that procedure can be invoked, either interactively, using a utility such as the Command Line Processor, or from a client application. Registered stored procedures are invoked by executing the `CALL` SQL statement. The basic syntax for this statement is:

```
CALL [ProcedureName] ( <[InputValue] | [OutputParameter] |
     NULL> ,...)
```

where:

ProcedureName — Identifies the name assigned to the procedure to be invoked. (Remember, the procedure name, not the specific name, must be used to invoke the procedure.)

InputValue — Identifies one or more parameter values that are to be passed to the procedure being invoked.

OutputParameter — Identifies one or more parameter markers or host variables that are to receive return values from the procedure being invoked.

Thus, the SQL procedure named GET_SALES that we created earlier could be invoked by connecting to the appropriate database and executing a `CALL` statement that looks something like this:

```
CALL GET_SALES (25, ?)
```

When this `SELECT` statement is executed, the value 25 is passed to the input parameter named QUOTA and a question mark (?) is used as a place-holder for the value that will be returned in the output parameter RETCODE. The procedure will then execute the SQL statements contained in it and return a result data set that looks something like this:

```
SALES_PERSON    TOTAL_SALES
--------------- -----------
GOUNOT                   50
LEE                      91

  2 record(s) selected.
"GET_SALES" RETURN_STATUS: "0"
```

Practice Questions

Question 1

Given the following CREATE TABLE statement:

```
CREATE TABLE EMPLOYEE
       (EMPNO       CHAR(3)  NOT NULL,
        FIRSTNAME   CHAR(20) NOT NULL,
        MIDINIT     CHAR(1),
        LASTNAME    CHAR(20) NOT NULL,
        SALARY      DECIMAL(10, 2))
```

Which of the following will retrieve the rows that have a missing value in the MIDINIT column?

❍ A. SELECT * FROM employee WHERE midinit = ' '

❍ B. SELECT * FROM employee WHERE midinit = NULL

❍ C. SELECT * FROM employee WHERE midinit = " "

❍ D. SELECT * FROM employee WHERE midinit IS NULL

Question 2

Given the following information:

```
CREATE TABLE table1 (c1  INTEGER, c2  INTEGER)
INSERT INTO table1 VALUES (123, 456)
UPDATE table1 SET c1 = NULL
```

What will be the result of the following statement?

SELECT * FROM table1

❍ A.
```
C1      C2
------  ------
123     456
1 record(s) selected.
```

❍ B.
```
C1      C2
------  ------
NULL    456
1 record(s) selected.
```

❍ C.
```
C1      C2
------  ------
-       456
1 record(s) selected.
```

❍ D.
```
C1      C2
------  ------
0       456
1 record(s) selected.
```

Question 3

Assuming the proper privileges exist, which of the following would NOT allow access to data stored in table TABLE1 using the name TAB1?

❍ A. CREATE ALIAS tab1 FOR table1

❍ B. CREATE TABLE tab1 LIKE table1

❍ C. CREATE SYNONYM tab1 FOR table1

❍ D. CREATE VIEW tab1 AS SELECT * FROM table1

Question 4

Given the following CREATE TABLE statement:

```
CREATE TABLE EMPLOYEE
        (EMPNO       CHAR(3) NOT NULL,
         FIRSTNAME   CHAR(20) NOT NULL,
         MIDINIT     CHAR(1),
         LASTNAME    CHAR(20) NOT NULL,
         SALARY      DECIMAL(10, 2))
```

Which of the following will cause EMPNO to be incremented automatically each time a row is inserted into the EMPLOYEE table?

❍ A. An index

❍ B. A view that was defined with the WITH CHECK OPTION clause specified

❍ C. A stored procedure

❍ D. A trigger

Question 5

Which of the following occurs if a server loses power while the DB2 Database Manager is in the middle of processing a transaction?

❍ A. All work done by the transaction up to that point is lost.

❍ B. All work done by the transaction up to that point is committed.

❍ C. All work done by the transaction up to that point is rolled back.

❍ D. All work done by the transaction up to that point is placed in "COMMIT PENDING" state.

Question 6

Which of the following can NOT be done using the ALTER TABLE statement?

- ❍ A. Add a new column
- ❍ B. Drop a check constraint
- ❍ C. Change a column's name
- ❍ D. Change the length of a VARCHAR column

Question 7

Assuming table TAB1 contains 100 rows, which of the following queries will return only half of the rows available?

- ❍ A. SELECT * FROM tab1 FIND FIRST 50 ROWS
- ❍ B. SELECT * FROM tab1 FETCH FIRST 50 ROWS ONLY
- ❍ C. SELECT * FROM tab1 WHILE ROW_NUM < 50
- ❍ D. SELECT * FROM tab1 MAXROWS 50

Question 8

Which two of the following statements are true about the HAVING clause?

- ❑ A. The HAVING clause is used in place of the WHERE clause.
- ❑ B. The HAVING clause uses the same syntax as the WHERE clause.
- ❑ C. The HAVING clause can only be used with the GROUP BY clause.
- ❑ D. The HAVING clause accepts wildcards.
- ❑ E. The HAVING clause uses the same syntax as the IN clause.

Question 9

Which of the following is a valid wildcard character in a LIKE clause of a SELECT statement?

- ❍ A. %
- ❍ B. *
- ❍ C. ?
- ❍ D. \

Question 10

Given the following set of statements:

```
CREATE TABLE tab1 (col1 INTEGER, col2 CHAR(20))
COMMIT
INSERT INTO tab1 VALUES (123, 'Red')
INSERT INTO tab1 VALUES (456, 'Yellow')
COMMIT
DELETE FROM tab1 WHERE col1 = 123
COMMIT
INSERT INTO tab1 VALUES (789, 'Blue')
ROLLBACK
INSERT INTO tab1 VALUES (789, 'Green')
ROLLBACK
UPDATE tab1 SET col2 = NULL
COMMIT
```

Which of the following records would be returned by the following statement?

```
SELECT * FROM tab1
```

❍ A.
```
COL1     COL2
-------- ----------
123      Red
1 record(s) selected.
```

❍ B.
```
COL1     COL2
-------- ----------
456      Yellow
1 record(s) selected.
```

❍ C.
```
COL1     COL2
-------- ----------
456        -
1 record(s) selected.
```

❍ D.
```
COL1     COL2
-------- ----------
789      Green
1 record(s) selected.
```

Question 11

Given the following two tables:

```
           TAB1
--------------------------------
COL_1              COL_2
---------          ---------
A                  10
B                  12
C                  14

           TAB2
--------------------------------
COL_A              COL_B
---------          ---------
A                  21
C                  23
D                  25
```

Assuming the following results are desired:

COL_1	COL_2	COL_A	COL_B
A	10	A	21
B	12	-	-
C	14	C	23
-	-	D	25

Which of the following joins will produce the desired results?

❍ A. SELECT * FROM tab1 INNER JOIN tab2 ON col_1 = col_a

❍ B. SELECT * FROM tab1 LEFT OUTER JOIN tab2 ON col_1 = col_a

❍ C. SELECT * FROM tab1 RIGHT OUTER JOIN tab2 ON col_1 = col_a

❍ D. SELECT * FROM tab1 FULL OUTER JOIN tab2 ON col_1 = col_a

Question 12

Given the following UPDATE statement:

UPDATE employees SET workdept =
(SELECT deptno FROM department WHERE deptno = 'A01')
WHERE workdept IS NULL

Which of the following describes the result if this statement is executed?

❍ A. The statement will fail because an UPDATE statement cannot contain a subquery.

❍ B. The statement will only succeed if the data retrieved by the subquery does not contain multiple records.

❍ C. The statement will succeed; if the data retrieved by the subquery contains multiple records, only the first record will be used to perform the update.

❍ D. The statement will only succeed if every record in the EMPLOYEES table has a null value in the WORKDEPT column.

Question 13

Given the following SQL statement:

GRANT INSERT, UPDATE, DELETE ON table1 TO user1

Which of the following describes what USERA is allowed to do?

❍ A. Create a read-only view using TABLE1

❍ B. Add new columns to TABLE1

❍ C. Add new rows to TABLE1

❍ D. Add a primary key to TABLE1

Question 14

Given the following table:

```
          TAB1
--------------------------------
COL_1           COL_2
---------       ---------
1               ABC
2               abc
3               DEF
4               def
```

Which of the following queries will find all rows where COL_2 contains the value 'DEF', regardless of its case?

❍ A. SELECT * FROM tab1 WHERE col_2 = 'DEF'

❍ B. SELECT * FROM tab1 WHERE LCASE(col_2) = 'def'

❍ C. SELECT * FROM tab1 WHERE IGNORE_CASE(col_2 = 'DEF')

❍ D. SELECT * FROM tab1 WHERE col_2 = 'DEF' WITH OPTION CASE INSENSITIVE

Question 15

Given the following table definition:

```
          EMPLOYEES
--------------------------------------------
EMPID           INTEGER
NAME            CHAR(20)
DEPT            CHAR(10)
SALARY          DECIMAL(10,2)
COMMISSION      DECIMAL(8,2)
```

Assuming the DEPT column contains the values 'ADMIN', 'PRODUCTION', and 'SALES', which of the following statements will produce a result data set in which all ADMIN department employees are grouped together, all PRODUCTION department employees are grouped together, and all SALES department employees are grouped together?

❍ A. SELECT name, dept FROM employees ORDER BY dept

❍ B. SELECT name, dept FROM employees GROUP BY dept

❍ C. SELECT name, dept FROM employees GROUP BY ROLLUP (dept)

❍ D. SELECT name, dept FROM employees GROUP BY CUBE (dept)

Question 16

Given the following two tables:

NAMES

NAME	NUMBER
Wayne Gretzky	99
Jaromir Jagr	68
Bobby Orr	4
Bobby Hull	23
Brett Hull	16
Mario Lemleux	66
Mark Messier	11

POINTS

NAME	POINTS
Wayne Gretzky	244
Jaromir Jagr	168
Bobby Orr	129
Brett Hull	121
Mario Lemleux	189
Joe Sakic	94

Which of the following statements will display the player name, number, and points for all players that have scored points?

❍ A. SELECT p.name, n.number, p.points FROM names n INNER JOIN points p ON n.name = p.name

❍ B. SELECT p.name, n.number, p.points FROM names n LEFT OUTER JOIN points p ON n.name = p.name

❍ C. SELECT p.name, n.number, p.points FROM names n RIGHT OUTER JOIN points p ON n.name = p.name

❍ D. SELECT p.name, n.number, p.points FROM names n FULL OUTER JOIN points p ON n.name = p.name

Question 17

USERA needs to be able to read and modify existing rows in TABLE1. Which of the following statements will give USERA only the privileges needed?

❍ A. GRANT ALL PRIVILEGES ON table1 TO usera

❍ B. GRANT SELECT ON table1 TO usera

❍ C. GRANT SELECT, MODIFY ON table1 TO usera

❍ D. GRANT SELECT, UPDATE ON table1 TO usera

Question 18

Given the following table definition:

```
                SALES
-------------------------------------------
SALES_DATE       DATE
SALES_PERSON     CHAR(20)
REGION           CHAR(20)
SALES            INTEGER
```

Which of the following SQL statements will remove all rows that had a SALES_DATE in the year 1995?

❍ A. DELETE * FROM sales WHERE YEAR(sales_date) = 1995

❍ B. DELETE FROM sales WHERE YEAR(sales_date) = 1995

❍ C. DROP * FROM sales WHERE YEAR(sales_date) = 1995

❍ D. DROP FROM sales WHERE YEAR(sales_date) = 1995

Question 19

A stored procedure has been created with the following statement:

CREATE PROCEDURE proc1 (IN var1 VARCHAR(10), OUT rc INTEGER)
SPECIFIC myproc LANGUAGE SQL ...

What is the correct way to invoke this procedure from the command line processor (CLP)?

❍ A. CALL proc1 ('SALES', ?)

❍ B. CALL myproc ('SALES', ?)

❍ C. CALL proc1 (SALES, ?)

❍ D. RUN proc1 (SALES, ?)

Question 20

Given the following table definitions:

EMPLOYEES

```
-------------------------------------------
EMPID          INTEGER
NAME           CHAR(20)
DEPTID         CHAR(3)
SALARY         DECIMAL(10,2)
COMMISSION     DECIMAL(8,2)
```

DEPARTMENTS

```
-------------------------------------------
DEPTNO         INTEGER
DEPTNAME       CHAR(20)
```

Which of the following statements will produce a result data set that satisfies all of these conditions:

Displays the total number of employees in each department
Displays the corresponding department name for each department ID
Sorted by department employee count, from greatest to least

- ❍ A. SELECT *, COUNT(empno) FROM departments, employees WHERE deptid = deptno GROUP BY deptname ORDER BY 2 DESC
- ❍ B. SELECT deptname, COUNT(empno) FROM departments, employees WHERE deptid = deptno GROUP BY deptname ORDER BY 2 DESC
- ❍ C. SELECT deptname, COUNT(empno) FROM departments, employees WHERE deptid = deptno GROUP BY deptname ORDER BY 2 ASC
- ❍ D. SELECT deptname, COUNT(*) FROM departments, employees WHERE deptid = deptno GROUP BY deptname ORDER BY 2

Question 21

Given the following table definition:

```
            EMPLOYEES
----------------------------------------
EMPID                INTEGER
NAME                 CHAR(20)
SALARY               DECIMAL(10,2)
```

If the following SQL statement is executed:

```
CREATE UNIQUE INDEX empid_ui ON employees (empid)
```

Which two of the following statements are true?

❑ A. Multiple null values are allowed in the EMPID column of the EMPLOYEES table.

❑ B. No null values are allowed in the EMPID column of the EMPLOYEES table.

❑ C. One (and only one) null value is allowed in the EMPID column of the EMPLOYEES table.

❑ D. No other unique indexes can be created on the EMPLOYEES table.

❑ E. Every value found in the EMPID column of the EMPLOYEES table will be different.

Question 22

Given the following statements:

```
CREATE TABLE table1 (col1 INTEGER, col2 CHAR(3))
CREATE VIEW view1 AS
      SELECT col1, col2 FROM table1
      WHERE col1 < 100
      WITH CHECK OPTION
```

Which of the following INSERT statements will execute successfully?

❍ A. INSERT INTO view1 VALUES (50, abc)

❍ B. INSERT INTO view1 VALUES(100, abc)

❍ C. INSERT INTO view1 VALUES(50, 'abc')

❍ D. INSERT INTO view1 VALUES(100, 'abc')

Question 23

Given the following table:

```
        CURRENT_EMPLOYEES
------------------------------------------
EMPID           INTEGER NOT NULL
NAME            CHAR(20)
SALARY          DECIMAL(10,2)

         PAST_EMPLOYEES
------------------------------------------
EMPID           INTEGER NOT NULL
NAME            CHAR(20)
SALARY          DECIMAL(10,2)
```

Assuming both tables contain data, which of the following statements will NOT successfully add data to table CURRENT_EMPLOYEES?

❍ A. INSERT INTO current_employees (empid) VALUES (10)

❍ B. INSERT INTO current_employees VALUES (10, 'JAGGER', 85000.00)

❍ C. INSERT INTO current_employees SELECT empid, name, salary FROM past_employees WHERE empid = 20

❍ D. INSERT INTO current_employees (name, salary) VALUES (SELECT name, salary FROM past_employees WHERE empid = 20)

Question 24

Which of the following is a NOT a valid reason for defining a view on a table?

❍ A. Restrict users' access to a subset of table data

❍ B. Ensure that rows entered remain within the scope of a definition

❍ C. Produce an action as a result of a change to a table

❍ D. Provide users with an alternate view of table data

Question 25

Given the following SQL statements:

```
CREATE TABLE tab1 (col1  INTEGER)
INSERT INTO tab1 VALUES (NULL)
INSERT INTO tab1 VALUES (1)

CREATE TABLE tab2 (col2 INTEGER)
INSERT INTO tab2 VALUES (NULL)
INSERT INTO tab2 VALUES (1)
INSERT INTO tab2 VALUES (2)
```

What will be the result when the following statement is executed?

```
SELECT * FROM tab1 WHERE col1 IN (SELECT col2 FROM tab2)
```

❍ A.
```
COL1
-------
1
1 record(s) selected.
```

❍ B.
```
COL1
--------
NULL
1
2 record(s) selected.
```

❍ C.
```
COL1
--------
-
1
2 record(s) selected.
```

❍ D.
```
COL1
--------
-
1 record(s) selected.
```

Question 26

Given the following table and the statements below:

TAB1

COL_1	COL_2
A	10
B	20
C	30
D	40
E	50

```
DECLARE c1 CURSOR WITH HOLD FOR SELECT * FROM tab1
 ORDER BY col_1
OPEN c1
FETCH c1
FETCH c1
FETCH c1
COMMIT
FETCH c1
CLOSE c1
FETCH c1
```

Which of the following is the last value obtained for COL_2?

❍ A. 20

❍ B. 30

❍ C. 40

❍ D. 50

Question 27

Given the following two tables:

NAMES

NAME	NUMBER
Wayne Gretzky	99
Jaromir Jagr	68
Bobby Orr	4
Bobby Hull	23
Mario Lemieux	66

POINTS

NAME	POINTS
Wayne Gretzky	244
Bobby Orr	129
Brett Hull	121
Mario Lemieux	189
Joe Sakic	94

How many rows would be returned if the following SELECT statement were executed?

SELECT * FROM names, points

❍ A. 0

❍ B. 5

❍ C. 10

❍ D. 25

Question 28

Given the following table definition:

```
            SALES
-----------------------------------
INVOICE_NO          CHAR(20) NOT NULL
SALES_DATE          DATE
SALES_PERSON        CHAR(20)
REGION              CHAR(20)
SALES               INTEGER
```

If the following SELECT statement is executed, which of the following describes the order of the rows in the result data set produced?

SELECT * FROM sales

❍ A. The rows are sorted by INVOICE_NO in ascending order.

❍ B. The rows are sorted by INVOICE_NO in descending order.

❍ C. The rows are ordered based on when they were inserted into the table.

❍ D. The rows are not sorted in any particular order.

Question 29

Given the following table:

```
           TAB1
----------------------------------
COL_1               COL_2
---------           ---------
A                   10
B                   20
C                   30
A                   10
D                   40
C                   30
```

Which of the following statements will return only one record for each set of repeated rows found in the final result data set produced?

❍ A. SELECT UNIQUE * FROM tab1

❍ B. SELECT DISTINCT * FROM tab1

❍ C. SELECT UNIQUE(*) FROM tab1

❍ D. SELECT DISTINCT(*) FROM tab1

Question 30

Given the following tables:

YEAR_2002

EMPID	NAME
1	Jagger, Mick
2	Richards, Keith
3	Wood, Ronnie
4	Watts, Charlie
5	Jones, Darryl
6	Leavell, Chuck

YEAR_1962

EMPID	NAME
1	Jagger, Mick
2	Richards, Keith
3	Jones, Brian
4	Wyman, Bill
5	Chapman, Tony
6	Stewart, Ian

If the following SQL statement is executed, how many rows will be returned?

```
SELECT name FROM year_2002
UNION
SELECT name FROM year_1962
```

❍ A. 0

❍ B. 6

❍ C. 10

❍ D. 12

Answers

Question 1

The correct answer is **D.** The proper way to test for a missing value (or null) is by using the NULL predicate with a WHERE clause, and answer D shows the correct way to construct such a WHERE clause. Keep in mind that NULL, zero (0), and blank (" ") are not the same value. NULL is a special marker used to represent missing information, while zero and blank (empty string) are actual values that can be stored in a column to indicate a specific value (or lack thereof).

Question 2

The correct answer is **C.** The UPDATE statement assigns a NULL value to column C1 and NULL values are displayed as a dash (-).

Question 3

The correct answer is **B.** The CREATE TABLE ... LIKE ... statement is used to create a new table that has the same structure as an existing table. On the other hand, an alias (a synonym is another name for an alias) and a view can be used to access data stored in a table, using an alternate name.

Question 4

The correct answer is **D.** A before trigger can be used to automatically generate a value for a column each time an insert operation is performed on a table.

Question 5

The correct answer is **C.** If the database or the DB2 Database Manager are terminated (for example, because of a hard disk failure or a loss of power), the DB2 Database Manager will try to roll back all open transactions it finds in the transaction log file the next time the database is restarted (which will take place automatically the next time a user attempts to connect to the database if the database configuration parameter *autorestart* has been set accordingly).

Question 6

The correct answer is **C.** Certain properties of an existing table can be changed, additional columns and constraints can be added, existing constraints can be removed, and the length of varying-length character data type values allowed for a particular column can be increased by executing the ALTER TABLE statement. However, the ALTER TABLE statement cannot be used to change a column's name.

Question 7

The correct answer is **B.** The FETCH FIRST clause is used to limit the number of rows that are returned to the result data set produced in response to a query. When used, the FETCH FIRST clause is followed by a positive integer value and the words ROWS ONLY. This tells the DB2 Database Manager that the user/application executing the query does not want to see more than *n* number of rows, regardless of how many rows might exist in the result data set that would be produced were the FETCH FIRST clause not specified.

Question 8

The correct answers are **B** and **C.** The HAVING clause is used to apply further selection criteria to columns that are referenced in a GROUP BY clause. This clause behaves like the WHERE clause, except that it refers to data that has already been grouped by a GROUP BY clause (the HAVING clause is used to tell the DB2 Database Manager how to select the rows that are to be returned in a result data set from rows that have already been grouped). And like the WHERE clause, the HAVING clause is followed by a search condition that acts as a simple test that, when applied to a row of data, will evaluate to TRUE, FALSE, or Unknown.

Question 9

The correct answer is **A.** The pattern of characters specified with the LIKE clause of a SELECT statement can consist of regular alphanumeric characters and/or special metacharacters that are interpreted as follows:

- The underscore character (_) is treated as a wild card character that stands for any single alphanumeric character.
- The percent character (%) is treated as a wild card character that stands for any sequence of alphanumeric characters.

Question 10

The correct answer is **C.** Table TAB1 is created, two rows are inserted, and the first row is deleted because a COMMIT statement follows each of these operations. The next two rows that are inserted are removed because a ROLLBACK statement follows their insertion. And finally, the value for COL2 of all rows is set to null—again because this operation is followed by a COMMIT statement.

Question 11

The correct answer is **D.** When a full outer join operation is performed, rows that would have been returned by an inner join operation and all rows stored in both tables of the join operation that would have been eliminated by the inner join operation are returned in the result data set produced.

Question 12

The correct answer is **B.** When the results of a query, or subselect, are used to provide values for one or more columns identified in the column name list provided for an UPDATE statement, the values retrieved from one base table or view are used to modify values stored in another. The number of values returned by the subselect must match the number of columns provided in the column name list specified, and only one record can be returned.

Question 13

The correct answer is **C.** USERA has been given the privileges needed to add data to TABLE1, update data stored in TABLE1, and delete data from TABLE1.

Question 14

The correct answer is **B.** The LCASE('*CharacterString*') or LOWER ('*CharacterString*') function returns a character string in which all of the characters in the character string value specified are converted to lowercase characters. By using this function to convert values before they are used in a WHERE clause, a table can be searched for a specific value, regardless of the case used to store it.

Question 15

The correct answer is **A.** The ORDER BY clause is used to tell the DB2 Database Manager how to sort and order the rows that are to be returned in a result data set produced in response to a query. In this example, all rows containing the value "ADMIN" in the DEPT column would be listed first, followed by all rows containing the value "PRODUCTION", followed by all rows containing the value "SALES".

Question 16

The correct answer is **C.** When a right outer join operation is performed, rows that would have been returned by an inner join operation, together with all rows stored in the rightmost table of the join operation (i.e., the table listed last in the OUTER JOIN clause) that would have been eliminated by the inner join operation are returned in the result data set produced. In this case, we want to see *all* records found in the POINTS table, along with any corresponding records found in the NAMES table, so a right outer join is the appropriate join operation to use.

Question 17

The correct answer is **D.** In order to read and modify data stored in a table, a user must have SELECT (to read) and UPDATE (to modify) privileges on that table. The GRANT statement shown in answer D is the appropriate statement to use to give USERA these privileges.

Question 18

The correct answer is **B.** The DELETE statement is used to remove specific records from a table (the DROP statement completely destroys the table object), and the correct syntax for the DELETE statement is DELETE FROM [*TableName*] ...

Question 19

The correct answer is **A.** The CALL statement is used to invoke a stored procedure, so answer D is wrong; because a stored procedure cannot be invoked using its specific name, answer B is wrong; and because SALES is a character string value that is being passed to the procedure, it must be enclosed in single quotes. Therefore, A is the correct answer.

Question 20

The correct answer is **B.** COUNT(empno) together with GROUP BY deptname displays the total number of employees in each department; SELECT deptname displays the corresponding department name for each department ID, and ORDER BY 2 DESC sorts the data by employee count (which is column 2) from greatest to least.

Question 21

The correct answers are **C** and **E.** When a unique index is created for a column, every value found in that column must be unique, and one of the column's unique values can be the null value.

Question 22

The correct answer is **C.** Because VIEW1 was created using a SELECT statement that only references rows that have a value less than 100 in COL1, and because VIEW1 was created with the WITH CHECK OPTION specified, each value inserted into COL1 (using VIEW1) must be less than 100. In addition, because COL2 was defined using a character data type, all values inserted into COL2 must be enclosed in single quotes. The INSERT statements shown in answers B and D will fail because the value to be assigned to COL1 exceeds 100; the INSERT statement shown in answer A will fail because the value abc is not enclosed in single quotation marks.

Question 23

The correct answer is **D.** Because the EMPID column was defined in such a way that it does not allow null values, a non-null value must be provided for this column anytime data is inserted into either table. The INSERT statement shown in answer D does not provide a value for the EMPID column of the CURRENT_EMPLOYEES table, so the statement will fail.

Question 24

The correct answer is **C.** A trigger is used to produce an action as a result of a change to a table. Views provide users with alternate ways to see table data. And because a view can reference the data stored in any number of columns found in the base table it refers to, views can be used, together with view privileges, to control what data a user can and cannot see. Furthermore, if a view is created with the WITH CHECK OPTION specified, it can be used to ensure that all rows added to a table through it conform to its definition.

Question 25

The correct answer is **A.** The IN predicate is used to define a comparison relationship in which a value is checked to see whether or not it matches a value in a finite set of values. This finite set of values can consist of one or more literal values coded directly in the SELECT statement, or it can be composed of the non-null values found in the result data set generated by a subquery. So in this example, the non-null values that appear in the result data set produced by the subquery are the values 1 and 2, and the only row in TAB1 that has a matching value in COL1 is the row with the value 1 in it.

Question 26

The correct answer is **C.** When a cursor that has been declared with the WITH HOLD option specified (as in the example shown) is opened, it will remain open across transaction boundaries until it is explicitly closed; otherwise, it will be implicitly closed when the transaction that opens it is terminated. In this example, the cursor is opened, the first three rows are fetched from it, the transaction is committed (but the cursor is not closed), another row is fetched from it, and then it is closed. Thus, the last value obtained will be:

TAB1	
COL_1	COL_2
D	40

Question 27

The correct answer is **D.** When a SELECT statement such as the one shown is executed, the result data set produced will contain all possible combinations of the rows found in each table specified (otherwise known as the Cartesian product). Every row in the result data set produced is a row from the first table referenced concatenated with a row from the second table referenced, concatenated in turn with a row from the third table referenced, and so on. The total number of rows found in the result data set produced is the product of the number of rows in all the individual table-references; in this case, 5 x 5 = 25.

Question 28

The correct answer is **D.** Data is stored in a table in no particular order, and unless otherwise specified (with an ORDER BY clause), a query only returns data in the order in which it is found.

Question 29

The correct answer is **B.** The DISTINCT clause of the SELECT statement must follow the word SELECT, and if used, duplicate records are removed from the result data set returned.

Question 30

The correct answer is **C.** When the UNION set operator is used, the result data sets produced by each individual query are combined and all duplicate rows are eliminated. Thus with this example, the results of both tables are combined (6 rows + 6 rows = 12 rows) and the duplicate rows for Jagger, Mick and Richards, Keith are removed (12 – 2 = 10 rows). So 10 rows are returned.

Working with DB2 UDB Objects

Nineteen percent (19%) of the DB2 UDB V8.1 Family Fundamentals certification exam (Exam 700) is designed to test your ability to identify the data types and constraints that are available with DB2 Universal Database, as well as to test your knowledge of when and how each one should be used in a table definition. The questions that make up this portion of the exam are intended to evaluate the following:

- Your knowledge of the DB2 UDB data types available and your ability to demonstrate when and how each of the data types available with DB2 UDB should be used.
- Your knowledge of the constraints available and your ability to identify when and how NOT NULL constraints, default constraints, check constraints, unique constraints, and referential integrity constraints should be used.
- Your ability to create a database table, using data types and constraints.
- Your ability to identify how operations performed on the parent table of a referential integrity constraint are reflected in the child table of the constraint.

This chapter is designed to introduce you to the data types and constraints that are available with DB2 Universal Database and to show you how to construct DB2 UDB base tables using any combination of each.

Terms you will learn:

Small Integer
SMALLINT
Integer
INTEGER
INT
Big Integer
BIGINT
Decimal
Sign
Precision
Scale
DECIMAL
DEC
NUMERIC
NUM
Single-Precision Floating-Point
REAL
Double-Precision Floating-Point
DOUBLE
DOUBLE PRECISION
FLOAT
Fixed-Length Character String
CHARACTER
CHAR
Varying-Length Character String
CHARACTER VARYING
CHAR VARYING
VARCHAR
Long Varying-Length Character String
LONG VARCHAR
Fixed-Length Double-Byte Character String
GRAPHIC
Varying-Length Double-Byte Character String

VARGRAPHIC
Long Varying-Length Double-Byte Character String
LONG VARGRAPHIC
Date
DATE
Time
TIME
Timestamp
TIMESTAMP
Binary Large Object
BLOB
Character Large Object
CLOB
Double-Byte Character Large Object
DBCLOB
DataLinks
DB2 Extender
User-Defined Data Type
NOT NULL Constraint
Default Constraint
Check Constraint
Unique Constraint
Referential Integrity Constraint
Referential Constraint
Foreign Key Constraint
Unique Key
Primary Key
Foreign Key
Parent Key
Parent Table
Parent Row
Dependent Table
Child Table
Dependent Row

Child Row
Descendant Table
Descendant Row
Referential Cycle
Self-Referencing Table
Self-Referencing Row
ON UPDATE NO ACTION
ON UPDATE RESTRICT
ON DELETE CASCADE
ON DELETE SET NULL
ON DELETE NO ACTION
ON DELETE RESTRICT
"Check Pending"
Base Table
Declared Temporary Table

Techniques you will master:

Recognizing the available built-in data types and understanding when each is to be used.

Understanding how NOT NULL constraints, default constraints, check constraints, unique constraints, and referential constraints are defined.

Understanding what NOT NULL constraints, default constraints, check constraints, unique constraints, and referential constraints are used for.

Understanding how a base table is created.

Recognizing how operations performed on the parent table of a referential integrity constraint are reflected in the child table of the constraint.

DB2 Universal Database's Data Types

If you stop and think about it, most of the "data" you encounter on a day-to-day basis falls into distinct categories. The money you buy coffee with and the change you get back is numerical in nature; the email messages you read and the replies you send back are composed of character strings; and many of the things you do, such as attending meetings, eating dinner, and going to bed revolve around time. Most of the data that gets stored in a DB2 UDB database can be categorized in a similar manner. To ensure that all data is stored as efficiently as possible, DB2 UDB comes equipped with a rich assortment of built-in data types. (In fact, 19 different built-in data types are available.) DB2 UDB also provides facilities that can be used to create an infinite number of user-defined data types, which can in turn be used to store complex, nontraditional data that might be found in a complex computing environment.

The built-in data types available with DB2 UDB are classified according to the type of data they have been designed to hold:

- Numeric data
- Character string data
- Date/Time data
- Large object data

In addition to these "traditional" types of data, special data types used with DataLinks and DB2 UDB Extenders are also available.

Numeric Data Types

As the name suggests, numeric data types are used to store numeric values—specifically, numeric values that have a *sign* and a *precision*. The sign is considered positive if the value is greater than or equal to zero and negative if the value is less than zero, while the precision is the actual number of digits used to present the value. Numeric data is stored using a fixed amount of storage space, and the amount of space required increases as the precision of the number goes up. Numeric data types include:

Small integer. The small integer data type is used to store numeric values that have a precision of 5 digits or less. The range for small integer values is –32,768 to 32,767 and 2 bytes of storage space is required for every small integer value stored. (Positive numbers have one less value in their range because they start at the value 0 while negative numbers start at –1.) The term SMALLINT is used to denote the small integer data type.

Integer. The integer data type is used to store numeric values that have a precision of 10 digits. The range for integer values is –2,147,483,648 to 2,147,483,647, and 4 bytes of storage space is required for every integer value stored. The terms INTEGER and INT are used to denote the integer data type.

Big integer. The big integer data type is used to store numeric values that have a precision of 19 digits. The range for big integer values is –9,223,372,036,854,775,808 to 9,223,372,036,854,775,807 and 8 bytes of storage space is required for every big integer value stored. The term BIGINT is used to denote the big integer data type. (This data type is typically used on systems that provide native support for 64-bit integers; on such systems, processing large numbers that have been stored as big integers is much more efficient, and any calculations performed are more precise.)

Decimal. The decimal data type is used to store numeric values that contain both whole and fractional parts, separated by a decimal point. The exact location of the decimal point is determined by the precision and the scale of the value (the scale is the number of digits used by the fractional part). The maximum precision allowed for decimal values is 31 digits, and the corresponding scale must be a positive number less than the precision of the number. The amount of storage space needed to store a decimal value can be determined by solving the following equation: *Precision* ÷ 2 (truncated) + 1 = *Bytes required*. (For example, the value 67.12345 has precision of 7, 7 ÷ 2 is 3, + 1 makes 4; therefore, 4 bytes are required to store the value 67.12345.) The terms DECIMAL, DEC, NUMERIC, and NUM are used to denote the decimal data type.

Single-precision floating-point. The single-precision floating-point data type is used to store a 32-bit *approximation* of a real number. This number can be zero, or it can fall within the range –3.402E+38 to –1.175E–37 or 1.175E–37 to 3.402E+38. Each single-precision floating-point value can be up to 24 digits in length, and 4 bytes of storage space is required for every value stored. The terms REAL and FLOAT are used to denote the single-precision floating-point data type.

Double-precision floating-point. The double-precision floating-point data type is used to store a 64-bit *approximation* of a real number. This number can be zero, or it can fall within the range –1.79769E+308 to –2.225E–307 or 2.225E–307 to 1.79769E+308. Each double-precision floating-point value can be up to 53 digits in length, and 8 bytes of storage space is required for every value stored. The terms DOUBLE, DOUBLE PRECISION, and FLOAT are used to denote the double-precision floating-point data type.

Character String Data Types

Character string data types are used to store values comprised of one or more alphanumeric characters. Together, these characters may form a word, a sentence, a paragraph, or a complete document. A variety of character string data types are available. Deciding on which one to use for a given situation primarily depends on the storage requirements of the data value to be stored. Character string data types include:

Fixed-length character string. The fixed-length character string data type is used to store character string values that are between 1 and 254 characters in length. The amount of storage space needed to store a fixed-length character string value can be determined by solving the following equation: (*Number of characters* x 1) = *Bytes required.* (A fixed amount of storage space is allocated, even if all of the space allocated is not needed—short strings are padded with blanks.) The terms CHARACTER and CHAR are used to denote the fixed-length character string data type.

Varying-length character string. The varying-length character string data type is used to store character string values that are up to 32,672 characters in length. However, the actual length allowed is governed by the tablespace page size used. For tables that reside in tablespaces that use 4K pages, varying-length character string values cannot be more than 4,092 characters in length; for tables that reside in a tablespaces that use 8K pages, varying-length character string values cannot be more than 8,188 characters in length, and so on. The amount of storage space needed to store a varying-length character string value can be determined by solving the following equation: (*Number of characters* x 1) + 4 = *Bytes required.* (Only the amount of storage space actually needed, plus four bytes for an "end-of-string" marker, is allocated—strings are not blank padded.) The terms CHARACTER VARYING, CHAR VARYING, and VARCHAR are used to denote the varying-length character string data type.

Long varying-length character string. The long varying-length character string data type is used to store character string values that are up to 32,700 characters in length, regardless of the tablespace page size used. The amount of storage space needed to store a long varying-length character string value can be determined by solving the following equation: (*Number of characters* x 1) + 24 = *Bytes required.* The term LONG VARCHAR is used to denote the long varying-length character string data type.

Fixed-length double-byte character string. The fixed-length double-byte character string data type is used to store DBCS (double-byte character set) character string values that are up to 127 characters in length. (Most Asian character sets are double-byte character sets.) The amount of storage space needed to store a fixed-length double-byte character string value can be determined by solving the following equation: (*Number of characters* x 2) = *Bytes required.* The term GRAPHIC is used to denote the fixed-length double-byte character string data type.

Varying-length double-byte character string. The varying-length double-byte character string data type is used to store DBCS character string values that are up to 16,336 characters in length. Again, the actual length allowed is governed by the tablespace page size used. For tables that reside in tablespaces that use 4K pages, varying-length double-byte character string values cannot be more than 2,046 characters in length; for tables that reside in a tablespaces that use 8K pages, varying-length double-byte character string values cannot be more than 4,094 characters in length; and so on. The amount of storage space needed to store a varying-length double-byte character string value can be determined by solving the following equation: (*Number of characters* x 2) + 4 = *Bytes required.* The term VARGRAPHIC is used to denote the varying-length double-byte character string data type.

Long varying-length double-byte character string. The long varying-length double-byte character string data type is used to store DBCS character string values that are up to 16,350 characters in length, regardless of the tablespace page size used. The amount of storage space needed to store a long varying-length double-byte character string value can be determined by solving the following equation: (*Number of characters* x 2) + 24 = *Bytes required.* The term LONG VARGRAPHIC is used to denote the long varying-length character string data type.

Date/Time Data Types

Data/Time data types are used to store values that represent dates and times. From a user perspective, these values appear to be character strings; however, they are physically stored as binary packed strings. Date/Time data types include:

Date. The date data type is used to store three-part values (year, month, and day) that represent calendar dates. The range for the year portion is 0001 to 9999; the range for the month portion is 1 to 12; and the range for the day portion is 1 to 28, 29, 30 or 31, depending upon the month value specified and whether or not the year specified is a leap year. Externally, date values appear to be fixed-length character string values 10 characters in length. However, only 4 bytes of storage space is required for every date value stored. The term DATE is used to denote the date data type.

Time. The time data type is used to store three-part values (hours, minutes, and seconds) that represent time, using a 24-hour clock. The range for the hours portion is 0 to 24; the range for the minutes portion is 0 to 59; and the range for the seconds portion is 0 to 59. Externally, time values appear to be fixed-length character string values 8 characters in length. However, only 3 bytes of storage space is required for every time value stored. The term TIME is used to denote the time data type.

Timestamp. The timestamp data type is used to store seven-part values (year, month, day, hours, minutes, seconds, and microseconds) that represent a specific calendar date and time (using a 24-hour clock). The range for the year portion is 0001 to 9999; the range for the month portion is 1 to 12; the range for the day portion is 1 to 28, 29, 30 or 31, depending upon the month value specified and whether or not the year specified is a leap year; the range for the hours portion is 0 to 24; the range for the minutes portion is 0 to 59; the range for the seconds portion is 0 to 59; and the range for the microseconds portion is 0 to 999,999. Externally, timestamp values appear to be fixed-length character string values 26 characters in length (this string is displayed in the form *YYYY-MM-DD-HH.MM.SS.NNNNNN*, which translates to Year-Month-Day-Hour.Minute.Second.Microseconds). However, only 10 bytes of storage space is required for every timestamp value stored. The term TIMESTAMP is used to denote the timestamp data type.

Because the representation of date and time values varies throughout the world, the actual string format used to present a date or a time value is dependant upon the territory code assigned to the database being used. Table 6–1 shows the date and time string formats that are available with DB2 UDB.

Table 6–1 DB2 UDB Date and Time Formats

Format Name	Abbreviation	Date String Format	Time String Format
International Standards Organization	ISO	YYYY-MM-DD	HH.MM.SS
IBM USA Standard	USA	MM/DD/YYYY	HH:MM AM or PM
IBM European Standard	EUR	DD.MM.YYYY	HH.MM.SS
Japanese Industrial Standard	JIS	YYYY-MM-DD	HH:MM:SS
Site Specific	LOC	Based on database territory and country code	Based on database territory and country code

For date formats, YYYY = Year, MM = Month, and DD = Day; for time formats, HH = Hour, MM = Minute, and SS = Seconds

Adapted from Tables 5 and 6 on Pages 101 and 102 of the DB2 SQL Reference – Volume 1 manual.

Large Object (LOB) Data Types

Large object (LOB) data types are used to store large amounts of unstructured data. Large object data types include the following:

Binary large object. The binary large object data type is used to store binary data values (such as documents, graphic images, pictures, audio, and video) that are up to 2 gigabytes in size. The terms BINARY LARGE OBJECT and BLOB are used to denote the binary large object data type. The amount of storage space set aside to store a binary large object value is determined by the length specification provided when a binary large object data type is defined. For example, 800 bytes of storage space would be set aside for a BLOB(800) definition.

Character large object. The character large object data type is used to store SBCS (single-byte character set) or MBCS (multibyte character set) character string values that are between 32,700 and 2,147,483,647 characters in length. The terms CHARACTER LARGE OBJECT, CHAR LARGE OBJECT, and CLOB are used to denote the character large object data type. The amount of storage space set aside to store a character large object value is determined by the length specification provided when a character large object data type is defined. For example, 800 bytes of storage space would be set aside for a CLOB(800) definition.

Double-byte character large object. The double-byte character large object data type is used to store DBCS (double-byte character set) character string values that are between 16,350 and 1,073,741,823 characters in length. The term DBCLOB is used to denote the double-byte character large object data type. The amount of storage space set aside to store a double-byte character large object value is determined by the length specification provided when a double-byte character large object data type is defined. For example, 800 bytes of storage space would be set aside for a DBCLOB(400) definition.

DataLinks

The DataLink data type is used to store encapsulated values that provide logical references to files that reside outside of the database and are controlled by a DB2 Data Links Server. (The DB2 Data Links Server is an add-on package that takes over control of the native file system on behalf of a DB2 UDB database.) DataLink values serve as "anchor values" that contain reference information allowing a database to establish and maintain a link to external data. The term DATALINK is used to denote the DataLink data type.

In File System Migrator (FSM), NT File System (NTFS), Journaled File System (JFS) and UNIX File System (UFS) environments, DataLink values consist of the name of the Data Links Manager server that contains the file to be externally linked, along with the name of the file itself, combined to create a Uniform Resource Locator (URL) address. This address may then be combined with descriptive comment text that can be up to 200 characters in length. However, the final DataLink value produced cannot exceed 200 bytes (200 bytes of storage space is required for every DataLink value stored).

Because DataLink values are encapsulated values that contain several pieces of information, they must be constructed, using the built-in function `DLVALUE()`. Once a DataLink encapsulated value has been created, specific information stored in that value can be updated or retrieved using one of the built-in DataLink functions provided (`DLCOMMENT()`, `DLLINKTYPE()`, `DLNEWCOPY()`, `DLPREVIOUSCOPY()`, `DLREPLACECONTENT()`, `DLURLCOMPLETE()`, `DLURLCOMPLETEONLY()`, `DLURLCOMPLETEWRITE()`, `DLURLPATH()`, `DLURLPATHONLY()`, `DLURLSCHEME()`, and `DLURLSERVER()`).

Extenders

The extender products that are available with DB2 UDB consist of unique sets of user-defined data types and user-defined functions that can be used to store and manipulate nontraditional data such as graphical images and audio/ video clips. Since many of the data types provided by the DB2 Extenders are based on built-in data types, the size limits and storage requirements of an extender data type often match those of their built-in data type counterparts—provided extender data is actually stored in the database. Some of the DB2 Extenders allow their data to be stored in external files that reside outside the database, while the location of the files themselves are stored in a database table. When this is the case, the storage requirements for an extender data type can be much lower than its built-in data type equivalent.

User-Defined Data Types

In Chapter 4, "Accessing DB2 UDB Data," we saw that user-defined data types (UDTs) are data types that are explicitly created by a database user. A user-defined data type can be a distinct data type that shares a common representation with one of the built-in data types provided with DB2 UDB, or it can be a structured type that consists of a sequence of named attributes, each of which have their own data type. Structured data types can also be created as subtypes of other structured types, thereby defining a type hierarchy.

User-defined data types are subject to strong data typing, which means that even though they may share the same representation as other built-in or user-defined data types, the value of one user-defined data type is only compatible with values of that same type (or of other user-defined data types within the same data type hierarchy). As a result, user-defined data types cannot be used as arguments for most built-in functions. However, user-defined functions and operators that duplicate the functionality provided by the built-in functions can be created.

Understanding Constraints

Within most businesses, data often must adhere to a certain set of rules and restrictions. For example, companies typically have a specific format and numbering sequence they use when generating purchase orders. Like triggers, constraints allow you to place the logic needed to enforce such business rules directly in the database rather than in applications that work with the database. Essentially, triggers are sets of actions that are to be executed whenever an insert, update, or delete operation is performed on a specific table.

Constraints, on the other hand, are rules that govern how data values can be added to a table, as well as how those values can be modified once they have been added. The following types of constraints are available:

- NOT NULL constraints
- Default constraints
- Check constraints
- Unique constraints
- Referential integrity constraints

Constraints are usually defined during table creation; however, constraints can also be added to existing tables using the `ALTER TABLE` SQL statement. (For more information, refer to Chapter 5, "Working with DB2 UDB Data.")

NOT NULL Constraints

With DB2 UDB, null values (not to be confused with empty strings) are used to represent missing or unknown data and/or states. And by default, every column in a table will accept a null value. This allows you to add records to a table when not all of the values that pertain to the record are known. However, there may be times when this behavior is unacceptable (for example, a tax identification number might be required for every employee that works for a company). When such a situation arises, the NOT NULL constraint can be used to ensure that a particular column in a base table is never assigned a null value; once the NOT NULL constraint has been defined for a column, any operation that attempts to place a null value in that column will fail. Figure 6–1 illustrates how the NOT NULL constraint is used.

Because NOT NULL constraints are associated with a specific column in a base table, they are usually defined during the table creation process.

Default Constraints

Just as there are times when it is objectionable to accept a null value, there may be times when it is desirable to have the system provide a specific value for you (for example, you might want to automatically assign the current date to a particular column whenever a new record is added to a table). In these situations, the default constraint can be used to ensure that a particular column in a base table is assigned a predefined value (unless that value is overridden) each time a record is added to the table. The predefined value provided could be null (if the NOT NULL constraint has not been defined for

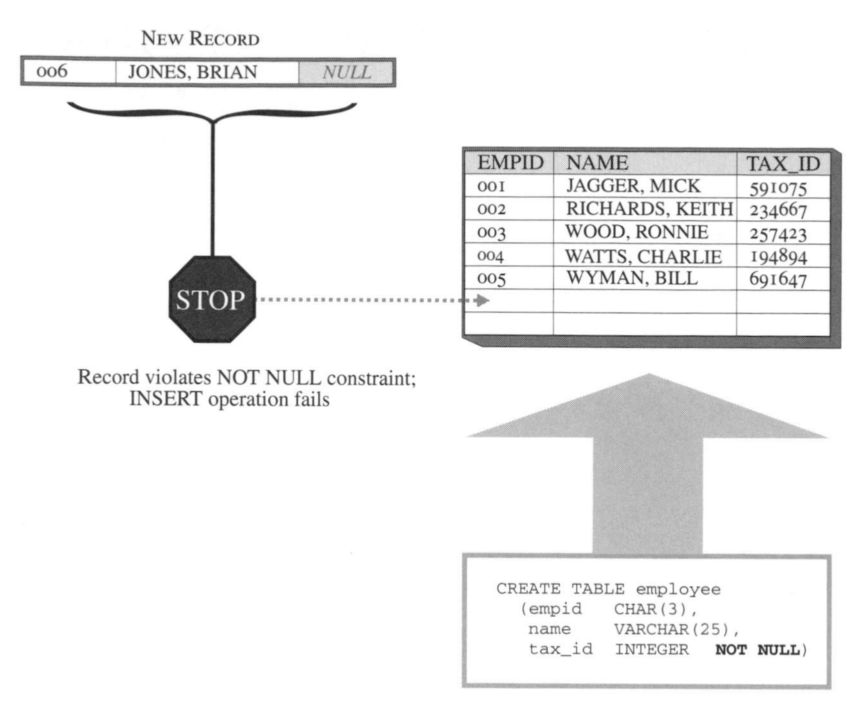

Figure 6–1 How the NOT NULL constraint prevents null values.

the column), a user-supplied value compatible with the column's data type, or a value furnished by the DB2 Database Manager. Table 6–2 shows the default values that can be provided by the DB2 Database Manager for the various DB2 UDB data types available.

Table 6–2 DB2 Database Manager-Supplied Default Values

Column Data Type	Default Value Provided
Small integer (SMALLINT)	0
Integer (INTEGER or INT)	0
Decimal (DECIMAL, DEC, NUMERIC, or NUM)	0
Single-precision floating-point (REAL or FLOAT)	0
Double-precision floating-point (DOUBLE, DOUBLE PRECISION, or FLOAT)	0
Fixed-length character string (CHARACTER or CHAR)	A string of blank characters

Table 6–2 DB2 Database Manager-Supplied Default Values *(Continued)*

Column Data Type	Default Value Provided
Varying-length character string (CHARACTER VARYING, CHAR VARYING, or VARCHAR)	A zero-length string
Long varying-length character string (LONG VARCHAR)	A zero-length string
Fixed-length double-byte character string (GRAPHIC)	A string of blank characters
Varying-length double-byte character string (VARGRAPHIC)	A zero-length string
Long varying-length double-byte character string (LONG VARGRAPHIC)	A zero-length string
Date (DATE)	The system date at the time the record is added to the table. (When a date column is added to an existing table, existing rows are assigned the date January 01, 0001.)
Time (TIME)	The system time at the time the record is added to the table. (When a time column is added to an existing table, existing rows are assigned the time 00:00:00.)
Timestamp (TIMESTAMP)	The system date and time (including microseconds) at the time the record is added to the table. (When a timestamp column is added to an existing table, existing rows are assigned a timestamp that corresponds to January 01, 0001 - 00:00:00.000000)
Binary large object (BLOB)	A zero-length string
Character large object (CLOB)	A zero-length string
Double-byte character large object (DBCLOB)	A zero-length string
Any distinct user-defined data type	The default value provided for the built-in data type the distinct user-defined data type is based on (typecast to the distinct user-defined data type).

Adapted from Table 2 on Page 51 of the DB2 SQL Reference – Volume 2 manual

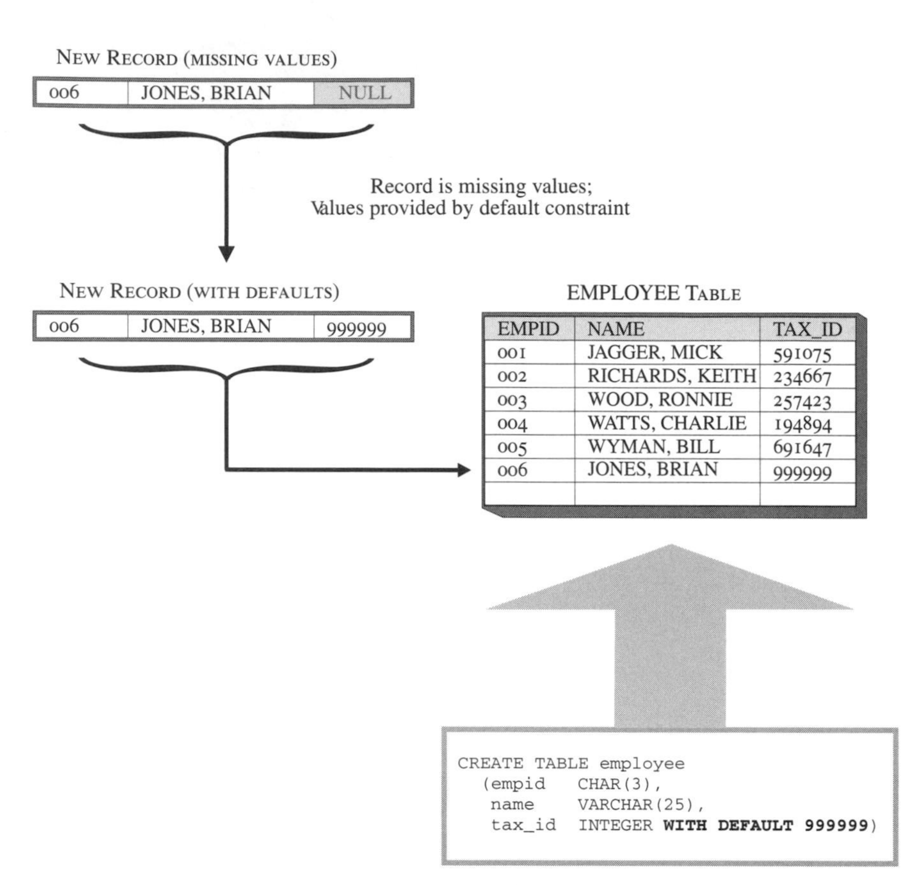

Figure 6–2 How the default constraint is used to provide data values.

Figure 6–2 illustrates how the default constraint is used.

Like NOT NULL constraints, default constraints are associated with a specific column in a base table and are usually defined during the table creation process.

Check Constraints

Sometimes, it is desirable to control what values will be accepted for a particular item and what values will not (for example, a company might decide that all nonexempt employees must be paid, at a minimum, the federal minimum wage). When this is the case, the logic needed to determine whether a value is acceptable can be incorporated directly into the data entry program being used to collect the data. A better way to achieve the same objective is by defining a check constraint for the column in the base table that is to receive the data value. A check constraint (also known as a *table check constraint*) can be used to ensure that a particular column in a base table is never assigned an unacceptable value—once a check constraint has been defined for a column, any operation that attempts to place a value in that column that does not meet specific criteria will fail.

Check constraints are comprised of one or more predicates (which are connected by the keywords AND or OR) that collectively are known as the *check condition.* This check condition is then compared with the data value provided and the result of this comparison is returned as the value "TRUE", "FALSE", or "Unknown". If the check constraint returns the value "TRUE", the value is acceptable, so it is added to the database. If, on the other hand, the check constraint returns the value "FALSE" or "Unknown", the operation attempting to place the value in the database fails, and all changes made by that operation are backed out of the database. However, it is important to note that when the results of a particular operation are rolled back because of a check constraint violation, the transaction that invoked that operation is not terminated, and other operations within that transaction are unaffected. Figure 6–3 illustrates how a simple check constraint is used.

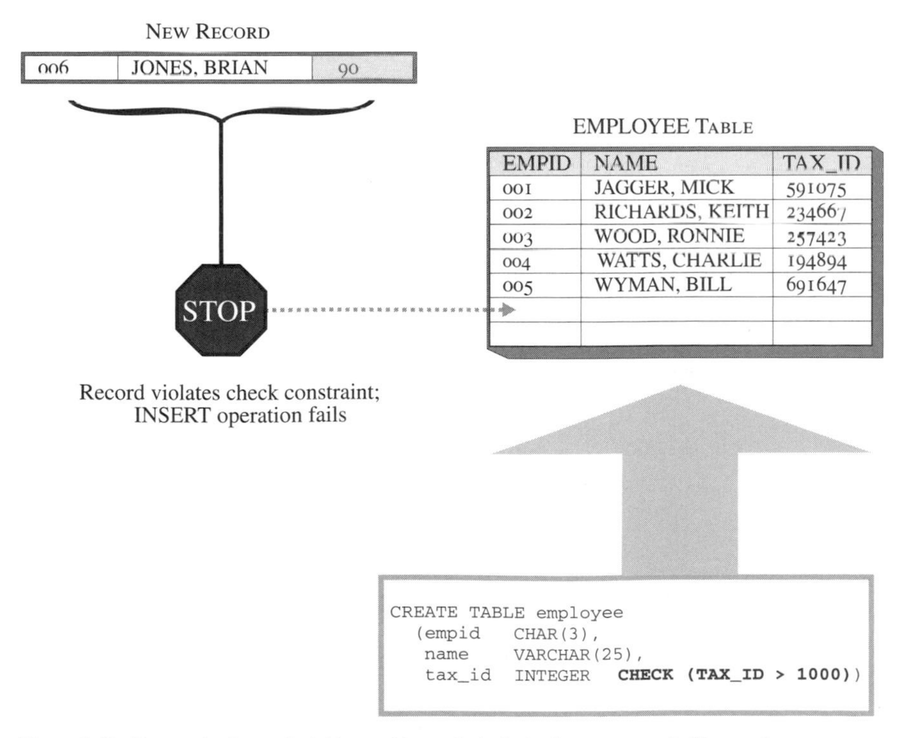

Figure 6–3 How a check constraint is used to control what values are accepted by a column.

Like NOT NULL constraints and default constraints, check constraints are associated with a specific column in a base table and are usually defined during the table creation process.

Unique Constraints

By default, records that are added to a base table can have the same values assigned to any of the columns available any number of times. As long as the records stored in the table do not contain information that should not be duplicated, this kind of behavior is acceptable. However, there are times when certain pieces of information that make up a record should be unique (for example, if an employee identification number is assigned to each individual that works for a particular company, each number used should be unique—two employees should never be assigned the same employee identification number). In these situations, the unique constraint can be used to ensure that the value(s) assigned to one or more columns when a record is added to a base table are always unique; once a unique constraint has been defined for one or more columns, any operation that attempts to place duplicate values in those columns will fail. Figure 6–4 illustrates how the unique constraint is used.

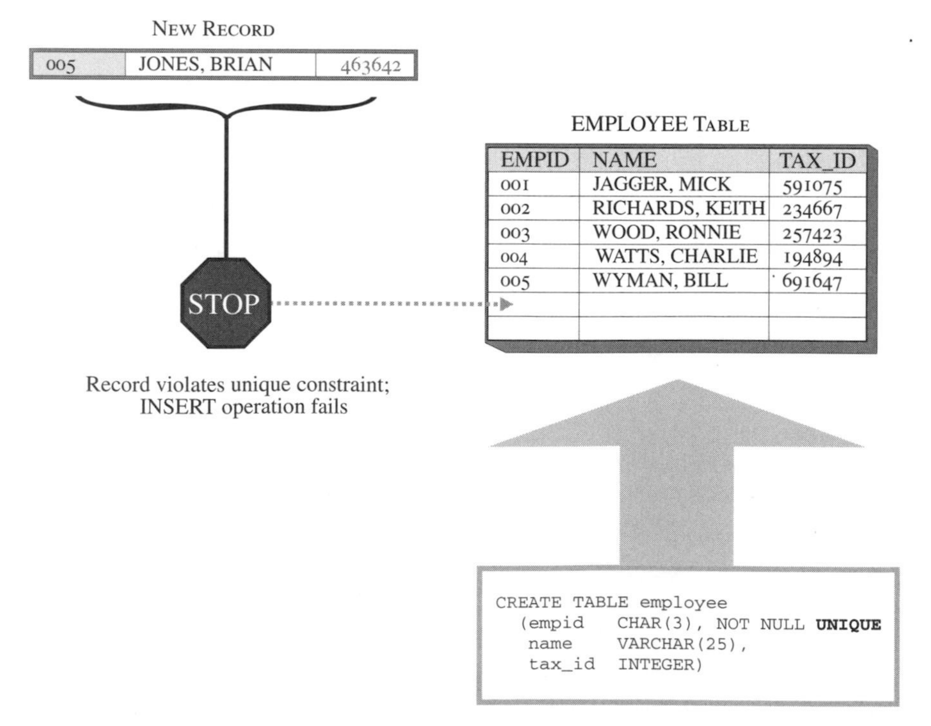

Figure 6–4 How the unique constraint prevents the duplication of data values.

Unlike NOT NULL constraints, default constraints, and check constraints, which are only associated with single columns in a base table, unique constraints can be associated with an individual column or with a group of columns. However, like the other constraints, unique constraints are usually defined during the table creation process.

Regardless of when a unique constraint is defined, when it is created the DB2 Database Manager looks to see if an index for the columns the unique constraint refers to already exists. If so, that index is marked as being unique and system-required. If not, an appropriate index is created and marked as being unique and system-required. This index is then used to enforce uniqueness whenever new records are added to the column(s) the unique constraint was defined for.

Although a unique, system-required index is used to enforce a unique constraint, there is a distinction between defining a unique constraint and creating a unique index. Although both enforce uniqueness, a unique index allows nullable columns and generally cannot be used in a referential constraint. (The value "NULL" means a field's value is undefined *and* distinct from any other value, *including* other NULL values.)

A *primary key*, which we will look at next, is a special form of unique constraint. Only one primary key is allowed per table, and every column that is used to define a primary key must be assigned the NOT NULL constraint. In addition to ensuring that every record added to a table has some unique characteristic, primary keys allow tables to participate in referential constraints.

A table can have any number of unique constraints; however, a table cannot have more than one unique constraint defined on the same set of columns. And because unique constraints are enforced by indexes, all the limitations that apply to indexes (for example, a maximum of 16 columns with a combined length of 255 bytes is allowed; none of the columns used can have a large object or long character string data type, etc.) apply to unique constraints.

Referential Integrity Constraints

If you've had the opportunity to design a database in the past, you are probably aware that data normalization is a technique used to ensure that there is only one way to get to a fact stored in a database. Data normalization is possible because two or more individual base tables can have some type of relationship with one another, and information stored in related base tables can be combined if necessary, using a join operation. Data normalization is also where referential integrity constraints come into play; referential integrity constraints (also known as referential constraints and foreign key constraints) are used to define required relationships between two base tables.

To understand how referential constraints work, it helps to look at an example. Suppose you own a small auto parts store, and you use a database to keep track of the inventory you have on hand. Many of the parts you stock will only work with a particular "make" and "model" of an automobile; therefore, your database has one table named MAKE to hold make information and another table named MODEL to hold model information. Since these two tables are related (every model must belong to a make), a referential constraint can be used to ensure that every record that is stored in the MODEL table has a corresponding record in the MAKE table; the relationship between these two tables is established by comparing values that are to be added to the "MAKE" column of the MODEL table (known as the *foreign key* of the *child table*) with the values that currently exist for the set of columns that make up the primary key of the MAKE table (known as the *parent key* of the *parent table*). To create the referential constraint just described, you would define a primary key, using one or more columns in the MAKE table, and you would define a foreign key for one or more corresponding columns in the MODEL table that reference the MAKE table's primary key. Assuming a column named MAKEID is used to create the primary key for the MAKE table and a column also named MAKEID is used to create the foreign key for the MODEL table, the referential constraint created would look something like the one shown in Figure 6–5.

In this example, a single column is used to define the parent key and the foreign key of the referential constraint. However, as with unique constraints, multiple columns can be used to define the parent key and the foreign key of a referential constraint.

The name of the column(s) used to create the foreign key of a referential constraint name do not have to be the same as the column(s) used to create the primary key of the constraint (as was the case in the previous example). However, the data types used for the column(s) that make up the primary key and the foreign key of a referential constraint must be identical.

As you can see, referential constraints are more complex than NOT NULL constraints, default constraints, check constraints, and unique constraints. In fact, they can be so complex that a set of special terms are used to identify the

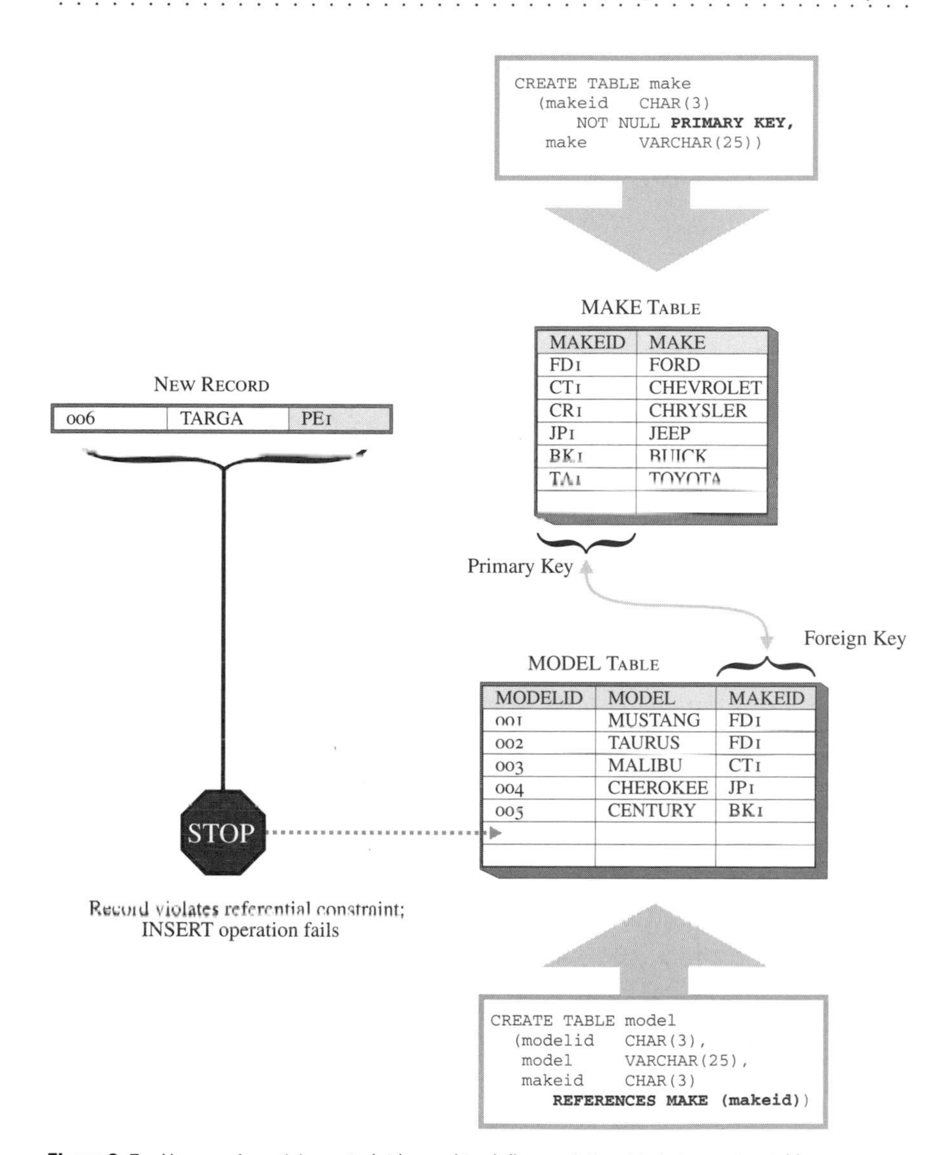

Figure 6–5 How a referential constraint is used to define a relationship between two tables.

individual components that can make up a single referential constraint. You may already be familiar with some of them; the complete list of terms used can be seen in Table 6–3.

The primary reason referential constraints are created is to guarantee that data integrity is maintained whenever one table object references another. As

Table 6–3 DB2 UDB Referential Integrity Constraint Terminology

Term	Meaning
Unique key	A column or set of columns in which every row of values is different from the values of all other rows.
Primary key	A special unique key that does not accept null values.
Foreign key	A column or set of columns in a child table whose values must match those of a parent key in a parent table.
Parent key	A primary key or unique key in a parent table that is referenced by a foreign key in a referential constraint.
Parent table	A table that contains a parent key of a referential constraint. (A table can be both a parent table and a dependent table of any number of referential constraints.)
Parent row	A row in a parent table that has at least one matching row in a dependent table.
Dependent or child table	A table that contains at least one foreign key that references a parent key in a referential constraint. (A table can be both a dependent table and a parent table of any number of referential constraints.)
Dependent or child row	A row in a dependent table that has at least one matching row in a parent table.
Descendent table	A dependent table or a descendent of a dependent table.
Descendent row	A dependent row or a descendent of a dependent row.
Referential cycle	A set of referential constraints defined in such a way that each table in the set is a descendent of itself.
Self-referencing table	A table that is both a parent table and a dependent table in the same referential constraint. (The constraint is known as a self-referencing constraint.)
Self-referencing row	A row that is a parent of itself.

long as a referential constraint is in effect, the DB2 Database Manager guarantees that, for every row in a child table that has a value in any column that is part of a foreign key, there is a corresponding row in the parent table. So what happens when an SQL operation attempts to manipulate data in a way that would violate a referential constraint? To answer this question, let's look at what could compromise data integrity if the checks and balances provided by a referential constraint were not in place:

- An insert operation could add a row of data to a child table that does not have a matching value in the corresponding parent table. (For example, using our MAKE/MODEL scenario, a record could be added to the MODEL table that does not have a corresponding value in the MAKE table.)
- An update operation could change an existing value in a child table such that it no longer has a matching value in the corresponding parent table. (For example, a record could be changed in the MODEL table so that it no longer has a corresponding value in the MAKE table.)
- An update operation could change an existing value in a parent table, leaving rows in a child table with values that no longer match those in the parent table. (For example, a record could be changed in the MAKE table, leaving records in the MODEL table that no longer have a corresponding MAKE value.)
- A delete operation could remove a value from a parent table, leaving rows in a child table with values that no longer match those in the parent table. (For example, a record could be removed from the MAKE table, leaving records in the MODEL table that no longer have a correspon-ding MAKE value.)

The DB2 Database Manager can either prohibit ("restrict") these types of operations from being performed on tables that are part of a referential constraint or it can attempt to carry out these actions in a way that will safeguard data integrity. In either case, DB2 UDB uses a set of rules to control the operation's behavior. Each referential constraint has its own set of rules (which consist of an Insert Rule, an Update Rule, and a Delete Rule), and the way a particular rule will function can be specified as part of the referential constraint creation process.

The Insert Rule for referential constraints

The Insert Rule guarantees that a value can never be inserted into the foreign key of a child table unless a matching value can be found in the correspon-ding parent key of the associated parent table. Any attempt to insert records into a child table that violates this rule will result in an error, and the insert operation will fail. In contrast, no checking is performed when records are added to the parent key of the parent table.

The Insert Rule for a referential constraint is implicitly created when the referential constraint itself is created. Figure 6–6 illustrates how a row that conforms to the Insert Rule for a referential constraint is successfully added to a child table; Figure 6–7 illustrates how a row that violates the Insert Rule causes an insert operation to fail.

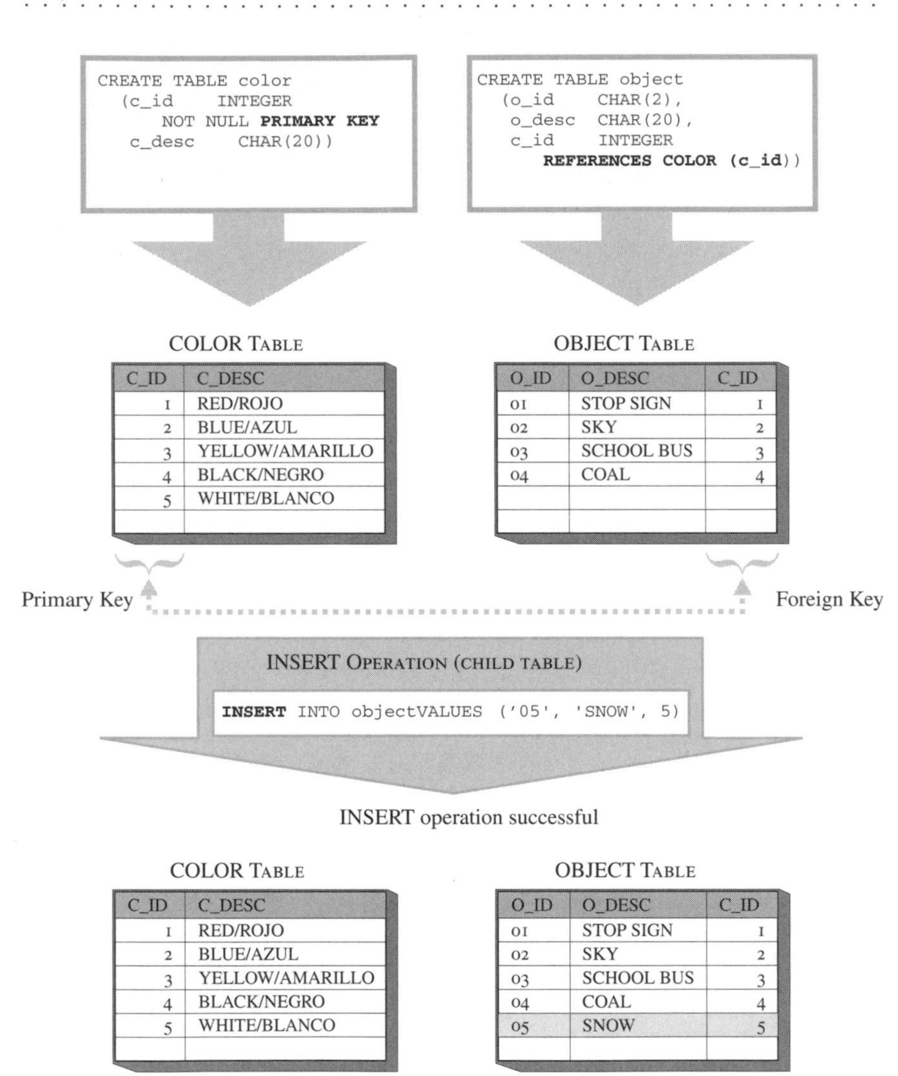

Figure 6–6 An insert operation that conforms to the Insert Rule of a referential constraint.

It is important to note that because the Insert Rule exists, records must be inserted in the parent key of the parent table before corresponding records can be inserted into the child table. (Going back to our MAKE/MODEL example, this means that a record for a new MAKE must be added to the MAKE table *before* a record that references the new MAKE can be added to the MODEL table.)

The Update Rule for referential constraints

The Update Rule controls how update operations performed against either table (child or parent) participating in a referential constraint are to be

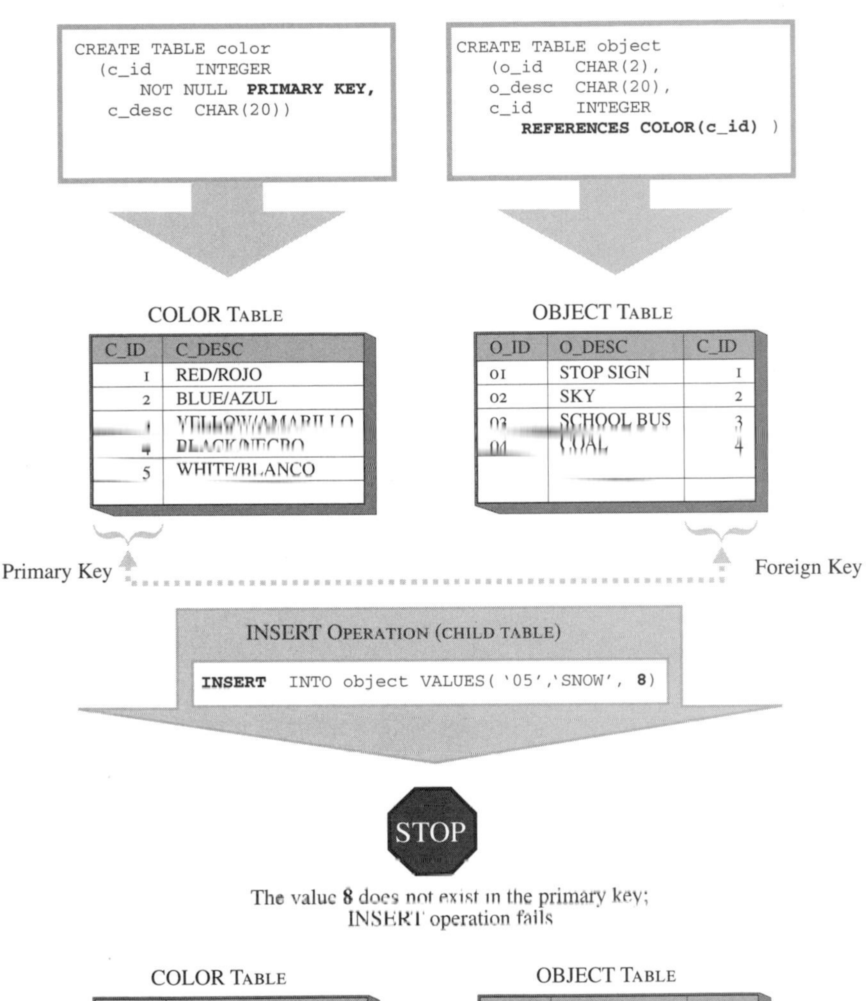

Figure 6–7 An insert operation that violates the Insert Rule of a referential constraint.

processed. The following two types of behaviors are possible, depending upon how the Update Rule is defined:

ON UPDATE NO ACTION. This definition ensures that whenever an update operation is performed on either table in a referential constraint, the value for the foreign key of each row in the child table will have a matching value in the parent key of the corresponding parent table; however, the value may not be the same as it was before the update operation occurred.

ON UPDATE RESTRICT. This definition ensures that whenever an update operation is performed on the parent table of a referential constraint, the value for the foreign key of each row in the child table will have the same matching value in the parent key of the parent table it had before the update operation was performed.

Figure 6–8 illustrates how the Update Rule is enforced when the ON UPDATE NO ACTION definition is used; Figure 6–9 illustrates how the Update Rule is enforced when the ON UPDATE RESTRICT definition is used.

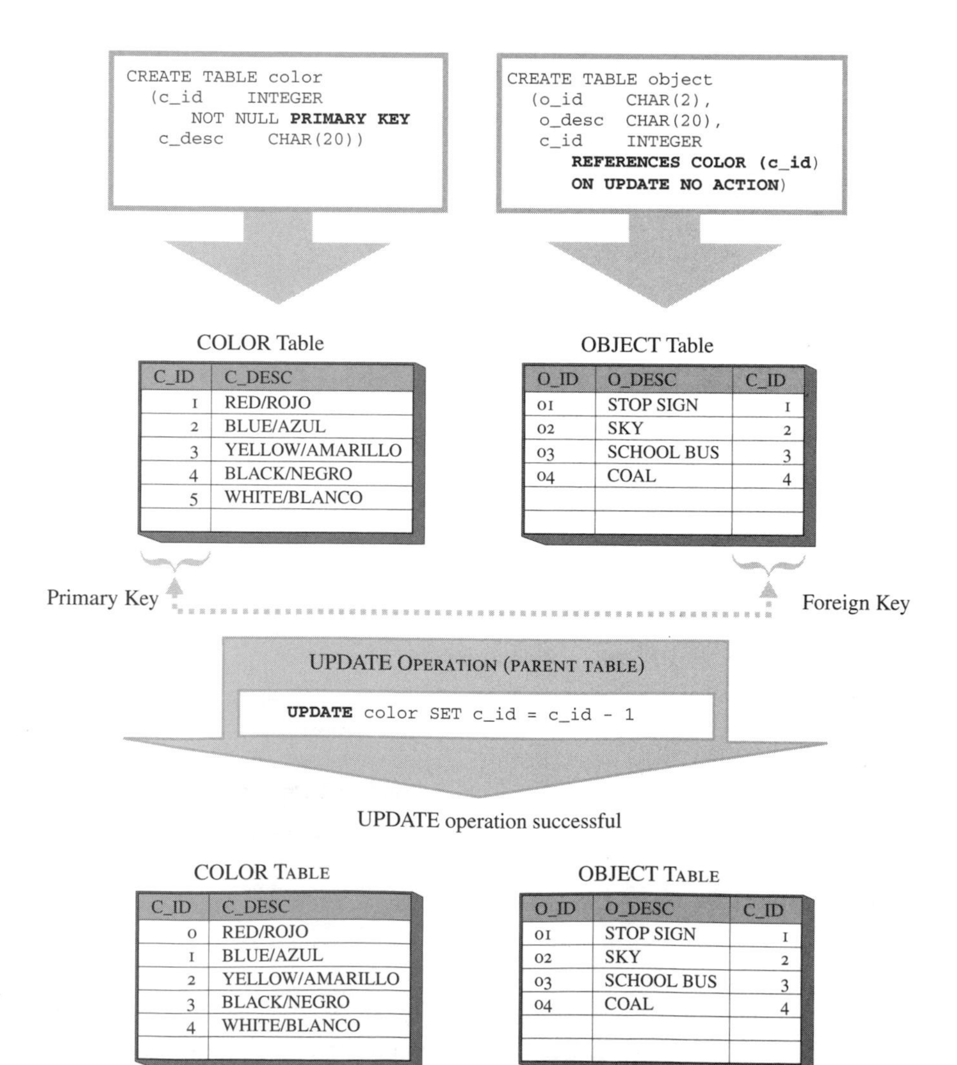

Figure 6–8 How the ON UPDATE NO ACTION Update Rule of a referential constraint is enforced.

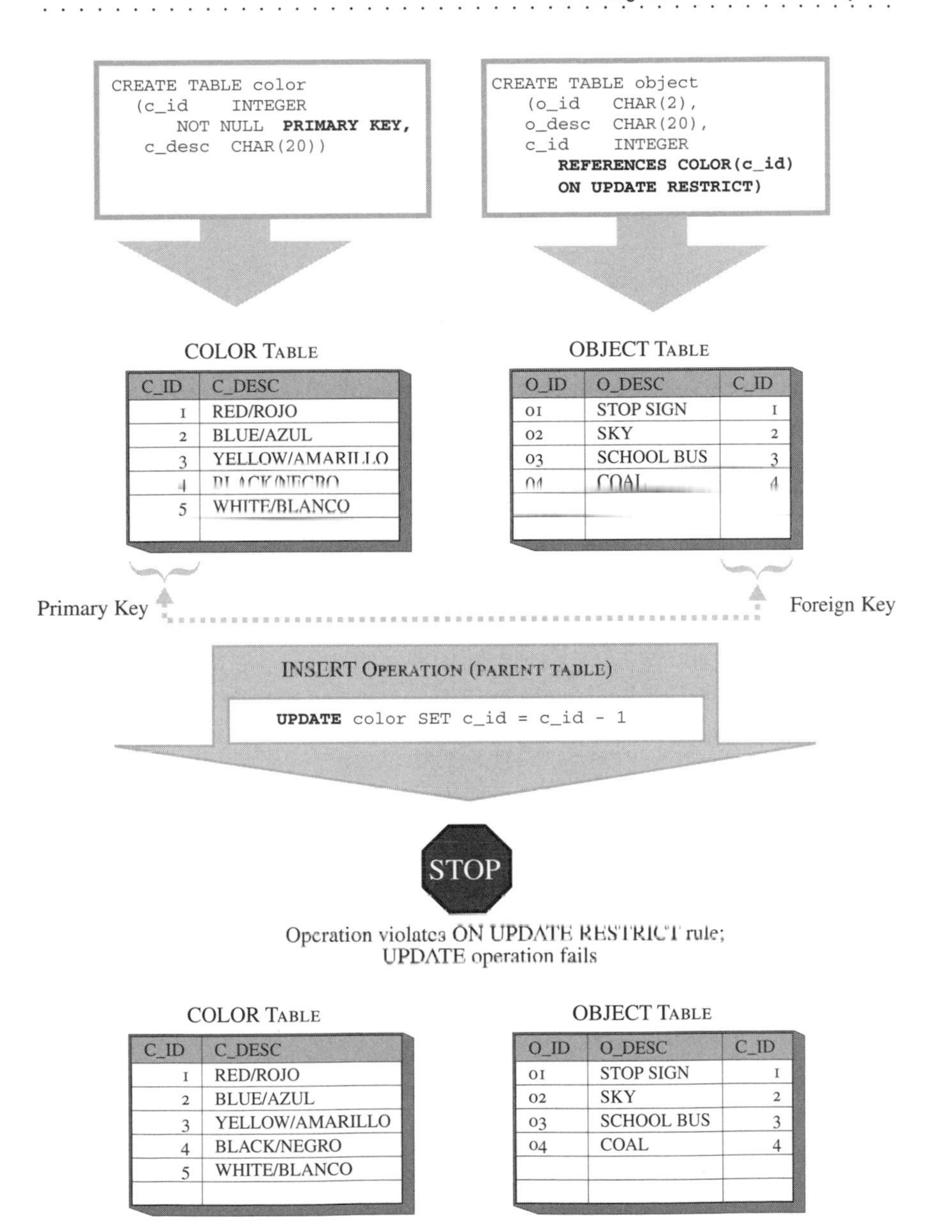

Figure 6–9 How the ON UPDATE RESTRICT Update Rule of a referential constraint is enforced.

Like the Insert Rule, the Update Rule for a referential constraint is implicitly created when the referential constraint itself is created. If no Update Rule definition is provided when the referential constraint is defined, the ON UPDATE NO ACTION definition is used as the default. Regardless of which form of the Update Rule is used, if the condition of the rule is not met, the update operation will fail, an error message will be displayed, and any changes made to the data in either table participating in the referential constraint will be backed out.

The Delete Rule for referential constraints

The Delete Rule controls how delete operations performed against the parent table of a referential constraint are to be processed. The following four types of behaviors are possible, depending upon how the Delete Rule is defined:

ON DELETE CASCADE. This definition ensures that when a parent row is deleted from the parent table of a referential constraint, all dependent rows in the child table that have matching primary key values in their foreign key are deleted as well.

ON DELETE SET NULL. This definition ensures that when a parent row is deleted from the parent table of a referential constraint, all dependant rows in the child table that have matching primary key values in their foreign key are located and their foreign key values are changed to null. Other values for the dependant row are not affected.

ON DELETE NO ACTION. This definition ensures that whenever a delete operation is performed on the parent table of a referential constraint, the value for the foreign key of each row in the child table will have a matching value in the parent key of the parent table (after all other referential constraints have been applied).

ON DELETE RESTRICT. This definition ensures that whenever a delete operation is performed on the parent table of a referential constraint, the value for the foreign key of each row in the child table will have a matching value in the parent key of the parent table (before any other referential constraints are applied).

Figure 6–10 illustrates how the Delete Rule is enforced when the ON DELETE CASCADE definition is used; Figure 6–11 illustrates how the Delete Rule is enforced when the ON DELETE SET NULL definition is used; Figure 6–12 illustrates how the Delete Rule is enforced when the ON DELETE NO ACTION definition is used; and Figure 6–13 illustrates how the Delete Rule is enforced when the ON DELETE RESTRICT definition is used.

Like the Insert Rule and the Update Rule, the Delete Rule for a referential constraint is implicitly created when the referential constraint itself is created. If no Delete Rule definition is provided when the referential constraint is defined, the ON DELETE NO ACTION definition is used as the default. No matter which form of the Delete Rule is used, if the condition of the rule is not met, an error message will be displayed, and the delete operation will fail.

If the ON DELETE CASCADE Delete Rule is used and the deletion of a parent row in a parent table causes one or more dependent rows to be delet-

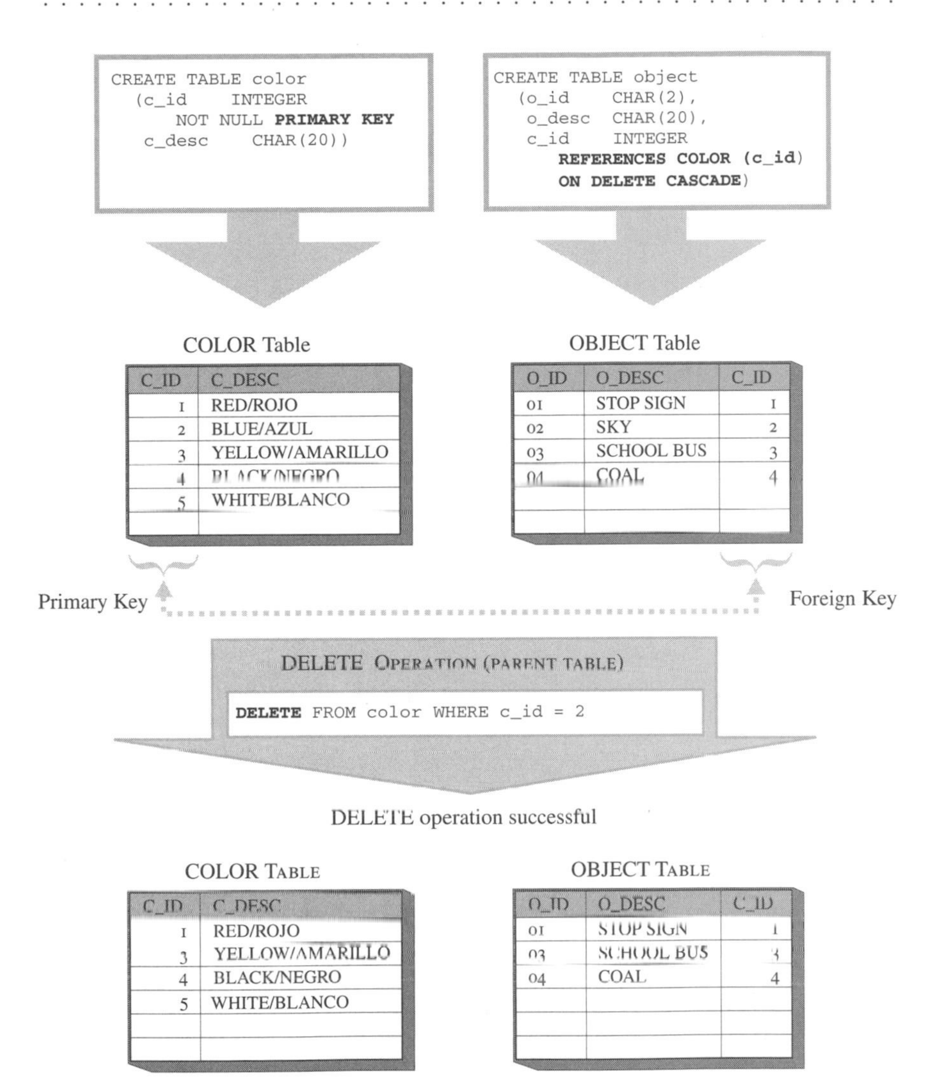

Figure 6–10 How the ON DELETE CASCADE Delete Rule of a referential constraint is enforced.

ed from the corresponding child table, the delete operation is said to have been *propagated* to the child table. In such a situation, the child table is said to be *delete-connected* to the parent table. Because a delete-connected child table can also be the parent table in another referential constraint, a delete operation that is propagated to one child table can, in turn, be propagated to another child table, and so on. Thus, the deletion of one parent row from a single parent table can result in the deletion of several hundred rows from any number of tables, depending upon how tables are delete-connected. Therefore, the ON DELETE CASCADE Delete Rule should be used with extreme caution when a hierarchy of referential constraints permeates a database.

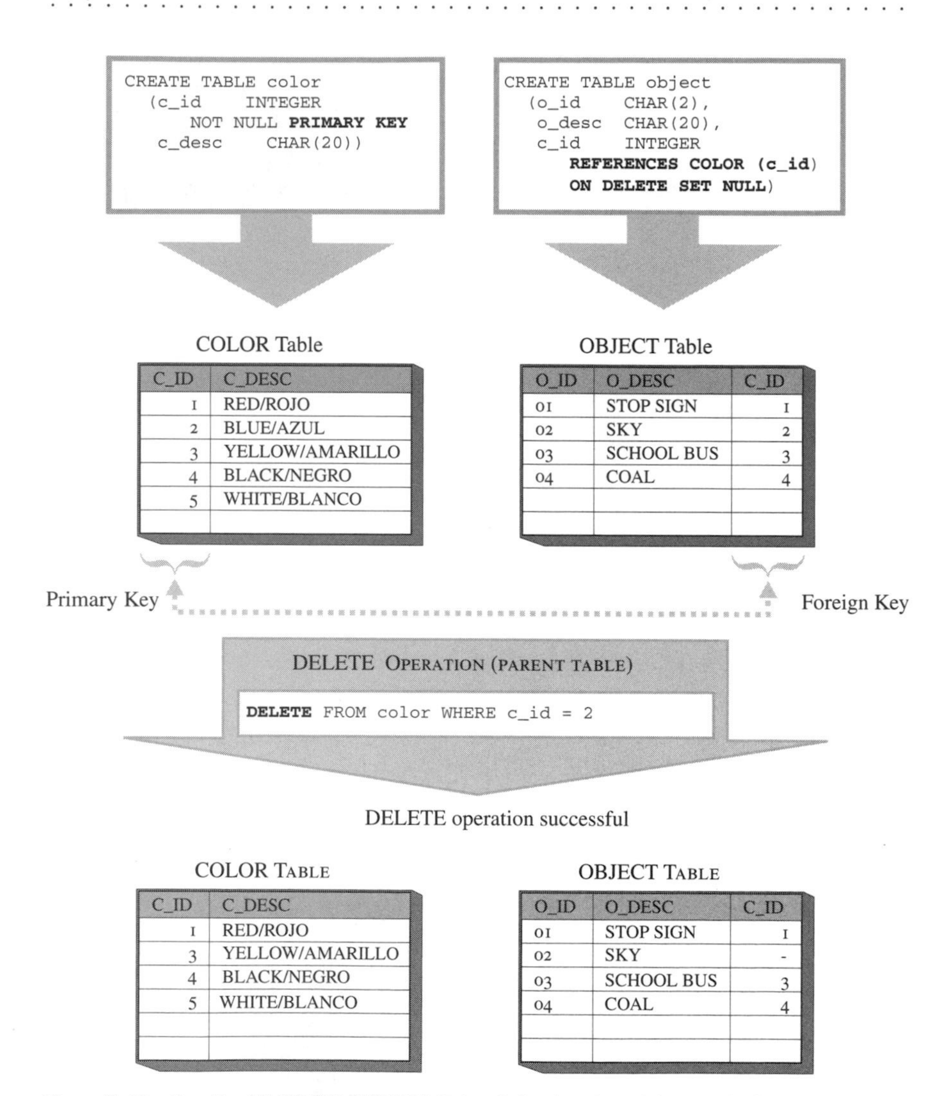

Figure 6–11 How the ON DELETE SET NULL Delete Rule of a referential constraint is enforced.

Temporarily Suspending Constraint Checking with the `SET INTEGRITY` SQL Statement

Although constraints provide a means of ensuring that some level of integrity is maintained as data is manipulated within a base table, their enforcement can prevent some types of operations from executing successfully. For example, suppose you want to bulk-load 10,000 rows of data into a base table using the LOAD utility. If the data that is to be loaded contains values that will vio-

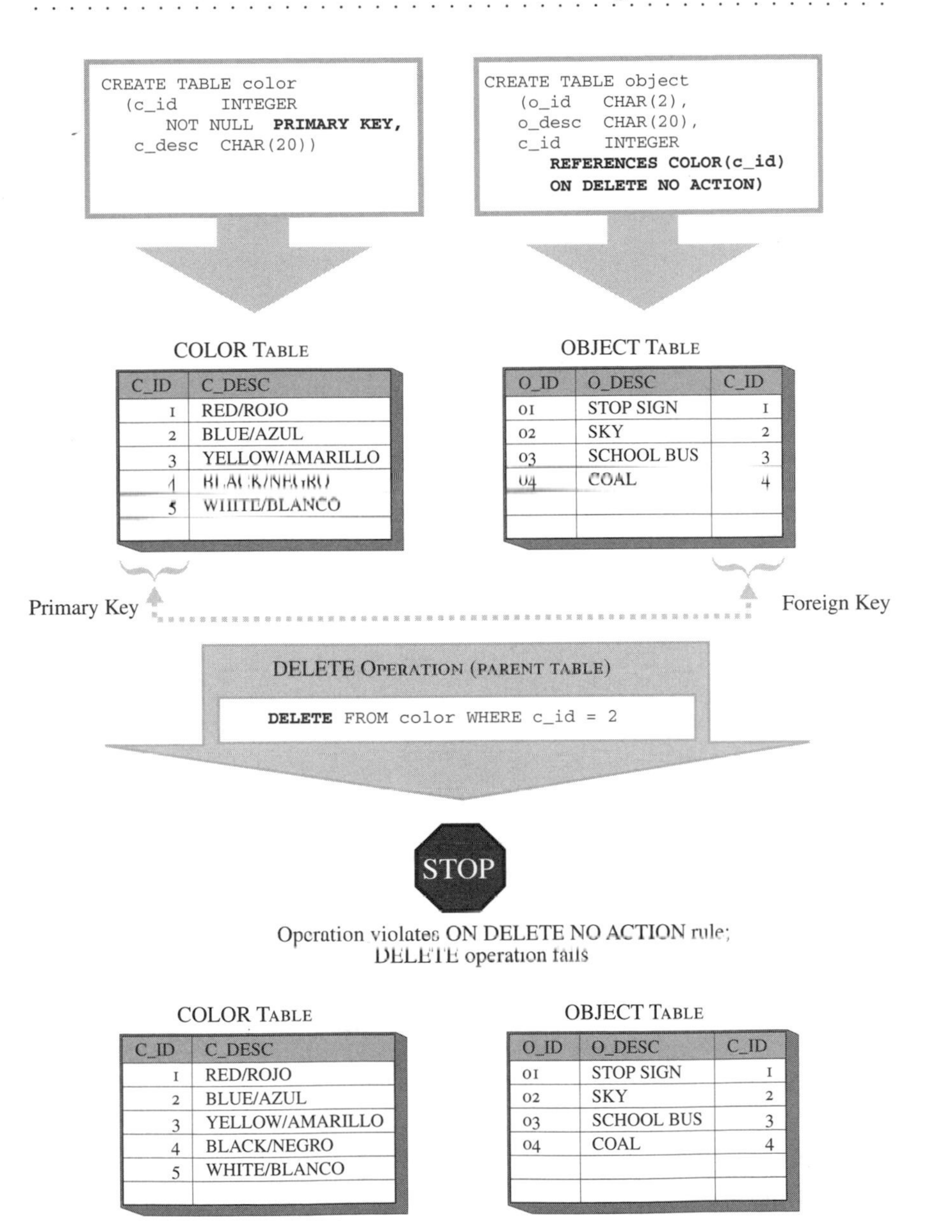

Figure 6–12 How the ON DELETE NO ACTION Delete Rule of a referential constraint is enforced.

late a constraint defined for the table the data is to be loaded into, the load operation will fail. Or suppose you wish to add a new constraint to an existing table that already contains several hundred rows of data. If one or more rows in the table contain data values that violate the constraint you wish to add, any attempt to add the constraint will fail. In situations like these, it can be advantageous to suspend constraint checking just long enough to perform

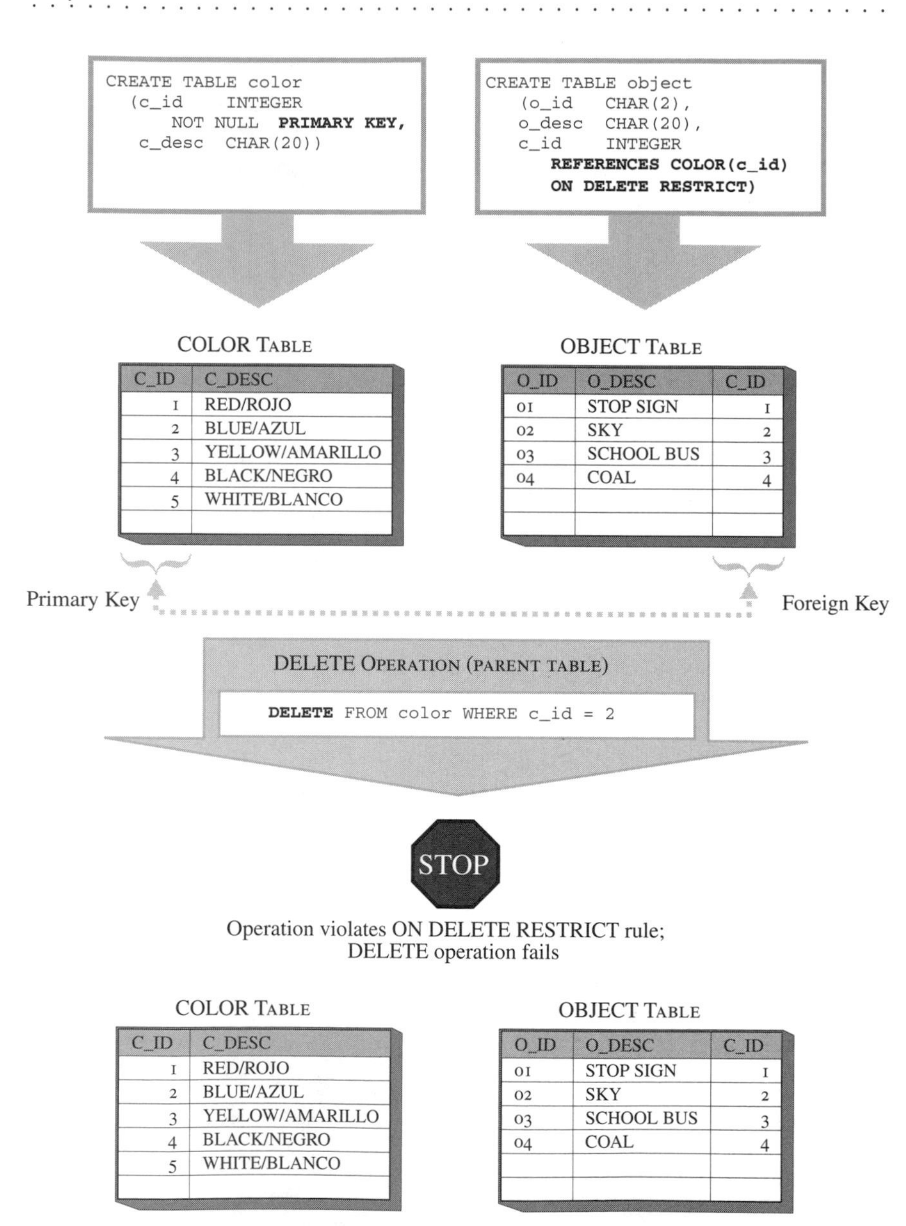

Figure 6–13 How the ON DELETE RESTRICT Delete Rule of a referential constraint is enforced.

the desired operation. However when constraint checking is suspended, at some point it must be resumed, and at that time, rows in the table that cause a constraint to be violated must be located and dealt with.

Constraint checking for a table can be suspended temporarily by executing the `SET INTEGRITY` SQL statement. When used to suspend constraint checking, the syntax for the simplest form of this statement is:

```
SET INTEGRITY FOR [TableName ,...] OFF <AccessMode>
```

where:

TableName — Identifies the name of one or more base tables that constraint checking is to be temporarily suspended for.

AccessMode — Specifies whether or not the table(s) specified can be accessed in read-only mode while constraint checking is suspended. (Valid values include NO ACCESS and READ ACCESS—if no access mode is specified, NO ACCESS is used as the default.)

So if you wanted to temporarily suspend constraint checking for a table named EMPLOYEES and deny read-only access to that table while constraint checking is turned off, you could do so by executing a `SET INTEGRITY` statement that looks something like this:

```
SET INTEGRITY FOR EMPLOYEES OFF
```

When constraint checking is suspended for a particular table, that table is placed in "Check Pending" state to indicate that it contains data that has not been checked (and that may not be free of constraint violations). While a table is in "Check Pending" state, it cannot be used in insert, update, or delete operations, nor can it be used by any DB2 UDB utility that needs to perform these types of operations. In addition, indexes cannot be created for a table while it is in "Check Pending" state, and data stored in the table can be retrieved only if the access mode specified when the `SET INTEGRITY` statement was used to place the table in "Check Pending" state allows read-only access.

Just as one form of the `SET INTEGRITY` statement is used to temporarily suspend constraint checking, another form is used to resume it. In this case, the syntax for the simplest form of the `SET INTEGRITY` statement is:

```
SET INTEGRITY FOR [TableName] IMMEDIATE CHECKED FOR
EXCEPTION [IN [TableName] USE [ExceptionTable] ,...]
```

or

```
SET INTEGRITY FOR [[TableName] [ConstraintType] ,...]
IMMEDIATE UNCHECKED
```

where:

TableName — Identifies the name of one or more base tables that suspended constraint checking is to be resumed for as well as one or more base tables where all rows that are in violation of a referential constraint or a check constraint are to be copied from.

ExceptionTable Identifies the name of a base table where all rows that are in violation of a referential constraint or a check constraint are to be copied to.

ConstaintType Identifies the type of constraint checking that is to be resumed. (Valid values include FOREIGN KEY, CHECK, DATALINK RECONCILE PENDING, MATERILIZED QUERY, GENERATED COLUMN, STAGING, and ALL.)

Thus, if you wanted to resume constraint checking for the EMPLOYEES table that constraint checking was suspended for in the previous example, you could do so by executing a `SET INTEGRITY` statement that looks something like this:

```
SET INTEGRITY FOR EMPLOYEES
IMMEDIATE CHECKED
```

When this particular form of the `SET INTEGRITY` statement is executed, the table named EMPLOYEES is taken out of the “Check Pending” state, and each row of data stored in the table is checked for constraint violations. If an offensive row is found, constraint checking is stopped, and the EMPLOYEES table is returned to the “Check Pending” state. However, if this form of the `SET INTEGRITY` statement is executed:

```
SET INTEGRITY FOR EMPLOYEES
IMMEDIATE CHECKED
FOR EXCEPTION IN EMPLOYEES USE BAD_ROWS
```

each row found that violates one or more of the constraints that have been defined for the EMPLOYEES table will be copied to a table named BAD_ROWS, where it can be corrected and copied back to the EMPLOYEES table if so desired. And finally, if this form of the `SET INTEGRITY` statement is executed:

```
SET INTEGRITY FOR EMPLOYEES ALL
IMMEDIATE UNCHECKED
```

the table named EMPLOYEES is taken out of the “Check Pending” state, and no constraint checking is performed. However, this is a very hazardous thing to do and should only be done if you have some independent means of ensuring that the EMPLOYEES table does not contain data that violates one or more constraints defined.

Creating Tables with the CREATE TABLE SQL Statement

In Chapter 4, we saw that a table is a logical database object that acts as the main repository in a database. We also saw that there are two ways a table can be created: by using the Create Table Wizard provided with the Control Center and by using the CREATE TABLE SQL statement.

Up until now, we've seen how to use a relatively simple form of the CREATE TABLE statement to construct very basic tables. Yet, the CREATE TABLE is probably the most complex SQL statement available (in fact, over 60 pages of the DB2 UDB SQL Reference manual are devoted to this statement alone). And because this statement is so complex, its syntax can be quite intimidating. Fortunately, you do not have to know all the nuances of the CREATE TABLE statement to pass the DB2 UDB V8.1 Family Fundamentals certification exam (Exam 700). Still, you do need to know the basics, and the remainder of this chapter is devoted to the CREATE TABLE statement and to the syntax you must be familiar with. With that said, let's begin by taking a look at the simplest form of the CREATE TABLE SQL statement.

In its simplest form, the syntax for the CREATE TABLE SQL statement is:

```
CREATE TABLE [TableName] ( [Element] ,...)
<IN [TablespaceName]>
<INDEX IN [TablespaceName]>
<LONG IN [TablespaceName]>
```

where:

TableName — Identifies the name to be assigned to the table to be created. (A table name must be unique within the schema the table is to be defined in.)

Element — Identifies one or more columns, unique/primary key constraints, referential constraints, and/or check constraints to be included in the table definition. The syntax used for defining each of these elements varies according to the element being defined.

TablespaceName — Identifies the tablespace that the table and its regular data, indexes, and/or long data/large object data is to be stored in. (Regular data, indexes, and long/large object data can only be stored in separate tablespaces if DMS tablespaces are used.)

The basic syntax used to define a column is:

```
 [ColumnName] [DataType]
<NOT NULL>
<WITH DEFAULT <[DefaultValue] | CURRENT DATE |
    CURRENT TIME | CURRENT TIMESTAMP>>
<UniqueConstraint>
<CheckConstraint>
<ReferentialConstraint>
```

where:

ColumnName	Identifies the unique name to be assigned to the column to be created.
DataType	Identifies the data type (built-in or user-defined) to be assigned to the column to be created; the data type specified determines the kind of data values that can be stored in the column. (Table 6–4 contains a list of the data type definitions that are valid).
DefaultValue	Identifies the value to be provided for the column in the event no value is supplied for the column when an insert or update operation is performed against the table.
UniqueConstraint	Identifies a unique or primary key constraint to be associated with the column.
CheckConsraint	Identifies a check constraint to be associated with the column.
ReferentialConstraint	Identifies a referential constraint to be associated with the column.

Table 6–4 Data Type Definitions That Can Be Used with the CREATE TABLE Statement

Data Type	Definition(s)
Small Integer	SMALLINT
Integer	INTEGER INT
Big Integer	BIGINT

Table 6–4 Data Type Definitions That Can Be Used with the CREATE TABLE Statement *(Continued)*

Data Type	Definition(s)
Decimal	DECIMAL(*Precision, Scale*) DEC(*Precision, Scale*) NUMERIC(*Precision, Scale*) NUM(*Precision, Scale*) where *Precision* is any number between 1 and 31; *Scale* is any number between 0 and Precision
Single-Precision Floating-Point	REAL FLOAT(*Precision*) where *Precision* is any number between 1 and 24
Double-Precision Floating-Point	DOUBLE FLOAT(*Precision*) where *Precision* is any number between 25 and 53
Fixed-Length Character String	CHARACTER(*Length*) <FOR BIT DATA>* CHAR(*Length*) <FOR BIT DATA>* where *Length* is any number between 1 and 254
Varying-Length Character String	CHARACTER VARYING(*MaxLength*) <FOR BIT DATA>* CHAR VARYING(*MaxLength*) <FOR BIT DATA>* VARCHAR(*MaxLength*) <FOR BIT DATA>* where *MaxLength* is any number between 1 and 32,672
Long Varying-Length Character String	LONG VARCHAR
Fixed-Length Double-Byte Character String	GRAPHIC(*Length*) where *Length* is any number between 1 and 127
Varying-Length Double-Byte Character String	VARGRAPHIC(*MaxLength*) where *MaxLength* is any number between 1 and 16,336
Long Varying-Length Double-Byte Character String	LONG VARGRAPHIC
Date	DATE
Time	TIME
	(*continued*)

<table>
<tr><th colspan="2">Table 6–4 Continued</th></tr>
<tr><th>Data Type</th><th>Definition(s)</th></tr>
<tr><td>Timestamp</td><td>TIMESTAMP</td></tr>
<tr><td>Binary Large Object</td><td>BINARY LARGE OBJECT(Size <K | M | G>)
BLOB(Size <K | M | G>)
where Length is any number between 1 and 2,147,483,647; if K (for kilobyte) is specified, Length is any number between 1 and 2,097,152; if M (for megabyte) is specified, Length is any number between 1 and 2,048; if G (for gigabyte) is specified, Length is any number between 1 and 2.</td></tr>
<tr><td>Character Large Object</td><td>CHARACTER LARGE OBJECT(Size <K | M | G>)
CHAR LARGE OBJECT(Size <K | M | G>)
CLOB(Size <K | M | G>)
where Length is any number between 1 and 2,147,483,647; if K (for kilobyte) is specified, Length is any number between 1 and 2,097,152; if M (for megabyte) is specified, Length is any number between 1 and 2,048; if G (for gigabyte) is specified, Length is any number between 1 and 2.</td></tr>
<tr><td>Double-Byte Character Large Object</td><td>DBCLOB(Size <K | M | G>)
where Length is any number between 1 and 1,073,741,823; if K (for kilobyte) is specified, Length is any number between 1 and 1,048,576; if M (for megabyte) is specified, Length is any number between 1 and 1,024; if G (for gigabyte) is specified, Length is must be 1.</td></tr>
<tr><td colspan="2">*If the FOR BIT DATA option is used with any character string data type definition, the contents of the column the data type is assigned to are treated as binary data. As a result, code page conversions are not performed if data is exchanged between other systems, and all comparisons made are done in binary, regardless of the collating sequence used by the database.</td></tr>
</table>

The syntax used to create a unique or primary key constraint as part of a column definition is:

```
<CONSTRAINT [ConstraintName]> [UNIQUE | PRIMARY KEY]
```

where:

ConstraintName Identifies the unique name to be assigned to the constraint to be created.

The syntax used to create a check constraint as part of a column definition is:

```
<CONSTRAINT [ConstraintName]> CHECK ( [CheckCondition] )
<ENFORCED | NOT ENFORCED>
<ENABLE QUERY OPTIMIZATION | DISABLE QUERY OPTIMIZATION>
```

where:

ConstraintName	Identifies the unique name to be assigned to the constraint to be created.
CheckCondition	Identifies a condition or test that must evaluate to TRUE before the value provided for the column will actually be stored in the table.

And finally, the syntax used to create a referential constraint as part of a column definition is:

```
<CONSTRAINT [ConstraintName]>
REFERENCES [PKTableName] < ( [PKColumnName] ,...) >
<ON UPDATE [NO ACTION | RESTRICT]>
<ON DELETE [CASCADE | SET NULL | NO ACTION |
RESTRICT]>
<ENFORCED | NOT ENFORCED>
<ENABLE QUERY OPTIMIZATION | DISABLE QUERY OPTIMIZATION>
```

where:

ConstraintName	Identifies the unique name to be assigned to the constraint to be created.
PKTableName	Identifies the name of the parent table that is to participate in the referential constraint.
PKColumnName	Identifies the column(s) that make up the parent key of the parent table that is to participate in the referential constraint.

Thus, if you wanted to create a table that had three columns in it, two of which use an integer data type and another that uses a fixed-length character string data type, you could do so by executing a CREATE TABLE SQL statement that looks something like this:

```
CREATE TABLE EMPLOYEES
     (EMPID   INTEGER,
      NAME    CHAR(50)
      DEPT    INTEGER)
```

If you wanted to create the same table such that the EMPID column had both the NOT NULL constraint and a unique constraint associated with it, you could do so by executing a CREATE TABLE statement that looks something like this:

```
CREATE TABLE EMPLOYEES
     (EMPID  INTEGER NOT NULL PRIMARY KEY,
      NAME   CHAR(50)
      DEPT   INTEGER)
```

And if you wanted to create the same table such that the DEPT column participates in a referential constraint with the DEPARTMENT table, you could do so by executing a CREATE TABLE statement that looks something like this:

```
CREATE TABLE EMPLOYEES
     (EMPID  INTEGER,
      NAME   CHAR(50)
      DEPT   INTEGER REFERENCES DEPARTMENT (DEPTID))
```

As you can see, a unique constraint, a check constraint, and/or a referential constraint that involves a single column can be defined as part of that particular column's definition. But what if you needed to define a constraint that encompasses multiple columns in the table? You do this by defining a constraint as another element, rather than as an extension to a single column's definition. The basic syntax used to define a unique constraint as an individual element is:

```
<CONSTRAINT [ConstraintName]> [UNIQUE | PRIMARY KEY]
( [ColumnName] ,...)
```

where:

ConstraintName	Identifies the unique name to be assigned to the constraint to be created.
ColumnName	Identifies one or more columns that are to be part of the unique or primary key constraint to be created.

The syntax used to create a check constraint as an individual element is the same as the syntax used to create a check constraint as part of a column definition:

```
<CONSTRAINT [ConstraintName]> CHECK ( [CheckCondition] )
<ENFORCED | NOT ENFORCED>
<ENABLE QUERY OPTIMIZATION | DISABLE QUERY OPTIMIZATION>
```

where:

ConstraintName	Identifies the unique name to be assigned to the constraint to be created.

CheckCondition Identifies a condition or test that must evaluate to TRUE before the value provided for the column will actually be stored in the table.

And finally, the syntax used to create a referential constraint as an individual element is:

```
<CONSTRAINT [ConstraintName]>
FOREIGN KEY ( [ColumnName] ,...)
REFERENCES [PKTableName] < ( [PKColumnName] ,...) >
<ON UPDATE [NO ACTION | RESTRICT]>
<ON DELETE [CASCADE | SET NULL | NO ACTION |
   RESTRICT]>
<ENFORCED | NOT ENFORCED>
<ENABLE QUERY OPTIMIZATION | DISABLE QUERY OPTIMIZATION>
```

where:

ConstraintName Identifies the unique name to be assigned to the constraint to be created.

ColumnName Identifies one or more columns that are to be part of the referential constraint to be created.

PKTableName Identifies the name of the parent table that is to participate in the referential constraint.

PKColumnName Identifies the column(s) that make up the parent key of the parent table that is to participate in the referential constraint.

Thus, a table that was created by executing a `CREATE TABLE` statement that looks something like this:

```
CREATE TABLE EMPLOYEES
    (EMPID  INTEGER NOT NULL PRIMARY KEY,
     NAME   CHAR(50)
     DEPT   INTEGER REFERENCES DEPARTMENT (DEPTID))
```

could also be created by executing a `CREATE TABLE` statement that looks something like this:

```
CREATE TABLE EMPLOYEES
    (EMPID  INTEGER NOT NULL,
     NAME   CHAR(50)
     DEPT   INTEGER,
     PRIMARY KEY (EMPID),
     FOREIGN KEY (DEPT) REFERENCES DEPARTMENT (DEPTID))
```

Creating Tables That Are Similar to Existing Tables

At times, it may be desirable to create a new table that has the same definition as an existing table. To perform such an operation, you could execute a CREATE TABLE statement that looks identical to the CREATE TABLE statement used to define the original table. Or better still, you could use a special form of the CREATE TABLE statement. The syntax for this form of the CREATE TABLE is:

```
CREATE TABLE [TableName] LIKE [SourceTable]
<[INCLUDING | EXCLUDING] COLUMN DEFAULTS>
<[INCLUDING | EXCLUDING] IDENTITY COLUMN ATTRIBUTES>
```

where:

TableName — Identifies the unique name to be assigned to the table to be created.

SourceTable — Identifies the name of an existing table whose structure is to be used to define the table to be created.

When this form of the CREATE TABLE is executed, the table that is ultimately created will have the same number of columns as the source table specified, and these columns will have the same names, data types, and nullability characteristics as those of the source table. In addition, unless the EXCLUDING COLUMN DEFAULTS option is specified, any default constraints defined for columns in the source table will be copied to the new table as well. However, no other attributes of the source table will be duplicated. Thus, the table that is created will not contain unique constraints, referential constraints, triggers, or indexes that have been defined for the source table used.

A Word about Declared Temporary Tables

Before we look at some more complex examples of the CREATE TABLE statement, another type of table that is commonly used should be mentioned. This type of table is known as a declared temporary table. Unlike base tables, whose descriptions and constraints are stored in the system catalog tables of the database to which they belong, declared temporary tables are not persistent and can only be used by the application that creates them—and only for the life of the application. When the application that creates a declared temporary table terminates, the rows of the table are deleted, and the description of the table is dropped. Whereas base tables are created with the CREATE

TABLE SQL statement, declared temporary tables are created with the DECLARE GLOBAL TEMPORARY TABLE statement.

CREATE TABLE SQL Statement Examples

Now that we've seen the basic syntax for the CREATE TABLE statement and have examined some simple examples of the CREATE TABLE statement's use, let's take a look at a few more complex CREATE TABLE statement examples and identify the characteristics of the resulting tables that would be created if each statement shown were executed.

Example 1

If the following CREATE TABLE statement is executed:

```
CREATE TABLE PROJECT
     (PROJNO     CHAR(6) NOT NULL,
      PROJNAME   VARCHAR(24) NOT NULL,
      DEPTNO     SMALLINT,
      BUDGET     DECIMAL(6,2),
      STARTDATE  DATE,
      ENDDATE    DATE)
```

A table named PROJECT will be created as follows:

- The first column will be assigned the name PROJNO and will be used to store fixed-length character string data that is six characters in length (for example, 'PROJ01', 'PROJ02', etc.).
- The second column will be assigned the name PROJNAME and it will be used to store variable-length character string data that can be up to 24 characters in length (for example, 'DB2 Benchmarks Tool', 'Auto-Configuration Tool', etc.).
- The third column will be assigned the name DEPTNO and will be used to store numeric values in the range of –32,768 to +32,767.
- The fourth column will be assigned the name BUDGET and will be used to store numerical values that contain both whole and fractional parts. Up to six numbers can be specified—four for the whole number part and two for the fractional part (for example, 1500.00, 2000.50, etc.).

- The fifth column will be assigned the name STARTDATE and will be used to store date values.
- The sixth column will be assigned the name ENDDATE and will also be used to store date values.
- Whenever data is added to the PROJECT table, values must be provided for the PROJNO column and the PROJNAME column. (Null values are not allowed because the NOT NULL constraint was defined for both of these columns.)
- The PROJECT table will be created in the tablespace USERSPACE1 (which was not specified, but is the default).

Example 2

If the following `CREATE TABLE` statement is executed:

```
CREATE TABLE SALES
      (PO_NUMBER   INTEGER NOT NULL CONSTRAINT UC1 UNIQUE,
       DATE         DATE NOT NULL WITH DEFAULT),
       OFFICE       CHAR(128) NOT NULL WITH DEFAULT 'HQ',
       AMT          DECIMAL(10,2) NOT NULL CHECK (AMT >
                    99.99)
      IN MY_SPACE
```

A table named SALES will be created as follows:

- The first column will be assigned the name PO_NUMBER (for Purchase Order Number) and will be used to store numeric values in the range of –32,768 to +32,767.
- The second column will be assigned the name DATE and will be used to store date values.
- The third column will be assigned the name OFFICE and will be used to store fixed-length character string data that can be up to 128 characters in length (for example, 'Baltimore/Washington', 'Dallas/Ft. Worth', etc.).
- The fourth column will be assigned the name AMT (for Amount) and will be used to store numerical values that contain both whole and fractional parts. Up to 10 numbers can be specified—eight for the whole number part and two for the fractional part (for example, 15000000.00, 20000000.50, etc.).
- Whenever data is added to the SALES table, values must be provided for the PO_NUMBER and the AMT columns. (Null values are not allowed

in any column because the NOT NULL constraint was defined for each column; however, default values are provided for two columns.)

- Every value provided for the PO_NUMBER column must be unique. (Because a unique constraint named UC1 was created for the PO_NUMBER column.)
- An index will automatically be created for the PO_NUMBER column. As data is added to the table, the values provided for the PO_NUMBER column will be added to the index, and the index will be sorted in ascending order.
- If no value is provided for the AMT column, the system date at the time a row is inserted into the SALES table will be written to the column by default (because a default constraint was created for the DATE column).
- If no value is provided for the OFFICE column, the value HQ will be written to the column by default (because a default constraint was created for the OFFICE column.).
- Every value provided for the AMT column must be greater than or equal to 100.00 (because a check constraint was created for the AMT column).
- The SALES table will be created in the tablespace MY_SPACE.

Example 3

If the following CREATE TABLE statements are executed:

```
CREATE TABLE EMPLOYEE
   (EMPID       INT NOT NULL PRIMARY KEY,
    EMP_FNAME   CHAR(30),
    EMP_LNAME   CHAR(30))

CREATE TABLE PAYROLL
    (EMPID         INTEGER,
     WEEKNUMBER   CHAR(3),
     PAYCHECK     DECIMAL(6,2),
   CONSTRAINT FKCONST FOREIGN KEY (EMPID)
      REFERENCES EMPLOYEE(EMPID) ON DELETE CASCADE,
   CONSTRAINT CHK1 CHECK (PAYCHECK > 0 AND WEEKNUMBER
      BETWEEN 1 AND 52))
```

A table named EMPLOYEE will be created as follows:

- The first column will be assigned the name EMPID (for Employee ID) and will be used to store numeric values in the range of –32,768 to +32,767.
- The second column will be assigned the name EMP_FNAME (for Employee First Name) and will be used to store fixed-length character string data that can be up to 30 characters in length (for example, 'Mark', 'Bob', etc.).
- The third column will be assigned the name EMP_LNAME (for Employee Last Name) and will be used to store fixed-length character string data that can be up to 30 characters in length (for example, 'Hayakawa', 'Jancer', etc.).
- Whenever data is added to the EMPLOYEE table, values must be provided for the EMPID column. (Null values are not allowed because the NOT NULL constraint was defined for this column.)
- Every value provided for the EMPID column must be unique (because a unique constraint was created for the EMPID column).
- An index will automatically be created for the EMPID column. As data is added to the table, the values provided for the EMPID column will be added to the index, and the index will be sorted in ascending order.
- The EMPLOYEE table will be created in the tablespace USERSPACE1.

A table named PAYROLL will also be created as follows:

- The first column will be assigned the name EMPID and will be used to store numeric values in the range of –32,768 to +32,767.
- The second column will be assigned the name WEEKNUMBER and will be used to store fixed-length character string data that can be up to three characters in length (for example, '1', '35', etc.).
- The third column will be assigned the name PAYCHECK and will be used to store numerical values that contain both whole and fractional parts. Up to six numbers can be specified—four for the whole number part and two for the fractional part (for example, 1500.00, 2000.50, etc.).
- An index will automatically be created for the EMPID column. As data is added to the table, the values provided for the EMPID column will be added to the index, and the index will be sorted in ascending order.
- Every value entered in the EMPID column must have a matching value in the EMPID column of the EMPLOYEE table created earlier (because a referential constraint in which the EMPID column of the EMPLOYEE

table is the parent key and the EMPID column of the PAYROLL table is the foreign key has been created—this referential constraint is assigned the name FKCONST).

- Whenever a row is deleted from the EMPLOYEE table created earlier, all rows in the PAYROLL table that have a value in the EMPID column matching the primary key of the row being deleted will also be deleted.
- Every value provided for the PAYCHECK column must be greater than 0 (because a check constraint named CHK1 was created for the PAY-CHECK and WEEKNUMBER columns).
- Every value provided for the WEEKNUMBER column must be greater than or equal to 1 and less than or equal to 52. (Again, a check constraint named CHK1 was created for the PAYCHECK and WEEKNUMBER columns.)
- The EMPLOYEE table will be created in the tablespace USERSPACE1.

Practice Questions

Question 1

Which of the following is not a valid DB2 data type?

- ❍ A. BIGINT
- ❍ B. SMALLINT
- ❍ C. IDENTITY
- ❍ D. INTEGER

Question 2

Which type of key is defined on the parent table to implement referential constraints?

- ❍ A. Unique key
- ❍ B. Primary key
- ❍ C. Foreign key
- ❍ D. Composite key

Question 3

Given the following tables:

TABLEA

empid	name
1	USER1
2	USER2

TABLEB

empid	weekno	payamt
1	1	1000.00
1	2	1000.00
2	1	2000.00

and the fact that TABLEB was defined as follows:

```
CREATE TABLE tableb ( empid      SMALLINT,
                      weekno     SMALLINT,
                      payamt     DECIMAL(6,2),
    CONSTRAINT const1 FOREIGN KEY (empid) REFERENCES
       tablea(empid)
    ON DELETE NO ACTION)
```

If the following command is issued:

```
DELETE FROM tablea WHERE empid=2
```

How many rows will be deleted from TABLEA and TABLEB?

- ❍ A. 0, 0
- ❍ B. 0, 1
- ❍ C. 1, 0
- ❍ D. 1, 1

Question 4

Which of the following DB2 UDB data types is used to store 1000 MB of single-byte character data as a single value?

- ❍ A. BLOB
- ❍ B. CLOB
- ❍ C. DBCLOB
- ❍ D. GRAPHIC

Question 5

Given the following CREATE TABLE statement:

CREATE TABLE newtable LIKE table1

Which two of the following would NOT occur as a result of the statement execution?

- ❑ A. NEWTABLE would have the same column names and column data types as TABLE1
- ❑ B. NEWTABLE would have the same column defaults as TABLE1
- ❑ C. NEWTABLE would have the same indexes as TABLE1.
- ❑ D. NEWTABLE would have the same nullability characteristics as TABLE1
- ❑ E. NEWTABLE would have the same referential constraints as TABLE1

Question 6

Which of the following DB2 data types should NOT be used to store double-byte character data?

- ❍ A. DBCLOB
- ❍ B. GRAPHIC
- ❍ C. VARCHAR
- ❍ D. VARGRAPHIC

Question 7

Given the statement:

```
CREATE TABLE tablea ( col1   INTEGER NOT NULL,
        CONSTRAINT const1 CHECK (col1 in (1, 2, 3))
```

Which of the following can be inserted into TABLEA?

- ❍ A. 0
- ❍ B. NULL
- ❍ C. 1
- ❍ D. '1'

Question 8

Which of the following deletion rules on CREATE TABLE will allow parent table rows to be deleted if a dependent row exists?

❍ A. ON DELETE RESTRICT

❍ B. ON DELETE NO ACTION

❍ C. ON DELETE SET NO VALUE

❍ D. ON DELETE CASCADE

Question 9

Given the following scenario:

Table TABLE1 needs to hold specific numeric values up to 9999999.999 in column COL1. COL1 is also used to perform arithmetic operations.

Which of the following would be the most appropriate DB2 data type to use for column COL1?

❍ A. INTEGER

❍ B. REAL

❍ C. NUMERIC(7, 3)

❍ D. DECIMAL(10, 3)

Question 10

Given the following statement:

```
CREATE TABLE tab1
        (col1  SMALLINT NOT NULL PRIMARY KEY,
         col2  VARCHAR(200) NOT NULL WITH DEFAULT NONE,
         col3  DECIMAL(5,2) CHECK (col3 >= 100.00),
         col4  DATE NOT NULL WITH DEFAULT)
```

Which of the following definitions will cause the CREATE TABLE statement to fail?

❍ A. COL1

❍ B. COL2

❍ C. COL3

❍ D. COL4

Question 11

Which of the following CANNOT be used to restrict specific values from being inserted into a column in a particular table?

❍ A. Index

❍ B. Check constraint

❍ C. Referential constraint

❍ D. Default constraint

Question 12

Which of the following is NOT a difference between a unique index and a primary key?

❍ A. A primary key is a special form of a unique constraint; both use a unique index.

❍ B. Unique indexes can be defined over one or more columns; primary keys can only be defined on a single column.

❍ C. A table can have many unique indexes but only one primary key.

❍ D. Unique indexes can be defined over one or more columns that allow null values; primary keys cannot contain null values.

Question 13

Which of the following DB2 data types CANNOT be used to store the time a scheduled flight left the departure gate?

❍ A. CLOB

❍ B. VARCHAR

❍ C. DATE

❍ D. TIMESTAMP

Question 14

Given the following statements:

```
CREATE TABLE table1 (col1   CHAR(3) PRIMARY KEY,
     CONSTRAINT const1 CHECK (col1 IN 'A01', 'B02', 'C03'))
INSERT INTO table1 VALUES('A02');
COMMIT
```

Which of the following occurs if the statements are executed in the order shown?

❍ A. The insert operation is rejected.

❍ B. The row is inserted with COL1 having a NULL value.

❍ C. The row is inserted with COL1 having a value of A02

❍ D. A user-defined function called CONST1 is activated to validate the data.

Answers

Question 1

The correct answer is **C.** Big integer (BIGINT), small integer (SMALLINT), and integer (INTEGER) are all valid DB2 UDB data types. IDENTITY is a keyword used with the CREATE TABLE statement to indicate that the DB2 Database Manager is to automatically generate values for a specific column.

Question 2

The correct answer is **B.** To create a referential constraint, you define a primary key, using one or more columns in the parent table, and you define a foreign key for one or more corresponding columns in the child table that reference the parent table's primary key.

Question 3

The correct answer is **A.** The ON DELETE NO ACTION definition ensures that whenever a delete operation is performed on the parent table in a referential constraint, the value for the foreign key of each row in the child table will have a matching value in the parent key of the parent table (after all other referential constraints have been applied). Therefore, no row will be deleted from TABLEA because a row exists in TABLEB that references the row the DELETE statement is trying to remove. And because the ON DELETE CASCADE definition was not used, no row will be deleted from TABLEB.

Question 4

The correct answer is **B.** The binary large object (BLOB) data type is used to store binary data, the double-byte character large object (DBCLOB) data type is used to store double-byte character data, and the fixed-length double-byte character string (GRAPHIC) data type is used to store double-byte character data strings. The character large object (CLOB) data type, on the other hand, is used to store single-byte character data.

Question 5

The correct answers are **C** and **E.** When the CREATE TABLE ... LIKE ... statement is executed, each column of the table that is created will have exactly the same name, data type and nullability characteristic as the columns of the source table used to create the new table. Furthermore, if the EXCLUDING COLUMN DEFAULTS option is not specified, all column defaults will be copied as well. However, the new table will not contain any unique constraints, foreign key constraints, triggers, or indexes that exist in the original.

Question 6

The correct answer is **C.** The variable-length character string (VARCHAR) data type is used to store single-byte character string data. The remaining data types—double-byte character large object (DBCLOB), fixed-length double-byte character string (GRAPHIC), and varying-length double-byte character string (VARGRAPHIC)—are used to store double-byte character data.

Question 7

The correct answer is **C.** The check constraint (CONST1) for TABLEA will only allow the values 1, 2, or 3 to be entered into column COL1. The NOT NULL constraint prohibits null values, the value 0 is not a valid value, and the value '1' is a character value (the column COL1 was defined using a numeric data type).

Question 8

The correct answer is **D.** The ON DELETE RESTRICT delete rule and the ON DELETE NO ACTION delete rule prevent the deletion of parent rows in a parent table if dependent rows that reference the primary row being deleted exist in the corresponding child table, and the ON DELETE SET NO VALUE delete rule is an invalid rule. On the other hand, the ON DELETE CASCADE delete rule will allow rows in the parent table to be deleted; if dependent rows that reference the primary row being deleted exist in the corresponding child table, they will be deleted as well.

Question 9

The correct answer is **D.** The decimal (DECIMAL or NUMERIC) data type is used to hold the number—the precision is 10 because 10 numbers will be displayed and the scale is 3 because the number contains three decimal places.

Question 10

The correct answer is **B.** Because column COL2 was defined using a varying-length character string (VARCHAR) data type, the default value provided for the default constraint must be enclosed in single quotes. Had the value 'NONE' been provided instead of the value NONE, the column COL2 would have been created. Instead, because column COL2 could not be created, the table TAB1 was not created.

Question 11

The correct answer is **D.** A unique index, a check constraint, and a referential constraint place restrictions on what can and cannot be stored in the column(s) they are associated with. A default constraint, however, is used to provide a default value for a particular column if no data is provided for that column when data is inserted into a table; if a value is provided for the column, the default value is ignored.

Question 12

The correct answer is **B.** Both primary keys and unique indexes can be defined over one or more columns in a table.

Question 13

The correct answer is **C.** The date (DATE) data type can only be used to store date values and time values must be stored in either time (TIME) data types or timestamp (TIMESTAMP) data types. However, a character representation of a date or time value can be stored in any of the character string data types available; the character large object (CLOB) data type and the varying-length character string (VARCHAR) data type are character string data types.

Question 14

The correct answer is **A.** Because the value 'A02' violates the check constraint CONST1 (the value provided for the column COL1 must be either 'A01', 'B02', or 'C03'), the INSERT operation will be rejected and an error code will be returned.

Database Concurrency

*E*leven percent (11%) of the DB2 UDB V8.1 Family Fundamentals certification exam (Exam 700) is designed to test your knowledge of the instruments DB2 Universal Database uses to allow multiple users and/or applications to interact with a database simultaneously without negatively affecting data consistency. The questions that make up this portion of the exam are intended to evaluate the following:

- Your ability to identify the appropriate isolation level to use for a given situation.
- Your ability to identify the characteristics of DB2 UDB locks.
- Your ability to list objects for which DB2 UDB locks can be acquired.
- Your ability to identify factors that can influence locking.

This chapter is designed to introduce you to the concept of data consistency and to isolation levels and locks—the mechanisms DB2 Universal Database uses to maintain data consistency in both single- and multiple-user database environments.

Terms you will learn:

Data Consistency
Inconsistency
Interleaved Transaction
Serializable Transaction
Concurrency
Lost Update

Dirty Read

Nonrepeatable Read

Phantom

Isolation Level

Repeatable Read

Read Stability

Cursor Stability

Uncommitted Read

Lock

Lock State

Lock Compatibility

Lock Conversion

Lock Escalation

Lock Wait

Deadlock Cycle

Conversion Deadlock

Techniques you will master:

Understanding how activities performed by transactions are isolated from each other in a multiuser environment.

Understanding how DB2 Universal Database provides concurrency control with isolation levels and locks.

Recognizing the types of isolation levels available and understanding when each is to be used.

Understanding what types of locks are available and how locks are acquired.

Understanding Data Consistency

In order to understand how DB2 Universal Database attempts to maintain data consistency in both single- and multi-user environments, you must first understand what data consistency is, as well as be able to identify what can cause a database to be placed in an inconsistent state. One of the best ways to learn both is by studying the following example:

Suppose your company owns a chain of hardware stores and a database is used to keep track of the inventory stored at each store. By design, this database contains an inventory table for each hardware store in the chain. Whenever supplies are received or sold at a particular store, the inventory table that corresponds to that store is updated accordingly. Now, suppose a case of hammers is physically moved from one hardware store to another. In order to reflect this inventory move, the hammer count value stored in the donating store's inventory table needs to be lowered, and the hammer count value stored in the receiving store's inventory table needs to be raised. If a user lowers the hammer count value in the donating store's inventory table, but fails to raise the hammer count value in the receiving store's inventory table, the data will become *inconsistent*. Now, the hammer inventory count for the entire chain of hardware stores is no longer accurate.

A database can become inconsistent if a user forgets to make all necessary changes (as in the previous example), if the system crashes while a user is in the middle of making changes (hammer count lowered in donating store's table, then system crash occurs before hammer count is raised in receiving store's table), or if, for some reason, a database application stops execution prematurely. Inconsistency can also occur when several users attempt to access the same data at the same time. For example, using the same hardware store scenario, one user might query the database and discover that no more hammers are available (when there really are) because the query read another user's changes before all tables affected by those changes had been properly updated. Reacting to this information, the user might then place an order for more hammers when none are needed.

To ensure that users and applications accessing the same data at the same time do not inadvertently place that data in an inconsistent state, DB2 UDB relies on two mechanisms, known as *isolation levels* and *locks*.

Isolation Levels

In Chapter 5, "Working with DB2 UDB Data," we saw that a transaction (otherwise known as a unit of work) is a recoverable sequence of one or more SQL operations grouped together as a single unit, usually within an application process. The initiation and termination of a single transaction defines points of data consistency within a database—either the effects of all SQL operations performed within a transaction are applied to the database and made permanent (committed) or the effects of all SQL operations performed are completely "undone" and thrown away (rolled back).

In single-user, single-application environments, each transaction runs serially and does not have to contend with interference from other transactions. However in multiuser environments, transactions can execute simultaneously, and each transaction has the potential to interfere with any other transaction that has been initiated but not yet terminated. Transactions that have the potential of interfering with one another are said to be *interleaved*, or *parallel*, while transactions that run isolated from each other are said to be *serializable*, which means that the results of running them simultaneously will be no different from the results of running them one right after another (serially). Ideally, every transaction should be serializable.

Why is it important that transactions be serializable? Consider the following: Suppose a travel agent is entering hotel reservation information into a database system at the same time a hotel manager is checking room availability for a conference planning committee. Now, suppose the travel agent blocks off two hundred rooms for a large tour group (to check availability get a price quote) but does not commit the entry. While the travel agent is relaying the price quote information to the tour group coordinator, the hotel manager queries the database to see how many rooms are available, sees that all but twenty rooms have been reserved, and tells the conference planning committee that he cannot accommodate their needs. Now, suppose the tour coordinator decides not to reserve the rooms because the quoted price is higher than anticipated. The travel agent rolls back the transaction because no reservations were made, and the two hundred rooms that had been marked as reserved are now shown as being available. Unfortunately, the damage has already been done. The hotel missed the opportunity to host a conference, and they have two hundred vacant rooms they need to fill. If the travel agent's transaction and the hotel manager's transaction had been isolated from each other (serialized), this problem would not have occurred. Either the travel agent's transaction would have finished before the hotel manager's transaction started, or the hotel manager's transaction would have finished before the travel agent's transaction started; in either case, the hotel would not have missed out on the opportunity to host the conference.

When transactions are not isolated from each other in multiuser environments, the following types of events (or phenomena) can occur:

> **Lost Updates.** This event occurs when two transactions read the same data, both attempt to update that data, and one of the updates is lost. For example: Transaction A and Transaction B both read the same row of data and calculate new values for that row based upon the original values read. If Transaction A updates the row with its new value and Transaction B then updates the same row, the update operation performed by Transaction A is lost.

Dirty Reads. This event occurs when a transaction reads data that has not yet been committed. For example: Transaction A changes a row of data and Transaction B reads the changed row before Transaction A commits the change. If Transaction A rolls back the change, Transaction B will have read data that theoretically never existed.

Nonrepeatable Reads. This event occurs when a transaction reads the same row of data twice, but gets different results each time. For example: Transaction A reads a row of data, and then Transaction B modifies or deletes that row and commits the change. When Transaction A attempts to reread the row, it will retrieve different data values (if the row was updated) or discover that the row no longer exists (if the row was deleted).

Phantoms. This event occurs when a row of data matches some search criteria but initially is not seen. For example: Transaction A retrieves a set of rows that satisfy some search criteria, and then Transaction B inserts a new row that contains matching search criteria for Transaction A's query. If Transaction A re-executes the query that produced the original set of rows, a different set of rows will be retrieved—the new row added by Transaction B will now be included in the set of rows returned.

Because several different users can access and modify data stored in a DB2 UDB database at the same time, the DB2 Database Manager must be able to allow users to make necessary changes while ensuring data integrity is never compromised. The sharing of resources by multiple interactive users or application programs at the same time is known as *concurrency*. One of the ways DB2 UDB enforces concurrency is through the use of *isolation levels*, which determine how data used in one transaction is "isolated from" other transactions. DB2 Universal Database recognizes and supports the following isolation levels:

- Repeatable Read
- Read Stability
- Cursor Stability
- Uncommitted Read

Table 7–1 shows the various phenomena that can occur when each of these isolation levels are used.

Table 7–1 DB2 Universal Database's Isolation Levels and the Phenomena That Can Occur When Each Is Used

Isolation Level	Phenomena			
	Lost Updates	Dirty Reads	Nonrepeatable Reads	Phantoms
Repeatable Read	No	No	No	No
Read Stability	No	No	No	Yes
Cursor Stability	No	No	Yes	Yes
Uncommitted Read	No	Yes	Yes	Yes

Adapted from Table 1 on Page 56 of the IBM DB2 Administration Guide – Performance manual.

The Repeatable Read Isolation Level

The Repeatable Read isolation level completely isolates one transaction from the effects of other concurrent transactions. When this isolation level is used, every row that is referenced *in any manner* by the isolated transaction is "locked" for the duration of that transaction. As a result, if the same SELECT SQL statement is issued two or more times within the same transaction, the result data set produced will always be the same. (Lost updates, dirty reads, nonrepeatable reads, and phantoms cannot occur.) In addition, transactions using the Repeatable Read isolation level will not see changes made to other rows by other transactions until those changes have been committed.

Transactions using the Repeatable Read isolation level can retrieve the same set of rows multiple times and perform any number of operations on them until terminated by performing either a commit or a rollback operation. However, no other transaction is allowed to perform any insert, update, or delete operation that would affect the set of rows being accessed by the isolating transaction—as long as that transaction remains active. To ensure that the data being accessed by a transaction running under the Repeatable Read isolation level is not adversely affected by other transactions, each row referenced by the isolating transaction is locked—not just the rows that are actually retrieved and/or modified. Thus, if a transaction scans 1,000 rows in order to retrieve 10, locks are acquired and held on all 1,000 rows scanned—not just on the 10 rows retrieved.

If an entire table or view is scanned in response to a query, the entire table or all table rows referenced by the view are locked. This greatly reduces concurrency, especially when large tables are used.

So how does this isolation level work in a real-world situation? Suppose you own a large hotel and you have a Web site that allows individuals to reserve rooms on a first-come, first-served basis. If your hotel reservation application runs under the Repeatable Read isolation level, whenever a customer retrieves a list of all rooms available for a given range of dates, you will not be able to change the room rate for those rooms during the date range specified, nor will other customers be able to make or cancel reservations that would cause the list to change if it were generated again—as long as the transaction that produced the list is active. (However, you can change room rates for any room that was not scanned in response to the first customer's query. Likewise, other customers can make or cancel room reservations for any room that was not scanned in response to the first customer's query.)

The Read Stability Isolation Level

Unlike the Repeatable Read isolation level, the Read Stability isolation level does not completely isolate one transaction from the effects of other concurrent transactions. That is because when the Read Stability isolation level is used, only rows that are actually retrieved by a single transaction are locked for the duration of that transaction. Thus when this isolation level is used, if the same SELECT SQL statement is issued two or more times within the same transaction, the result data set produced may not always be the same. (Lost updates, dirty reads, and nonrepeatable reads cannot occur; phantoms, however, can and may be seen.) In addition, transactions using the Read Stability isolation level will not see changes made to other rows by other transactions until those changes have been committed.

Transactions using the Read Stability isolation level can retrieve a set of rows and perform any number of operations on them until terminated by performing either a commit or a rollback operation. However, no other transaction is allowed to perform any update or delete operation that would affect the set of rows that were retrieved by the isolating transaction—as long as that transaction exists. (However, other transactions can perform insert operations, and if the transaction running under the Read Stability isolation level executes the same query multiple times, rows inserted between each query by other concurrent transactions may appear in subsequent result data sets produced. As mentioned earlier, such rows are called "phantoms.")

Unlike the Repeatable Read isolation level, where every row that is referenced in any way by the isolating transaction is locked, when the Read Stability isolation level is used, only the rows that are actually retrieved and/or modified by the isolating transaction are locked. Thus, if a transaction scans 1,000 rows in order to retrieve 10, locks are only acquired and held on the 10 rows retrieved—not on all 1,000 rows scanned. (And because fewer locks are acquired, more transactions can run concurrently.)

So how does this isolation level change the way our hotel reservation application works? Now when a customer retrieves a list of rooms available for a given range of dates, you will be able to change the room rate for any room in the hotel that does not appear on the list, and other customers will be able to cancel room reservations for rooms that had been reserved for the date range specified by the first customer's query. Therefore, if the customer generates the list of available rooms again (before the transaction that submitted the query terminates), the list produced may contain new room rates and/or rooms that were not available the first time the list was generated.

The Cursor Stability Isolation Level

The Cursor Stability isolation level is even more relaxed than the Read Stability isolation level in the way it isolates one transaction from the effects of other concurrent transactions. When the Cursor Stability isolation level is used, only the row that is currently being referenced by a cursor is locked. The lock acquired remains in effect until the cursor is repositioned—more often than not by executing the `FETCH` SQL statement—or until the isolating transaction terminates. (If the cursor is repositioned, the lock being held on the last row read is released and a new lock is acquired for the row the cursor is now positioned on.).

When a transaction using the Cursor Stability isolation level retrieves a row from a table via an updatable cursor, no other transaction can update or delete that row while the cursor is positioned on it. However, other transactions can add new rows to the table, as well as perform update and/or delete operations on rows positioned on either side of the locked row, provided the locked row itself was not accessed using an index. Furthermore, if the isolating transaction modifies any row it retrieves, no other transaction can update or delete that row until the isolating transaction is terminated, even when the cursor is no longer positioned on the modified row. As you might imagine, when the Cursor Stability isolation level is used, if the same `SELECT` SQL statement is issued two or more times within the same transaction, the results returned may not always be the same. (Lost updates and dirty reads cannot occur; nonrepeatable reads and phantoms, on the other hand, can and may be seen.) In addition, transactions using the Cursor Stability isolation level will not see changes made to other rows by other transactions until those changes have been committed.

Once again, let us see how this isolation level affects our hotel reservation application. Now when a customer retrieves a list of rooms available for a given range of dates, then views information about each room on the list produced (one room at a time), you will be able to change the room rate over any date range for any room in the hotel with the exception of the room the customer is currently looking at. Likewise, other customers will be able to make or cancel reservations over any date range for any room in the hotel; however, they will not be able to do anything with the room the first customer is currently looking at. When the first customer views information about another room in the list, the same holds true for the new room the customer is looking at; you will now be able to change the room rate for the room the first customer was just looking at and other customers will be able to reserve that particular room—provided the first customer did not reserve the room for themselves.

The Uncommitted Read Isolation Level

While the Repeatable Read isolation level is the most restrictive of the isolation levels available, the Uncommitted Read isolation level is the least intrusive isolation level provided. In fact, when the Uncommitted Read isolation level is used, rows that are retrieved by a single transaction are only locked if another transaction attempts to drop or alter the table from which the rows were retrieved. Because rows often remain unlocked when this isolation level is used, dirty reads, nonrepeatable reads, and phantoms can occur. Therefore, the Uncommitted Read isolation level is commonly used for transactions that access read-only tables/views or transactions that execute queries on which uncommitted data from other transactions will have no adverse affect.

In most cases, transactions using the Uncommitted Read isolation level can read changes made to rows by other transactions before those changes have been committed. However, such transactions can neither see nor access tables, views, or indexes created by other concurrent transactions until those transactions themselves have been terminated. The same applies to existing tables, views, or indexes that have been dropped—transactions using the Uncommitted Read isolation level will only learn that these objects no longer exist when the transaction that dropped them is terminated. There is one exception to this behavior: When a transaction running under the Uncommitted Read isolation level uses an updatable cursor, the transaction will behave as if it is running under the Cursor Stability isolation level, and the constraints of the Cursor Stability isolation level will apply.

So how does the Uncommitted Read isolation level affect our hotel reservation application? Now when a customer retrieves a list of rooms available for a given range of dates, you will be able to change the room rate for any room in the hotel, and other customers will be able to make or cancel reservations over any date range for any room. Furthermore, the list produced for the first customer may contain rooms that other customers have chosen to cancel reservations for, but whose cancellations have not yet been committed to the database.

Choosing the Proper Isolation Level

In addition to controlling how well the DB2 Database Manager provides concurrency, the isolation level used also determines how well applications running concurrently will perform. As a result, using the wrong isolation level for a given situation can have a significant negative impact on both concurrency and performance. So how do you determine which isolation level to use for a given situation? You start by identifying the concurrency phenomena that can arise and determining what phenomena are tolerable and what phenomena are not. Then you select an isolation level that will prevent any unacceptable phenomena from occurring. Typically, you should:

- Use the Repeatable Read isolation level if you are executing queries and you do not want other concurrent transactions to have the ability to make changes that could cause the same query to return different results if run more than once.
- Use the Read Stability isolation level when you want some level of concurrency between applications, yet you also want qualified rows to remain stable for the duration of an individual transaction.
- Use the Cursor Stability isolation level when you want maximum concurrency between applications, yet you do not want queries to return uncommitted data values.
- Use the Uncommitted Read isolation level if you are executing queries on read-only databases, or if you do not care if a query returns uncommitted data values.

Specifying the Isolation Level to Use

Although isolation levels control concurrency at the transaction level, they are actually set at the application level. Therefore in most cases, the isolation level specified for a particular application is applicable to every transaction initiated by that application. (It is important to note that an application can be constructed in several different parts, and each part can be assigned a different isolation level, in which case the isolation level specified for a particular part is applicable to every transaction that is created within that part.)

For embedded SQL applications, the isolation level to be used is specified at precompile time or when the application is bound to a database (if deferred binding is used). The isolation level for embedded SQL applications written in a supported compiled language (such as C and C++) is set through the `ISOLATION` option of the `PRECOMPILE PROGRAM` and `BIND` commands. The isolation level for Open Database Connectivity (ODBC) and Call Level Interface (CLI) applications is set at application runtime by calling the `SQLSetConnectAttr()` function with the `SQL_ATTR_TXN_ISOLATION` connection attribute specified. Alternatively, the isolation level for ODBC/CLI applications can be set by assigning a value to the `TXNISOLATION` keyword in the *db2cli.ini* configuration file; however, this approach does not provide the flexibility of changing isolation levels for different transactions within the application that the first approach does. The isolation level for JDBC and SQLJ applications is set at application runtime by calling the `setTransactionIsolation()` method that resides within DB2 Universal Database's *java.sql* connection interface.

When the isolation level for an application is not explicitly set using one of these methods, the Cursor Stability isolation level is used as the default. This holds true for commands, SQL statements, and scripts executed from the Command Line Processor, as well as for embedded SQL, ODBC/CLI, JDBC, and SQLJ applications. Therefore, it is also possible to specify the isolation level to be used for any transaction that is to be executed by the Command Line Processor. In this case, the isolation level is set by executing the `CHANGE ISOLATION` command before a connection to a database is established.

Locking

The one thing that all four isolation levels have in common is that they control how data is accessed by concurrent transactions through the use of locks. So just what is a lock? A *lock* is a mechanism used to associate a data resource with a single transaction, for the sole purpose of controlling how other transactions interact with that resource while it is associated with the transaction that has it locked. (The transaction that has a data resource associated with it is said to "hold" or "own" the lock.) Essentially, locks in a database environment serve the same purpose as they do in a house or a car: They determine who can and cannot gain access to a particular resource—in the case of a data resource, this is one or more tablespaces, tables, and/or rows. The DB2 Database Manager imposes locks to prohibit "owning" transactions from accessing uncommitted data that has been written by other transactions and to prevent other transactions from making data modifications that might adversely affect the owning transaction. When an owning transaction is terminated (by being committed or by being rolled back), any changes made to the resource that was locked are made permanent or removed, and all locks on the resource that had been acquired by the owning transaction are released. Once unlocked, a resource can be locked again and manipulated by

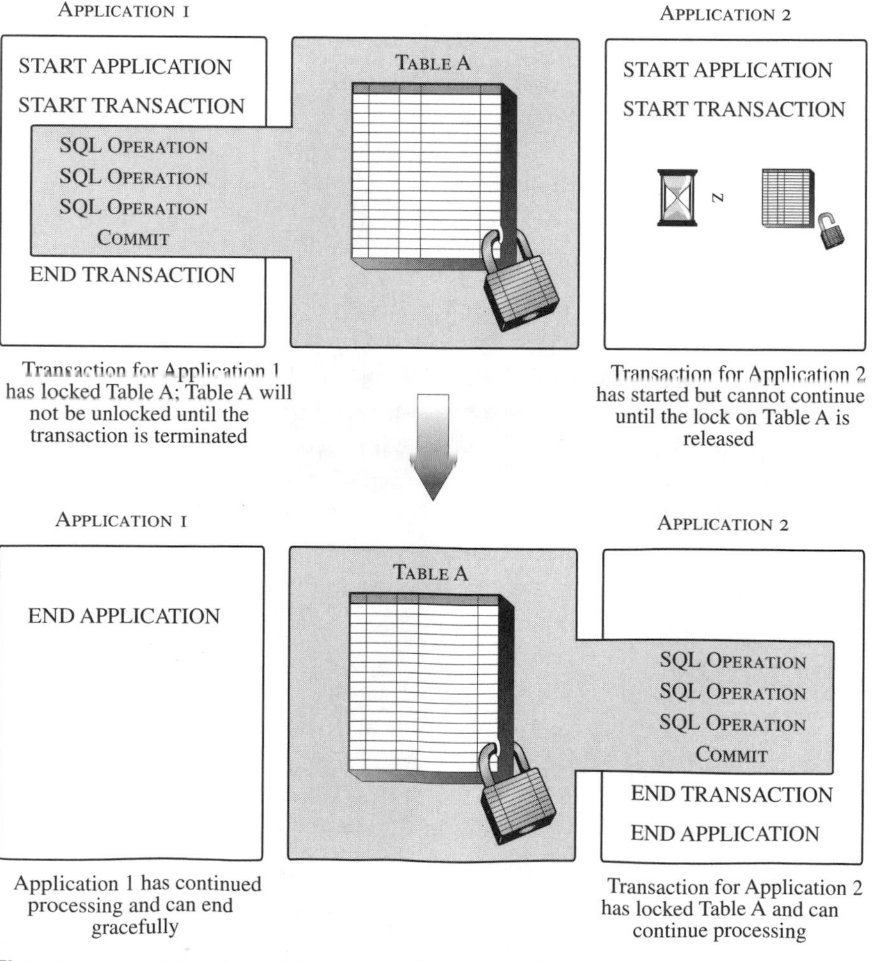

Figure 7–1 How DB2 Universal Database prevents uncontrolled concurrent access to a resource through the use of locks.

another active transaction. Figure 7–1 illustrates the principles of transaction/ resource locking.

Lock Attributes and Lock States

All DB2 Universal Database locks have the following basic attributes:

Object. This attribute identifies the data resource that is being locked. The DB2 Database Manager implicitly acquires locks on data resources (specifically, tablespaces, tables, and rows) whenever they are needed.

Size. This attribute identifies the physical size of the portion of the data resource that is being locked. A lock does not always have to control an entire data resource. For example, rather than giving an application exclusive control over an entire table, the DB2 Database Manager can elect to give an application exclusive control over one or more specific rows in a table.

Duration. This attribute identifies the length of time a lock is held. The isolation level used has a significant impact on the duration of a lock. (For example, the lock acquired for a Repeatable Read transaction that accesses 500 rows is likely to have a long duration if all 500 rows are to be updated; on the other hand, the lock acquired for a Cursor Stability transaction is likely to have a much shorter duration.)

State (or Mode). This attribute identifies the type of access allowed for the lock owner, as well as the type of access permitted for concurrent users of the locked data resource. Table 7–2 shows the various lock states available (along with their effects) in order of increasing control.

How Locks Are Acquired

Except for occasions where the Uncommitted Read isolation level is used, it is never necessary for a transaction to explicitly request a lock. That's because the DB2 Database Manager implicitly acquires locks as they are needed (and once acquired, these locks remain under the DB2 Database Manager's control until they are no longer needed). By default, the DB2 Database Manager always attempts to acquire row-level locks. However, it is possible to control whether the DB2 Database Manager will always acquire row-level locks or table-level locks on a specific table resource by executing a special form of the

Table 7–2 Lock States

Lock State (Mode)	Applicable Objects	Lock Owner Access	Concurrent Transaction Access	Other Locks Acquired
Intent None (IN)	Tablespaces, Tables	Lock owner can read all data, including uncommitted data, stored in the locked resource; however, lock owner cannot modify data stored in the locked resource. Intent None locks are typically acquired for read-only transactions that have no intention of modifying data (thus, additional locks will not be acquired on the transaction's behalf).	Other transactions can read and modify data stored in the locked resource, however, they cannot delete data stored in the locked resource.	None
Intent Share (IS)	Tablespaces, Tables	Lock owner can read all data (excluding uncommitted data) stored in the locked resource; however, lock owner cannot modify data stored in the locked resource. Intent Share locks are typically acquired for transactions that do not convey the intent to modify data (transactions that execute SELECT FOR UPDATE, UPDATE WHERE, and/or INSERT statements convey the intent to modify data).	Other transactions can read and modify data stored in the locked resource.	If the lock is held on a table, a Share (S) or a Next Key Share (NS) lock is acquired on each row read from that table.

Next Key Share (NS)	Rows	Lock owner can read all data (excluding uncommitted data) stored in the locked resource; however, lock owner cannot modify data stored in the locked resource. Next Key Share locks are typically acquired in place of a Share (S) lock for transactions that are running under the Read Stability (RS) or Cursor Stability (CS) isolation level.	Other transactions can read all data (excluding uncommitted data) stored in the locked resource; however, they cannot modify data stored in the locked resource.	None
Share (S)	Tables, Rows	Lock owner can read all data (excluding uncommitted data) stored in the locked resource; however, lock owner cannot modify data stored in the locked resource. Share locks are typically acquired for transactions that do not convey the intent to modify data (transactions that execute SELECT FOR UPDATE, UPDATE WHERE, and/or INSERT statements convey the intent to modify data) that are running under the Repeatable Read (RR) isolation level.	Other transactions can read all data (excluding uncommitted data) stored in the locked resource; however, they cannot modify data stored in the locked resource.	Individual rows in a table can be Share (S) locked, provided the table itself is not Share (S) locked. (If the table is Share (S) locked, row-level locks cannot be acquired.)

(*continued*)

Table 7–2 Lock States *(Continued)*

Lock State (Mode)	Applicable Objects	Lock Owner Access	Concurrent Transaction Access	Other Locks Acquired
Intent Exclusive (IX)	Tablespaces, Tables	Lock owner can read and modify data stored in the locked resource. Intent Exclusive locks are typically acquired for transactions that convey the intent to modify data (transactions that execute `SELECT FOR UPDATE`, `UPDATE WHERE`, and/or `INSERT` statements convey the intent to modify data).	Other transactions can read and modify data stored in the locked resource.	When the lock owner works with an Intent Exclusive (IX) locked table, a Share (S) or a Next Key Share (NS) lock is acquired on every row read from that table, and both an Update (U) and an Exclusive (X) lock is acquired on every row to be modified.
Share With Intent Exclusive (SIX)	Tables	Lock owner can read and modify data stored in the locked resource. Share With Intent Exclusive locks are typically acquired when a transaction holding a Share (S) lock on a resource attempts to acquire an Intent Exclusive (IX) lock on the same resource (or vice versa).	Other transactions can read all data (excluding uncommitted data) stored in the locked resource; however, they cannot modify data stored in the locked resource.	When the lock owner works with a Share With Intent Exclusive (SIX) locked table, an Exclusive (X) lock is acquired on every row in that table that is to be modified.
Update (U)	Tables, Rows	Lock owner can modify all data (excluding uncommitted data) stored in the locked resource; however, lock owner cannot read data stored in the locked resource.	Other transactions can read all data (excluding uncommitted data) stored in the locked resource; however, they cannot modify data stored in the locked resource.	When the lock owner works with an Update (U) locked table, an Exclusive (X) lock is acquired on every row to be modified in that table.

		Update locks are typically acquired for transactions that modify data with `INSERT`, `UPDATE`, and/or `DELETE` statements.		
Next Key Exclusive (NX)	Rows	Lock owner can read all data (excluding uncommitted data) stored in the locked resource; however, lock owner cannot modify data stored in the locked resource Next Key Exclusive locks are typically acquired on the next available row in a table whenever a row is deleted from or inserted into any index associated with the table.	Other transactions can read all data (excluding uncommitted data) stored in the locked resource; however, they cannot modify data stored in the locked resource.	None
Next Key Weak Exclusive (NW)	Rows	Lock owner can read all data (excluding uncommitted data) stored in the locked resource; however, lock owner cannot modify data stored in the locked resource. Next Key Weak Exclusive locks are typically acquired on the next available row in a table whenever a row is inserted into any index of a non-catalog table.	Other transactions can read all data (excluding uncommitted data) stored in the locked resource; however, they cannot modify data stored in the locked resource.	None

(*continued*)

Table 7–2 Lock States *(Continued)*

Lock State (Mode)	Applicable Objects	Lock Owner Access	Concurrent Transaction Access	Other Locks Acquired
Exclusive (X)	Tables, Rows	Lock owner can read and modify data stored in the locked resource. Exclusive locks are typically acquired for transactions that retrieve data with `SELECT` statements and then modify the data retrieved with `INSERT`, `UPDATE`, and/or `DELETE` statements.	Transactions using the Uncommitted Read isolation level can read all data, including uncommitted data, stored in the locked resource; however they cannot modify data stored in the locked resource. All other transactions can neither read, nor modify data stored in the locked resource.	Individual rows in a table can be Exclusive (X) locked, provided the table itself is not Exclusive (X) locked.
Weak Exclusive (WE)	Rows	Lock owner can read and modify data stored in the locked resource. Weak Exclusive locks are typically acquired on a row when it is inserted into a nonsystem catalog table.	Transactions using the Uncommitted Read isolation level can read all data, including uncommitted data, stored in the locked resource; however, they can-not modify data stored in the locked resource. All other transactions can neither read nor modify data stored in the locked resource.	None

Super Exclusive (Z)	Tablespaces, Tables	Lock owner can read and modify data stored in the locked resource. Super Exclusive locks are typically acquired on a table whenever the lock owner attempts to alter that table, drop that table, create an index for that table, drop an index that has already been defined for that table, or reorganize the contents of the table (while the table is offline) by running the REORG utility.	Other transactions can neither read nor modify data stored in the locked resource.	None

Adapted from Table 3 on Pages 62 - 63 of the IBM DB2 Administration Guide – Performance manual.

ALTER TABLE SQL statement. The syntax for this form of the ALTER TABLE statement is:

```
ALTER TABLE [TableName] LOCKSIZE [ROW | TABLE]
```

where:

TableName Identifies the name of an existing table for which the level of locking that all transactions are to use when accessing it is to be specified.

For example, if executed, the SQL statement

```
ALTER TABLE EMPLOYEE LOCKSIZE TABLE
```

would force the DB2 Database Manager to acquire table-level locks for every transaction that accesses the table named EMPLOYEE. On the other hand, if the SQL statement

```
ALTER TABLE EMPLOYEE LOCKSIZE ROW
```

was executed, the DB2 Database Manager would attempt to acquire row-level locks (which is the default behavior) for every transaction that accesses the table named EMPLOYEE.

But what if you don't want every transaction that works with a particular table to acquire table-level locks? What if you instead only want one specific transaction to acquire table-level locks, and you want all other transactions to acquire row-level locks when working with that table? In this case, you leave the default locking behavior alone (in which case row-level locking is used), and you use the LOCK TABLE SQL statement to acquire a table-level lock for the appropriate individual transaction. The syntax for the LOCK TABLE statement is:

```
LOCK TABLE [TableName] IN [SHARE | EXCLUSIVE] MODE
```

where:

TableName Identifies the name of an existing table to be locked.

As you can see, the LOCK TABLE statement allows a transaction to acquire a table-level lock on a particular table in one of two modes: SHARE mode and EXCLUSIVE mode. If a table is locked using the SHARE mode, a table-level Share (S) lock is acquired on behalf of the requesting transaction, and other concurrent transactions are allowed to read, but not change the data stored in the locked table. On the other hand, if a table is locked using the EXCLUSIVE mode, a table-level Exclusive (X) lock is acquired, and other concurrent transactions can neither access nor modify data stored in the locked table.

For example, if executed, the SQL statement

```
LOCK TABLE EMPLOYEE IN SHARE MODE
```

would acquire a table-level Share (S) lock on the EMPLOYEE table on behalf of the current transaction (provided no other transaction holds a lock on this table), and other concurrent transactions would be allowed to read, but not change, the data stored in the table. On the other hand, if the SQL statement

```
LOCK TABLE EMPLOYEE IN EXCLUSIVE MODE
```

were executed, a table-level Exclusive (X) lock would be acquired, and no other concurrent transaction would be allowed to read or modify data stored in the EMPLOYEE table.

Which Locks Are Acquired

Although it is possible to control whether the DB2 Database Manager will acquire row-level locks or table-level locks, it is not possible to control what type of lock will actually be acquired for a given transaction. Instead, the DB2 Database Manager implicitly makes that decision by analyzing the transaction to determine what type of processing it has been designed to perform. For the purpose of deciding which particular type of lock is needed for a given situation, the DB2 Database Manager places all transactions into one of the following categories:

- Read-Only
- Intent-to-Change
- Change
- Cursor-Controlled

The characteristics used to assign transactions to these categories, along with the types of locks that are acquired for each, are shown in Table 7–3.

It is important to keep in mind that some transactions are actually composed of two or more transaction types. For example, a transaction that contains an SQL statement that performs an insert operation against a table using the results of a subquery actually does two different types of processing: Read-Only and Change. Thus, the locks needed for the resources referenced in the subquery are determined by the rules for Read-Only transactions, while

Table 7–3 Types of Transactions Available and Their Associated Locks

Type of Transaction	Description	Locks Acquired
Read-Only	Transactions that contain SELECT SQL statements (which are intrinsically read-only), SELECT SQL statements that have the FOR READ ONLY clause specified, or SQL statements that are ambiguous, but are presumed to be read-only because of the BLOCKING option specified as part of the precompile and/or bind process.	Intent Share (IS) and/or Share (S) locks for tablespaces, tables, and rows.
Intent-to-Change	Transactions that contain SELECT SQL statements that have the FOR UPDATE clause specified or SQL statements that are ambiguous, but are presumed to be intended for change because of the way they are interpreted by the SQL precompiler.	Share (S), Update (U), and Exclusive (X) locks for tables; Update (U), Intent Exclusive (IX), and Exclusive (X) locks for rows.
Change	Transactions that contain INSERT, UPDATE, and/or DELETE SQL statements but not UPDATE WHERE CURRENT OF or DELETE WHERE CURRENT OF SQL statements.	Intent Exclusive (IX) and/or Exclusive (X) locks for tablespaces, tables, and rows.
Cursor-Controlled	Transactions that contain UPDATE WHERE CURRENT OF and/or DELETE WHERE CURRENT OF SQL statements.	Intent Exclusive (IX) and/or Exclusive (X) locks for tablespaces, tables, and rows.

the locks needed for the target table of the insert operation are determined by the rules for Change transactions.

Locks and Performance

Although the DB2 Database Manager implicitly acquires locks as they are needed and, aside from using the ALTER TABLE and LOCK TABLE SQL statements to force the DB2 Database Manager to acquire table-level locks, locking is out of your control, there are several factors that can affect locking that you need to be aware of. These factors include:

- Lock compatibility
- Lock conversion
- Lock escalation
- Lock waits and timeouts
- Deadlocks
- Concurrency and granularity

Knowing what these factors are and understanding how they can affect overall performance can assist you in designing database applications that work well in multiuser database environments and, indirectly, give you more control over how locks are used.

Lock compatibility

If the state of a lock placed on a data resource by one transaction is such that another lock can be placed on the same resource by another transaction before the first lock acquired is released, the two locks (or lock states) are said to be *compatible.* Anytime one transaction holds a lock on a data resource and another transaction attempts to acquire a lock on the same resource, the DB2 Database Manager will examine the two lock states to determine if they are compatible. If both locks are compatible, the second lock is acquired on behalf of the requesting transaction. On the other hand, if the locks are incompatible, the requesting transaction must wait for the owning transaction to release the lock it holds before it can gain access to the resource and acquire the lock that is needed. This is known as a *lock wait event.* When a lock wait event occurs, the transaction attempting to access the locked resource simply stops execution until the owning transaction terminates (and releases the incompatible lock) or until a *lock timeout event* occurs (we will look at lock timeout events shortly). Table 7–4 contains a lock compatibility matrix that identifies which locks are compatible and which are not.

Lock conversion

If a transaction holds a lock on a resource and needs to acquire a more restrictive lock on the same resource, the DB2 Database Manager will attempt to change the state of the existing lock to the more restrictive state, rather than acquire a second lock. The action of changing the state of an existing lock to a more restrictive state is known as *lock conversion.* Lock conversion occurs because a transaction can hold only one lock on a specific data resource at any given time. Figure 7–2 illustrates a simple lock conversion process.

Table 7–4 Lock Compatibility Matrix

Lock Requested by Second Transaction	Lock State	Lock Held by First Transaction											
		IN	IS	NS	S	IX	SIX	U	NX	NW	X	WE	Z
	IN	Yes	Yes	Yes	Yes	Yes	Yes	Yes	Yes	Yes	Yes	Yes	No
	IS	Yes	Yes	Yes	Yes	Yes	Yes	Yes	No	No	No	No	No
	NS	Yes	Yes	Yes	Yes	No	No	Yes	Yes	Yes	No	No	No
	S	Yes	Yes	Yes	Yes	No	No	Yes	No	No	No	No	No
	IX	Yes	Yes	No	No	Yes	No	No	No	No	No	No	No
	SIX	Yes	Yes	No	No	No	No	No	No	No	No	No	No
	U	Yes	Yes	Yes	Yes	No	No	No	No	No	No	No	No
	NX	Yes	No	Yes	No	No	No	No	No	No	No	No	No
	NW	Yes	No	Yes	No	No	No	No	No	No	No	Yes	No
	X	Yes	No	No	No	No	No	No	No	No	No	No	No
	WE	Yes	No	No	No	No	No	No	No	Yes	No	No	No
	Z	No	No	No	No	No	No	No	No	No	No	No	No

Yes	Locks are compatible; therefore, the lock request is granted
No	Locks are not compatible; therefore, the requesting transaction must wait for the held lock to be released or for a lock timeout to occur before the lock request can be granted.

Lock Types:

IN	Intent None
IS	Intent Share
NS	Next Key Share
S	Share
IX	Intent Exclusive
SIX	Share With Intent Exclusive
U	Update
NX	Next Key Exclusive
NW	Next Key Weak Exclusive
X	Exclusive
WE	Weak Exclusive
Z	Super Exclusive

Adapted from Table 4 on Page 73 of the IBM DB2 Administration Guide – Performance manual.

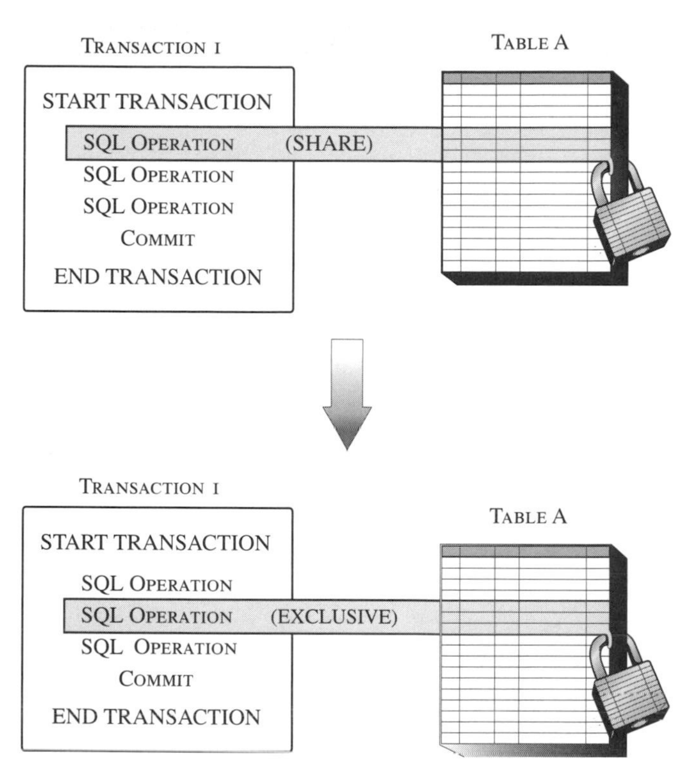

Figure 7–2 A simple lock conversion scenario—a Share (S) lock is converted to an Exclusive (X) lock.

In most cases, lock conversion is performed on row-level locks, and the conversion process is fairly straightforward. For example, if an Update (U) lock is held and an Exclusive (X) lock is needed, the Update (U) lock will be converted to an Exclusive (X) lock. However, Share (S) locks and Intent Exclusive (IX) locks are special cases, since neither lock is considered more restrictive than the other; if one of these locks is held and the other is requested, the held lock is converted to a Share With Intent Exclusive (SIX) lock. With all other conversions, the lock state of the current lock is changed to the lock state being requested—provided the lock state being requested is a more restrictive state. (Lock conversion only occurs if a held lock can increase its restriction.) Once a lock has been converted, it stays at the highest level attained until the transaction holding the lock is terminated and the lock is released.

Lock escalation

When a connection to a database is first established, a specific amount of memory is set aside to hold a structure that DB2 UDB uses to manage locks. This structure is called the *lock list*, and this is where the locks held by all applications concurrently connected to a database are stored after they are acquired. (The actual amount of memory that gets set aside for the lock list is determined by the *locklist* database configuration parameter.)

Because a limited amount of memory is available, and because this memory must be shared by everyone, the DB2 Database Manager imposes a limit on the amount of space in the lock list each transaction can use for its own locks (which is defined by the *maxlocks* database configuration parameter). To prevent a specific database agent from exceeding its space limitations, a process known as *lock escalation* is performed whenever too many locks (regardless of their type) have been acquired on behalf of a single transaction. During lock escalation, space in the lock list is freed by converting several row-level locks into a single table-level lock. Figure 7–3 illustrates a simple lock escalation process.

So just how does lock escalation work? When a transaction requests a lock and the database's lock list is full, one of the tables associated with the transaction is selected, a table-level lock is acquired, all row-level locks for that

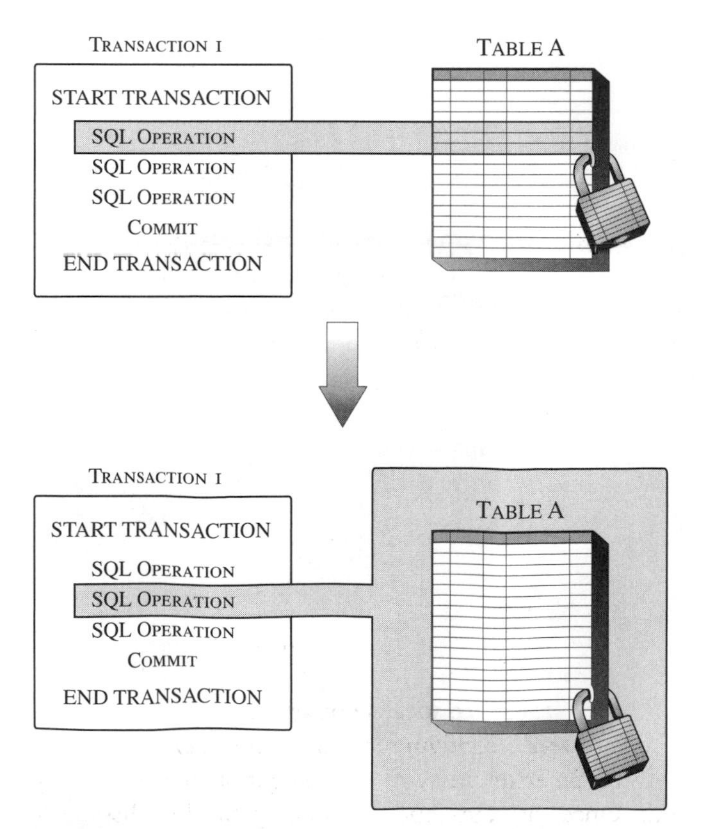

Figure 7–3 Lock escalation—several individual row-level locks are changed to a single table-level lock.

table are released to create space, and the table-level lock acquired is added to the lock list. If this process does not free up the storage space needed to acquire the lock that was requested, another table is selected and the process is repeated until enough free space is made available—only then will the requested lock be acquired and the transaction be allowed to resume execution. However, if the lock list space needed is still unavailable after all the transaction's row-level locks have been escalated, an SQL error code is generated, all changes that have been made to the database since the transaction was initiated are rolled back, and the transaction is gracefully terminated. If a database is configured properly, lock escalation events rarely occur.

Use of the `ALTER TABLE` SQL statement or the `LOCK TABLE` SQL statement does not prevent normal lock escalation from occurring. However, it may reduce the frequency with which lock escalations take place.

Lock waits and timeouts

Any time a transaction holds a lock on a particular resource (tablespace, table, or row), other transactions may be denied access to that resource until the owning transaction terminates and frees all locks it has acquired. Because of this behavior, without some sort of lock timeout detection mechanism in place, a transaction might wait indefinitely for a lock to be released. For example, if a transaction in one user's application was waiting for a lock being held by a transaction in another user's application to be released, and the other user left their workstation without performing some interaction that would have allowed their application to terminate the owning transaction and release all locks held, the application waiting for the lock to be released would be unable to continue processing for an indeterminable amount of time. Unfortunately, it would also be impossible to terminate the application that was waiting for the lock to be released without compromising data consistency.

To prevent situations like these from occurring, an important feature known as *lock timeout detection* has been incorporated into the DB2 Database Manager. When used, this feature prevents applications from waiting indefinitely for a lock to be released in an abnormal situation. By assigning a value to the *locktimeout* configuration parameter in the appropriate database configuration file, you can control when lock timeout detection occurs. This parameter controls the amount of time that any transaction will wait to obtain a requested lock; if the requested lock is not acquired before the time interval specified in the *locktimeout* configuration parameter has elapsed, the waiting application receives an error message, and the transaction requesting the lock is rolled back. Once the transaction requesting the lock has been rolled back, the waiting application will, by default, be terminated. (This behavior prevents data inconsistency from occurring.)

By default, the *locktimeout* configuration is set to –1, which means that applications will wait forever to acquire the locks they need. In many cases, this value should be changed to something other than the default. In addition, applications should be written such that they capture any timeout (or deadlock) SQL return code returned by the DB2 Database Manager and respond appropriately.

Deadlocks

We just saw how one transaction can make another transaction wait indefinitely for a lock to be released and how this situation can be resolved by establishing lock timeouts. Unfortunately, there is one situation where contention for locks by two or more transactions cannot be resolved by a lock timeout. This situation is known as a *deadlock*, and the best way to illustrate how a deadlock can occur is by example: Suppose Transaction 1 acquires an Exclusive (X) lock on Table A, and Transaction 2 acquires an Exclusive (X) lock on Table B. Now, suppose Transaction 1 attempts to acquire an Exclusive (X) lock on Table B, and Transaction 2 attempts to acquire an Exclusive (X) lock on Table A. We have already seen that processing by both transactions will be suspended until their second lock request is granted. However, because neither lock request can be granted until one of the owning transactions releases the lock it currently holds (by performing a commit or rollback operation), and because neither transaction can perform a commit or rollback operation because they both have been suspended (and are waiting on locks), a deadlock situation has occurred. Figure 7–4 illustrates this deadlock scenario.

A deadlock is more precisely referred to as a *deadlock cycle*, because the transactions involved form a circle of wait states; each transaction in the circle waits for a lock held by another transaction in the circle to be released (see Figure 7–4). When a deadlock cycle occurs, all transactions involved will wait indefinitely for a lock to be released unless some outside agent steps in and breaks the deadlock cycle. With DB2 Universal Database, this agent is a background process, known as the *deadlock detector*, whose sole responsibility is to locate and resolve any deadlocks found in the locking subsystem.

Each database has its own deadlock detector, which is activated as part of the database initialization process. Once activated, the deadlock detector stays "asleep" most of the time but "wakes up" at preset intervals and examines the locking subsystem to determine whether a deadlock situation exists. Normally, the deadlock detector wakes up, sees that there are no deadlocks in the locking subsystem, and goes back to sleep. If, however, the deadlock detector dis-

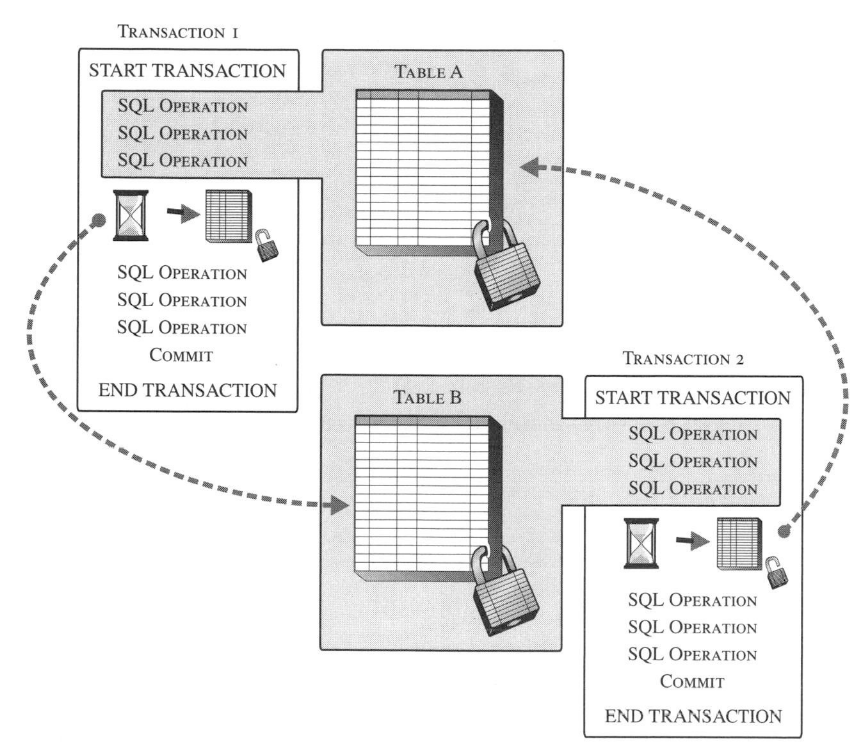

Figure 7–4 A deadlock scenario—Transaction 1 is waiting for Transaction 2 to release its lock on Table B, and Transaction 2 is waiting for Transaction 1 to release its lock on Table A; however, neither transaction can release their respective locks because they have been suspended and are waiting to acquire other locks.

covers a deadlock cycle in the locking subsystem, it randomly selects one of the transactions in the cycle to roll back and terminate. The transaction chosen receives an SQL error code, and every lock it had acquired is released. The remaining transaction(s) can then proceed, because the deadlock cycle has been broken. It is possible, but very unlikely, that more than one deadlock cycle exists in a database's locking subsystem. However, if several deadlock cycles exist, the detector locates each one and terminates one of the offending transactions in the same manner, until all deadlock cycles have been broken. Eventually, the deadlock detector goes back to sleep, only to wake up again at the next predefined interval and reexamine the locking subsystem.

While most deadlock cycles involve two or more resources, a special type of deadlock, known as a *conversion deadlock*, can occur on one individual resource. Conversion deadlocks occur when two or more transactions that already hold compatible locks on an object request new, incompatible locks on that same object. This typically takes place when two or more concurrent transactions search for rows in a table by performing an index scan, and then try to modify one or more of the rows retrieved.

Concurrency and granularity

As we have already seen, any time a transaction holds a lock on a particular resource, other transactions may be denied access to that resource until the owning transaction is terminated. Therefore, row-level locks are usually better than table-level locks, because they restrict access to a much smaller resource. However, because each lock acquired requires some amount of storage space (to hold) and some degree of processing time (to manage), there is usually considerably less overhead involved when a single table-level lock is used, rather than several individual row-level locks.

Earlier, we saw that the granularity of locks (i.e. whether row-level locks or table-level locks are used) can be controlled through the use of the `ALTER TABLE` and `LOCK TABLE` SQL statements—the `ALTER TABLE` statement is used to control granularity at a global level, while the `LOCK TABLE` statement is used to control granularity at an individual transaction level. (In both cases, only Share (S) locks or Exclusive (X) locks are acquired whenever explicit table-level locking is performed.) So when is it more desirable to control granularity at the global level rather than at an individual transaction level? It all depends on the situation. Suppose you have a read-only table lookup table that is to be accessed by multiple concurrent transactions. Forcing the DB2 Database Manager to globally acquire Share (S) table-level locks for every transaction that attempts to access this table could improve overall performance without negatively influencing other concurrent transactions. On the other hand, suppose you have a table that is to be accessed frequently by read-only transactions and periodically by a single transaction designed to perform basic maintenance. Forcing the DB2 Database Manager to only acquire an Exclusive (X) table-level lock whenever the maintenance transaction executes makes more sense than forcing the DB2 Database Manager to globally acquire Exclusive (X) table-level locks for every transaction that needs to access the table. If the former approach is used, the read-only transactions are locked out of the table whenever the maintenance transaction runs, but in all other situations, they can access the table concurrently while requiring very little locking overhead.

Practice Questions

Question 1

Which of the following isolation levels will lock all rows scanned to build a result data set?

❍ A. Uncommitted Read

❍ B. Cursor Stability

❍ C. Read Stability

❍ D. Repeatable Read

Question 2

For which two of the following database objects can locks NOT be acquired?

❑ A. Buffer pools

❑ B. Tablespaces

❑ C. Tables

❑ D. Rows

❑ E. Columns

Question 3

Which of the following DB2 UDB isolation levels will only lock rows during read processing if another transaction tries to drop the table the rows are being read from?

❍ A. Repeatable Read

❍ B. Read Stability

❍ C. Cursor Stability

❍ D. Uncommitted Read

Question 4

A transaction is using the Repeatable Read isolation level. A table is scanned twice within the same transaction. Which of the following can be seen the second time the table is scanned?

- ❍ A. The same rows that were seen the first time the table was scanned
- ❍ B. Rows added to a result set by other processes
- ❍ C. Rows changed in a result set by other processes
- ❍ D. Rows with uncommitted changes made by other processes

Question 5

A transaction is using the Read Stability isolation level. Which of the following releases an Update (U) lock that has been acquired by the transaction?

- ❍ A. When the cursor accessing the row is closed
- ❍ B. When the transaction executes a COMMIT statement
- ❍ C. When the cursor accessing the row is moved to the next row
- ❍ D. Immediately after the UPDATE statement is executed

Question 6

Which of the following modes, when used with the LOCK TABLE statement, will cause the DB2 Database Manager to acquire a table-level lock that prevents other concurrent transactions from accessing data stored in the table while the owning transaction is active?

- ❍ A. SHARE MODE
- ❍ B. ISOLATED MODE
- ❍ C. EXCLUSIVE MODE
- ❍ D. RESTRICT MODE

Question 7

A transaction using the Read Stability isolation level scans the same table multiple times before it terminates. Which of the following can occur within this transaction's processing?

- ❍ A. Uncommitted changes made by other transactions can be seen from one scan to the next.
- ❍ B. Rows removed by other transactions that appeared in one scan will no longer appear in subsequent scans.
- ❍ C. Rows added by other transactions that did not appear in one scan can be seen in subsequent scans.
- ❍ D. Rows that have been updated can be changed by other transactions from one scan to the next.

Question 8

A database contains a read-only lookup table. In order to provide optimum read concurrency, transactions accessing this table should be run using which of the following isolation levels?

- ❍ A. Repeatable Read
- ❍ B. Read Stability
- ❍ C. Cursor Stability
- ❍ D. Uncommitted Read

Question 9

An application is bound to a database using the Repeatable Read isolation level. A transaction within the application issues a request that retrieves 100 rows out of 10,000 in the table. Which of the following describes the rows that are locked as a result of this request?

- ❍ A. None of the rows are locked.
- ❍ B. All rows scanned are locked.
- ❍ C. All rows returned to the result data set produced are locked.
- ❍ D. The last row accessed is locked.

Question 10

A table contains a list of all seats available at a football stadium. A seat consists of a section number, a seat number, and whether or not the seat has been assigned. A ticket agent working at the box office generates a list of all unassigned seats. When the agent refreshes the list, it should only change if another agent assigns one or more unassigned seats. Which of the following is the best isolation level to use for this application?

- ❍ A. Repeatable Read
- ❍ B. Read Stability
- ❍ C. Cursor Stability
- ❍ D. Uncommitted Read

Answers

Question 1

The correct answer is **D.** The Repeatable Read isolation level will lock all rows scanned in response to a query. (The Read Stability isolation level will only lock the rows returned in the result data set; the Cursor Stability isolation level will only lock the row in the result data set that the cursor is currently pointing to; and the Uncommitted Read isolation level will not lock any rows during normal read processing.)

Question 2

The correct answers are **A** and **E.** Locks can only be acquired for tablespaces, tables, and rows.

Question 3

The correct answer is **D.** Usually, locks are not acquired during processing when the Uncommitted Read isolation level is used. However, rows that are retrieved by a transaction using the Uncommitted Read isolation level will be locked if another transaction attempts to drop or alter the table from which the rows were retrieved.

Question 4

The correct answer is **A.** To ensure that the data being accessed by a transaction running under the Repeatable Read isolation level is not adversely affected by other transactions, each row referenced by the isolating transaction is locked. As a result, if the same SELECT SQL statement is issued two or more times within the same transaction, the result data set produced will always be the same.

Question 5

The correct answer is **B.** When the Repeatable Read and Read Stability isolation levels are used, all locks acquired are released when the owning transaction terminates by performing a commit or a rollback operation. (When the Cursor Stability isolation level is used, a lock is held on the row the cursor is pointing to, and when the cursor is moved to a new row, the lock for the old row is released and a lock for the new row is acquired; when the Uncommitted Read isolation level is used, locks are usually not acquired.)

Question 6

The correct answer is **C.** The LOCK TABLE statement allows a transaction to acquire a table-level lock on a particular table in one of two modes: SHARE and EXCLUSIVE. If a table is locked using the SHARE mode, a table-level Share (S) lock is acquired on behalf of the transaction, and other concurrent transactions are allowed to read, but not change, the data stored in the locked table. If a table is locked using the EXCLUSIVE mode, a table-level Exclusive (X) lock is acquired, and other concurrent transactions can neither access nor modify data stored in the locked table.

Question 7

The correct answer is **C.** When the Read Stability isolation level is used by a transaction that executes a query, locks are acquired on all rows returned to the result data set produced, and other transactions cannot modify or delete the locked rows; however, they can add new rows to the table that meet the query's search criteria. If that happens, and the query is run again, these new rows will appear in the new result data set produced.

Question 8

The correct answer is **D.** If a table is marked as read-only, there is no need to use a restrictive isolation level when accessing it; since no transaction can modify its data, queries against the table should always return the same result data set each time they are run. Therefore, if the least restrictive isolation level (which is Uncommitted Read) is used, more applications can access the table at the same time (concurrently).

Question 9

The correct answer is **B.** When the Repeatable Read isolation level is used, every row that is referenced *in any manner* by the isolated transaction is "locked" for the duration of that transaction. Thus, if a transaction scans 10,000 rows in order to retrieve 100, locks are acquired and held on all 10,000 rows scanned—not just on the 100 rows retrieved. (If the Read Stability isolation level is used, only the rows returned to the result data set are locked; if the Cursor Stability isolation level is used, only the last row accessed is locked; and if the Uncommitted Read isolation level is used, no rows are locked.)

Question 10

The correct answer is **C.** If the Repeatable Read isolation level is used, other agents will be unable to assign seats as long as the transaction that generated the list remains active; therefore, the list will not change when it is refreshed. If the Read Stability isolation level is used, other agents will be able to unassign currently assigned seats (and these unassigned seats will show up when the list is refreshed), but they will not be able to assign any seat that appears in the list as long as the transaction that generated the list remains active. If the Uncommitted Read isolation level is used, other agents will be able to unassign currently assigned seats, as well as assign unassigned seats; however, uncommitted seat unassignments/assignments will show up when the list is refreshed, and the agent may make an inappropriate change based on this data. Therefore, the best isolation level to use for this particular application is the Cursor Stability isolation level.

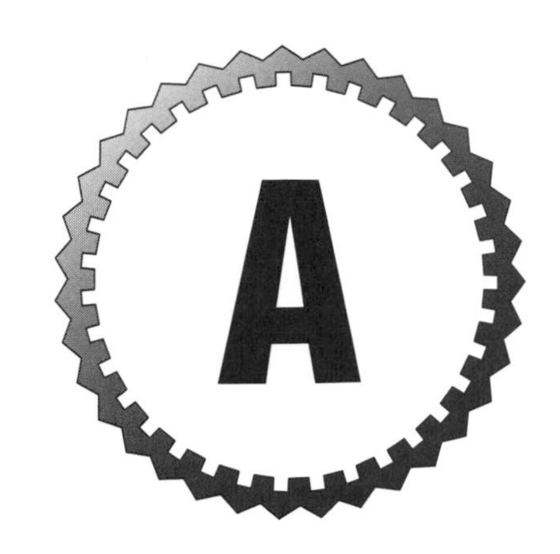

DB2 UDB V8.1 Family Fundamentals Exam (Exam 700) Objectives

The DB2 UDB V8.1 Family Fundamentals exam (Exam 700) consists of 54 questions, and candidates have 75 minutes to complete the exam. A score of 61% or higher is required to pass this exam.

The primary objectives the DB2 UDB V8.1 Family Fundamentals exam (Exam 700) is designed to cover are as follows:

Planning (15%)

- Knowledge of DB2 UDB products (client, server, etc.)
- Knowledge of the features provided by DB2 tools such as DB2 Extenders, the Configuration Assistant, Visual Explain, the Command Center, the Control Center, Relational Connect, the Replication Center, the Development Center, and the Health Center
- Knowledge of Data Warehouse and OLAP concepts
- Knowledge of nonrelational data concepts (extenders, etc)

Security (9%)

- Knowledge of restricting data access
- Knowledge of the different privileges available

Accessing DB2 UDB Data (15%)

- Ability to identify and locate DB2 UDB servers
- Ability to access and manipulate DB2 UDB objects
- Ability to create basic DB2 UDB objects

Working with DB2 UDB Data (31%)

- Knowledge of transactions
- Given a DDL SQL statement, knowledge to identify results
- Given a DML SQL statement, knowledge to identify results
- Given a DCL SQL statement, knowledge to identify results
- Ability to use SQL to SELECT data from tables
- Ability to use SQL to SORT or GROUP data
- Ability to use SQL to UPDATE, DELETE, or INSERT data
- Ability to call a procedure

Working with DB2 UDB Objects (19%)

- Ability to demonstrate usage of DB2 UDB data types
- Given a situation, ability to create table
- Knowledge to identify when referential integrity should be used
- Knowledge to identify methods of data constraint
- Knowledge to identify characteristics of a table, view or index

Data Concurrency (11%)

- Knowledge to identify factors that influence locking
- Ability to list objects on which locks can be obtained
- Knowledge to identify characteristics of DB2 UDB locks
- Given a situation, knowledge to identify the isolations level that should be used

Index

D

E

F

G

H

I

J

K

L

T

U

V

W

X

Y

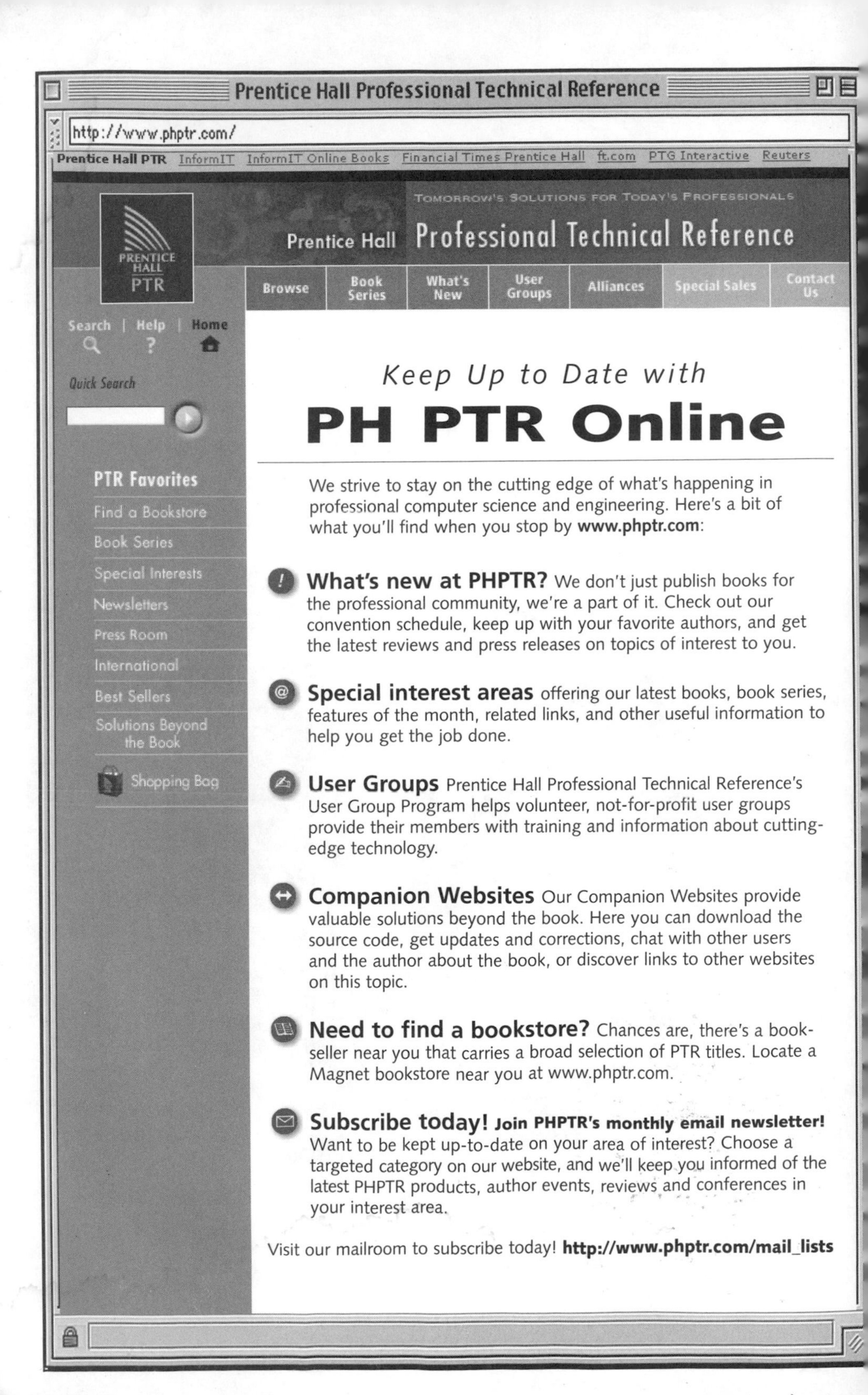

Prentice Hall Professional Technical Reference
http://www.phptr.com/
Prentice Hall PTR
InformIT
InformIT Online Books
Financial Times Prentice Hall
ft.com
PTG Interactive
Reuters
TOMORROW'S SOLUTIONS FOR TODAY'S PROFESSIONALS
PRENTICE HALL PTR
Prentice Hall Professional Technical Reference
Browse
Book Series
What's New
User Groups
Alliances
Special Sales
Contact Us
Search
Help
Home
Quick Search
PTR Favorites
Find a Bookstore
Book Series
Special Interests
Newsletters
Press Room
International
Best Sellers
Solutions Beyond the Book
Shopping Bag
Keep Up to Date with
PH PTR Online
We strive to stay on the cutting edge of what's happening in professional computer science and engineering. Here's a bit of what you'll find when you stop by www.phptr.com:
What's new at PHPTR? We don't just publish books for the professional community, we're a part of it. Check out our convention schedule, keep up with your favorite authors, and get the latest reviews and press releases on topics of interest to you.
Special interest areas offering our latest books, book series, features of the month, related links, and other useful information to help you get the job done.
User Groups Prentice Hall Professional Technical Reference's User Group Program helps volunteer, not-for-profit user groups provide their members with training and information about cutting-edge technology.
Companion Websites Our Companion Websites provide valuable solutions beyond the book. Here you can download the source code, get updates and corrections, chat with other users and the author about the book, or discover links to other websites on this topic.
Need to find a bookstore? Chances are, there's a bookseller near you that carries a broad selection of PTR titles. Locate a Magnet bookstore near you at www.phptr.com.
Subscribe today! Join PHPTR's monthly email newsletter!
Want to be kept up-to-date on your area of interest? Choose a targeted category on our website, and we'll keep you informed of the latest PHPTR products, author events, reviews and conferences in your interest area.
Visit our mailroom to subscribe today! http://www.phptr.com/mail_lists